Unsung Hollywood
Musicals of the
Golden Era

ALSO BY EDWIN M. BRADLEY

The First Hollywood Musicals: A Critical Filmography of 171 Features, 1927 through 1932
(McFarland, 1996; softcover 2004)

The First Hollywood Sound Shorts, 1926–1931
(McFarland, 2005; softcover 2009)

Unsung Hollywood Musicals of the Golden Era

50 Overlooked Films and Their Stars, 1929–1939

EDWIN M. BRADLEY

McFarland & Company, Inc., Publishers
Jefferson, North Carolina

LIBRARY OF CONGRESS CATALOGUING-IN-PUBLICATION DATA

Names: Bradley, Edwin M., 1958– author.
Title: Unsung Hollywood musicals of the golden era : 50 overlooked films and their stars, 1929–1939 / Edwin M. Bradley.
Description: Jefferson, North Carolina : McFarland & Company, Inc., Publishers, 2016. | Includes bibliographical references and index. | Includes filmography.
Identifiers: LCCN 2016002322 | ISBN 9780786498338 (softcover : acid free paper) ∞
Subjects: LCSH: Musical films—United States—History and criticism.
Classification: LCC PN1995.9.M86 B75 2016 | DDC 791.43/750973—dc23
LC record available at http://lccn.loc.gov/2016002322

BRITISH LIBRARY CATALOGUING DATA ARE AVAILABLE

ISBN (print) 978-0-7864-9833-8
ISBN (ebook) 978-1-4766-2400-6

© 2016 Edwin M. Bradley. All rights reserved

No part of this book may be reproduced or transmitted in any form or by any means, electronic or mechanical, including photocopying or recording, or by any information storage and retrieval system, without permission in writing from the publisher.

Front cover image of Chick Chandler and Patricia Ellis (top) lead the "Two Little Flies on a Lump of Sugar" number in *Harold Teen* (Ron Hutchinson/The Vitaphone Project)

Printed in the United States of America

McFarland & Company, Inc., Publishers
  Box 611, Jefferson, North Carolina 28640
    www.mcfarlandpub.com

To Kathy, James, and Andrew

Table of Contents

Preface   1

1. Early Sound Rediscoveries   5
2. Failed, Fallen, and One-Shot Stars   38
3. Slumming with the Songsters   88
4. Big Ideas, Bigger Casts ... and Some Oddities   127
5. Dancing Down Poverty Row   166

Chapter Notes   197
Bibliography   208
Index   211

Preface

For all the famous musicals that emerged from Hollywood before the passing of the 1930s, there are as many or more that are all but forgotten. In the idiosyncratic roster of 50 feature films described in these pages, I have chosen to encompass (mainly) efforts by short-lived stars of (mainly) secondary movie musicals during the first decade or so of the genre. These performers were talented singers and dancers who were new to acting before the camera; personalities from other showbiz realms; star actors shoehorned into songfests, even if they didn't, or couldn't, sing themselves; or supporting players who were never quite star-quality. You'll learn about Dorothy Dell, Lee Dixon, Peggy Fears, Lawrence Gray, Jeanne Madden, Joe Morrison, the mother-daughter team of Myrt and Marge, and a producer named Lou Brock (not the baseball player), among others. And when I write about *International House*, the W.C. Fields musical comedy that is hardly a forgotten film, it's from the angle of seldom-recalled co-star Peggy Hopkins Joyce; there are plenty of books about Fields and other big names. These "lesser" folks—and their films—deserve to be rescued from obscurity, even if only in this account.

Thus, although this *is* a book about pre–1940 movie musicals, you *won't* find any of the films of Fred Astaire, Alice Faye, Eddie Cantor, Al Jolson, Mae West, Deanna Durbin, Mickey Rooney, Judy Garland, Jeanette MacDonald and/or Nelson Eddy. No Bing Crosby or Bob Hope. There is one Ruby Keeler effort—but her last at the company where she became a movie star. One Ginger Rogers film—before Fred. One from Shirley Temple—only because of the tragic fate of one of her co-stars. Just a single Busby Berkeley-Dick Powell project between them—hardly their best, and here because of the presence of a lesser performer. None of the titles herein include the word pairings "Big Broadcast," "Broadway Melody," or "Gold Diggers."

Some more about what's not here: With two borderline exceptions, there are no Westerns—plenty has been written about the singing cowboy pictures. Short subjects of the era have spawned a few books—one of which was my *The First Hollywood Sound Shorts*—and another full-length follow-up would be worthy, but not in these pages. And because I have sought to spotlight mostly forgotten, seldom-revived features, you'll notice a low percentage from Metro-Goldwyn-Mayer and Warner Bros. because many of their musicals have played frequently on Turner Classic Movies or home video. This book is, without apology, skewed toward minor musicals from Fox, Paramount, Universal, and smaller companies that aren't so easy to find these days. (Sadly, an all-but-lost musical such as Fox's *It's Great to Be Alive*, from 1933, will have to be saved for a future book if we can ever get a look at it.) Although many of them are little known, the films included here made lots of money; lost lots (I'm looking at you, *Down to Their Last Yacht*); created scandals; spawned lawsuits; and launched, ruined, and revived careers.

Song plays varying roles of importance in our 50 titles, meaning that some are more fully realized musicals than others. Some readers will argue that some of the selections here have music that is more interpolated than integrated into the plots, but I have tried to be broader than narrower in defining what makes a musical. Inclusiveness is the point, so I'm not inclined to get hung up on the differences between a "musical" and a comedy or drama "with songs." Also, although some of these films were shot in New York by Eastern-based personnel, and many studios were corporately headquartered in New York City, we use "Hollywood" in our title as representative of the American movie industry as a whole.

This book is organized into five categories that, for the select films herein, serve as points of entry:

- those that showcased short-time Hollywood musical stars;
- those that starred established actors or rising stars, especially those not strictly classifiable as musical performers;
- productions from the low-budget, independent "Poverty Row" studios;
- oddities or novelties that fall into a looser classification, mainly because of strange or unusual storylines or large/interesting casts; and
- a few "encores" and discoveries from the early years of sound.

That fifth category ties back to my 1996 book *The First Hollywood Musicals*, a study of feature films from the first wave of the genre in 1927–32. A few features covered in that book have subsequently resurfaced for appraisal, and thus are re-evaluated here. As for the title of this book, "unsung" can mean what you want it to. A good but underappreciated musical can be described as "unsung," but so—with a change in syllabic accenting—can a lousy one. You'll definitely find a mixed bag of films here in terms of quality, but learning where they fall is part of the fun. Much of the coverage herein comes from periodicals of the day, in which reporting on Hollywood and its stars was sometimes as effective as a studio flack or press agent or embellishing interviewer could make it, but it does reflect the context of the times, even if some of it may not be fully believed.

Thanks to David Pierce and his invaluable Digital Media History Library, which has made online access to important research material a real asset. So have archival websites for the Margaret Herrick Library and major publications such as *Variety* and *The New York Times*. Chuck Anderson's comprehensive "Old Corral" website (www.b-westerns.com) has great information on minor players and Poverty Row, and sources such as Newspapers.com, NewspaperArchive.com, Google News, the Internet Movie Database (but approach with caution), Ancestry.com, and the ProQuest database also have helped. Regarding the discography information included with many entries, I have listed 78-rpm recordings made by people involved with the film at (roughly) the time of the film. Especially valuable to me in compiling these listings were Brian Rust's book-length discographies and the exhaustive Online 78 rpm Discographical Project (78discography.com).

Even with a single name on the cover, this project was no solo effort. Thank-yous must go to the Vitaphone Project (Ron Hutchinson); the George Eastman Museum, International Museum of Photography and Film (Nancy Kauffman, Sophia Lorent); the University of Southern California Archives of the Cinematic Arts (Sandra Garcia-Myers); the New York State Archives (William Gorman); and the Wisconsin Center for Film and Theatre Research (and Gregory T. Smith). Don Dahlstrom read the manuscript and made helpful suggestions. Also, here's to Roy Blakey, Ken Bloom, Jeff Cohen, Richard Finegan, Mark Forer, Mark Roth, and the late Cole Johnson. A forever thanks to the late Marion Shilling Cook, whom I interviewed in 1993 regarding her participation in *Lord Byron of Broadway*, and George Burns, who briefly commented to me about his 1930s musicals during a 1992 interview on other matters.

Special gratitude goes to my wife, Kathy, and my children, Andrew and James. Andrew sat through many viewings of these films with me and aided in research. Perhaps he'll write a book of his own someday.

1. Early Sound Rediscoveries

Of all the forgotten movies that found new audiences as vintage cinema transitioned to cable television and home video, perhaps the most interesting subset is from the advent of sound. Many of these films, produced with primitive technique, became technologically obsolete upon release as talkie methods improved, practically by the month, as the 1920s passed into the '30s. These works were locked away into vaults and left to crumble, often literally, or were "orphaned" because of copyrights not renewed. Nobody seemed to want to see most of them again, although some popped up, in murky prints chopped up by commercials, on TV late-late shows in the 1950s and '60s. Some, originally made fully or partly in color, survived only in monochrome or were lost altogether. Few with influence saw a need to bring the ancient talkies back with care, until programming was needed for movie-centric cable networks. The vaults began to open—wide enough for more than a peek.

And of those faded pictures mocked, more with nostalgia than derision, in *Singin' in the Rain* for microphones hidden in flowerpots and actors huddled close enough to be heard, many of the best came out of a film genre born with the dawn of sound: the musical. Boy, was it born ... the first wave of the Hollywood musical went tidal, with nearly 200 releases in the five years after Al Jolson opened his mouth in 1927 in *The Jazz Singer*! Add in scores of other films with incidental songs, and it was no wonder that audiences grew wary until the *42nd Street*-led reboot of 1933 rejuvenated a Depression-stagnant box office. This meant that some good pre-'33 musicals got lumped in with the bad, and were unjustly ignored, and that some interesting performers were unfairly cast aside. But cable and video—not just some historian who told us what to think—allowed us to decide if we liked Marilyn Miller or Irene Bordoni or Morton Downey. When I was researching my book *The First Hollywood Musicals* in the early 1990s, I had to travel around the country to visit film archives to view many titles that could have been seen—at (sigh!) much less expense—on TNT or TCM not long after. Even now, thanks to specialized TV channels, devoted archivists, forward-thinking video companies, and the grey market of

Polly Moran loses her dignity—and more—in the failed RKO musical *Down to Their Last Yacht* (1934) (courtesy Ron Hutchinson/The Vitaphone Project).

collectors, new attractions from the era are coming to light. Hence, this chapter in this book.

I have been diving into early sound musicals ever since discovering them on the nascent TNT, circa 1988. But in revisiting the titles in this chapter, I was struck at how uncomfortable the major studios remained—well past the talkies' halting first months—with the presentation of non-diegetic sound, that not from a source visible or implied on the screen. This was more easily explained in the earliest sound musicals, mainly "backstagers" in which song numbers were proffered within a performance context—in other words, we could see Jolson sing or George Olsen lead a band, and be comforted by knowing where the noise was coming from. But as studios and audiences became savvy to music, it's difficult to explain something like *Queen High* [q.v.]—a 1930 late-summer release, at that. Why should a song number be signaled by the handing of a ukulele to someone, or, later, why should the male lead (in the case of *Queen High*, Stanley Smith) signal to viewers by telling a restaurant violinist, "In about three minutes, play our tune"? No ... just sing!

This recalls a sad truth: Much of the same public that will accept spontaneity from a live music performance cannot accept it on the screen. Given the paucity of present-day movie musicals, this seems as much the case now as in 1930.

Weary River
(First National; January 24, 1929)

Director: Frank Lloyd. Producer: Richard A. Rowland. Screenplay: Bradley King, based on the short story by Courtney Ryley Cooper. Dialogue: Tom J. Geraghty. Titles: Paul Perez. Photography: Ernest Haller. Special Photography: Alvin Knechtel. Editing: Edward Schroeder, James Gibbon. Art Director: John J. Hughes. Musical Director: Louis Silvers. Costumes: Max Rée. Sets: Ray Moyer. Running Time: 86 minutes (part-talking; also released as silent).

Cast: Richard Barthelmess (Jerry Larrabee); Betty Compson (Alice Gray); William Holden (warden); Louis Natheaux (Spadoni); George E. Stone (Blackie); Ray Turner (elevator operator); Gladden James (Jerry's manager); Robert Emmett O'Connor (police sergeant); Robert Kortman (prison guard); Blue Washington (prisoner in bathtub); Edwards Davis (prison chaplain); Brooks Benedict (Jerry's guest at Literary Club); Richard Cramer (radio announcer); Ernie Adams (ex-convict in alley); Pat Harmon (bartender); Jack Richardson (police officer); Jim Farley (police detective); Virginia Sale (noisy audience member); Harry Semels (informer on telephone); Sally Eilers (hat check girl); Ernest Hilliard (Literary Club host); Randolph Scott (theater patron); Johnny Murray (voice double for Barthelmess); Frank Churchill (piano double for Barthelmess).

Songs: "It's Up to You" [Barthelmess, dubbed by Murray and Churchill], "Weary River" [Barthelmess, four times, dubbed by Murray and Churchill] (Grant Clarke, Louis Silvers); "Dolly Dimples" [band] (Louis Alter); "Ruy Blas" Overture [band] (Felix Mendelssohn).

Academy Award Nomination: Best Director (Frank Lloyd).
Home Video: Warner Archive DVD.

The Story: Bootlegger Jerry Larrabee is sent to prison after being framed by rival gangster Spadoni. Jerry's girlfriend, Alice, tries to visit him but is kept away from the warden, who wants to protect Jerry from bad influences. Jerry turns to music and leads a prison band, whose music—especially Jerry's self-penned "Weary River," inspired by a sermon by the prison chaplain—becomes popular on the radio. Jerry *wins an early parole and enters vaudeville as "The Master of Melody," but reminders of his past make him uncomfortable before live audiences, and he returns to his gang, vowing revenge on Spadoni. Police intervene to prevent a gang shootout. Through the kindness of the warden and the love of Alice, Jerry makes good.*

Produced near the start of the "theme song" craze that strongly impacted early talkies, the part-talking Weary River was a gangster drama that might not have been given a strong melodic angle even a few months later, but its oft-delivered title song was more than just incidental, conveying the film's primary theme of personal redemption through music. Weary River also merits at least a footnote in the annals of film musicals for spawning the first controversy over one performer's singing being doubled by another's.

That dubbed performer, Richard Barthelmess (1895–1963), was no singer at all, but one of the most popular actors in Hollywood when he made Weary River for his home studio, First National, with esteemed director Frank Lloyd. Barthelmess began in movies as a boyish hero of D.W. Griffith productions a decade before, but his acting had improved, and his features hardened just

Despite publicity to the contrary, Richard Barthelmess neither sang nor played the piano in Weary River (1929) (courtesy George Eastman Museum, International Museum of Photography and Film).

enough, to put him in his prime when his first talkie came 'round. *Weary River* was based on a short story by Courtney Ryley Cooper that was published in *Collier's* magazine on August 11, 1928. Cooper was a popular writer of crime and circus stories, and this one combined both, although Bradley King's screenplay removed the big-top elements and turned the protagonist into a convicted bootlegger trying to turn around the "weary river" of his life through singing, songwriting, and playing piano while in prison. In Cooper's short story, the "weary river" reference is specific to lines from the A.G. Swinburne poem "The Garden of Proserpine": "That even the weariest river/winds somewhere safe to sea." The film paraphrases the same passage, in dialogue and song lyrics, although without mentioning the name of the poet.[1]

Like all the majors in late 1928, First National was turning the corner into sound films, and *Weary River* was announced in September as an all-sound picture—albeit one with sizable portions, totaling about one-third of the film, without dialogue but with synchronized sound. Warner Bros. was in the midst of acquiring all of First National's assets—Barthelmess was arguably the latter's biggest star—although the acquired company remained a separate entity for now. Forty-five of the 86 or so features released by Warner Bros. in 1929—among them *Weary River*—went out under the First National brand, per the agreement between the companies; at the time, FN releases brought higher rentals from theaters than Warners'.[2] *Weary River* was filmed at Warners' new sound facility in Burbank in November and December 1928; it was the first sound feature made there.

Theme songs were becoming practically *de rigueur* in Hollywood at this point, even in otherwise non-musical films, and in this department, *Weary River* delivered, with a Grant Clarke and Louis Silvers-penned title tune that reflected the inner conflict of its main character. For the aurally oriented magazine *Sound Waves*, the noise was good news in advance: "The next First National picture to star Richard Barthelmess will be ultra-modern in romantic possibilities. The radio being as modern as today itself, the entire structure of *Weary River* is built upon the axis of a voice over the ether waves."[3] However, "Weary River" the song had to be "sold" through repeated renditions, so the studio dared to dub Barthelmess' tenor and piano playing from a singer and musician who performed before off-screen microphones as the actor struck the keys on a sound-deadened keyboard. This bit of deception didn't deter First National from advertising *Weary River* as showcasing "two great stars at once":

> All these years the wealth of Richard Barthelmess' rich voice has been concealed. Now, VITAPHONE unearths this hidden treasure for you to enjoy. VITAPHONE brings you a Barthelmess so much greater it's like discovering a new star.... You and millions of others have gone just to see him act. Now you can HEAR him TALK and play the piano.

At least they were right about the talking part—on which the actor was more than adequate—but note that the ads didn't say anything about singing. For the film-going public, what it did hear was more than enough despite the dishonesty. *Weary River* did big business, even in New York City, where it drew crowds despite a lofty $2.50 admission price at a top Broadway theater, and it drew record houses in other cities. "Weary River"—formally rendered four times within the film's 86 minutes (plus repeated instrumental hearings in the background score, and again in the instrumental exit music)—became a big hit, recorded by Rudy Vallee and Gene Austin, among many others. *Photoplay* named Barthelmess' performance, and the picture itself, among the best of the season, although *The New York Times* provided a minority opinion about its star being wasted in a "hopeless hodgepodge."[4] Many of the laudatory early reviews of *Weary River* cited the effectiveness of Barthelmess' voice, but how different would their tone have been had their authors known the truth?

A look at the film eight decades later reveals that the *Times*' verdict was too harsh; *Weary River* is a slickly made piece of box office, not as potent or edgy as the films from the gangster cycle Warner Bros. would initiate a couple of years later, but it offers a convincing performance by Barthelmess as a hood who is both cultured and menacing, and is capable of self-awareness. The decision to make *Weary River* as a sound film from the start makes its frequent transitions from intertitles to dialogue and back pretty smooth among hybrid films, especially in contrast with a more slapdash project like *Lucky Boy* [q.v.]. Betty Compson (1897–1974), who had co-starred with Barthelmess in FN's *Scarlet Seas* in 1928, contributes good chemistry with the leading man, and William Holden, not the future Oscar winner but an elderly character actor, is a standout as the gangster's warden mentor. A final-reel shootout is arguably the best part of the film, even with no audible talk.

The dubbing was revealed early on in the trades—*Weary River* opened in New York on January 24, and *Variety* ran a tiny item before month's end about the singing and piano not being that of Barthelmess.[5] Fans and reviewers in the hinterlands were kept unaware of this in the film's advertising, but the fan magazine *Photoplay* went into more detail in a July article headlined "The TRUTH About Voice Doubling." It revealed that one Johnny Murray, a former cornetist at Los Angeles' Cocoanut Grove club, sang in *Weary River* and Frank Churchill, a pianist in a Hollywood theater orchestra, did the keyboard work—and that Barthelmess, embarrassed by the publicity, had asked his bosses at First National that he not sing in any future pictures.[6] By this time, as the *Photoplay* story pointed out, other dubbed performers had been found out: Laura La Plante in Universal's *Show Boat*, Corinne Griffith in First National's *The Divine Lady*, Barry Norton in Fox's *Mother Knows Best*. And even Al Jolson's voice had been replaced in the worship scenes of *The Jazz Singer* by Cantor Josef Rosenblatt.

But that Jolson film was comparatively long ago. *Weary River* was the big box-office picture of the newer bunch, and it got the most ink. Barthelmess may have been upset, but his bosses couldn't quite make good on his request not to appear in another musical, for near the end of 1929, he was part of the voluminous cast of the Warners studio revue *The Show of Shows*. The actor, likely ordered to appear, looked glum and uncomfortable during a brief introduction of a song number called "Meet My Sister." The only other time Barthelmess appeared in anything approaching a musical was RKO's *The Mayor of 44th Street* (1942). This time Barthelmess was the heavy, but it was the same kind of gangsters-and-songs opus that began his dialogue career.

As Jeff Cohen has noted on his Vitaphone Varieties website, the impact of *Weary River* extended beyond disposable entertainment. For example, an editorial by a newspaper in Chillicothe, Missouri, about whether movie houses should be open on Sundays used the film to make a positive argument:

> American opinion has fast left behind the idea that there is anything harmful or disgraceful in a clean theater. Some of the great church men in the country have realized the value in the talking picture in helping them to teach their own divine doctrines. Recently, a famous pastor said, "I have never preached a sermon stronger than the film *Weary River*." If there are devout men who can say such things sincerely, can we be honest and farseeing in our objections to Chillicothe theaters opening for Sunday performances?[7]

In other quarters, *Weary River* was criticized for making its protagonist too sympathetic. A memo in the archive of the Motion Picture Producers and Distributors of America shows that Mayor Ralph S. Bauer in Lynn, Massachusetts, banned the Barthelmess film, along with the FBO crime drama *Gang War*, from local theaters on the grounds that it "tended to make crooks heroes in the eyes of the younger generation, and he also said in doing so he refused to take any chances of Lynn 'growing into a Chicago overnight.'"[8] This may have been a minority view in 1929, but it was not limited to small cities in Massachusetts. As gangster films became more graphic, such complaints would escalate, and *Weary River* seems tame compared to the Cagney/Raft/Edward G. Robinson pictures that arrived in the next few years.

Fortunately for enthusiasts of early sound cinema, *Weary River* was restored in 1996 by Warner Bros., the UCLA Film and Television Archive, and the Library of Congress Motion Picture, Broadcasting, and Recorded Sound Division. In 2010, it even came to DVD as part of the Warner Archive series.

Lucky Boy
(Tiffany-Stahl; February 2, 1929)

Directors: Norman Taurog, Charles C. Wilson. Dialogue Director/Director of Sound Sequences: Rudolph Flothow. Scenario: Isadore Bernstein, based on the story "The

Schlemiehl" by Viola Brothers Shore. Dialogue: George Jessel. Titles: Harry Braxton, George Jessel. Photography: Harry Jackson, Frank Zucker. Editors: Desmond O'Brien, Russell Shields. Art Director: Hervey Libbert. Set Director: George Sawley. Musical Arrangements: Hugo Riesenfeld. Musical Director: Sasha Bunchuk. Running Time: 77 minutes (part-talking; also released as silent).

Cast: George Jessel (Georgie Jessel); Gwen Lee (Mrs. Ellis); Richard Tucker (Mr. Ellis); Gayne Whitman (Mr. Trent); Margaret Quimby (Eleanor); Rosa Rosanova (Momma Jessel); William H. Strauss (Jacob Jessel); Mary Doran (Bella); Edwin Jerome (Ziegbert); Glenda Farrell (Ziegbert's secretary); William Gargan (man in Ziegbert's office); Sig Rumann (bridge player); Charles C. Wilson (amateur night host); Abel Baer (piano player in music store); Ted Athey (stage manager); Ray Turner (porter); Patty and Fields, Joe Sevely (amateur-night acts).

Songs: "In My Bouquet of Memories" [Jessel], "Old Man Sunshine" [Jessel], "You're My Real Sweetheart" [Jessel] (Sam M. Lewis, Joe Young, Harry Akst): "Lucky Boy" [Jessel, chorus], "My Mother's Eyes" [Jessel, four times, first with Baer at piano] (L. Wolfe Gilbert, Abel Baer); "Keep Sweeping the Cobwebs off the Moon" [Patty and Fields] (Sam M. Lewis, Joe Young, Oscar Levant); "My Blackbirds Are Bluebirds Now" [Jessel] (Irving Caesar, Cliff Friend).

Working Titles/Also Known As: *The Ghetto; The Schlemiehl.*

Disc: Victor 21852 ("My Mother's Eyes," George Jessel).

Home Video: Reel Classic DVD.

The Story: Georgie Jessel works in his father's jewelry store in the Bronx and dreams of making it in show business, even though he is rebuffed by Broadway producer Ziegbert. His mother gives him her earrings to sell for the cash needed to rent a theater for his own show, but "Georgie Jessel's Bronx Follies" is canceled on opening night when Georgie runs out of money. Georgie goes to San Francisco, where he performs in an amateur night and gets his big break when he sings "My Mother's Eyes." Now a success in a San Francisco cabaret, Georgie falls for socialite Eleanor, whose sister, Mrs. Ellis, is carrying on an affair with Trent. Trent gives Mrs. Ellis a valuable ring; Georgie nearly catches her in a lie but keeps quiet and is rewarded for it. Georgie's mom is taken ill, but she gets better after he sings "My Mother's Eyes" to her over the radio. Georgie stars in Ziegbert's new hit, "Lucky Boy," and wins Eleanor.

When it was believed lost, *Lucky Boy* was known as the low-budget consolation prize for which George Jessel settled after turning down the role in the landmark movie version of *The Jazz Singer*—the Broadway play in which Jessel originated the lead—and then watching Al Jolson's career rise to new heights. Now that Jessel's so-called prize has resurfaced, there is more to the story, although this transitional part-talkie—which had an unusual production history—retains a second-hand air.

For a time, it seemed as if Jessel (1898–1981) would be rewarded by Warner Bros.' plan to remain financially solvent by making a feature-length picture with synchronized underscoring and sound effects in its new Vitaphone process.

The studio had done this to great success with the non-dialogue John Barrymore romantic drama *Don Juan*, but the new project, an adaptation of the stage drama *The Jazz Singer*, was to have song numbers added. Jessel not only was starring in the stage version, he had national recognition from vaudeville and Broadway, and he seemed a natural to reprise his role of a cantor's son conflicted by show-business fame and familial tradition. Jessel was signed by Warner Bros. in 1926 with *The Jazz Singer* in mind, but he first appeared for the studio in an ethnic comedy feature, *Private Izzy Murphy*, and a short subject, *George Jessel in a Theatrical Booking Office*.

But Jolson ended up being contracted for *The Jazz Singer*. Jolson was older, a bigger name than Jessel, and had impressed with his own short, *Al Jolson in a Plantation Act*, which joined the Jessel one-reeler in Vitaphone's second-ever theatrical shorts program in October 1926. Jessel's claimed explanation for the snub, albeit some years later:

> Harry Warner offered me $25,000 in cash and $75,000 in stock to do the picture. But he wouldn't ever put the deal on paper.... Warner wouldn't do it because he and his brothers didn't have any money.... One morning, Jolson got up early [he was sharing a hotel suite with Jessel] and he said, "You go back to sleep, kid. I'm going to play golf." Instead, he went straight to the studio and signed the contract to do *The Jazz Singer*. I didn't even know that he had been approached.... When we talked about it, I said, "How did you get the picture?" (He said,) "I put up about a million dollars of my own money."[9]

The 1927 film, released with Jolson's trademark gusto in song and (limited) dialogue delivery, put Warner Bros. on firm financial footing and changed the course of Hollywood history. It prompted an unofficial follow-up by Warners and Jolson, the part-talking *The Singing Fool* (1928), an even bigger box-office hit. Meanwhile, Jessel, presumably still smarting over the *Jazz Singer* snub, made three minor silents for WB and one for Fox, then went to the lower-rung Tiffany-Stahl studio for what were to be two more non-audible comedies. One, *George Washington Cohen*, was released near the end of 1928. The other, titled *The Ghetto* and based on a story by novelist/playwright/short-story writer Viola Brothers Shore, was filmed in Hollywood in 12 days in April 1928 by Norman Taurog, making his debut in features after years of directing comedy shorts. Jessel played a fictionalized version of himself in *The Ghetto*, right down to his character's name of Georgie Jessel, a jeweler's son from the Bronx who overcomes his father's resistance to make it big in showbiz. This Georgie was described in promotional ads as "a poor fool who blunders into the lives of others and brings happiness to all."

But the talkie revolution—and perhaps Warners' impending release of *The Singing Fool*—altered Tiffany-Stahl's plans for *The Ghetto*, which sat on the shelf while the studio decided what to do with it. In September, the trades reported that, after lengthy negotiations, Jessel had "finally given in" to Tiffany, via a "bag of gold," to add singing and talking sequences to *The Ghetto*.[10] For what was retitled *Lucky Boy*, those scenes were shot between mid–November and early December in a hastily assembled studio facility in New York City using RCA's fledgling Photophone sound process. Taurog was back in Hollywood, having been signed by Fox to make comedy shorts, so the dialogue and song sequences—which made up nearly 40 minutes, or about half the film—were directed by actor Charles C. Wilson and/or dialogue director Rudolph Flothow. Jessel and female lead Margaret Quimby (1904–1965) seem to have been the only players from *The Ghetto* who participated in the sound sections.

Jessel was doing double duty at this point; he was starring live at the National Theatre in *The War Song*, a comedy-drama he'd co-written, in the evenings while finishing his movie by day. He wrote the titles and dialogue himself for *Lucky Boy*, which was all the more his production because much of the *War Song* cast was brought in to appear in the movie. Those actors included not only Wilson, who played a small role in *Lucky Boy* as a stage emcee in addition to directing, but also Edwin Jerome, who portrayed a Ziegfeldian producer; Ted Athey, who was Jessel's longtime stage manager; Sig Rumann, who would go on to appear in *A Night at the Opera* and many other features; and William Gargan, whose movie career began with a bit part here.[11] Another future star, Glenda Farrell, played a secretary in *Lucky Boy*. To add to the impromptu casting, Abel Baer—who co-wrote the film's theme song, "My Mother's Eyes"—made a rare in-person appearance as a music-store piano player. Meanwhile, for scenes set at an amateur-night performance, Jessel dispatched theatrical agent Abe Meyer to find some markedly untalented acts to contrast with the star's talent; two of such, acrobat Joe Sevely and sister duo Patty and Fields, were signed for the film.[12]

George Jessel's shortcomings as a movie star were apparent in his first sound film, the part-talkie *Lucky Boy* (1928).

With full- and part-talking films in full swing at many studios as 1929 dawned, Tiffany-Stahl made swift plans to get its first talkie into release, and the timing was good, even for a hybrid like *Lucky Boy*. With Jessel's name as a big draw as "The Original Jazz Singer," Tiffany pacted with the Loew's theater chain for first-run bookings—a heady move for an indie—and arranged for a national ad tie-in with the American Tobacco Company to promote endorsements by Jessel on the Saturday night "Lucky Strike Hour" radio program.[13] Tiffany announced *Lucky Boy* as the lead attraction in its first roster of talking pictures; among the others were *Molly and Me* and *My Lady's Past*, both of which paired screen newcomer Joe E. Brown with established star Belle Bennett, and *Midstream*, a rejuvenation drama with Ricardo Cortez as an elderly man who undergoes an experimental operation to be restored to youth.

Tiffany-Stahl spent a lot (for Tiffany-Stahl) on *Lucky Boy*, but the investment was worth it, with solid box office and generally positive reviews, although too many of the latter compared Jessel with Jolie. *The Film Daily*, for example, praised "My Mother's Eyes" but predicted it "as a runner-up" for "Sonny Boy," referring to the hit tune from *The Singing Fool*.[14] Reviewers also liked the comedy, among which was a quip by Jessel about alleged anti–Semite Henry Ford and his new brand of car: "Only one trouble with it—if you speak Jewish in the back seat, it stops immediately." Another number that attracted attention was the strongly sentimental "In My Bouquet of Memories," a pop song that Jessel turns into a tribute to recently departed stage performers such as Sam Bernard, Robert Mantell, and Eddie Foy, even imagining dialogues with the deceased. ("Save your money!" is the advice to Jessel from the singer's version of the "German"-accented Jewish comedian Bernard.)

The frequency with which "My Mother's Eyes" was heard came in for scrutiny; in the 77-minute print viewed by the author (the film originally may have been as long as 90 minutes), Jessel delivers the tune four times. He gets right to it, the first rendition coming within the first five minutes. At another point, he sings it as his parents (who are shown in the silent footage shot six months prior) listen to the song over the radio. Of course, Jessel ends the film with "My Mother's Eyes"; needing material for an encore for his Broadway opening-night triumph, he balks at Quimby's suggestion for the tune before being reminded by a stage manager (played by real-thing Ted Athey): "Listen, young fella, I've been hanging around the show business for 40 years, and a song about mother is never too old!"

Lucky Boy is worth watching to see Jessel at his peak as an entertainer. It is less accomplished as an achievement in the advancement of sound in film, but its aural awkwardness is part of what makes it interesting. The initial sound sequence is conveniently set in a music store, where there is a piano handy to accompany Jessel; he need only bark at Abel Baer to "play the blackbirds song!" ("My Blackbirds Are Bluebirds Now") or "play me the mother song!" ("My Mother's Eyes"). Also highlighting the primitive nature of the production is a transition from silent footage of a bridge game, set in a mansion and filmed on a fancy set, to a short dialogue sequence involving Jessel and Sig Rumann shot in front of a crude tapestry mounted on a wall and a plain table lamp, and then back to the bridge game with Jessel, Gwen Lee, Margaret Quimby, and others speaking through title cards with underscoring resumed. This was enough to satiate audiences in the first months of 1929, but they would not be so undemanding for long.

Tiffany-Stahl planned to make more movies with its new star—presumably with more mother songs—but the company, always needing cash, gave in to an offer from Fox to buy Jessel's contract in March 1929.[15] At Fox, Jessel made only two pictures before his contract was discreetly bought out—perhaps with the realization that he really wasn't suited to be a film star, no matter his talent. Tiffany would declare bankruptcy within a couple of years, and Jessel would outlast his first sound movie employer by nearly 50 years. Perhaps his most lasting contribution to the Hollywood film was his stint as a producer at 20th Century–Fox, where he brought the stories of many of his vaudeville colleagues to the screen in the 1940s and '50s.

Jessel was long departed when *Lucky Boy* was rediscovered, and it was shown in 1994 at UCLA along with the just-restored 1929 Vitaphone short *Baby Rose Marie, the Child Wonder*. Rose Marie was in attendance, sitting next to Ron Hutchinson of the Vitaphone Project. When the third rendition of "My Mother's Eyes" began, she leaned over to Hutchinson and said, "I can't take it another time," and exited the theater. She wasn't the only one who had the same urge upon viewing *Lucky Boy*.

The Battle of Paris
(Paramount; November 30, 1929)

Director: Robert Florey. Producer: Monta Bell. Story/Dialogue: Gene Markey. Photography: William Steiner. Editor: Emma Hill. Sound: Edward Schebbehar. Running Time: 68 minutes.

Cast: Gertrude Lawrence (Georgie Manners); Charles Ruggles (Zizi); Walter Petrie (Tony Trent); Gladys DuBois (Suzanne); Arthur Treacher (Harry); Joe King (Jack); Luis Alberni (waiter); Charles Esdale (café host); Jules Epailly (mustached café proprietor); Charles LaTorre (crook); Louise Mackintosh (nurse); Warren Ashe, Herbert Miller (soldiers); Barry Curran, Rita LaTenza (Apache dancers); The New Yorkers; The Singing Marines.

Songs: "Here Comes the Band Wagon" [Lawrence, band], "They All Fall in Love" [Lawrence, chorus] (Cole Porter); "What Makes My Baby Blue?" [Lawrence, chorus], "When I Am Housekeeping for You" [Lawrence, three times] (Howard Dietz, Jay Gorney); "The Boys With the Little Red Drum" [chorus] (Eugene Field, Gibson); "Give Me the Moonlight, Give Me the Girl" [Ruggles, chorus] (Lew Brown, Albert Von Tilzer); "It's a Long Way to Tipperary" [Lawrence, chorus, reprised by band]

(Jack Judge, Harry Williams); "Madelon" [chorus] (Louis Bousquet, Alfred Bryan, Camille Robert); "Mademoiselle from Armentieres" ("Hinky Dinky Parlez Vous") [chorus, danced by Lawrence] (authorship uncertain); "Sous les Pontsch Paris" [Lawrence, chorus] (Jean Rodor, Vincent Scotto).
Working Title: *The Gay Lady.*

The Story: Georgie, an English girl who sings on the streets of Paris, meets American artist Tony Trent. They are parted when he enlists in the Great War, although she keeps his apartment. Now a Red Cross nurse at a military hospital, Georgie is reunited with her old pal Zizi, a pickpocket-turned-soldier. Georgie reconnects with Tony, now an officer, who is pursued by the possessive Suzanne while on leave. Zizi and fellow soldiers Harry, an Englishman, and Jack, an American, "borrow" a dress for Georgie so she can entertain café patrons and attract Tony's attention. Georgie is told Tony has been injured in an accident; she is taken to a seedy club and kidnapped by Suzanne and her minions. Tony and the "Musketeers" rescue Georgie just as the Armistice is announced.

How could Paramount have the services of English revue star Gertrude Lawrence, composer extraordinaire Cole Porter, and visionary director Robert Florey—and make such a botch? Hard to believe, but *The Battle of Paris*, was criticized by *Variety* as "perhaps the poorest picture to come out of a major studio this season."[16]

Ah, but the play's the thing, and *The Battle of Paris* wielded a 10-cent script by Gene Markey to go with its million-dollar names. This was no less than the fifth 1929 musical Markey had a hand in writing—the others were Paramount's Nancy Carroll-Buddy Rogers hit *Close Harmony* and three Morton Downey vehicles in RKO's *Syncopation* and Pathé's *Lucky in Love* and *Mother's Boy*—but he must have been running out of ideas. This one was a tale about a penniless singer who falls for an American artist, loses him to the Great War, and then finds him again through a ridiculous unfolding of events in the Montmartre.

Perhaps not inappropriately, Lawrence (1898–1952) had one of her few stage flops to thank for her first feature film appearance. *Treasure Girl*, a musical comedy with a George and Ira Gershwin score, closed on Broadway in early 1929 after only two months, and Lawrence hung around New York hoping for another job offer before her return to London. The call came from Paramount for a film called *The Gay Lady*, to be shot at the studio's Long Island facility at Astoria, New York, under the direction of Florey. The Paris-born Florey initially came to prominence as an avant-garde filmmaker—his shorts *The Life and Death of 9413, a Hollywood Extra* and *Skyscraper Symphony* were strongly influenced by German expressionism—but Paramount had signed him to make more-conventional fare. At Astoria earlier in 1929, he helmed *The Hole in the Wall*, a suspense thriller with some inventive use of sound, and co-directed the

Marx Brothers' debut, *The Cocoanuts*, a mainly stage-bound production with a few visual flourishes, such as kaleidoscopic overhead shots and unusual ground-level views of production numbers, and dancing girls shown in photo-negative images. Unfortunately, Florey did not bring the same creativity to *The Gay Lady*, which was renamed *The Battle of Paris* shortly after wrapping production in the summer of 1929.

Reminiscing years later, well into a filmmaking career that would last into the 1960s, the director called the *Battle of Paris* scenario "afflicted ... ridiculous ... stupid," and said he made the film "the best I knew how but without any particular enthusiasm."[17] According to Florey, who threatened to walk out on the production, Lawrence didn't have much interest in the project, either, for when he asked her what she thought of the screenplay, he found that she hadn't paid much attention to it, favoring instead the score and the period costumes.[18] Another drawback was that *The Battle of Paris* had to be shot at night, due to the busy production schedule at Astoria, where 10 features and nearly 50 shorts were made between mid–1928 and mid–'29.[19]

The company was on this topsy-turvy schedule when a reporter from *The New York Times*, which considered Lawrence's stay in the city as big news, visited the set early in July to watch scenes of the finale in which Lawrence's character is kidnapped by toughs from the Paris underworld and held in a back room of a seedy café. The writer decided that this star, even dirtied up, was foremost a star: "She held up a piece of her evening gown that had been torn from her in the struggle. She appeared very chic, even after many rehearsals, during which she was carelessly thrown against dirty wine casks and maltreated by ruffians whose countenances resembled gargoyles."[20] According to the *Times* account, the crooks were played by cab drivers hired as extras.

The shooting schedule had to be difficult for the company, but for those who lived near the studio, the night-time activity led to an expected holiday treat:

> A day before the Fourth of July, residents of Astoria ... were treated to a display of fireworks that rivaled the famous "Last Days of Pompeii." This unusual pyrotechnic display took place in the back yard of the Paramount Long Island studio for the war scenes in *The Gay Lady*.... The scenes depicted an air raid on Paris. Star shells burst in the air, bombs exploded, searchlights cast beams of light into the dark sky, and all manner of confusion was generated to give realistic atmosphere.... More than a thousand residents of Astoria lined the streets around the studio to watch the display.[21]

Other publicity spawned by the set doings stemmed from Lawrence's hands-across-the-water generosity toward her new colleagues, as shown by this account in a fan magazine:

> I have yet to find anyone who doesn't get dizzy in digging up their best adjectives to describe Gertrude Lawrence. She has been making *The Gay Lady* at the Paramount studio on Long Island, and the company is one of those happy-family affairs where

everyone thinks the star is simply swell. While the company worked at night, she took the whole troupe to see *Show Girl* [the Broadway musical] in the afternoon, crowded them all into her apartment for luncheon, and herded them to the theater like a young teacher with a lot of high-spirited pupils.[22]

Lawrence's supporting cast was made up of obscure New York talent, few of which had much movie experience. For Walter Petrie and Gladys DuBois, *The Battle of Paris* would be their only substantive film acting credit. Arthur Treacher came to the cast directly from the Broadway stage; this was his only feature prior to 1933, when the native Britisher began a lengthy career as Hollywood's ideal butler. *The Battle of Paris*' primary comic, Charles Ruggles, would fare better on screen more quickly; based on his work in *The Battle of Paris* and the Astoria-shot features *Gentlemen of the Press* and *The Lady Lies*, he was inked to a long-term contract by Paramount. This kept him in the East making *Queen High* [q.v.] and other titles.

Ruggles affects a broad French accent as the charming pickpocket of *The Battle of Paris*, which must have made his performance all the more endearing to non-discerning audiences, but there's little in Lawrence's work to suggest her lofty reputation, save for a sufficiently animateed rendition of Porter's "They All Fall in Love." The number, set in a cabaret, is the film's highlight, despite it sounding like a rehash of the composer's hit "Let's Do It," written the previous year for the Broadway musical *Paris*. "They All Fall in Love" was one of only two songs Porter wrote in his first foray into movies, despite his being the only credited songwriter on screen. The emphasis on Porter obscured the work of two Paramount staff songwriters, lyricist Howard Dietz (then writing under the pseudonym Dick Howard) and composer Jay Gorney, whose "When I Am Housekeeping for You" and "What Makes My Baby Blue?" are given more screen time. Film work was secondary to writing for the stage for Dietz and Gorney at this point—they'd worked on the Broadway show *Merry-Go-Round*—and their efforts here suggest a certain indifference.

Its cheap-looking sets and claustrophobic feel hardly suit *The Battle of Paris*, but the worst asset is the script, in which the possessive rival for the affections of Lawrence's boyfriend is an out-and-out psycho who resorts to imprisonment to keep her man. DuBois plays the role complete with weirdly dark eyebrows that look painted on; if she'd had a moustache, she would be twirling it for such awful dialogue—spoken to Lawrence as she's held captive by her nasty-looking cohorts—as "I'm giving a little party for you tonight. Meet some *charming* men! ... Are these *common* enough for you?"[23] (A more-substantial contribution by DuBois to showbiz was as co-lyricist of—wait for it—"You Call It Madness, But I Call It Love.")

The Battle of Paris put up little fight at the box office. It was initially slated to premiere in New York at the high-end Paramount Theater, but the studio sat on its release there for some time.[24] According to Lawrence biographer Sheridan Morley, Paramount sent a dispatch to its distributors that said, "Sell strongly on songs and clothing of G. Lawrence," not mentioning the story.[25] Paramount must have known it had a stinker; the film played in hamlets such as Alton, Illinois; Escanaba, Michigan; and Portsmouth, New Hampshire, in late 1929 before being sent, like a lamb to slaughter, to New York grindhouses in February 1930. (The *Times*, which a few months before deemed the film worthy of a feature story, didn't bother to review it.) Lawrence returned to the stage, and in her last 23 years made only eight feature films. She was most memorable on camera as Amanda Wingfield in *The Glass Menagerie* (1950), a year before her Broadway triumph in *The King and I* and two years before her death from liver cancer.

In 1994—65 years after *The Battle of Paris* debuted—author, playwright, producer, director and musical theater historian Ken Bloom found an unpublished Cole Porter song written for the film. It was a ballad called "Without You," located by Bloom in manuscript form in the Paramount music library. By its (re-)discoverer's account, it wasn't much of a song, which seems an appropriate postscript for such a cinematic mediocrity.

Lord Byron of Broadway
(Metro-Goldwyn-Mayer; February 28, 1930)

Directors: Harry Beaumont, William Nigh. Dialogue/Continuity: Crane Wilbur, Willard Mack, based on the novel by Nell Martin. Photography: Henry Sharp. Editor: Anne Bauchens. Dance Director: Sammy Lee. Ballet Staging: Albertina Rasch. Sound: Douglas Shearer. Art Director: Cedric Gibbons. Costumes: David Cox. Running Time: 77 minutes. Technicolor sequences.

Cast: Charles Kaley (Roy Erskine); Ethelind Terry (Ardis Trevelyan); Marion Shilling (Nancy Clover); Cliff Edwards (Joe Lundeen); Gwen Lee (Bessie); Benny Rubin (Phil); Drew Demorest (Edwards); John Byron (Millaire); Rita Flynn (Redhead); Hazel Craven (Blondie); Gino Corrado (Riccardi); Paulette Paquet (Marie); James Burroughs; Albertina Rasch Ballet; Jack Benny (radio announcer); Mary Doran (woman on street); Ann Dvorak (chorus girl); Eddie Kane (Abe); Virginia Sale (dowager at party); Larry Steers (Larry).

Songs: "A Bundle of Old Love Letters" [Edwards; reprised by Kaley, Edwards], "Old Pal, Why Did You Leave Me?" [Kaley], "Only Love Is Real" [Edwards; reprised by Terry], "Should I?" [Kaley; reprised by Terry], "The Woman in the Shoe" [Terry, off-screen male vocalist, chorus; reprised by male trio], "You're the Bride and I'm the Groom" [Kaley] (Arthur Freed, Nacio Herb Brown); "Blue Daughter of Heaven" [Burroughs, Rasch girls] (Raymond B. Egan, Dimitri Tiomkin); "The Doll Dance" [danced by Flynn, Craven] (Nacio Herb Brown); "The Japanese Sandman" [Edwards] (Raymond B. Egan, Richard A. Whiting).

Also Known As: *What Price Melody?*
Disc: Brunswick 4718 ("Should I?"/"A Bundle of Old Love Letters," Charles Kaley).
Home Video: Warner Archive DVD.

The Story: Roy Erskine, a café pianist, is prompted to write "A Bundle of Old Love Letters" during an encounter with a girlfriend, Bessie. He teams with singer Joe Lundeen and piano player Nancy Clover in vaudeville, and Roy's songwriting career flourishes as he continues to derive inspiration from romantic exploits. Roy meets Broadway headliner Ardis Trevelyan and falls for her, but she fails to tell him she is Joe's estranged wife. Roy, Joe, and Nancy are hired to perform in Ardis' new show, in which she sings Roy's "The Woman in the Shoe." After a falling-out with Roy over Ardis, Joe is killed in an auto accident. Roy writes "Old Pal, Why Did You Ever Leave Me?" after Joe's death but is made aware of his callousness by an angry Nancy. Racked by guilt, Roy falls into a personal and professional tailspin, but Nancy's love rejuvenates him—as does a new song, "Only Love Is Real."

To most fanciers of the early Hollywood musical, *Lord Byron of Broadway* is what it was to most analysts in 1930: an expensive flop sunk by career-killing performances by two cinematically inexperienced leads and a mind-numbingly familiar backstage milieu. Here's one vote for a second look ... because it's actually much more enjoyable than its reputation might suggest, with built-in big-studio sheen and, especially, a terrific score out of the MGM songbook. Those go a long way toward balancing the casting ... uh, difficulties and a topsy-turvy production saga marred by hasty decisions and bad timing.

Lord Byron of Broadway began life as a widely read 1928 novel by Nell Martin, a former vaudevillian and newspaper reporter, about a fellow of whom there were more than a few in showbiz but very few of in print: an egotistical songwriter, this one an out-and-out heel who exploits his love life—and the misfortune of those around him—to mine his material. Perhaps sensing the growing need for movie musical fare, Metro bought the screen rights to Martin's book in November 1928 and set out to put together a project that needed strong personalities in the top roles. This turned out to be easier said than done—William Haines and Bessie Love, the latter newly acclaimed for her work in the MGM musical *The Broadway Melody* (1929), were initially announced as the leads, the female headline character being the big-time star who makes the composer's tunes sing.[26] Neither actor worked out—although one can envision resident smart-aleck Haines in the role—and neither did Charles King, Love's *Broadway Melody* co-star, who instead was reteamed with Love in the studio's "other" big *Melody* follow-up, *Chasing Rainbows*.

Production was set to begin in the late spring of 1929 under director William Nigh, and songs were penned by *Broadway Melody* tunesmiths Nacio Herb Brown and Arthur Freed, but the calendar moved into late summer with no *Lord Byron*. Broadway singer Frances Williams was cast, then took a stage role, opening the door for blues chanteuse Marion Harris. Still, nothing—a *Variety* report curiously cites a delay until Harris "gains some weight."[27] That might have been code for studio displeasure at the casting, but this would soon

Stage stars Charles Kaley and Ethelind Terry (right) fizzled in *Lord Byron of Broadway* (1930), but ingenue Marion Shilling (left) enjoyed a longer Hollywood career.

change. Ethelind Terry, star of the 1921 *Music Box Revue* and the blockbuster Broadway musicals *Rio Rita* (as the original Rita) and *Kid Boots* (for Flo Ziegfeld), was signed during what an MGM puff piece described as an intended two-day vacation in Los Angeles. She was said to have been introduced at a club to the makers of *Lord Byron* and asked to test. "There has been a lot of hectic telephoning and testing … to find a beautiful young actress with a voice suitable to a difficult role," reported the *Los Angeles Times* upon Terry's addition in August. "…Now there is peace around the lot, as Miss Terry fills the bill quite nicely."[28]

A Philadelphia-born daughter of the president of the Hires Root Beer Company, Terry (1899–1984) was a brunette with large, dark eyes and a vaguely exotic look. She had been raised in comfort and was drawn to the theater at an early age. In contrast to performers who were schooled to be modest and self-deprecating in press interviews, Terry admitted that she loved being a celebrity. "I just love publicity—I never have been able to get enough of it to satisfy me," she told a newspaper wire service reporter while making *Lord Byron*. "…I am in pictures largely because of the enormous salary I can earn."[29] Terry's yen for high living also was reflected in a statement she reportedly made in 1927 while romancing the real estate mogul who would be her first husband: "None but millionaires will be considered matrimonially."[30]

Terry's cinematic male counterpart had yet to be found, and time was growing short. In September, MGM announced the signing of Charles Kaley after auditions by a reported "60 Hollywood and stage actors."[31] Kaley (1902–1965) was a former violinist and tenor with Abe Lyman's band who had become a recording artist, revue performer (in Earl Carroll's *Vanities*), and, most notably, a master of ceremonies and orchestra leader in Chicago theaters. Alternately known as "The Singing Band Leader" or, when he really needed a push, "The World's Premiere Singing Director," Kaley was noticed for his resemblance to Hollywood star Richard Arlen. He had warmed up in real life for his status as a singer with sex appeal in *Lord Byron of Broadway* by having married the then–16-year-old singer Hannah Williams (Jack Dempsey's future wife) in 1927, and then, one month after that brief union had been annulled, eloping with, and then deserting, another woman within a few weeks.[32] During his stay in Hollywood, he was linked to Carole Lombard, among others.

With key supporting players Marion Shilling, a new Metro find cast as the third member of the film's love triangle, and recording star Cliff "Ukelele Ike" Edwards, shooting on *Lord Byron* finally began in late September and was finished in less than a month. Except that it didn't finish: By the end of October, the film's ending was being reshot per orders from MGM production supervisor Harry Rapf.[33] As Marion Shilling (1910–2004) told this book's author in 1993:

> The [stock] market had just crashed when ... Harry Rapf returned from New York having lost a fortune in a few days. You can imagine his mood when he looked at the first rough cut.... He ordered an almost complete remake. William Nigh was replaced as director by Harry Beaumont. All of Nigh's cronies in the cast were replaced, and Benny Rubin was recruited to lighten the mood. My wardrobe was entirely remade, as skirts had taken a plunge along with the stocks.[34]

Shilling—who would go on to a steady Hollywood career, mainly in low-budget films, before retiring for motherhood in 1936—said she had good memories of her experience on the *Lord Byron* set:

> Charles Kaley and Ethelind Terry couldn't have been more pleasant to work with. Cliff Edwards was the life of the set. A wit, a wag, preoccupied with sex, he made racy comments at every opportunity. I was the special object of his jokes, his ideal foil. Having had a sheltered upbringing by a strict mother, I was naïve even by the standards of that innocent era. Benny Rubin was a dear—intelligent, clean-cut.[35]

The new footage shot by *Broadway Melody* director Beaumont supposedly made Kaley's character more sympathetic, and it provided comic relief by Rubin as a vaude manager with typical mis-sayings such as "Pardon me while I consummate!" It didn't keep *Lord Byron of Broadway* from opening, in February

1930, to mainly negative reactions. Ever-grumpy critic Mordaunt Hall of *The New York Times* found that "the dialogue is hopeless and most of the work of the players is amateurish."[36] Other descriptions termed the film "slipshod," "completely lacking," and a "capital offense," and *The Film Daily* called Kaley's performance "a little too phlegmatic"—not exactly a reviewer's typical adjective, but perhaps true of his flat characterization.[37]

Variety had a more perceptive opinion: "Backstage stuff and romances built around songwriters have grown stale since talkers, but in *Lord Byron of Broadway*, Metro has applied a refreshing touch to such material."[38] This, at its core, might have been the biggest hindrance for audiences—they weren't used to seeing a hero quite this unsympathetic in a musical film. In a satirical straight (non-musical) play, yes, but in what MGM was advertising, antiheroes were not welcome, *Pal Joey* being some years away. True, there were no real "star" names to sell the film, and Terry's performance can be charitably described as "offbeat"—or, if you're Richard Barrios, as "a thing of bizarre inflections, illiterate body language, and unfathomable hauteur."[39] With flowery dialogue like "You have created beauty—I'm only the interpreter!" she was a tough sell to viewers who were starting to tire of stage people hijacking their movies from movie stars. Had *Lord Byron* made its original production deadline and been released earlier, people might have been more accepting.

Ah ... but there's the music, and in *Lord Byron*, there's plenty—and it's great. The biggest song hit to emerge from the film was Brown and Freed's "Should I?"—which became one of the season's most-played and hummed-to tunes. MGM plugged it well in advance of the film's release, so the backlash against the film didn't hurt sales. Old-timey fare is represented by Edwards' rendition of "The Japanese Sandman"—which the singer had covered years before—and a duet hoofing to "The Doll Dance." Two new tunes are showcased in separate Technicolor sequences.[40] One, "Blue Daughter of Heaven," is a kitschy, Chinese-style floor-show ballet partially revealed in lingering, pre–Busby Berkeley overhead camera shots; the music, co-written by the young Dimitri Tiomkin, is danced by his wife's Albertina Rasch girl troupe.

Significantly better is the other color piece, Brown and Freed's "The Woman in the Shoe," which was clearly intended to match the splendor of the same writers' "Wedding of the Painted Doll" number from *Broadway Melody*. The two "story" songs are staged similarly; here, Ethelind Terry doubles as the fairy-tale matron in the "Shoe" verse, singing about her plight of too many children and not enough food. A "fairy prince" waves his wand, transforming the woman's tattered boot into a sleek, modern, high-heeled shoe perched atop a stairway of gold. A now-gowned Terry and a chorus of butchers, bakers, Jack and Jill, a ballerina, and a dancing row of "four-and-twenty female blackbirds" finish the song with a tricky display of Sammy Lee's cinematography.

Despite such flair, the enmity toward Kaley and Terry was too much to overcome. Only a year later, the two actors were dismissed by *Variety*—in a story headlined "Talker Stars for a Day: Quick Fadeouts After Big Push"—with the comment that *Lord Byron* "was their first and last picture."[41] It might as well have been, but the record indicates otherwise. Kaley hung around in Hollywood after his *Byron* washout long enough to appear in a pair of 1930 Pathe two-reel musical comedies, *Red Heads* and *The Beauties*. Later, he made a Warner Bros. color short, *Pickin' a Winner* (1932), and played an uncredited bit as a bandleader in the First National comedy *Bright Lights* (1935). His final film role, for tiny Spectrum Pictures in 1937, backed cowboy star Fred Scott in *The Singing Buckaroo*. As an embezzling stockbroker, he utters lines like "So you thought you could get away with it, huh!" with the same lack of conviction as he told Cliff Edwards to get lost in *Lord Byron*. Kaley's career as an emcee/bandleader included a lengthy stint in San Francisco in the late '30s and early '40s, and then in Nevada. There, in 1943, he married his fourth wife, to whom he was wed when he died.[42]

Terry went right back to the musical stage after *Lord Byron*, starring in the Sigmund Romberg operetta *Nina Rosa* on Broadway in 1930–31 and in *Sons o' Guns* in L.A. right after. Her only other documented film appearance was as a singer in a 1937 Tex Ritter oater, *Arizona Days*.[43] She experienced a stormy seven-month marriage to actor Dick Purcell—who divorced her in 1942 on grounds of mental cruelty—before gaining some of the publicity she once craved when found working as a stock clerk in an aircraft plant in 1943.[44] Newspaper photographs that showed her working on an assembly line at the Burbank, California, plant were accompanied by this caption: "As a Ziegfeld beauty her salary was $2,500 a week. But she is happy to be doing her bit." Terry was in Florida when she died at age 84.

Lord Byron of Broadway didn't exactly disappear after 1930, either. It received periodic TV showings in the 1960s and attracted a new (and not uniformly appreciative) audience through airings on Turner Network Television and Turner Classic Movies, and even a Warner Archive DVD release. (Thank you!) Even if it veers a little too closely to the early talkie parody so amusingly presented in Metro's own *Singin' in the Rain*, it's a valuable reminder of both the good and bad of the earliest film musicals.

Oh, Sailor, Behave!
(Warner Bros.; July 4, 1930)

Director: Archie Mayo. Screenplay/Dialogue: Joseph Jackson, Sid Silvers, Ole Olsen, Chic Johnson, based on the play *See Naples and Die* by Elmer Rice (New York opening, September 24, 1929; 62 performances). Photography: Dev Jennings. Editing:

Robert Crandall. Sound: Clare A. Riggs. Musical Direction: Ermo Rapee. Costumes: Earl Luick. Running Time: 67 minutes.
Cast: Irene Delroy (Nancy Dodge); Charles King (Charlie Carroll); Ole Olsen (Simon); Chic Johnson (Peter); Lowell Sherman (Prince Kosloff); Noah Beery (General Skulany); Lotti Loder (Luisa); Charles Judels (De Medici); Vivien Oakland (Kunegundi); Elsie Bartlett (Mitzi); Lawrence Grant (Hugo Klaus); Gino Corrado (Stepan).
Working Titles: *Nancy From Naples*; *See Naples and Die*.
Disc: Brunswick 4840 ("Love Comes in the Moonlight"/"Highway to Heaven," Charles King); Brunswick 4849 ("Leave a Little Smile," Charles King).
Home Video: Warner Archive DVD.
Songs: "Highway to Heaven" [King, Delroy, Judels, Olsen, Johnson, Loder, chorus; reprised by King, Delroy. chorus], "Leave a Little Smile" [Oakland, King; reprised by Oakland, King, chorus], "When Love Comes in the Moonlight" [King, Delroy, twice; reprised by Olsen, Johnson, Delroy, King]; "Which One Do You Love?" [Olsen, Johnson] (Al Dubin, Joe Burke); "The Laughing Song" [Olsen, Johnson, Judels] (Ole Olsen, Chic Johnson).

The Story: American sailors Simon and Peter are on leave in Naples, where they search for a wooden-legged man who has stolen from the Navy storehouse, but they are distracted by a local miss, Luisa. Meanwhile, Paris Herald reporter Charlie Carroll, in the city to interview General Skulany from Montenegro, meets and falls in love with fellow American Nancy Dodge. Nancy loves him, too, but Charlie learns that Nancy has married a Russian prince, and he allows himself to be seduced by Kunegundi, who has promised to help him get his interview. Nancy explains to Charlie that she married Prince Kosloff only to save her sister from disgrace. Kosloff kidnaps Nancy to keep her from securing a divorce; Skulany holds Charlie captive after accusing him of infidelity with Kuni. Simon, Peter, and Luisa must save the day. Kosloff is shot during an assassination attempt on the general, and Charlie and Nancy are free to marry.

In the second full year of sound pictures, Warner Bros. set out to make a musical called *See Naples and Die*, headlined by Broadway singing stars Charles King and Irene Delroy. That it was released as *Oh, Sailor, Behave!*—with the vaudeville comedy team of Olsen and Johnson billed above the title—tells us something about the state of the Hollywood musical during 1930.

There was little to hint at this film's hectic pre-release history in February, when *See Naples and Die* was announced as a musical version of the same-titled comic play by Elmer Rice, and King and Delroy were signed as the romantic leads. Delroy (1900–1985) was a newcomer to films who joined in the exodus of musical performers to Hollywood after having starred on Broadway in the likes of *Follow Thru*, *Hitchy Koo*, *The Greenwich Village Follies*, and the *Ziegfeld Follies of 1927*. A vivacious brunette, the former Josephine Sanders of Bloomington, Illinois, was enjoying a fairytale career that saw her named "Queen of Musical Comedy" by the *New York Daily Mirror* in 1927, and the silver screen was her next field to conquer.[45] Warners signed her in January 1930 and would tout her selection by a Los Angeles newspaper critic as the "Typical Girl of 1930" for her "ultra-modern ... snap and pop, the indefinable elan of this present year of grace."[46]

Manhattan-born King (1886?–1944) had made the transition from stage (*Hit the Deck, Present Arms*) to film as the male lead of the first all-talking musical, MGM's *The Broadway Melody* (1929). The cheerful song-and-dance man was prominently featured in Metro's *Hollywood Revue of 1929* and cast in a follow-up with his *Melody* co-star Bessie Love called *Road Show*, but that film encountered production delays and was not released until early 1930, as *Chasing Rainbows*, to a tepid response. MGM also used King in another kitchen-sink revue, *The March of Time*, but the studio got cold feet over its lack of story and never released it. Described as "one of those perennial juveniles who will never, no matter how old they may be, grow up," King was nonetheless no youngster, and his stature as family man—with a wife and three small children—earned him positive fan-magazine space.[47] Perhaps preferring younger leading men to exploit, Metro loaned King to Warner Bros. for *See Naples and Die* and director Archie Mayo. Al Dubin and Joe Burke, the songwriting team behind "Tiptoe Through the Tulips," "Painting the Clouds With Sunshine," and other hits, were engaged to pen the score for *See Naples and Die* and another WB release, *Top Speed*, in what was reported as a mere three weeks.[48]

See Naples and Die, a not-terribly-successful New York production for Pulitzer Prize–winning *Street Scene* author Rice, concerned a romance between two Americans amid a revolution in a fictional Eastern European country. There were no sailors, behaved or not. This changed for the screen, thanks to Ole Olsen (1892–1965) and Chic Johnson (1891–1962), who were brought in to provide comedy relief, as two seamen on shore leave amid the foreign intrigue, and impressed WB brass enough to merit greater attention. No sophisticates or critics' darlings, these native Midwesterners were especially popular in flyover country, with silly on-stage routines with props like fired shotguns and portable bathtubs to attract belly laughs. No wonder they were billed in vaudeville as "The Mad Monarchs of Monkey Business." By April 1930, after completing their scenes in their film debut, Olsen and Johnson were signed to a long-term studio contract. By May, the title of *See Naples and Die* was changed to *Nancy From Naples*—at least to prevent it from being mistaken for a murder mystery—but this, too, would be temporary.[49] It didn't help that straight-up musicals were starting to lose their surefire box office, potentially lessening the appeal of juvenile and ingénue types like King and Delroy.

Warner Bros. actually premiered the film as *Nancy From Naples* at its Hollywood theater over the Fourth of July weekend, with Delroy earning front-page feature coverage in the *Los Angeles Times* arts section. *Variety* reported

Chic Johnson (left) and Ole Olsen double-team lovely Lotti Loder in the comedy duo's film debut, *Oh! Sailor Behave!* (1930) (courtesy Ron Hutchinson/The Vitaphone Project).

decent box-office returns initially, although a deluxe live revue from dance director Larry Ceballos was thought to have inflated the L.A. money numbers.[50] In any case, Warners grew concerned and, before showing the movie to the rest of the world, changed its title to *Oh, Sailor, Behave!*—signaling emphasis on the Olsen-Johnson critic-proof comedy over the King-Delroy singing romance. What's more, Olsen and Johnson received above-the-title first billing in the opening titles as "America's Craziest Clowns." Perhaps noting Olsen and Johnson's heartland following, the studio played *Oh, Sailor, Behave!* mainly in smaller markets, and it never received a formal New York City premiere.

A look at the film—a 2014 Warner Archive DVD release after years in vault purgatory—reveals the logic of Warner Bros.' game plan. Similar to the early movies of Wheeler and Woolsey when they were teamed with romantic co-stars in conventional musicals such as *Rio Rita* and *The Cuckoos*, Olsen and Johnson seem to exist in a different universe than King and Delroy. The two acting pairs aren't on the screen much at all together, with the comics cavorting with luscious local talent Lotti Loder and jumpy café owner Charles Judels, and King and Delroy interacting with vampy Vivien Oakland, effete Lowell Sherman, and tough-guy Noah Beery. Sherman (1888–1934) may well be the film's best player as a weakling Russian prince dismissed by Delroy as "the thing I married," and Oakland (1895–1958) has an unexpectedly meaty role that showed she could be more than just a foil to Laurel and Hardy or Edgar Kennedy (which she otherwise frequently was). But there is little doubt that this is an Olsen and Johnson showcase, as evidenced by the film's trade-ad boast: "Thar's gold in them thar gobs!"

O&J's first interaction with King introduces one of the film's running jokes: the sailors' preoccupation with finding a man with a wooden leg who has robbed the Navy storehouse. King just happens to be at the wrong street corner when the gobs fire a pea-shooter at his lower limb. That King feels the pain tells us he isn't the culprit, and the boys move on to other exploits punctuated by Johnson's trademark giggle and a rendition of their familiar theme, "The Laughing Song." As for the new vocal material, King and Delroy duet nicely aboard a gondola on "When Love Comes in the Moonlight," an opening number that charmingly establishes the Neapolitan setting, but O&J provide an upstaging counterpoint with a peppy reprise. King recorded "Moonlight" and two other songs from the film, "Highway to Heaven" and "Leave a Little Smile," for Brunswick Records, further plenishing the Dubin-Burke coffers. Olsen and Johnson did not commit the same composers' duet "Which One Do You Love?" to wax, but it's a catchy ditty in which the boys serenade Loder (1910–1999) with romantically questionable lyrics such as "I'm Simon, I'm Peter, you sweet garlic eater."

Even as it signals the decline of the early Hollywood musical, *Oh, Sailor, Behave!* is quite watchable, undeserving of *Photoplay*'s complaint that "[a] few more like this, and song writers and song birds will be going back to Broadway."[51] An unmerited slap, maybe, but not untrue about the songsters. Delroy made three more features at Warner Bros.—among them the all-but-aborted Jerome Kern-Otto Harbach musical *Men of the Sky* (1931)—before leaving the screen for marriage. Dropped by MGM after one final credit, the William Haines comedy *Remote Control*, King would be back in New York by the year of 1930's final fade as part of the Cole Porter hit revue *The New Yorkers*. All would not be rosy, as King declared bankruptcy in 1935, but he made a Broadway comeback in *Panama Hattie* in 1940. He would be a casualty of war: Aboard a USO ship bound for England in 1944, he contracted pneumonia and succumbed shortly after arriving in London.

As for Olsen and Johnson, Warners kept them on for *Fifty Million Frenchmen* (1931), an erstwhile stage musical issued in Technicolor without songs, and *Gold Dust Gertie* (1931), with brassy comic co-star Winnie Lightner. Despite stints at Republic in the late 1930s and Universal in the 1940s, the latter including a filming of their stage smash *Hellzapoppin,*' this duo never really found a footing on celluloid.

Paradise Island
(Tiffany; July 15, 1930)

Director: Bert Glennon. Screenplay: Monte Katterjohn. Story: M. B. Deering. Photography: Max Dupont. Editor: Byron Robinson. Musical Direction: Al Short. Sets: Ralph M. DeLacy. Sound: Dean Daily. Running Time: 69 minutes.

Cast: Kenneth Harlan (Jim Thorne); Marceline Day (Ellen Bradford); Tom Santschi (Mike Lutze); Paul Hurst (Beauty); Betty Boyd (Poppi); Victor Potel (Swede); Gladden James (Roy Armstrong); Will Stanton (Limey).

Songs: "Drinking Song" [Harlan, chorus], "I've Got a Girl in Every Port" [Harlan, chorus, reprised by Harlan], "Just Another Dream" [Day], "Lazy Breezes" [Harlan, chorus] (Val Burton, Will Jason).

Home Video: Alpha DVD.

The Story: Ellen Bradford arrives on a South Seas island intending to marry her fiancé, Roy Armstrong, but Roy has been cheated out of his plantation riches—and lulled into drunkenness—by local saloon owner Lutze. An appalled Ellen postpones the wedding, and Roy is pursued by native girl Poppi. Jim Thorne, a carefree sailor, is attracted to Ellen, and with the help of his comic sidekick, Beauty, thwarts the plans of Lutze, who also desires Ellen and has led Roy to his demise. Thorne and Ellen are united.

If you lived in Kokomo, Indiana, in the fall of 1930, you might have opened the local *Tribune* one evening to read an advertisement for the local Colonial Theater that promised this: "One lone white girl on a South Sea island—and three men who desire her." Tell me ... could you resist? The movie at play was *Paradise Island*, an hour-and-change mix of action, comedy, melodrama, and romance. With a few songs, which is why we're writing about it.

A production of the Tiffany company (formerly known as Tiffany-Stahl), *Paradise Island* was unpretentious fare best enjoyed in neighborhood houses and small cities like Kokomo—where, as late as the second half of 1930, movies were promoted as "all-talking with music" in case the potential audience needed to know the difference.[52] The cast was populated with the typical Tiffany roster of mid-level and/or on-the-way-down talent. In the forefront were Kenneth Harlan (1895–1967), the star of the 1923 version of *The Virginian*, and Marceline Day (1908–2000), a former co-star with Lon Chaney and Buster Keaton.

Director Bert Glennon, on loan from Columbia, was in the midst of a lackluster period in the set's top chair—from whence he supervised such mediocrities as *Gang War, Girl of the Port,* and *Syncopation*—before his return to a distinguished career as a cinematographer (*Stagecoach, Drums Along the Mohawk, Young Mr. Lincoln*). Glennon's cameraman for *Paradise Island*, Max Dupont, could claim to know the territory, as the reported owner of a cocoanut plantation in Tahiti. Glennon gathered a cast and crew of 50 or so for location shooting at Catalina Island for the outdoor scenes of *Paradise Island*; much of the rest was shot in April and May of 1930 on a standing tropical village set recently used for Tiffany's all-Technicolor drama *Mamba*.

Wherever shooting was at a given time, there were natural hazards unforeseen by a domesticized cast and crew. According to a trade-publication news item, Tiffany's chief property man, George Sawley, was delivering large bunches of bananas to the *Paradise Island* set before filming was to commence one day when an unexpected critter was spotted by a jittery extra.

> "Oh, kill that ugly spider!" screamed one of the bronze-limbed extra girls, covering three yards in one leap. Sawley slapped a flat board on the insect with such venom that the sound engineers objected to the unexpected hard explosive noise. "That was an 'ugly spider,' all right, but in some places they call 'em 'tarantulas.'"[53]

With plenty of work to be done by Glennon and company, there came the necessity for activity well into one late Saturday afternoon on Catalina. Day, hoping to get back to Hollywood in time for a family birthday party, left the set at 4 p.m. in a car she hired to drive her across the 27-mile length of the island, over treacherous mountain roads, to get to a steamship in time for its departure to the mainland. But she arrived at the harbor to see the vessel already pulling out, and she was unsuccessful in convincing a seaplane pilot to remove her as an alternative. Wanting to make sure she wouldn't be stranded by the evening, Day asked her driver to race her back to the *Paradise Island* set in hopes of catching one of the company's two boats that were about to depart for captivity. She barely made it in time, to a rousing welcome by her colleagues already aboard. "Lovely scenery along the ridge," the actress reportedly said in response. "You should see it sometime—but go slowly. All I saw clearly was when we slowed down for curves."[54]

Day ignored the elements and travel concerns sufficiently to portray the woman whose future is in question on the titular island. She has come to the South Seas—where, she is told, "the natives are too lazy and the whites are not interested"—to marry a wealthy man. However, her fiancé has lost his riches to a crooked, cigar-chomping saloon owner, and she has to be rescued by Harlan's singing sailor. All three men covet this rare Caucasian visitor, although the fiancé is seduced by native siren "Poppi" (Betty Boyd). The fiancé, played by Gladden James (1888–1948), and the saloon owner, portrayed by Tom Santschi (1878–1931), climax the film with a thrilling brawl. Longtime action heavy Santschi had ample experience in such fisticuffs, as a participant in the most famous fistfight in the silents, with William Farnum in 1914's *The Spoilers*. Sadly, Santschi would be dead of a heart ailment within a few months of the initial release of *Paradise Island*. Joining the hero in the battle here is a dimwitted ruffian played by Paul Hurst (1888–1953) as the type of fellow who can get into a fight and then can't remember why.

Of the four forgettable—and generally unnecessary—Val Burton-Will

In *Paradise Island* (1930), the heroine (Marceline Day) looks on as the hero (Kenneth Harlan) is accosted on a South Seas island.

Jason songs, three are sung by Harlan (or possibly a voice double) with an adequate tenor. The music does develop the plot: "I've Got a Girl in Every Port" and "Drinking Song" establish his character as a carefree sort; later, the tender "Lazy Breezes" is delivered once he's found his romantic match. For Harlan, *Paradise Island* may have been best remembered as the film he was making when he married the third of what may have been as many as nine wives. (Or seven, or eight, depending on which account you believe.) At this point, Harlan had divorced actress Marie Prevost to unite with Doris Hilda Booth, a Massachusetts socialite who was reportedly a childhood sweetheart of the actor. Harlan and Booth were kaput a year later. The actor was soon to graduate to villainous roles in Westerns and serials.

Paradise Island was mainly dismissed by critics: *The Film Daily* thought it "too much on the cut and dried order for wise audiences," *Motion Picture News* saw it as "very weak," and *Variety* termed it as "a punkaroo from the beginning."[55] But pictures like this were made not for critics, but for "regular folk" who had some time to kill.

Which brings us back to Kokomo ... would you have stayed away from the movie house after being teased by the premise of the white girl and her three rowdy suitors? What if we told you that the rest of that night's Colonial Theater bill was a Laurel and Hardy two-reeler (*Night Owls*), plus a Mickey Mouse cartoon? Yeah, we thought so. Fifteen cents could buy you a lot of entertainment in 1930.

Queen High
(Paramount; August 8, 1930)

Director: Fred Newmeyer. Dialogue Director: Daniel Reed. Producers: Frank Mandel, Laurence Schwab. Adaptation: Frank Mandel. Based on the musical play, book by Laurence Schwab and B.G. DeSylva, lyrics by DeSylva and others, music by Lewis Gensler and James Hanley (New York opening, September 8, 1926; 378 performances), based on the play *A Pair of Sixes* by Edward H. Peple (New York opening, March 17, 1914; 237 performances). Photography: William Steiner. Editor: Barney Rogan. Art Director: William Saulter. Costumes: Caroline Putnam. Sound: C.A. Tuthill. Musical Arrangements: Johnny Green. Running Time: 87 minutes.

Cast: Charles Ruggles (T. Boggs Johns); Frank Morgan (George Nettleton); Stanley Smith (Dick Johns); Ginger Rogers (Polly Rockwell); Helen Carrington (Nellie Nettleton); Theresa Maxwell Conover (Eva Rockwell); Betty Garde (Florence Cole); Nina Olivette (Coddles); Rudolph Cameron (Cyrus Vanderholt); Tom Brown (Jimmy O'Keefe); Theresa Klee, Dorothy Walters (cooks); Eleanor Powell, Edith Shelton (dancing garter models); Marta DeVeaux.

Songs: "Brother! Just Laugh It Off!" [Rogers, Morgan, Ruggles, chorus] (E.Y. Harburg, Arthur Schwartz, Ralph Rainger); "I'm Afraid of You" [Smith, Rogers] (Edward Eliscu, Arthur Schwartz, Ralph Rainger); "I Love a Girl in My Own Peculiar Way" [Ruggles] (E.Y. Harburg, Henry Souvain); "Seems to Me" [Smith, Rogers] (Howard Dietz, Ralph Rainger).

The Story: Polly Rockwell rejects a marriage proposal from attorney Cyrus Vanderholt and finagles a job as a stenographer from her uncle, George Nettleton, at his garter business. George's bickering business partner, T. Boggs Johns, has already brought his nephew, Dick, into the firm. Polly and Dick fall in love. George and Boggs want to end their partnership, so Cyrus proposes they play a hand of poker, with the winner to take over the business for a year and the loser to become the other's butler. Boggs loses the hand; two weeks later, he is toiling at the Rockwell estate with man-hungry maid Coddles. George invites Boggs' fiancée, Florence, to the mansion to embarrass him on his birthday; the servant responds by flirting with George's wife, Nellie, at Polly's suggestion. Cyrus admits the contract from the bet isn't legally binding, life returns to normal for the partners, and Polly and Dick are reunited.

Upon its release, *Queen High* was recognized as a triumph for Charles Ruggles in reprising his Broadway musical comedy role. But if it's remembered now (not much), it's for the presence of its 19-year-old ingénue—Ginger Rogers—in her very first feature-length movie musical.

Rogers (1911–1995) spent much of 1930—her first full year in films—shuttling between the Broadway stage and Paramount's New York sound stages. She had come to prominence in 1929 as a squeaky-voiced, Helen Kane–type comedienne in the legit musical comedy *Top Speed*, and RKO, Pathe, and Paramount snapped her up for side work in short subjects. A few weeks into the new year, *Variety* was already predicting that Rogers, who "one year ago ... was unknown to Broadway ... is now on the brink of what looks like a successful screen career."[56] And this before anyone had seen her in a feature film.

During 1930, Rogers took part in five features in New York for Paramount—the first was the comedy *Young Man of Manhattan*, in which she sang a little and introduced the catchphrase "Cigarette me, big boy!" After *Top Speed* closed in March, she set to work on her second full-lengther, *Queen High*, at Paramount's Astoria Long Island facility, with veteran stage actors Ruggles and Frank Morgan and prolific movie juvenile Stanley Smith under the direction of former Harold Lloyd collaborator Fred Newmeyer. A Kansas City–born, Hollywood-bred banker's son, Smith (1903–1974) had practically beaten a path between Los Angeles and New York. Having parlayed the need for handsome, young tenors into prominent parts, he was touring the studios in 1929 and 1930 in roles for Paramount (*Honey, Sweetie, Love Among the Millionaires, Paramount on Parade*); MGM (*Good News*); Fox (*Soup to Nuts*); Universal (*King of Jazz*); and Pathé (*The Sophomore*).

Queen High was a 1926 stage hit from the highly successful production team of Frank Mandel and Laurence Schwab, who had mounted *The Desert Song, Follow Thru, Good News*, and *New Moon*, among others, and had signed a deal with Paramount to produce some of those for the screen. While Paramount was shooting an all-Technicolor version of *Follow Thru* in Los Angeles in the spring of 1930 under Schwab's partial supervision, Mandel was in the East overseeing *Queen High*.[57] The latter was in capable hands, with Ruggles (1886–1970) reprising his acclaimed role as a garter-factory mogul reduced to serving as a butler for his hostile business partner through the losing of a hand at poker.

Not only was Ruggles comfortable with the screen part, the screen audience was comfortable with him, already having liked his work in *Young Man of Manhattan, The Battle of Paris* [q.v.], and others so much that Paramount had seen fit to place him under long-term contract. Meanwhile, Morgan (1890–1949) was just returning to pictures after having made a few silents, and the silver screen's future Wizard of Oz admitted some indifference toward the refitted medium to a *New York Times* reporter during the filming of *Queen High*, explaining "that he liked [talking] films, had already appeared in two of them, but had never seen a single audible photoplay in his life."[58]

In a businessman-to-butler role, Charles Ruggles makes mirth in Paramount's production of the stage musical *Queen High* (1930).

Queen High survives for appraisal as little more than a filmed play in the familiar mode of early-century musical comedy, which was full of lightweight concoctions in which mainly affluent people with punchy names slammed doors, mistook identities, and fell in or out of love at the drop of a phrase, either spoken or tuneful. The perceived necessity of long shots for this film—perhaps to achieve a more theatrical look—led to some technical complications as in ... where to hide the microphones. In a scene set in an office, one microphone was hidden in a waste-paper basket and another in an inkwell, and the sound from a solo by Rogers was captured by cutting a hole in a restaurant table and positioning the "mike" behind a sugar bowl.[59]

Reviewers overlooked such primitive sound technique, and most liked the film for its comedic situations, especially for the interplay between the characters played by Ruggles, a cagey type whose bluster—and moustache—are suddenly lost with a bad hand of draw poker, and Morgan, who wastes his good luck with worry and insecurity. The pivotal poker scene is great fun—the best example of what *The New York Times*, in praising *Queen High*, called "a rich fund of fun," not just with the two principals but also through the work of Rudolph Cameron, as the attorney whose trick on his clients gets out of hand, and future screen juvenile Tom Brown, as a wisecracking office boy.[60]

Others in the cast are less familiar to the modern viewer. Loose-limbed Nina Olivette, the future mom to actors Guy and Dean Stockwell, plays to the balconies in reprising her *Queen High* stage role as a flirtatious maid. Betty Garde, two decades before being seen as nasty old broads in the likes of *Call Northside 777* and *Caged*, makes an effective rare early screen appearance as Ruggles' love interest. Garde was a well-respected and versatile stage and radio player whose between-takes renditions of her own comic song compositions reportedly kept the cast entertained on the set of *Queen High*.[61] For all she accomplished before the footlights and cameras, Garde (1905–1989) remains most recognized as Aunt Eller in the original stage production of *Oklahoma!* Besides Ruggles and Olivette (1911–1971), a third member of the *QH* stage cast—Helen Carrington, as Morgan's wife—reprised her role in the film.

Stanley Smith shows why he was cast in so many movies of this type; he's earnest and unthreatening, with a pleasant-enough voice. He also was an early casualty of the end of the first film musical wave; Smith did a few films in 1932–33 with dwindling presences, became an orchestra leader for a while, and returned briefly for small screen roles in the early '40s. A chance at a strong Hollywood comeback fell through in 1933, when Warner Bros. announced Smith as a likely replacement for an ailing Dick Powell for *Footlight Parade*, then decided to wait until Powell had recovered from pneumonia to use him in the film.[62]

That Rogers' screen career outlasted all the others from *Queen High* wasn't just a function of her youth. The cutie brings the film great energy as she's handed three of the four songs—all newly written, as the stage score was jettisoned. The one song she doesn't sing is the bizarre "I Love a Girl in My Own Peculiar Way"—in which Ruggles scares the bejesus out of the household help with his account of the joys of wife-killing! The most notable of Rogers' offerings is "Brother, Just Laugh It Off!"—in which she dances for the first time in a feature. The executive-suite setting includes young and healthy members of the "workforce" on hand for a chorus—among the group, and plainly visible for a few seconds, is an uncredited 17-year-old Eleanor Powell, who had lately introduced her rapid-fire, highly athletic dance style to audiences in the stage *Follow Thru*. Powell wears a bob haircut that's hard to see, as her head is cut off during much of the number. She wouldn't gain a foothold on the screen until Fox's *George White's 1935 Scandals*, which directly preceded her long run at MGM.

Rogers made three more 1930 Paramount features (*The Sap From Syracuse, Follow the Leader, Honor Among Lovers*) at Astoria before triumphing on Broadway again with the musical *Girl Crazy* and then moving on to Hollywood. Watchers of *Queen High* might not have known what Rogers had, even if "it" wouldn't be obvious until Fred Astaire came on the scene.

2. Failed, Fallen, and One-Shot Stars

When it came to movie stardom in the 1930s, as in any other time, many were called and few were chosen. They were summoned to Hollywood from Broadway stages, vaudeville houses, nightclubs, radio studios, even amateur theatrics. Inking a signature on a film studio contract fulfilled many a dream, but that was just part of the process. Film being a collaborative art, a performer was—and is—dependent on material. A bad script could sink the most well-intentioned project, a poor director could fail to elicit the right tone of mood and performance, and unflattering camera work could literally make someone look bad.

In musical filmmaking, issues were more complicated. Ideally, a performer would be able to sing, dance, and act—but the right amount of one of the three talents was enough to get noticed, and many a lead-footed singer or tone-deaf dancer could be exploited effectively by masquerading deficiencies. However, there was still the matter of resources—the right stories and plots had to be secured for lasting success. And we haven't even considered the quality of physical appearance, which was a particular issue with personalities from radio, whose appeal derived almost totally from how they sounded and little, if at all, from how they actually looked.

As radio captivated audiences—and drew them away from their neighborhood movie theaters and home victrolas—Hollywood brought in many names from the airwaves, at the least for novelty value. Among the biggest of the radio-related musicals was Paramount's *The Big Broadcast* (1932), in which Bing Crosby, George Burns, Gracie Allen, and a raft of other personalities appeared in a revue-style comedy. For some of these names, it was a given that novelty would be all, for as *Hollywood Reporter* editor W.R. Wilkerson stated in a 1933 column: "*The Big Broadcast* and the Kate Smith feature, *Hello, Everybody!*, are all right in the smaller communities where people are curious to see what radio stars look like. But the personal appearances of these stars have taken the edge off the interest in big cities."[1] If a performer had a very specific talent or limited repertoire, he or she risked using it all on celluloid and ruining appeal as a live act.

Crosby lasted—but what of his sexier crooning contemporary, Russ Columbo? A brassy blonde like Alice Faye could alight to stardom in a hurry, but not Dorothy Dell. Columbo and Dell had the bad luck of dying young. Opera stars were tough sells in the hinterlands. Kate Smith didn't click for obvious reasons. Other would-be headliners would see the fickle public never warm to them, or fall away after getting their fill for a few pictures; they retreated into their specialties, to lower reaches of showbiz, and even out of the public eye.

This chapter features some notable 1930s musicals with short-lived stars. Some of those folks were operating on second chances; others would never get them. But at least they got chances.

Hello, Everybody!
(Paramount; January 27, 1933)

Director: William A. Seiter. Associate Producer: William LeBaron. Screenplay: Dorothy Yost, Lawrence Hazard. Story: Fannie Hurst. Photography: Gilbert Warrenton. Editor: James Smith. Sound: Jack A. Goodrich. Running Time: 69 minutes.

Cast: Kate Smith (Kate Smith); Randolph Scott (Hunt Blake); Sally Blane (Lily Smith); Charley Grapewin (Jed); George Barbier (Marshall); Julia Swayne Gordon (Mrs. Smith); Wade Boteler (Parker); Erville Alderson (Horton); Paul Kruger (Lindle); Ted Collins (Ted Collins); Frank Darien (Henry Thompson); Fern Emmett (Ettie); Jerry Tucker (Bobby Smith); Marguerite Campbell (Bettina Smith); Edwards Davis (Sinclair Eldridge); Frank McGlynn, Sr. (Jonathan Reed); Hallene Hall (Mrs. Thompson); Jack Pennick (Joe), Lon Poff (constable); Russell Simpson (townsman); Irving Bacon (radio announcer); Frank Jenks (orchestra leader at company show); Frederick Sullivan (company executive).

Songs [all performed by Smith]: "Moon Song (That Wasn't Meant for Me)" [twice], "My Queen of Lullaby Land," "Out in the Great Open Spaces," "Pickaninnies' Heaven," "Twenty Million People" [twice] (Sam Coslow, Arthur Johnston); "When the Moon Comes Over the Mountain" (Harry Woods, Howard Johnson); "Dinah" (Sam M. Lewis, Joe Young, Harry Akst).

Working Titles: *Queen of the Air; Moon Song; Cheerful; Nice Girl.*

Disc: Brunswick 6496 ("My Queen of Lullaby Land"/"Twenty Million People," Kate Smith); Brunswick 6497 ("Moon Song"/"Pickaninnies' Heaven," Kate Smith).

The Story: Kate Smith runs her family farm and leads the efforts of her townspeople to resist selling their land to the General Power & Water Company, which wants to build a new dam. Company agent Hunt Blake quits his job after he falls in love with Kate's sister Lily. Kate is invited to sing on a company-sponsored radio broadcast ("Out in the Great Open Spaces"). Talent agent Ted Collins hears the broadcast *and invites Kate to come East and perform on the Nationwide Broadcasting System, which she does when she realizes her compensation can finance the town's court battle against the utility. Kate becomes a radio star ("Twenty Million People"), but when a protest in her hometown turns ugly, she intercedes to keep peace.*

"The Voice That Brought Romance Into the Homes of America Now Brings a New Kind of Romance to the Talking Screen!" blared ads for Paramount's new musical *Hello, Everybody!* in early 1933. "The Voice" was Kate

Rotund Kate Smith cooks up a not-so-tasty meal in her only starring film, *Hello, Everybody!* (1933).

Smith, the gifted singer of radio renown. The "New Kind of Romance" was necessitated by the fact that the voice was Kate Smith's.

Smith (1907–1986) was beloved over the airwaves as "The Songbird of the South," but given her rotund appearance—at 200 pounds plus—she was no movie star. But she did have a personality, and she'd had some success as an actress. A discovery of hoofer Eddie Dowling, with whom she debuted on Broadway in the 1926 musical comedy *Honeymoon Lane*, the native Virginian drew raves as a featured player in such stage hits as *Hit the Deck* and *Flying High*, but she was better advised by her new manager, record executive Ted Collins, to concentrate on a singing career than be comic fat-girl fodder for the likes of Bert Lahr.

The cheerful, folksy Smith delivered honesty and sincerity in both her speaking voice and her robust contralto, which made her immensely popular on radio and record. She even made the transition to film with a couple of Vitaphone shorts, *Kate Smith, the Songbird of the South* (1929), and a one-reeler that introduced Jerry Wald's *Rambling 'Round Radio Row* series in 1932. For the latter, Smith filmed the tune "Whistle and Blow Your Blues Away" at Warner Bros.' Brooklyn studio that spring, then journeyed across town to Paramount's Astoria facility a few weeks later to sing "It Was So Beautiful" and her theme song, "When the Moon Comes Over the Mountain," for Paramount's first feature-length radio revue, *The Big Broadcast*. Paramount signed the 25-year-old performer in September 1932 to make a starring feature, the title of which would come from Smith's trademark greeting to her audiences.

"We made the long jump across the continent to Hollywood for *Hello, Everybody*, my first picture" [sic], Smith was credited as saying in a "tell-all" for *Radio Mirror* magazine:

> I was thrilled, and although I worked hard I had a marvelous time. Ted, Mrs. Collins and I rented (actor) Monte Blue's beautiful house in Beverly Hills. There was a swimming pool and tennis court on the estate, and we all spent as much time in the sunshine as possible.... Without a doubt the biggest social event of my life was the party the film folks gave for me at (the Cocoanut Grove). I am quite a movie fan myself, so it was a thrill and a joy to meet so many of the stars. I am sure I was as curious as a high school kid to find out whether they resembled the characters they played on the screen.[2]

But what to do with Kate Smith for anything beyond a few minutes of song? Paramount bought *Moon Song*, an original story by famed novelist Fannie Hurst (*Back Street, Imitation of Life*), to mold into something workable, which turned out to be a how-she-came-to-be tale, a slice of hokum about family farmer Kate Smith becoming a radio star to save her hometown from economic ruin perpetrated by a greedy utility company. This version of Kate can do it all, as her longtime farmhand (Charley Grapewin) acknowledges in an opening-reel chat.

SMITH: "The old farm's in good repair now."
GRAPEWIN: "Yup, you've done mighty fine for a girl, Kate."
SMITH: "Well, when there's no one to do it but a girl, she just does it, I guess."
GRAPEWIN: "You mean ... *your* kind of a girl does, Kate."
SMITH: "Aw, Jed, if I didn't know you so well, I'd think you were flirting with me!"

Smith could not be convincingly paired with the actual male lead, Randolph Scott (1898–1987), so Scott's character was written to fall in love with Smith's fictional sister, played by Sally Blane (whose real sis was movie star Loretta Young) as a surrogate of sorts. As she looks out her bedroom window to watch Scott and Blane in an evening embrace, Smith sings regretfully about a "love dream that could never be" in "Moon Song (That Wasn't Meant for Me)," one of five Sam Coslow–Arthur Johnston tunes in the film. It's a good number, and Smith's shockingly nimble footwork during a brief rendition of "Dinah" also is a highlight (and a redo of the "hot dance" Smith performed in vaudeville).

Both of the above, however, are negated by Coslow and Johnston's cringeworthy "Pickaninnies' Heaven," in which Smith's performance at the mike is accompanied by shots of glum-looking black children shown in an orphanage. They, the song goes, ought to be cheered by a utopia of giant watermelons and pork chop bushes and a Swanee River made of lemonade—even if their mammys are dead. That sequence alone would be enough to earn *Hello, Everybody!* an entry under "Disastrous Debuts" in the 1984 Harry and Michael Medved book *The Hollywood Hall of Shame*. According to the Medveds' account, longtime film distributor Arthur Mayer, a Paramount publicist in the 1930s, told them the studio spent more than $2 million on *Hello, Everybody!*, making it the most expensive movie musical production to that point.[3] One drain on the budget might have been Smith's contractual request for Paramount to pay the $3,600 weekly to wire her radio programs to the East Coast from KNX, the station on the studio lot, between November 1932 and early January 1933.[4]

In an interview with the Medveds, Blane (1910–1997) described the discomfort for, and with, Smith on the set:

> She was very different than picture people. I'd been here since I was 5 or 6 years old, and it just felt like Kate Smith didn't belong, as far as I could see. You got the feeling that she didn't approve of Hollywood; she just wanted to take their money. It felt to us like an intrusion. She came with her whole entourage. California was supposed to be for actors, everyone was supposed to be good-looking and pretty, and here we had this big stout woman who just had nothing to do with us.[5]

Critics of 1933 were a bit more charitable about Smith. "The picture, needless to say, will be a terrible bore to those who don't relish taking their radio-singers straight, but when one considers the difficulty of tailoring a story to suit this particular songbird, there is much to be said in praise," wrote *The Hollywood Reporter*.[6] *The Film Daily* was more blunt: "Miss Smith sings with her usual pleasing charm, but the illusion is destroyed that puts her over on the radio. You see her in the flesh, and so much of it does not harmonize with songs of sentiment and romance."[7] Business wasn't favorable, and the studio's precarious financial condition at the time precluded another potentially expensive investment in a Smith picture. In a 1968 interview with radio host Joe Franklin, Smith would admit that her only starring film was "horrible ... it was a mess. I was so homesick for the East I couldn't wait to go back home again. I really didn't like motion pictures."[8]

Smith would return to the big screen only periodically; her only other appearance in a feature was a cameo in the 1943 musical *This Is the Army*. In that film, she sang "God Bless America," the patriotic Irving Berlin song with which she would become closely associated, especially as she prodigiously sold war bonds in the '40s, and which could be heard with her recorded voice at sporting events 30 years after her death. The failure of *Hello, Everybody!* wasn't going to prevent Kate Smith from becoming an American icon.

Broadway Thru a Keyhole
(20th Century/United Artists; November 1, 1933)

and *Wake Up and Dream*
(Universal; October 1, 1934)

Broadway Thru a Keyhole

Director: Lowell Sherman. Producer: Darryl F. Zanuck. Screenplay: Gene Towne, Graham Baker. Story: Walter Winchell. Photography: Barney McGill, Peverell Marley. Editing: Maurice Wright. Musical Director: Alfred Newman. Dance Director: Jack Haskell. Art Directors: Richard Day, Joseph Wright. Costumes: Ernest Rotchy. Running Time: 90 minutes.

Cast: Constance Cummings (Joan Whelen); Paul Kelly (Frank Rocci); Russ Columbo (Clark Brian); Blossom Seeley (Sybil Smith); Gregory Ratoff (Max Mefoofsky); Texas Guinan (Tex Kaley); Abe Lyman and His Band (Klub Kaley band); Hugh O'Connell (Chuck Haskins); Hobart Cavanaugh (Peanuts Dinwiddie); Frances Williams (herself); Eddie Foy, Jr. (himself); Barto and Mann (club dancers); George Mann (himself); C. Henry Gordon (Tim Crowley); William Burress (Thomas Barnum); Helen Jerome Eddy (Esther Whelen); Bradley Ward (Willie Stacko); John Kelly (Louie); Andrew Tombes (press agent); Arthur Franklin (pianist); Fred Santley (Pierre); Wheeler Oakman (Sam); Charles Lane (columnist); Theresa Harris (maid); Ronnie Cosby, Marceline Medcalf (children in "Bike" number); Lucille Ball, Edith Allen (girls with Louie); Walter Winchell (himself, voice only).

Songs: "Doin' the Uptown Lowdown" [Williams, chorus, danced by Barto and Mann],

"I Love You Prince Pizzicato" [Columbo, Cummings, band], "When You Were a Girl on a Scooter and I Was a Boy on a Bike" [Cummings, Foy, chorus], "You're My Past, Present, and Future" [Columbo, band, reprised by Cummings, Foy] (Mack Gordon, Harry Revel).
Working Title: *Broadway Love.*
Also Known As: *Walter Winchell's Broadway Thru a Keyhole.*
Disc: Brunswick 6672 ("You're My Past, Present, and Future," Abe Lyman Orchestra); Brunswick 6674 ("Doin' the Uptown Lowdown"/"When You Were a Girl on a Scooter and I Was a Boy on a Bike," Abe Lyman Orchestra).

The Story: Racketeer Frank Rocci, president of the American Poultry Protective Association, deals out "protection" from "hoodlums" in New York City. He helps aspiring dancer Joan Whelen get a job in the chorus of Tex Kaley's nightclub show. Frank buys the club as a hangout for his boys, orders director Max to make Joan the show's star, and sets her up in a fancy apartment. Joan reluctantly accepts Frank's marriage proposal, but while visiting Florida, she falls for crooner-bandleader Clark Brian. She must choose between the two men as Frank becomes increasingly embroiled in gang warfare.

Wake Up and Dream

Director: Kurt Neumann. Producer: B. F. Zeidman. Story/Screenplay: John Meehan, Jr. Photography: Charles Stumar, Harold Smith. Special Photography: John P. Fulton. Additional Music and Orchestrations: Howard Jackson. Editing: Daniel Mandell. Musical Director: Sam K. Wineland. Art Direction: Harrison Wiley. Running Time: 76 minutes.

Cast: Russ Columbo (Paul Scotti); Roger Pryor (Charlie Sullivan); June Knight (Toby Brown); Catherine Doucet (Madame Rose); Henry Armetta (Giovanni Cellini); Wini Shaw (Mae La Rue); Andy Devine (Joe Egbert); Spencer Charters (Earl Craft); Richard Carle (Roger Babcock); Gavin Gordon (Harold Seabrook); Rollo Lloyd (Richard Little); Clarence H. Wilson (Tom Hilderbrand); Paul Porcasi (Polopolis); Maurice Black (Tom Romero); Arthur Hoyt (George Spelvin); Philip Dakin (John Richards); Eddie Prinz (Joe); Matt McHugh (Craft's assistant); Jane Darwell (landlady); James Flavin (detective); James Donlan (Jim); Florence Enright (maid); Sam Flint (theater patron); Edmund Cobb (waiter); Eddie Kane (ad man); Edward Hearn (reporter).

Songs: "Too Beautiful for Words" [Columbo, reprised by Columbo, Knight, then by Columbo, Shaw, then by Columbo, Knight], "When You're in Love" [Columbo, reprised by Knight, Doucet, Armetta, Columbo] (Russ Columbo, Bernie Grossman, Jack Stern); "Let's Pretend There's a Moon" [Columbo, Knight] (Russ Columbo, Grace Hamilton, Jack Stern); "Wake Up and Dream" [Columbo, Knight, Pryor] (Gordon Clifford, Sidney Cutner).

Working Titles: *Castles in the Air; The Love Life of a Crooner; Tonight's the Night.*

The Story: Struggling vaudeville act Paul Scotti, Toby Brown, and Charlie Sullivan think they've finally gotten a break when Charlie talks revue producer Earl Craft into hiring Paul as a leading man, but then Charlie gets into trouble with the law. Charlie goes wire-walking in New York City for the newsreel cameras to earn money for the trio's passage to California; on the bus West, they meet Joe and his moneyed fortune-teller "aunt," Madame Rose, who pursues the trio's pal Giovanni. Another lost opportunity: Paul's crooning of "When You're in Love" impresses theater owner Polopolis ... who unfortunately has just sold all of his theaters. In Los Angeles, Paul is hired by motion picture producer Babcock to star opposite his protege, Mae La Rue, and becomes "Hollywood's Newest Screen Sensation." He high-hats his old friends, and Charlie must confront him over Toby's affections.

At the time of his death in 1934, Russ Columbo stood in the triumvirate of famous pop crooners, as testified to by the song "Crosby, Columbo, and Vallee." A handsome vocalist, violinist, bandleader, and composer who rose to the top of his profession in the span of five years, he would, inevitably, try his hand as an actor. As a solo performer, Columbo's cinematic acting resume encompasses a two-reel short subject; a singing cameo in the feature *Moulin Rouge* [q.v.]; and his only two substantial roles, in the full-length musicals *Broadway Thru a Keyhole* and *Wake Up and Dream*. The last came to theaters mere weeks after his passing at age 26.

Born Ruggerio de Rodolfo Columbo in 1908, the future superstar initially made the big time as a violinist and, eventually, featured soloist in Gus Arnheim's Ambassadors, replacing Crosby in the latter role. Columbo played with the Arnheim band in two 1927–28 Vitaphone shorts and in the 1929 RKO musical *Street Girl*, and sang solo, but unbilled, in 1929's *Dynamite* (MGM) and *Wolf Song* (Paramount). Composer Con Conrad became Columbo's manager and pushed him hard toward a solo career. Columbo became famous on his own, cutting such hits as "My Love," "Prisoner of Love," "Sweet and Lovely," and his theme song, "You Call It Madness, But I Call It Love." He also received major exposure on NBC as "The Romeo of Radio" or, given his ethnicity and good looks, "The Valentino of Radio."

A falling-out with Conrad led to the cancellation of Columbo's recording contract with RCA, however, so when Columbo brought his soothing voice to the Vitaphone two-reeler *That Goes Double*, filmed in late 1932 and released in July 1933, it was regarded as a comeback of sorts. The short makes sport of Columbo's seeming ubiquity by casting him in a dual role as himself and a meek accountant whom the songster hires as an imposter for select social events, including an outing in the home of a pretty girl. There's even a pushy theatrical agent on hand to remind insiders of Conrad, then tangling with Columbo in court. *That Goes Double* was liked enough to bring future film work—and intensify the comparisons in the "Battle of the Baritones" with Crosby.

Columbo and Crosby would be closely associated during this period; they recorded many of the same songs, and both had shows at NBC. Crosby biographer Gary Giddins notes the older crooner's influence on the younger's career: "If Bing represented a synthesis of jazz and pop, Columbo was a limited stylist who held his notes a tad too long. Yet, Russ echoes throughout Bing's developing years like a night wind, pursuing him in every medium—the first of many celebrated singers to consciously imitate Bing, affirming and codifying his influence."[9] Columbo biographers Joseph Lanza and Dennis Penna reject that condescending view, noting that Columbo and Crosby were markedly different in style; the younger man was smoother, more romantic—Perry Como or Vic Damone—but no worse: "Many other crooners sang the praises and dirges of love found and lost, but Columbo's songs are among the most purified hymns to the secular religion of romance."[10] Still, Crosby now had a film career that was taking off at Paramount, and Columbo was curious about his own prospects, even if they paid a fraction of what he could earn as a live performer.

In July 1933, Columbo signed to play a second lead in *Broadway Thru a Keyhole*, one of the earliest productions of Darryl F. Zanuck's new 20th Century Pictures (later to be merged into 20th Century–Fox). As Clark Gregg, a hypochondriac singer-bandleader who falls for the nightclub performer girlfriend (Constance Cummings) of a New York racketeer (Paul Kelly), he was given two Mack Gordon–Harry Revel songs, "I Love You Prince Pizzicato" and "You're My Past, Present, and Future." Columbo capably flexes his acting muscles in a dramatic scene in which Clark overcomes his cowardice and asserts his love for the girl to the gangster-with-the-heart-of-gold who also loves her. "I love her more than my own life, and whatever happens to me doesn't matter if I can't have her," he says of Cummings' character, and viewers believed him. Off screen, Columbo was romantically linked with actresses Dorothy Dell, Sally Blane, Mary Brian, or, most conspicuously (and, accurately, at this point), Carole Lombard.

Although *Broadway Thru a Keyhole* retains a pre–Code punch, the love-triangle premise seems a comedown from the promised insider's look at Big Apple brass. Columbo was only a small part of the interesting history of a film packed with interesting players who were seeing little movie work elsewhere— and which generated a behind-the-scenes mini-scandal. The film was based on an autobiographical story by Broadway columnist Walter Winchell, and after word got out that said story was uncomfortably close to the real-life affairs of Al Jolson, Jolson's dancer wife Ruby Keeler, and New York gangster Johnny "Irish" Costello, it prompted a much-publicized confrontation between Jolson and Winchell at a boxing match in Hollywood on July 21, 1933. Winchell, who denied the story was based on Jolson and Keeler, alleged that Jolson punched him once, in the neck; Jolson said he hit the newspaperman more than that, and decked him four or five times. "Was that a press stunt when Al Jolson took a smack at Walt Winchell?" *The Film Daily* wondered.[11]

Winchell sued Jolson for $50,000, alleging assault and damages. Jolson kept up his public complaints, so Darryl Zanuck issued a statement—which functioned as a press release—that was reported in one trade publication as such:

> We refuse to admit that Al Jolson or Ruby Keeler are among these characters [in *Broadway Thru a Keyhole*]. Let Mr. Jolson wait until he sees the picture. If then he is convinced that he was right, he will have no reason to feel that Mrs. Jolson has been done an injustice, for the chorus girl in our story is ... always shown in an admirable light.... Since the accusation has become a matter of public record ... let the public be the judge when it sees the picture.[12]

Meanwhile, the *Keyhole* cast was being filled with some interesting personalities. Paul Kelly (1899–1956) was playing one of his first film roles after a two-year prison stretch for manslaughter in connection with the death of his lover's husband. Legendary New York nightclub owner Texas Guinan was hired to portray a variation on herself, and another old pro, Blossom Seeley, was rushed in for a supporting role after the first two players cast, Peggy Hopkins Joyce and Lilyan Tashman, became unavailable. Joyce, the model/dancer/professional celebrity/occasional actress, was said to have walked off the set after

Paul Kelly and Constance Cummings are the main romantic pairing in 20th Century Pictures' punchy *Broadway Thru a Keyhole* (1933).

a day's work because her man-hungry character hit uncomfortably close to home.[13] Tashman's problem was legitimate—she'd had what was reported as an appendectomy, but which was more likely the onset of the abdominal cancer that would kill her in 1934 while she was filming *Frankie and Johnnie* [q.v.].

Seeley was a vaudeville headliner—the "Queen of Syncopation"—who made very few films, and although Guinan had appeared in silent shorts (as a cowgirl star!), she made no talkies besides the now-lost Warner Bros. feature *Queen of the Night Clubs* (1929). Thus, their presences here are particularly welcome, if only for their rarity. Guinan died of an intestinal infection at 49, four days after the November 1, 1933, New York premiere of *Broadway Thru a Keyhole*, so her utterances of her catchphrases "Hello, suckers!" and "Give that little girl a great big hand!" in the film serve as historical documentation of Prohibition-era ballyhoo.

As the sidekick to Cummings' character, Seeley (1891–1974) had a meatier role. The work prompted talk of her as a Mae West type, and 20th Century signed Seeley for a second film appearance, which turned out to be her last, *Blood Money* (1933). In *Broadway Thru a Keyhole*, she gets to give her younger charge advice from a sage trouper: "You know, I'll never forget the night that Minsky's sweet-chested prima donna got the gout. I went on with a minute's notice to save the show with influenza and a worn-out, patched fig leaf. And was I a hit! I got my name in lights and my body in the hospital with double pneumonia. The only one who remembers my big moment when I gave my all was the doctor, and he still sends me bills!" In the Ships Passing in the Night Department, Lucille Ball can be seen in a brief scene set at a Florida beach, in the first film appearance for the bleached blonde who would become the world's most famous redhead.[14]

Aided by all the off-screen publicity, *Broadway Thru a Keyhole* brought in many curious patrons. According to Winchell biographer Neal Gabler, Zanuck was enthusiastic enough after screening a preview to send the columnist a wire praising the film as "the best picture I've been associated with in the past two years. Makes *42nd Street, Golddiggers* [sic] (*of 1933*) look like a trailer and I mean it sincerely," and asking Winchell to come up with an idea for a sequel.[15] Winchell apparently had second thoughts about the film's quality and griped in his column: "[T]he next time I sell a picture, if ever, I won't take coin for merely suggesting the theme. Nor would I permit a company to rush a picture of mine just because it wanted to cash in on some front-page publicity."[16] Winchell would even make up with Al Jolson, although their reconciliation wouldn't come until many years later.

Even if *Broadway Thru a Keyhole* didn't make Winchell a mogul, it did help Russ Columbo, whom *Variety* praised as the "surprise of the picture…. He screens unusually well and suggests a type who, with development and tutelage, may go places. In *Keyhole*, he shows traces of camera shyness and unfinished delivery, but has not been favored with dialog."[17] The director of *Keyhole*, Lowell Sherman, praised the singer's cinematic "possibilities as great as Rudolph Valentino had. This boy ... with his gentle, crooning voice, his handsome Latin beauty, and lovable personality, is headed straight for stardom."[18] Universal offered more exposure with a contract, but then let Columbo sit for a few months while trying to find a suitable project as the singer stewed and threatened to break from the studio. The studio even tried to convince him to take a non-singing role, opposite Constance Cummings and Paul Lukas in *Glamour*, under William Wyler's direction. Paramount reportedly offered Columbo a part as the Mock Turtle in its fairytale extravaganza *Alice in Wonderland*, but the role was played by Cary Grant. During this period, 20th Century borrowed Columbo back for what amounted to a walk-on in *Moulin Rouge*, a musical comedy in which he sang "Coffee in the Morning and Kisses in the Night" with the film's star, Constance Bennett.

The "suitable" project at Universal turned out to be *The Love Life of a Crooner*, which was retitled *Wake Up and Dream* during production in July. Under any title, this was no way for Columbo to go out. Indifferently directed by Kurt Neumann, it survives as a dull, episodic, listless saga of a vaudeville trio's coast-to-coast struggle for success amid love-triangle complications. Columbo plays the big talent of the three, who ultimately goes to Hollywood and big-times his old cohorts—played by Roger Pryor and cute-as-a-button former Ziegfield Girl June Knight (1913–1987)—before being brought down to earth by a good talking-to. Columbo's acting is passable and his singing—especially on "Too Beautiful for Words"—is good, and "When You're in Love" (the tune that finally brought Columbo back to the recording studio) became a strong seller. But the comic interludes between Henry Armetta, doing his angry-Italian schtick, and romance-minded Catherine Doucet are interminable.

Shooting wrapped on *Wake Up and Dream* in the middle of August, and Universal was optimistic enough about the film that it put out a press release in which Columbo, whose career seemed to be back running on all cylinders, was quoted thusly: "At 26, I find that I have just about everything I want from life and am pretty happy the way things have turned out for me."[19] On the last evening of August, he and Carole Lombard discreetly attended a Hollywood sneak preview of *Wake Up and Dream*. But this was a project that was doomed before anyone could pay money to see it, for Columbo died on September 2, 1934. In what was called a bizarre accident, he was struck in the head by a bullet from an antique pistol discharged by a close friend, photographer Lansing Brown. Brown, who said he was playing with the pistol while talking to Columbo in Brown's home, was absolved of guilt by authorities.

As expected, talk of its star's death dominated reviews of *Wake Up and*

Doomed crooner Russ Columbo muddles through *Wake Up and Dream* (1934) as the object of affection of two women: Wini Shaw, center, and June Knight.

Dream, as in Frank Nugent's *New York Times* account, headlined "A Musical Without Surprises": "On the whole it is an insipid musical comedy, built along stock lines and, through no fault of the producers, possessed of a morbid quality.... The story ... [is] entirely indistinguishable from countless others dragged from studio shelves in the past."[20] As poor as it was, *Wake Up and Dream* could hardly hint at what could have been for Columbo, as actor and singer. NBC had just brought him back to the ether in a coveted Sunday night time slot. Universal had started discussing him to co-star in its prestige musical *Show Boat*.[21] We'll never know, but perhaps the course of American pop music history—and even the history of the Hollywood musical—was changed with a single gunshot.

Myrt and Marge
(Universal; December 4, 1933)

Director: Al Boasberg. Producer: Bryan Foy. Story/Screenplay: Beatrice Banyard. Additional Dialogue: Al Boasberg. Photography: Joseph A. Valentine. Editing: Arthur

Hilton. Sound: Lambert E. Day. Musical Director: Paul Van Loan. Dance Director: Jack Haskell. Art Director: W. L. Vogel. Running Time: 65 minutes.
Cast: Myrtle Vail (Myrt Spear); Donna Damerel (Marge Minter); Ray Hedge (Clarence); Eddie Foy, Jr. (Eddie Hanley); Grace Hayes (Grace); Trixie Friganza (Mrs. Minter); J. Farrell MacDonald (Grady); Thomas E. Jackson (Johnny Jackson); Ted Healy (Mullins); Howard, Fine and Howard [Moe Howard, Larry Fine, Curly Howard aka Ted Healy's Stooges] (stagehands); Bonnie Bonnell (Sue); Jimmy Conlin (comedian); Peter Lind Hayes (radio station employee); Tom McGuire (police detective); The Colenette Ballet; Bo-Ching; Bo-Ling.
Songs: "Draggin' My Heels Around" [performed by Vail, Foy, chorus; reprised by Healy, then by Bo-Ching, Bo-Ling; then by Foy, Bonnell, chorus], "Isle of Blues" [Hayes, Colenette Ballet], "What Is Sweeter Than the Sweetness of I Love You?" [Damerel, Foy; reprised by Damerel, Foy, Healy, Stooges; then by Vail, Damerel] (Joan Jasmyn, M. K. Jerome).
Working Titles: *My Lady's Legs*; *The New Deal*.

The Story: Aging performer Myrt Spear attempts to rejuvenate a struggling stage musical, "My Lady's Legs," by hiring cocky song-and-dance man Eddie Hanley and persuading old friend Johnny Jackson to fund the production. Stagehand Mullins, his three assistants, and gate-crashing Sue vie to join the cast. In the sticks, Eddie discovers a promising ingénue, Marge Minter, who joins the tour over the objections of her overly protective mother. Despite Marge's and Eddie's talents, Jackson's unwanted affections toward Marge nearly stop the show before it can get to New York, but help comes from an unexpected source.

The story behind *Myrt and Marge* is a tale of two famous showbiz acts, only one of which was Myrt and Marge. One was so popular in 1933 that its name alone could serve as the title of a film, although "Radio's Sweethearts" are virtually forgotten today. The other was near the bottom of the credits eight decades ago, but it would soon be retooled to mature into a unit that would carry on for nearly 40 more years, and delight audiences well into the next millennium. In '33, however, people went to see *Myrt and Marge* for Myrt and Marge—and not for Howard, Fine, and Howard ... the Three Stooges.

And who could blame those people? The mother-daughter duo of Myrtle Vail (1888–1978) and Donna (Marge) Damerel (1912–1941) had one of the most popular shows on the airwaves. Sponsored by the company owned by chewing gum magnate Philip K. Wrigley, "Myrt and Marge" debuted in 1931 on CBS and was a rare "soap opera"–type show to air in prime time; the network didn't move it to a less prestigious, female-audience daytime slot until 1937. A former vaudevillian, Vail wrote the scripts for the series—which was about the travails of chorus girls Myrt Spear and Marge Minter (think "Spear-Mint" gum)—based on her real-life experiences. The stories were adventurous enough to expand beyond typical backstage fare to edgier stuff like crime-related scenarios. A year after the show debuted, Damerel was named radio's typical "It" girl—edging out vocal favorite Ruth Etting—in a national poll by *Radio Guide* magazine.[22]

Vail and Damerel got their screen break when they were signed by independent producer Bryan Foy, now on his own between lengthy stints at Warner Bros., where he directed and produced scores of short subjects and low-budget features. With Bryan's brother Eddie Foy, Jr. (1905–1983)—another of the "Seven Little Foys" of vaudeville fame—in the cast, the film was shot for Universal release in June 1933 under the working titles *The New Deal* and *My Lady's Legs*. Also on hand: Ray Hedge, who played the girls' fey friend, Clarence, on the radio; veteran troupers Grace Hayes (the Foys' sister-in-law), Trixie Friganza, and Ted Healy; and Healy's longtime professional "stooges," Moe Howard, Larry Fine, and Curly Howard. The knockabout trio had been Healy's foils on stage and screen for a decade, sometimes with the Howards' brother Shemp in Curly's stead. Bryan Foy signed Healy and the Stooges to star in four features, of which *Myrt and Marge* was to be the first, but ended up being the only.[23]

Veteran gagman Al Boasberg helmed what would be his only feature as a director; he had been writing lines for the flickers since the middle '20s and was known as the "Hollywood Ghost Writer" for all the uncredited work he did for the movies and radio. Bryan Foy was so happy with Boasberg's work on *Myrt and Marge* that he gifted the filmmaker with a new car as a token of the esteem of Foy Productions, Ltd.[24] *Myrt and Marge* screenwriter Beatrice Banyard was a sometime actress married to longtime playwright-producer-actor Willard Mack; among her writing credits was the Marie Dressler comedy *Reducing*. (Mack and Banyard can be seen on screen together in the 1929 MGM talkie *The Voice of the City*.)

In its publicity material, Universal boasted that *Myrt and Marge* was at the vanguard of an invasion of Hollywood by radio stars:

> Those with an ear to the ground for signs and portents in the movies declare that *Myrt and Marge* has started a new cycle in motion picture production. It is a behind-the-mike cycle with one or more radio personalities of note and lots and lots of atmosphere and technology of the radio studio.... Universal is in the forefront of the cycle with *The Love Life of a Crooner* and one of radio's most attractive personalities in Russ Columbo as its star. Other companies have also started on the new behind the mike cycle.[25]

Perhaps to account for their visually obvious age difference, Vail and Damerel were cast as performers on opposite ends of the experience spectrum; this makes their characters more believable but limits their interaction. (They sing together only once.) Game but aging as her show struggles to survive, Myrt is so old by showbiz standards that, a snide patron jokes, "my grandfather went to West Point with her son." More daring, even for pre–Code fare, was the humor in the depiction of Clarence, the costume designer for "My Lady's Legs," as unabashedly gay. When the show's original producer (J. Farrell MacDonald) informs the cast he's bowing out, Clarence bids him farewell: "I hope you stick this lovely coat in your ... assets." The now-former money man replies: "You wouldn't wear it unless it had lace on it!" Later, when Myrt hands the young man a fancy headdress to put away after a performance, she warns him to "put that in the trunk ... and don't wear it!" Clarence looks at the headdress and complains: "Selfish!"

Besides Hedge's swishy turn, Healy and his stooges give Myrt and Marge its prime watchability. Much of their interaction plays off the premise that his three helpers do all of Mullins' work for him; he's too involved with dumbbell stage-door wannabe Sue (Bonnie Bonnell), who spends the film trying to join the show. Bonnell, a third-tier Gracie Allen, was working with Healy and the stooges on stage and in the MGM shorts; I'll leave it to the viewer as to whether she was actually as untalented as she played, or whether she was entirely too convincing as an actress.[26] She does tend to grow on you, even with predictable patter. (Healy: "This may be a personal question, but what do you call your daddy?" Bonnell: "Oh, we don't call him. He has an alarm clock.") Bonnell is absent for the film's best number, Ted and the boys' close-harmony rendition of "What Is Sweeter Than the Sweetness of I Love You?"—one of three songs written for the film (and which is oft-repeated in it). The number begins with Foy and Damerel performing in a theater, and it expands when the four comics pick up the lyrics behind the curtain as the actors continue to dance out front.

When Universal brought *Myrt and Marge* out of mothballs for a few cable TV airings in 1988, Stooge fans may have been disappointed by the function of future acknowledged comic genius Curly Howard as a prop for headliner Healy's violent slaps, but this was a document of how the proto–Stooges interacted. An example:

HEALY: "Ya gettin' tired, Curly?"
CURLY: "Yes, I'm so tired I need a rest."
HEALY (nodding toward Larry): "Why don't you get some old clothes and spend a couple of weeks in his hair? ... You know, you guys are gettin' to be a burden.... You know what a burden is, don't ya?"
LARRY: "Yeah, burden in the hand is worth two in the bush." (Moe hits Larry in the nose; Healy slaps Curly in the head.)
HEALY: "You know, you're goin' to regret these sarcastic remarks someday."
CURLY: "Startin' when?"
HEALY: "Right now!" (Hits Curly on the head again.)

In mid–1934, Fine and the Howards split from Healy (1896–1937) and went to Columbia to launch what would become a long-running shorts series—and pop-culture immortality. Myrtle Vail and Donna Damerel weren't so blessed. Although their show continued to flourish, their movie did not. The grosses were indifferent and the reviews mixed, with less of the praise going to the headliners than to their support. Wrote *The Film Daily*: "Unpretentious from a production standpoint and lacking name value unless the radio following of Myrt and Marge can be considered substantial enough to mean something, this picture should just about get by as a programmer.... Ted Healy and his stooges provide some of their familiar comedy."[27]

Others agreed about Healy and his gang. "Ted Healy and his Stooges, by sticking to their own vaudeville technique ... come through with the minimum of stilted moments," wrote a *Variety* critic.[28] Opined *Motion Picture Daily*: "Ted Healy and his gang furnish all the laughs with Eddie Foy, Jr., assisting with his neat routine of dance and song. Some of the gags are a bit spicy.... First class entertainment. There are plenty of exploitation possibilities."[29] Less kind were the New York critics: "It seems to be a particular misfortune of radio personalities to make their screen debuts in productions so old-fashioned that they seem quaint" (*Sun*) ... "One is apt to conclude that they are particularly suited to radio entertaining" (*Times*) ... "Nothing but a farce, choppy and lacking pep. Most of the gags are old" (*News*).[30] Perhaps anticipating this reaction, Universal withheld *Myrt and Marge* from any Big Apple theaters until mid–January 1934, nearly a month after its premiere. The film fared better in smaller markets like Denver, where it broke house records at multiple theaters, and in the Midwest and South.

Myrt and Marge acknowledges its novelty value by ending in a radio studio; the scenario we've seen play out over 65 minutes is revealed to be a broadcast of a Vail-Damerel show, and the cast members break the fourth wall to take bows before the camera. Had this pleasant, unpretentious film been made when the musical was younger, it might've been a success. To patrons accustomed to a newly elaborate genre led by the likes of Busby Berkeley, its conventional backstage stuff was old hat. Vail and Damerel went back to radio full time. Their partnership, and the heart of their show, stopped beating in 1941 when Damerel died in childbirth.

Even if we're seeing it just to watch the Three Stooges, *Myrt and Marge* gives us a sense of why people loved Myrt and Marge—even if they didn't care for this movie.

Harold Teen
(Warner Bros.; April 7, 1934)

Director: Murray Roth. Producer: James Seymour. Screenplay: Paul Gerard Smith, Al Cohn, based on the comic strip by Carl Ed. Photography: Arthur L. Todd. Editing: Terry Morse. Art Director: John Hughes. Running Time: 65 minutes.

Cast: Hal LeRoy (Harold Teen); Rochelle Hudson (Lillian "Lillums" Lovewell); Patricia Ellis (Mimi); Guy Kibbee (Pa Lovewell); Hugh Herbert (Ed Rathburn); Hobart Cavanaugh (Pop); Chick Chandler (Lilacs); Douglass Dumbrille (Snatcher); Eddie Tamblyn (Shadow); Clara Blandick (Ma Lovewell); Mayo Methot (Sally LaSalle); Richard Carle (Parmalee); Charles C. Wilson (McKinsey); Ethel Wales (Miss Gilly); Spec O'Donnell (Jones); Harriett Forbstein (Sadie); Sidney Miller (student); Harry Seymour (Yost); Eddie Shubert (Morris); Sammy Fain (vocalist at dance).

Songs: "Collegiate Wedding" [Chandler, Hudson, LeRoy, Cavanaugh, chorus], "Farewell Covina" [chorus], "How Do I Know It's Sunday?" [Chandler, Hudson, Tamblyn, Forbstein, chorus; reprised by orchestra], "Simple and Sweet" [Fain, orchestra], "Two Little Flies on a Lump of Sugar" [Ellis, Chandler] (Irving Kahal, Sammy Fain).

The Story: Harold Teen, an absent-minded cub reporter for the Covina Crier, is assigned to cover the graduation ceremony at Covina High School, where his former classmate, and now girlfriend, Lilliums, is in the outgoing class. H.H. Snatcher, new in town to take over its failing bank, becomes a mentor to Harold but also a competitor for Lillums' attention. Snatcher's citified daughter, Mimi, organizes a Junior League show, "Covina Junior Gaieties," and vies with Lillums for its star part. At the show, Lilacs and Mimi sing "Two Little Flies on a Lump of Sugar," but Mimi misses her cue in the big "Collegiate Wedding" finale. Harold, who secretly has been taking mail-order dancing lessons from Rathburn, the show's choreographer, steps in to lead the number. Harold and Lillums get married, this time for real.

"Harold Teen," Carl Ed's slangy comic strip about small-town high school life, was touted by its owner, the Chicago Tribune Newspapers Syndicate, for its "trivial tragedies and humorous highlights of the very young man in the serio-comic throes of calf love." Harold loved the girls and hung out at his local malt shop, and he would be considered a forerunner of sorts to the most famous of teen funny-paper characters, Archie Andrews in the strip *Archie*. Harold made it the movies twice during his four-decade run on paper from 1919 to 1959. First National adapted it as a 1928 silent that starred Arthur Lake as Harold. Warner Bros., which by this time had incorporated FN, brought it back to the screen six years later as a musical comedy with young dancer Hal LeRoy (1913–1985) in his only starring role in a feature.

LeRoy's frenzied footwork made him a hit on Broadway in *The Gang's All Here* and *Ziegfeld Follies of 1931*, as well as in vaudeville, and he earned a shot at the movies with a series of 17 Vitaphone shorts filmed at Warners' Brooklyn studio between 1931 and 1939. He appeared opposite his stage dancing partner, Mitzi Mayfair, in many of these two-reelers, and a raft of starlets: Dorothy Dare, Dawn O'Day, Grace Bradley, June Preisser, Toby Wing, and even the young June Allyson and Betty Hutton. LeRoy popped up occasionally in features, at Warners-First National (*Wonder Bar*) and elsewhere (*Start Cheering* at Columbia and *Too Many Girls* at RKO). Helmed by longtime Vita shorts director Murray Roth and produced by *42nd Street* co-screenwriter James Seymour,

Harold Teen may have been LeRoy's most important screen assignment. However, Paul Gerard Smith and Al Cohn's script, in which lead-footed teen Harold takes secret dance lessons via mail order, forced him to hide LeRoy's eccentric tap work until the final reel.

The lanky LeRoy—born John LeRoy Schotte in Cincinnati—sometimes combined dancing with drumming in his routines. He seemed so carefree as a performer that when he appeared in the Broadway show *Strike Me Pink* in 1933, *New York Times* critic Brooks Atkinson said the lad "dances like an inspired schoolboy on a holiday"; another writer described him as having "the face of a hick and the feet of a genius."[31] LeRoy seemed like a natural to play Carl Ed's insouciant teenager, and the assignment sent him on one of his periodic jaunts away from his East Coast base. A few months past his 20th birthday in December 1933 when he came to Hollywood chaperoned by his lumber executive father, he took time to tell an Associated Press reporter about his singlemindedness: "I could have studied law or medicine or anything—but all I wanted to do was dance. I never liked school, and dad let me choose the work I have my heart set on."[32]

While in Hollywood in December and January, LeRoy shot his part in the "Goin' to Heaven on a Mule" number for *Wonder Bar*, the Al Jolson WB musical, and excited would-be visitors to the set of *Harold Teen* in nearby Van Nuys, California. Van Nuys was about 30 miles from Covina, the Los Angeles-area community that inspired the setting for the comic strip. A *Film Daily* report noted: "Youngsters are certainly interested in *Harold Teen*.... While on location, the company ... had three motorcycle cops busy, so that 'shooting' could be done."[33]

Warner Bros. worked to keep interest in *Harold Teen* for all ages: It signed a deal with seven leading manufacturers to sponsor 50,000 window displays of merchandise from the film, and arranged a newspaper series of tap-dance lessons. It included *Harold Teen* as part of its National Trade Exhibit of studio product in key cities; among other titles in the showcase were *Jimmy the Gent* (with James Cagney and Bette Davis), *Gambling Lady* (with Barbara Stanwyck) and the aforementioned *Wonder Bar*. There also was a promotional short subject, *Hollywood Newsreel*, which debuted a couple of weeks before the feature premiered and showed LeRoy, co-star Patricia Ellis, and *Harold Teen* songwriters Irving Kahal and Sammy Fain singing and dancing. (*Harold Teen* is absent from DVD and Blu-Ray at this writing, but *Hollywood Newsreel* can be seen as an extra on the disc of Warners' *42nd Street*.)

This was an especially eventful period in LeRoy's life; he married a model named Betty Dodd in April 1934 in what would be a lasting union. On the less happy side, in January 1935, a few months after the marriage, LeRoy sued his father, George Schotte—who was his longtime manager. The dispute was over

2. Failed, Fallen, and One-Shot Stars 57

$70,000 held in a joint bank account, set up by his late mother, that the performer accused his dad of keeping from the couple. In July, the suit was resolved in court in LeRoy's hometown of Cincinnati with the announcement of a "satisfactory" settlement, although no details were released[34]

What of *Harold Teen*? Upon its New York City debut, *Variety* panned the film as "too childish even for the boys and girls to whom the appeal apparently is directed. LeRoy looks the part ... but does not carry the interest."[35] *The Hollywood Reporter* thought it strayed too far from its roots and didn't allow its star to hoof enough: "The whole aim ... is to introduce Hal LeRoy ... as an extraordinary dancer.... The trouble is they have tried to get a feature picture out of a single dance."[36] The verdict from this writer is that it plays much less like the strip than people might have liked in 1934, but that the studio-infused musical angle lifts this modest little film.

Kahal and Fain supply two catchy tunes, "How Do I Know It's Sunday?" and "Simple and Sweet," the latter sung on camera by Fain, on hand as a pianist at a Covina High dance, and their "Collegiate Wedding" finale is neatly staged, if derivative of football-themed song numbers like those found in *Good News*

Rochelle Hudson is beckoned to participate in the climactic "Collegiate Wedding" number in *Harold Teen* (1934) (courtesy Ron Hutchinson/The Vitaphone Project).

or *Sweetie*. Chick Chandler (1905–1988), borrowed from RKO to play a school hipster—and rival for ingénue Rochelle Hudson (1916–1972)—brings energy in introducing the "Sunday" number amid libido-driven "merriment and high blood pleasure" at the kids' fave soda shop, the Sugar Bowl. And it wouldn't be a Warner Bros. musical without some Depression-era topicality to balance the sweetness: Lillums' father (Guy Kibbee) complains to his wife about being broke, and the city slicker (Douglass Dumbrille) brought in to reorganize Covina's failing bank admits to reporter Harold that he needs the spreading of some "propaganda" to revitalize local commerce.

Still, there would be no Harold Teen series, and Hal LeRoy went right back to Brooklyn to do more shorts and stage work. He remained active by performing in supper clubs, summer stock, and television, as well as directing and producing shows, until shortly before his death. A sampling of his talents—his short subjects were oft-aired in the early years of Turner Classic Movies—reveals that he may have been underused in the movies.

Little Miss Marker
(Paramount; May 18, 1934)
and *Shoot the Works*
(Paramount; July 6, 1934)

Little Miss Marker

Director: Alexander Hall. Producer: B. P. Schulberg. Screenplay: William R. Lipman, Sam Hellman, Gladys Lehman, based on the short story by Damon Runyon. Photography: Alfred Gilks. Editing: William Shea. Sound: Earl S. Hayman. Art Directors: Hans Dreier, John B. Goodman. Running Time: 80 minutes.

Cast: Adolphe Menjou (Sorrowful Jones); Dorothy Dell (Bangles Carson); Charles Bickford (Big Steve); Shirley Temple (Marky); Lynne Overman (Regret); Warren Hymer (Sore Toe); Sam Hardy (Benny the Gouge); John Kelly (Canvas Back); Frank McGlynn, Sr. (Doc Chesley); John Sheehan (Sun Rise); Frank Conroy (Dr. Ingalls); Edward Earle (Marky's father); Tammany Young (Bugs); Willie Best [Sleep 'n Eat] (Dizzy); Crawfurd Kent (doctor); Mildred Gover (maid).

Songs: "I'm a Black Sheep Who's Blue" [Dell], "Laugh You Son of a Gun" [Dell, Temple], "Low Down Lullaby" [Dell] (Leo Robin, Ralph Rainger); "The Bowery" (Overman, chorus) (Charles H. Hoyt, Percy Gaunt); "The Sidewalks of New York" [Overman, chorus] (James W. Blake, Charles B. Lawlor).

Working Title: *Halfway Decent.*
Also Known As: *The Girl in Pawn.*
Home Video: Universal DVD/VHS.

The Story: The gambling operation run by horse race-fixing gangster and cabaret owner "Big Steve" Halloway accepts a little girl, nicknamed "Marky," as an I.O.U.

from her penniless father. Steve's girlfriend, Bangles, befriends and protects Marky after she is sent to live with bookie Sorrowful Jones after the death of her father. After an accident, Marky requires a blood transfusion for a life-saving operation; Steve donates the blood, then forgives Sorrowful and Bangles, who have fallen in love and plan to marry and adopt the girl.

Shoot the Works

Director: Wesley Ruggles. Producer: Albert Lewis. Screenplay: Howard J. Green, Claude Binyon, based on the play *The Great Magoo* by Ben Hecht and Gene Fowler (New York opening, December 2, 1932; 11 performances). Photography: Leo Tover. Art Directors: Hans Dreier, Robert Usher. Running Time: 81 minutes.

Cast: Jack Oakie (Nicky Nelson); Ben Bernie (Joe Davis); Dorothy Dell (Lily Racquel); Alison Skipworth (The Countess); Roscoe Karns (Sailor Burke); Arline Judge (Jackie); William Frawley (Larry Hale); Lew Cody (Axel Hanratty); Paul Cavanagh (Alvin Ritchie); Ben Bernie's Lads (Davis band); Frank Prince [Fred Lawrence] (singer); Lee Kohlmar (Professor Jones); Monte Vandergrift (board of health man); Jill Dennett (Wanda); Tony Merlo (head waiter); Ben Taggart (detective); Charles McAvoy (cop); Ann Sheridan (Hanratty's secretary).

Songs: "In the Good Old Winter Time" [band], "Were Your Ears Burning—Baby?" [Bernie, band], "With My Eyes Wide Open I'm Dreaming" [Oakie, reprised by Dell, Oakie, then three times by Dell, band] (Mack Gordon, Harry Revel); "Do I Love You?" [Dell, Prince, Bernie, Karns, band], "Take a Lesson From the Lark" [band] (Leo Robin, Ralph Rainger); "A Bowl of Chop Suey and You-ey" [Bernie, Karns, band] (Ben Bernie, Alyce Goering, Walter Bullock).

Working Titles: *The Great Magoo; Thank Your Stars.*

The Story: New York huckster Nicky Nelson scratches out a living with his band of small-time colleagues: bandleader Joe Davis, daredevil Sailor Burke, Sailor's girlfriend Jackie, and the ever-loyal "Countess." He meets singer Lily Racquel, and the two fall in love ("With My Eyes Wide Open I'm Dreaming") while rehearsing their vaudeville act. Davis and his band break from Nicky, with Lily as vocalist, via radio promoter Ritchie, who wants to marry Lily. Newspaper columnist Joe Hale attempts to smear Davis; Nicky beats up the writer in response, and Hale has a change of heart. Nicky joins Davis' radio program as master of ceremonies.

In 1934, Paramount took a failed Broadway play, sanitized its seedy showbiz melodrama into a musical comedy vehicle for funnyman Jack Oakie and bandleader Ben Bernie, and watched it enjoy nearly as short a life on celluloid as it had in New York.[37] It didn't help that the female lead—a rising star at age 19—was dead by the time *Shoot the Works* came to theaters.

The tragedy of Dorothy Dell, who died in an auto accident less than a month before the debut of *Shoot the Works*—and a week after the national release of the second of her three feature films, *Little Miss Marker*—cast a pall, of course. But a re-evaluation of *Shoot the Works* 80 years later reveals that Dell couldn't lift a movie that simply wasn't very good. Based on *The Great Magoo*, an unsuccessful Ben Hecht-Gene Fowler play, *Shoot the Works* derives much of its humor from the shenanigans of its protagonist, Nicky Nelson, whose reliance on the smelly whale carcass in his 42nd Street "Leviathan" exhibit for income shows how low he is on the entertainment food chain.[38] Nicky (Oakie, in the role played on Broadway by Paul Kelly) also employs a daredevil act (Roscoe Karns) for whom he is always trying to find new exploitation angles. Stunt man "Sailor," however, balks at Nicky's latest idea: "I've clung buildings for ya, and I've sat on flagpoles, but I ain't holding no fork in my mouth to catch no apple that's thrown from the 15th floor of the Empire State Building." So there.

Nicky manages a talented band, run by Joe Davis (Bernie), and discovers a beautiful blonde singer, Lily Racquel (Dell), only to lose them both to the bigger time—and be reduced to running a flea circus—over the course of most of 81 minutes. Audiences in the sticks could grow tired of the film's cynicism; big-city folks, such as the *New York Times* reviewer Andre Sennwald, could complain of the watering down of a hot property just as the Production Code was coming in for prime enforcement:

Blonde beauty Dorothy Dell made a splash in the movies opposite Jack Oakie and Alison Skipworth in *Shoot the Works* (1934), but her success came posthumously.

The program of liquidation involves the selection of Jack Oakie to play the part of Nicky, the drunk-sodden spieler, and the consequence is Portrait No. 43,389 in the series devoted to the lovable bad boy who loves a girl who nearly marries another man but realizes in time that the lead is not the rascal he seems.[39]

Shoot the Works is more watchable for personalities than plot, not least if you're interested in the talents of Ben Bernie, the bandleader, violinist, composer, and radio attraction best known for his "Yowsah!" catchphrase and "The Old Maestro" moniker. Both are heard in *Shoot the Works*, which doesn't care to expand Bernie's character beyond the real Ben. This includes a parody of Bernie's long-running feud—mainly for show—with acidic newspaper columnist Walter Winchell, played in this film by William Frawley under the name "Larry Hale." The real-life "feud" is reflected in Davis' and Hale's cinematic sniping.

DAVIS (on stage spotting Hale in a nightclub audience as the band plays "Take a Lesson From the Lark"): "Hi, Larry, how does it feel to be among nice people?"
HALE (referring to Davis' violin): "Are you really playing that thing or are you just cooling it off for a friend?"
DAVIS: "What, this? Don't you know this is a Mickey Mouse fiddle. Always acts that way around cheese!"

Bernie (1891–1943) did this kind of thing better with the real Winchell in two 1937 20th Century–Fox films, *Love and Hisses* and *Wake Up and Live*, in which they played themselves.[40] Unlike Winchell, Bernie died fairly young, and *Shoot the Works* helps us understand his elusive appeal. Meanwhile, Arline Judge is on hand as Karns' unintentionally slutty girl; she was married to Wesley Ruggles, the director of *Shoot the Works*, at the time. But the more impactful female presence belongs to Dell (1915–1934), who is heard to good advantage singing Ralph Rainger and Leo Robin's "With My Eyes Wide Open I'm Dreaming," as a solo and with co-star Oakie (1903–1978), and projects vulnerability as well as sass.

Born Dorothy Dell Goff, she grew up in New Orleans (as a childhood friend of future star Dorothy Lamour), and won the 1930 Miss Universe contest. This catapulted her into a featured role in the 1931 *Ziegfeld Follies*. In that show, she sang the suggestive ditty "Was I Drunk, and Was He Handsome?" in a rich contralto, evoking descriptions as a Mae West type—at age 16, no less. Dell debuted in movies in a 1932 Brooklyn-shot Vitaphone short, *Passing the Buck*, opposite baritone Alexander Gray. She came West after being signed by Paramount in September 1933 for a Bing Crosby project. Instead, she was assigned to a routine drama, *Wharf Angel*, released in March 1934, in which she did well enough to earn a long-term studio contract.

The fan mag *Picture Play* was duly impressed:

As soon as you see Dorothy Dell in her first picture you will like her. Shortly afterward you will admire her and before the end you will be enthusiastic. She has the beauty of the "Follies" girl she used to be, the ability of a real actress and a voice that is not only haunting but is used with the skill of a trained speaker.[41]

Paramount prepared to promote Dell's career as one of its "Stars of Tomorrow," along with Ida Lupino, Ethel Merman, Larry "Buster" Crabbe, and Lanny Ross. The Damon Runyon–inspired comedy *Little Miss Marker* followed, and as club singer "Bangles" Carson, Dell was paired with top-billed Adolphe Menjou (1890–1963)—and performed three Leo Robin–Ralph Rainger songs. But both stars were upstaged by the fourth-billed Shirley Temple, playing a little girl held as collateral by a band of gangsters. Temple was a 6-year-old prodigy who was alighting to stardom on the strength of this and two almost concurrently released films from her home Fox lot: *Stand Up and Cheer!* and *Baby Take a Bow*. Fox had rescued the tyke from short-subject oblivion and was so impressed by her work in the all-star musical *Stand Up and Cheer!* that it locked her up to a long-term contract, then loaned her to Paramount for the spreading of further charm, even amid a band of cagey character actors and a comely emerging star. Audiences made a big hit of *Little Miss Marker*, which was more of the Runyonesque tough-guys-with-hearts-of-gold fare that made a big screen success out of Columbia's *Lady for a Day* the year before.

Dell and Temple dueted on "Laugh You Son of a Gun" and Dell sang Temple's "Marky" to sleep with "Low Down Lullaby." The two befriended each other off the screen as well. During the filming of a scene in which little "Marky" is supposed to be insolent, Dell broke into laughter and as Temple (1928–2014) would recall in her autobiography, "we held hands, enjoying the sense of impromptu gaiety. I felt treated as an equal.... Time and time again during the film, she turned out to be a splendid foil for my energy and exuberance."[42] Dell might have reappeared with Temple on screen, but fate would intervene.

Little Miss Marker opened in New York City on May 18 and nationally on the first day of June, but the drama behind *Shoot the Works* was just beginning, as cast member Lew Cody died in his sleep from a heart attack on May 31 at age 50. Dell attended Cody's wake, and in the early hours of June 8 was a passenger in a car driven by her new boyfriend, oral surgeon Carl Wagner, whom she had met when he treated her mother during a bout with pneumonia. Their car went off the road at a high speed near Pasadena, California. Dell was killed almost instantly, and Wagner survived only a few hours more. "Nineteen years old—everything ahead of her—then a sharp turn in the road—and oblivion," eulogized *Photoplay*.[43] A day later, the actress's wake was held in the same chapel as Cody's. (Her former beau, crooner Russ Columbo, who stayed away from Dell's funeral, would himself die suddenly before summer's end.)

On the set of her picture *Now and Forever* at Paramount, Shirley Temple was shielded from news of the tragedy, but, as Temple wrote in her autobiography;

We were set to film when someone, perhaps advertently, spilled the sad news about Dell. I burst into tears. Mother was momentarily off the set, so everyone milled around helplessly. Everyone but the director, who quickly called for a camera to focus on me where I lay slumped, sobbing away.... Mother returned, observed the splendid performance, and resumed watching while the camera continued to roll. Only I knew it was more fun to shed fake tears than real ones.[44]

When patrons heard Dell sing the haunting "With My Eyes Wide Open I'm Dreaming" in *Shoot the Works*, or the tender "Low Down Lullaby" in *Little Miss Marker*, it would remind them of dreams unrealized and promise unfilled.[45] Paramount didn't have Dorothy Dell any more, but it wasn't done with the *Great Magoo/Shoot the Works* property. The studio remade it in 1939 as a Bob Hope comedy, *Some Like It Hot*, with drummer Gene Krupa as the new Ben Bernie and Shirley Ross in the Dell part. *Little Miss Marker* was also redone at Paramount with Hope, as 1949's *Sorrowful Jones*, with Lucille Ball, and then twice by Universal, as *40 Pounds of Trouble* (1962), with Tony Curtis, and *Little Miss Marker* (1980), with Walter Matthau and Julie Andrews.

One Hour Late
(Paramount; December 14, 1934)

and *Love in Bloom*
(Paramount; April 20, 1935)

One Hour Late

Director: Ralph Murphy. Producer: Bayard Veiller. Screenplay: Kathryn Scola, Paul Gerard Smith. Story: Libbie Block. Photography: Ben Reynolds. Sound: Philip Wisdom. Art Directors: Hans Dreier, John B. Goodman. Running Time: 75 minutes.

Cast: Joe Morrison (Eddie Blake); Helen Twelvetrees (Betty [Bessie] Dunn); Conrad Nagel (Stephen Barclay); Arline Judge (Hazel); Ray Walker (Cliff Miller); Edward Craven (Maxie); Toby Wing (Maizie); Gail Patrick (Eileen Barclay); Edward Clark (Mr. Zeller); Raymond [Ray] Milland (Tony St. John); George E. Stone (Benny); Jed Prouty (Finch); Arthur Hoyt (Barlow); Charles Sellon (Simpson); Jack Mulhall (Whittaker); Bradley Page (Jim); Sidney Miller (Orville); Gladys Hulette (Gertrude); Billy Bletcher (Gerald); Betty Farrington (Miss Jones); Phil Tead (Wally); Diana Lewis (sick woman's daughter); John Howard (elevator operator); Ann Sheridan (girl); Frank Mayo (Kearney); Jack Norton (manager).

Songs: "(I Can't Imagine) Me Without You" [Morrison], "With My Eyes Wide Open I'm Dreaming" [Walker, Morrison; reprised by Walker] (Leo Robin, Lewis Gensler); "A Little Angel Told Me So" [Morrison, twice] (Sam Coslow); "The Last Round-Up" [Morrison] (Billy Hill).

Working Title: *Me Without You*.

Disc: Brunswick 7347 ("[I Can't Imagine] Me Without You"/"A Little Angel Told Me So," Joe Morrison).

The Story: Eddie Blake, a file clerk at Marsden & Barclay Electrical Engineers, becomes jealous after his girlfriend, stenographer Bessie Dunn, is asked by their boss, Stephen Barclay, to do an hour of extra work with him each day. Eddie auditions for a local radio program, but the broadcast cuts out before listeners can hear him sing "A Little Angel Told Me So." Eddie gets stuck in an elevator, where he performs "(I Can't Imagine) Me Without You." Meanwhile, Bessie's brother-in-law, Jim, borrows money from Eddie, and Barclay's wife carries on an affair with Tony St. John. When Barclay invites Bessie to his home to get caught up on work, Eddie impulsively asks co-worker Hazel to marry him. Another stuck elevator allows Eddie to become a hero, patch things up with Bessie, and get a job singing over the airwaves.

Love in Bloom

Director: Elliott Nugent. Producer: Benjamin Glazer. Screenplay: Frank R. Adams. Adaptation: J. P. McAvoy, Keene Thompson. Additional Dialogue: John P. Medbury. Photography: Leo Tover. Editing: William Shea. Art Directors: Hans Dreier, Robert Odell. Costumes: Travis Banton. Running Time: 75 minutes.

Cast: George Burns (George Downey); Gracie Allen (Gracie Downey); Joe Morrison (Larry Deane); Dixie Lee (Violet Downey); J. C. Nugent (Colonel "Dad" Downey); Lee Kohlmar (Pop Heinrich); Richard Carle (Sheriff); Mary Foy (Mrs. Cassidy); Wade Boteler (motorcycle cop); Marian Mansfield (Edith Bowen); Julia Graham (waitress); Sam Godfrey (cashier); Jack Mulhall (beggar); Douglas Blackley [Robert Kent] (man who buys song); Benny Baker (man who buys radio); Harry C. Bradley (sexton); Douglas Wood (rector); Charlotte Ogden (carnival troupe member).

Songs: "Got Me Doin' Things!" [Lee], "Let Me Sing You to Sleep With a Love Song" [Morrison], "(Lookie, Lookie, Lookie) Here Comes Cookie" [Allen], "My Heart Is an Open Book" [Morrison, reprised by Lee, Morrison, then instrumentally in montage, then by Morrison] (Mack Gordon, Harry Revel); "None But the Weary Heart" (aka "None But the Lonely Heart") [Morrison] (Lev Mey, Pyotr Ilyich Tchaikovsky).

Working Title: *Win or Lose.*

Disc: Brunswick 02014 ("Got Me Doin' Things!"/"My Heart Is an Open Book," Dixie Lee with Orville Knapp Orchestra).

Home Video: Universal DVD/VHS.

The Story: The carnival owned by Colonel "Dad" Downey is grounded when "Dad" is jailed in the sticks for nonpayment of bills. His son, George, and George's wife, Gracie, who performs as the "exotic" dancer Fatima, set out for New York City to find Violet, Dad's daughter and George's sister, to help fund the carnival back into solvency. Vi, who has run away from her family to make her own way, is bailed out of financial trouble by aspiring musician/songwriter Larry Deane. The two find jobs in Pop's sheet music store, where Larry writes a catchy tune, "My Heart Is an Open Book," and Vi proves to be an astute salesperson. Larry wants to marry Vi, but she feels unworthy of him because of her background—especially after confrontations with George and her drunken father—and she returns to her family. However, Larry finds a publisher for his song, and he comes to fetch Vi from carny life.

2. Failed, Fallen, and One-Shot Stars 65

A clean-cut, boyish tenor, Joe Morrison wasn't a one-shot movie luminary—he appeared in six 1934–35 features at Paramount, plus three later short subjects at other studios. That many movies might not quite make him a failed star. But he became so forgotten that until well into the 21st century, movie historians didn't know for sure if he was alive or dead.

Morrison (1904–1972) toiled in the minor leagues of showbiz for many years—more than he might have let on, given the untruths told about his age—before hitting big with a huge song hit that brought him a movie contract. He acted opposite W.C. Fields, George Burns and Gracie Allen, Richard Barthelmess, and Ray Milland. He appeared in only two bona fide musical features: *One Hour Late*, the first of his two films with top-of-the-cast billing, and *Love in Bloom*, in which he and Dixie Lee were billed behind Burns and Allen. Morrison never reached the career heights of Bing Crosby, but at least he got to woo Crosby's wife, Dixie Lee, on screen.

Morrison may have been a cheerful sort in public during his Hollywood stay, but his smile was hard-won. Starting in 1927, the Michigan native had knocked around in vaudeville with a partner named Eddie Vine—they were billed as Eddie Vine and Brother—and Vine would become Morrison's manager. A well-attended benefit appearance landed Morrison a slot as "The Beloved Vagabond" on radio; eventually, he went to George Olsen's orchestra as a vocalist. One night in 1933, they attempted a rendition of an obscure Western song, "The Last Round-Up." It didn't go over well, but Morrison wasn't going to give up. As a magazine writer would recount:

> At few weeks later, they were playing an engagement in Pittsburgh. Joe was sitting at a table with Ethel Shutta, who is Olsen's wife, waiting for his turn to go on. "Whatever became of that cowboy song you tried out?" Miss Shutta asked. "George never plays it anymore," Joe answered. They dug it out of the pile of music and sang it again. People stopped dancing to crowd around the platform and listen. Returning to New York for an engagement at the Paramount Theater, they tried it again. The next day, a banner stretched across Broadway announcing "JOE MORRISON." And that, my friends, is what is really known as an overnight sensation.[46]

The Morrison-Olsen recording of the haunting tune about a cowhand's impending demise topped national charts, spawning remakes by Bing Crosby, Guy Lombardo, and Gene Autry, and making Paramount take notice. Morrison traveled in February 1933 to Hollywood, where his first assignment was the juvenile role in the Fields comedy *The Old Fashioned Way*, released in July. Morrison acquitted himself well in singing the ballad "Rolling in Love" to co-star Judith Allen but wasn't about to overshadow the film's distinctive headliner. More songs were to come in *One Hour Late*, in which Morrison played a cocky file clerk overly jealous of the professional relationship between his girl (Helen Twelvetrees, 1908–1958) and their boss (Conrad Nagel, 1897–1970). "She works in his office from 9 to 5 ... but from 5 to 6 she worked on him!" was the insinuating poster text for the film.

One Hour Late packs too much plot into 75 minutes, which remains its biggest drawback despite being passable entertainment. Nagel's wife (Gail Patrick) is having an affair with a handsome socialite (Ray Milland), but they're hardly seen. Twelvetrees lives in a crowded flat with an alcoholic mooch of a brother-in-law (Bradley Page), her sister, and four yowling kids, but this thread is dropped halfway through. Morrison's "boy nightingale"—who vows that "someday I'm going to be getting fan mail from Bing Crosby" but refuses to be "crawling around" to radio tryouts—finally puts his ego aside for an audition. Adding to the thespian lineup are Ray Walker, as an egotistical would-be baritone whose singing is compared to hog-calling, and perennially wisecracking Arline Judge, as an office flirt. Starlet Toby Wing is seen as a binge-eating coworker, of all things.

Morrison's theme song, "A Little Angel Told Me So," is heard multiple times in a studio setting, but there's also a cute radio parody in which Morrison visits a broadcast of "America's Sweethearts, Geraldine and Gerald, in 'Terrors of the Jungle,'" complete with sound effects and two actors physically ill-suited for their robust over-the-air characters; "Gerald" yawns between his lines while "Geraldine" knits while at the mike. Morrison also sings "With My Eyes Wide Open I'm Dreaming," lately introduced in *Shoot the Works* [q.v.], and, while his character risks his life to climb into an elevator shaft in the finale, "The Last Round-Up." The latter was what the public wanted, if only to enjoy the in-joke. In its favorable review of *One Hour Late*, the fan magazine *Hollywood* dared to invoke the C-word: "It looks as if Bing Crosby has a rival.... The boy has what it takes."[47] Morrison was tied enough to the cowboy song brand that Paramount threw him into a cameo to sing the title tune in its Zane Grey Western *Home on the Range* in early 1935. A melodrama, *Four Hours to Kill*, with fading star Barthelmess, followed.

Love in Bloom arrived for April release; the title came from the mega-hit Leo Robin-Ralph Rainger song from the recent Crosby musical *She Loves Me Not*, but audiences expecting that song in the new film would not hear a note. ("Love in Bloom" would become even more famous as Jack Benny's trademark tune.) Instead, Gracie Allen got to sing "(Lookie, Lookie, Lookie) Here Comes Cookie" while posing as an exotic dancer in a seedy carnival, and Morrison was handed two other Mack Gordon-Harry Revel tunes, "Let Me Sing You to Sleep With a Love Song" and "My Heart Is an Open Book," plus a higher-brow rendition of Tchaikovsky's "None But the Weary Heart." *Love in Bloom* pushes "Open Book" the most, but "Sing You to Sleep" provides a welcome sensitive moment as Morrison sings Dixie Lee into slumber when both are practically homeless and forced to sleep in a music store.

2. Failed, Fallen, and One-Shot Stars   67

Joe Morrison and Dixie Lee can't believe their good fortune in *Love in Bloom* (1935); Lee Kohlmar looks on.

Burns (1896–1996)—who is hardly believable as a sibling of the 15-years-younger Lee—and Allen (1895–1964) were heavily promoted as the stars of *Love in Bloom*, which was described as "a shoddy tale" by *The New York Times*, but it's essentially a Morrison-Lee vehicle.[48] It was part of a widely publicized return to the screen for Lee, a former Fox contractee who had stepped away from her acting career not long after marrying Bing Crosby in 1930, when she was much more famous than he. In *Love in Bloom*, she capably sings "Got Me Doin' Things!" During her "comeback," Lee also appeared in a Poverty Row romance, *Manhattan Love Song* (made in two weeks while she was pregnant with twins born in 1934), and a minor 1935 Fox musical, *Redheads on Parade*, before resuming her focus on raising the Crosby brood. She did some radio and cut a couple of records with her husband thereafter, but that was it professionally. Troubled by bouts with stage jitters, alcoholism, and depression, she died of cancer in 1952, just short of her 41st birthday.

Joe Morrison's own cinematic record would be complete in short order. He was top-lined in *It's a Great Life*, a 1935 "B" about Civilian Conservation Corps workers, then was dropped by Paramount, losing a potential assignment in *The Big Broadcast of 1936* because of his diminishing box office returns. He can be seen singing in two MGM-issued Technicolor shorts, *La Fiesta de Santa Barbara* (1935, with "The Last Round-Up" again) and *Hollywood Party* (1937). He returned to the stage and radio, but in 1936, *Variety* reported Morrison had filed for personal bankruptcy.[49] Ships passed in a few nights in 1939 when the former music hit-maker opened for headlining comic Milton Berle in a New York theater variety show.

Morrison's career slowly declined with age, as a 1950 *Billboard* review of a Seattle club performance seemed to indicate:

> Headliner Joe Morrison managed to pull a couple of real old ones out of the fire to only fair mitts.... [He] hit strongest on his version[s] of "Peg o' My Heart" and "Daddy's Little Girl." Morrison still has a lot of charm, but his falsetto transitions were unsteady and unsure. Crowd was beginning to warm to him after his final [Irving] Berlin medley.[50]

If you believe the studio bios from the '30s, Morrison would've been 42 in 1950, but he apparently shaved four years off his age, making it difficult for researchers to find information about him; his relatively common name didn't help. In 2014, research of Social Security Index death records revealed that Morrison had died in 1972—42 years before—in Flushing, Queens. A misplaced player had been found, but fans who enjoyed watching Morrison in VHS and DVD releases of *Love in Bloom* and *The Old Fashioned Way* had never lost the charming singer with the big voice and easy smile.

Lottery Lover
(Fox; January 4, 1935)

Director: William [Wilhelm] Thiele. Producer: Al Rockett. Screenplay: Franz Schulz, Billie [Billy] Wilder. Story: Sig Herzig, Maurice Hanline. Additional Dialogue: Sam Hellman. Photography: Bert Glennon. Editing: Dorothy Spencer. Sound: Joseph E. Aiken. Musical Director: Arthur Lange. Dance Director: Jack Donohue. Art Director: William Darling. Costumes: René Hubert, William Lambert. Running Time: 83 minutes.

Cast: Lew Ayres (Cadet Frank Harrington); Pat Paterson (Patty); Peggy Fears (Gaby Aimee); Sterling Holloway (Cadet Harold Stump); Walter [Woolf] King (Prince Midanoff); Alan Dinehart (Edward Arthur "Tank" Tankersley); Reginald Denny (Captain Payne); Edward Nugent (Gibbs); Nick [Dick] Foran (Cadet Allen Taylor); Rafaela Ottiano (Marie); Gaston Glass (Andre); Rolfe Sedan (barber); Ray Turner (bootblack); Armand Kaliz (Frenchman); Paul Weigel (attendant); Thomas Beck (cadet).

Songs: "Close Your Eyes and See" [Paterson], "There's a Bit of Paree in You" [Foran, Holloway, chorus; reprised by Ayres, Denny, Fears; then danced by Paterson, chorus], "Ting-a-Ling-a-Ling" [Fears, chorus; reprised by Ayres, Foran, Holloway, Nugent, chorus] (Don Hartman, Jay Gorney).

Working Titles: *Love Can Be Fun*; *Weak in Paris*.

The Story: As they begin leave in Paris, U.S. Navy cadets—among them bookish Frank Harrington—become smitten with French revue star Gaby Aimee after her garter comes into their possession. With their American guide, "Tank" Tankersley, the boys watch Gaby in her new show; so does their commander, Captain Payne, an old beau of Gaby's. The cadets pool their money for a lottery to decide which of them will pursue Gaby, and Frank is the winner. Tank hires Patty, a Canadian actress, to learn the ways of romance; Frank is mainly ignored by Gaby but falls for Patty, who tries to tell Frank that she loves him ("Close Your Eyes and See"). Tank arranges for Frank to dine with Gaby in her villa, but Frank unwittingly confesses his love for Patty. French soldiers challenge the cadets to a duel, which ends amicably.

There weren't many female "hyphenates" in Hollywood in 1935, but Peggy Fears could claim to be one of them.

Fears (1903–1994) was a Ziegfeld Follies showgirl and musical comedy star who—with her land developer/theatrical promoter husband, A.C. Blumenthal—produced the 1932–33 Broadway show *Music in the Air*, which came to the movies for Fox in 1934. Fox put Fears before the camera in the 1935 release *Lottery Lover*, an acting-only assignment, although she reportedly was under contract as an actress, writer, director, producer, and costume designer.[51] *Lottery Lover*, a musical comedy that co-starred Lew Ayres (1908–1996) and Pat Paterson, was just another product off the Fox assembly line, and it would be Fears' only credit in an abbreviated film career that was overshadowed by her tumultuous off-screen life.

Co-scripted by Billy Wilder (billed on screen as "Billie") and directed by Wilhelm (William) Thiele, *Lottery Lover* concerns a group of U.S. Navy cadets on a five-day shore leave in Paris. Despite being told by their commander (Reginald Denny) to "look at them—and leave them!" when it comes to women, the sailors (Ayres, Edward Nugent, Sterling Holloway, and Dick Foran among them) hold a lottery to win the affections of revue star Gaby Aimee (Fears). The mere mention of her name prompts the boys to break into Don Hartman and Jay Gorney's "There's a Bit of Paree in You." The lottery winner is Ayres' character, Cadet Frank Harrington. After being spurned by Gaby, he falls for a showgirl played by Paterson, while Gaby locates a former beau, who happens to be the cadets' aforementioned commander. The sailors engage in a climatic swordsmanship duel with a band of Frenchmen that turns into a dance number to a reprise of "There's a Bit of Paree in You."

Lottery Lover was somewhat of a troubled production. Originally announced co-star Lilian Harvey walked off another picture and out of Hollywood (she was replaced by Paterson), and its initially announced director, Hanns Schwartz, bowed out in July 1934 when he was stricken with appendicitis. William (born Wilhelm) Thiele, who like Schwartz had been a filmmaker in Germany, was the replacement in his first American film as a director. Thiele helped Wilder, a former screenwriter in Germany who was struggling to make a name in America (the script for *Music in the Air* [q.v.] was Wilder's only previous U.S. credit), get the co-writing job on *Lottery Lover*. Wilder received a mere $200 a week for five weeks' work with his collaborator, fellow German Franz Schulz.[52] Biographer Kevin Lally has written that the only recognizable Wilder touch in *Lottery Lover* is a repetition of a visual gag from *Mauvaise Graine*, a 1934 French film directed and co-written by Wilder, in which a passing truck obscures an open-air seduction (in *Lottery Lover*, it's between Walter King and Pat Paterson).

Meanwhile, Fears was being mentioned as one of 10 Fox players being "groomed for stardom" in early 1934—among the others were future *Lottery Lover* co-stars Pat Peterson and Nick (later to be known as Dick) Foran, plus Alice Faye and little Shirley Temple.[53] And *Motion Picture* magazine was gushing in a portrait of Fears:

> This girl has blazed a new trail of accomplishments for women in America as a successful writer, producer, actress, and businesswoman. Her philosophy of dress is based on a study of the effect of clothes upon New York's leading society women on famous actresses, on chorus girls, and on herself. And now she is translating what she has learned to the screen, so that her styles can be copied by any of us.[54]

Fears declared that fashion was the key to her own success:

> What happens to a woman is 65 per cent due to her clothes. In my own case, I should say about 85 per cent.... And especially is this true in pictures—because nowhere on earth are clothes so important as on the screen.[55]

Filmed in the fall of 1934, *Lottery Lover* would aid the careers of some of its minor players: Alan Dinehart, who played the cadets' American mentor (a role originally intended for Ned Sparks), earned a long-term contract from Fox. Walter Woolf King, who made an impact as Gaby's dimwitted Russian beau (think Erik Rhodes' comic work in the Fred Astaire–Ginger Rogers pictures at RKO), landed a new Fox pact as well. King, a longtime Broadway leading man, debuted in films as Walter Woolf as the male lead of the infamous Warner Bros. operetta *Golden Dawn* (1930), then was dropped from the studio after musicals fell out of favor. When the actor sued for breach of contract, Warners alleged that his singing voice was unsuitable for talkies. Woolf/King won the judgment, and his return to Hollywood for what would be a 40-year stay, mainly with billing as Walter Woolf King, put to rest that dubious assertion.

Lottery Lover was a routine assignment for Lew Ayres, but it did mark something of a personal highlight, for publicity photos of him and a visiting Ginger Rogers on the set—she was there to see him and the ensemble in the sailors' dance—presaged their marriage on November 13, 1934. *Lottery Lover* also did not advance Peggy Fears' Hollywood career. She solos passably on a

Lew Ayres can't make a good match for co-star Peggy Fears in her only film, *Lottery Lover* (1935).

verse of Don Hartman and Jay Gorney's "Ting-a-Ling-a-Ling," but leaves the heavy lifting to her choristers; later, she duets more agreeably with Denny (1891–1967) in a brief rendition of "There's a Bit of Paree in You." Otherwise, she walks through her part, especially in the scenes where she's supposed to be angry at Ayres, and one wonders what there is about Gaby that would make opposing bands of military men fight a duel over her.

Fears earned some positive reviews—*The Film Daily* called her "personable and talented"—and the use of "Lottery" in the film's title was thought to be a draw of sorts, for all throughout 1934, debate raged nationally over the legality, and morality, of drawing lots for prizes, especially in the context of the "bank night" contests held at many movie theaters to attract patrons.[56] But *Lottery Lover* tanked. "Should be one that you might want to cancel," *Harrison's Reports* advised theater owners shortly after the film's release in January 1935, reporting later that the paybox returns were "universally poor," and *Photoplay*'s review declared that "Peggy Fears undresses well and wears lots of diamonds. No actress...."[57] This movie was no triumph for its producer, Al Rockett, whose contract was bought out by Fox after he had supervised Hollywood product for more than a decade; Rockett was said to be unhappy with the quality of the casts he was being assigned.[58] The former head of production at First National, Rockett would officially produce only once more, in *Follow the Boys* (United Artists, 1944), before settling into a new career as a prominent agent.

Fears enjoyed a lavish but stormy lifestyle as the frequently estranged wife of "Blumie" Blumenthal, to whom she was married from 1927 to 1950, and her Hollywood sojourn was marked primarily by activity away from the camera. Fears opened a gown shop in Los Angeles, and syndicated newspaper columnist Dan Thomas reported in February 1935 that Fears, costume designer Charles Lemaire, and actress Lili Damita "are making up Hollywood's latest threesome. They're practically inseparable. And they've got everyone guessing as to just where the romance lies."[59] Then there was this strange July 1935 report in the fan magazine *Modern Screen*:

> Peggy Fears has devoted her time to startling staid Hollywoodites since her arrival here some time ago. Between outlandish garb, sable bedspreads, and nine greyhounds on a leash, the gal's succeeded nobly, too. But her latest idea of midnight airplane jaunts to Palm Springs and other points of interest in the state have not made such a hit with her friends. Last week her party narrowly escaped disaster when the plane made a forced landing in the desert, with a landing wheel knocked awry on a ledge of rock as they came down. It wasn't the first forced landing for Peggy and pals, but it was the first time that the entire group of them were found shivering in a disabled plane, listening to coyote obligatos [sic] until the cold, gray dawn.[60]

By this time, Fears' six-month "four-way" contract with Fox had expired, and the studio declined to renew. Fears would return to more familiar haunts, eventually settling on Fire Island, where she would overcome periodic financial reverses—as early as 1938, according to the Associated Press, she was "pawning and selling my jewelry to eat."[61] She built and owned a hotel and endured a tempestuous relationship with television personality Tedi Thurman. In the meantime, Pat Paterson would leave her screen career by the end of the 1930s to concentrate on her marriage to movie star Charles Boyer.

At least Lew Ayres—and, of course, Billy Wilder—would go on to bigger efforts than time-killers like *Lottery Lover*.

The Music Goes 'Round
(Columbia; February 19, 1936)

Director: Victor Schertzinger. Producer: Sol Lesser. Screenplay: Jo Swerling. Story: Sidney Buchman. Photography: Joseph Walker. Editing: Gene Milford. Sound: Lodge Cunningham. Musical Director: Howard Jackson. Dance Director: Larry Ceballos. Art Director: Stephen Goosson. Costumes: Samuel Lange. Running Time: 85 minutes.

Cast: Harry Richman (Harry Wallace aka Harry Linden); Rochelle Hudson (Susanna Courtney); Walter Connolly (Hector Courtney); Douglass Dumbrille (Bishop); Lionel Stander (O'Casey); Henry Mollison (Stephen); Etienne Girardot (Brewster); Walter Kingsford (Cobham); Wyrley Birch (Josh); Victor Kilian (Marshall); Dora Early (Eleanora); John Mack (manager); Michael Bartlett (himself); Herman Bing (himself); Gene Morgan (Nelson); Eddie "Rochester" Anderson (Lucifer); Erville Alderson (irate show boat patron); Irving Bacon (stutterer); Jack Pennick (man at audition); Fred "Snowflake" Toones (garage attendant); Ian Wolfe (doctor); Al Bridge (police inspector); Russell Hicks (Cohn); Peppino and Rhoda (dancers); Edward Farley & Michael Riley and Their [Onyx Club] Band (themselves).

Songs: "Let's Go" [Richman], "Rolling Along" [Richman, twice], "Susannah I'm Betting on You" [Anderson, chorus], "There'll Be No South" [Richman, Peppino and Rhoda, chorus] (Lew Brown, Harry Akst, Harry Richman); "Life Begins When You're in Love" [Richman; reprised by Anderson, chorus; then by chorus; then by Richman] (Lew Brown, Victor Schertzinger); "The Music Goes 'Round and Around" [Farley, Riley, band; reprised by Bing; then by Bartlett; then by Richman, chorus] (Red Hodgson, Edward Farley, Michael Riley).

Working Titles: *Moonlight on the River; The Music Goes 'Round and 'Round; Rolling Along.*

Disc: Brunswick 02161, Decca 700 ("Life Begins When You're in Love"/"Let's Go," Harry Richman); Brunswick 02162, Decca 701 ("Suzannah I'm Betting on You"/ "There'll Be No South," Harry Richman); Decca 578 ("The Music Goes 'Round and Around," Edward Farley and Michael Riley).

The Story: On the eve of the opening of his latest Broadway revue, "Bishop's Follies of 1936," singer Harry Wallace disappears from public view to journey cross-country ("Rolling Along"). On a lark, and posing as "Harry Linden," he gets a job in a struggling Mississippi River show boat production supervised by Hector Courtney and his daughter, Susanna. Harry asks his producer, Bishop, and agent, O'Casey, to come to Mississippi to see the troupe's melodrama, "Love Conquers Pride," which he envisions taking to New York as a "comedy sensation." With Harry's secret backing, Bishop acquires the show; Harry feels guilty because he has fallen for Susanna ("Life Begins When You're in Love"). The revue opens with the big number "The Music Goes 'Round and Around." The show boat section gets big laughs, and the Courtneys leave New York in embarrassment, but Harry begs Susanna's forgiveness.

Six years after failing to stick in the movies with his Hollywood debut, nightclub singer Harry Richman made a second attempt. But his star turn in *The Music Goes 'Round* was overshadowed by the enormous song hit—one not even originated by Richman, and barely sung by him on screen—that gave the film its real box-office value.

Richman (1895–1972) was immensely talented, although few remember him today. He sang with a swagger and confidence that matched his idol and contemporary, Al Jolson, but with more edge and less sentimentality. Like Jolson, he had no lack of ego—his autobiography, immodestly titled *A Hell of a Life*, bragged about numerous sexual conquests and other achievements. As Anthony Slide described in his book *The Encyclopedia of Vaudeville*, Bob Hope recalled co-starring with Richman on stage in *Say When* in 1934 when the latter was involved with gangsters and radio-type payola. When Hope asked, "Who let those mugs in?," referring to the notorious Lucky Luciano and his gang, Richman replied, "They're the backers and you better be funny—or you get a concrete overcoat."[62]

Still, Richman was a hell of a song stylist, even if he wasn't movie-star handsome. Producer Joseph M. Schenck gave Richman a shot at films with a big-budget musical, *Puttin' on the Ritz*, a 1930 United Artists release in which the vocalist popularized Irving Berlin's title song but was regarded as too stiff a thespian. (The film, which survives in a truncated version, is much better than its reputation at the time, thanks to Richman's gusto as a vocalist and its elaborate production numbers.) The craze for movie musicals abated, and Richman headed back East to find more profitable vehicles for his abilities.

In the summer of 1935, Richman signed to make another movie, initially titled *Moonlight on the River* and then renamed *Rolling Along*, which would be ambitious by the standards of the second-tier Columbia studio. Contractee Ann Sothern was announced to co-star, but she would be replaced by the more winsome Rochelle Hudson; director Victor Schertzinger had recently made Columbia's musical success *One Night of Love* with opera star Grace Moore. Jo Swerling's screenplay for *Rolling Along* had echoes of *Show Boat*: Big-name singer Harry Wallace joins, then tries to exploit the unintentional comedy of, a floating small-time acting company, while falling in love with the daughter (Hudson) of the troupe's manager (Walter Connolly). By mid–December 1935,

2. *Failed, Fallen, and One-Shot Stars* 75

Rolling Along was nearing completion with river-set dance scenes—complete with a cast and crew of 700—being shot at Columbia's 40-acre ranch in Burbank, California.[63]

But something happened to change the course—and the title—of Richman's film. In September 1935, jazz trombonist Michael Riley and trumpeter

Rochelle Hudson and Harry Richman have a candid moment on the set of *The Music Goes 'Round* (1936).

Edward Farley recorded with their band a novelty song they'd written, "The Music Goes 'Round and Around." The tune gained airplay, then skyrocketed after Riley and Farley played it on New Year's Eve in a much-listened-to live radio broadcast from New York's Onyx Club, where they regularly appeared.[64] The nonsensical ditty describing how the music comes out of a French horn became a radio staple within days and a love-it-or-hate-it thing—one wag derided it as "the song hit that makes pessimists about America's destiny so merry."[65] Columbia got the bright idea to buy the rights to the song to put it in the Richman film and, for exploitation purposes, provide its new title, although the extra "Around" was ditched to save space on theater marquees. Studio trade ads in mid–January trumpeted the deal—"COLUMBIA SCOOPS THE SHOW WORLD! Columbia Pictures Scores an Electrifying Beat by Acquiring Rights to the World-Rocking Song Sensation"—which also put the Onyx Club boys under contract.

In late January, Riley, Farley, and their band journeyed to Hollywood to shoot a special sequence for *The Music Goes 'Round*, in advance of its world premiere in Miami Beach on February 19 and national release two days later. Riley and Farley embarked on a series of personal appearances to accompany bookings of the film in key cities. As this was happening, a third claimant to the creation of "The Music Goes 'Round and Around," Chicago bandsman William "Red" Hodgson, sued Riley and Farley for credit. He settled out of court but was considered to be the "official" lyricist. Also, Hodgson unsuccessfully asked for a share of the profits from *The Music Goes 'Round* and to appear with Riley and Farley in the movie.[66]

"At least," complained *New York Times* reviewer Frank Nugent, "The Music Goes 'Round and Around" number

> makes no pretense of being anything but a musical interlude dragged in by the scruff of its neck to illustrate the devastating effect upon the public of some anonymous young busybody's question about the workings of a three-value sax horn. Like the "March of Time," it preserves in film the stark record of a social phenomenon—in this case, the conversion of a song hit into a plague, like Japanese beetles or chain letters.[67]

The nine-minute "musical interlude" remains the highlight of *The Music Goes 'Round*, Richman's improved emoting and ever-assured singing (especially in the blackface number "There'll Be No South") aside. During the revue, Harry introduces the Onyx Club act, and Riley sings a chorus of the song while "demonstrating" the lyrics to Farley. "These are the boys responsible," Harry tells the house, then spots real-life comic actor Herman Bing in a seat and has him deliver a chorus in his sputtering style, then "recruits" grand opera performer Michael Bartlett to do the same in highbrow mode. Harry completes the "comes out here" song with the collective vocal help of the audience.

Although the title song was already starting to lose its popularity when many patrons viewed *The Music Goes 'Round*, the novelty value, and the community-singing angle, helped the film to decent business. Columbia signed Richman to do another film. But it didn't get made, and the singer's third and final screen acting appearance would be in a 1938 British musical, *Kicking the Moon Around* (aka *The Playboy*), the film debut of a very young Maureen O'Hara. Richman may have been distracted by non-showbiz pursuits in 1936. In September, he funded a trans-Atlantic flight for him and pilot Dick Merrill from New York City to England. They set a record for such a flight by completing it in 18 hours, 36 minutes. The return was rockier; a panicked Richman dumped a large volume of fuel, and the plane had to make a forced landing in Newfoundland before returning to New York 19 days after they'd left. The adventure, which cost Richman a reported $360,000, became known as "The Ping Pong Flight" because some 40,000 table tennis balls were carried on the plane as a flotation aid.

"The Music Goes 'Round and Around" would become a pop-jazz standard, recorded by the likes of Ella Fitzgerald, Tommy Dorsey, and Hal Kemp, and its life in the movies would surpass Richman's when it reappeared as sung by Danny Kaye and Susan Gordon in the 1959 musical *The Five Pennies*. Music historian Thomas C. Hischak has called it "arguably the most successful nonsense song in the history of Tin Pan Alley."[68] Its presence in *The Music Goes 'Round* does nothing to refute that claim.

Stage Struck
(Warner Bros.–First National; August 28, 1936)

and *Talent Scout*
(Warner Bros.–First National; July 24, 1937)

Stage Struck

Director: Busby Berkeley. Dialogue Director: Irving Rapper. Screenplay: Tom Buckingham, Pat C. Flick. Story: Robert Lord. Photography: Byron Haskin. Editing: Thomas Richards. Sound: Oliver S. Garretson. Musical Director: Leo F. Forbstein. Orchestral Arrangements: Ray Heindorf. Special Photography Effects: Fred Jackman. Art Director: Robert Haas. 91 minutes.

Cast: Dick Powell (George Randall); Joan Blondell (Peggy Revere); Warren William (Fred Harris); Frank McHugh (Sid); Jeanne Madden (Ruth Williams); The Yacht Club Boys ("The Mexican Serenaders"); Carol Hughes (Grace); Craig Reynolds (Gilmore Frost); Hobart Cavanaugh (Wayne); Johnny Arthur (Oscar Freud); Spring Byington (Mrs. Randall); Thomas Pogue (Dr. Stanley); Andrew Tombes (Burns Heywood); Lulu McConnell (Toots O'Connor); Ernie Stanton (Marley); Val Stanton (Cooper); Edward Gargan (Riordan); Libby Taylor (Yvonne); Mary Gordon (Mrs.

Cassidy); George Offerman, Jr. (Wilbur); Mary Treen (clerk); Katherine Clare Ward (landlady); Iris Adrian (Miss DeRue); Rosalind Marquis (Miss LaReno); Jane Wyman (Bessie Funfnick); John Alexander (red cap); Charles King (Alexander); Leo White (waiter); Sidney Miller (kid on street).
Songs: "Fancy Meeting You" [Powell, Madden], "In Your Own Quiet Way" [Powell, Val Stanton, reprised by Madden], "She's in Love" [McHugh, chorus] (E.Y. Harburg, Harold Arlen); "The Body Beautiful" [Yacht Club Boys], "The Income Tax" [Yacht Club Boys] (The Yacht Club Boys).

The Story: Dance director George Randall is fired from his latest Broadway show after insulting its new lead, socialite "husband-killer" Peggy Revere. Small-town girl Ruth tries to lobby George for a big break. Producer Fred Harris signs George to a contract for his new revue, "Words and Music," which also happens to star Peggy, its main backer. George and Ruth visit a museum of natural history ("Fancy Meeting You"); he loves her but doesn't want to see her corrupted by showbiz. Peggy's paramour, ham actor Gilmore Frost, gets Ruth a job as a dancer in the show anyway. Ruth sees George singing "In Your Own Quiet Way" to Peggy and erroneously thinks they're in love. Early reviews for "Words and Music" are poor, and Peggy is indisposed, which means a new star must step in for the Broadway opening.

Talent Scout

Director: William Clemens. Producer: Bryan Foy. Dialogue Director: Joseph Graham. Screenplay: George R. Bilson, William Jacobs. Story: George R. Bilson. Photography: Rex Wimpy. Editing: Terry Morse. Art Director: Esdras Hartley. Running Time: 62 minutes.
Cast: Donald Woods (Steve Stewart); Jeanne Madden (Mary Brannigan, later known as Doris Pierce); Fred Lawrence (Raymond Crane); Rosalind Marquis (Bernice Fox); Joseph Crehan (A.J. Lambert); Charles Halton (M.B. Carter); Teddy Hart (Moe Jerome); Mary Treen (Janet Morris); David Carlyle [Robert Paige] (Bert Smith); Al Herman (Jack Scholl); Helen Valkis [Joan Valerie] (Ruth); John Pearson (Jed Hudkins); Frank Faylen (master of ceremonies); John Harron (Charlie); Mary Doyle (Miss Grant); Harry Fox (Robert Donnolly); Eddie Acuff (Musselman); Donald Kerr (Twerp); Glenn Cavender (furniture salesman); Claudia Coleman (Mrs. Carter); Wilfred Lucas (director); Frank Orth (theater manager); Larry Steers (maître d').
Songs: "Born to Love" [Madden, Lawrence, reprised by Madden, Lawrence, chorus], "I Am the Singer, You Are My Song" [Madden, twice], "In the Silent Picture Days" [Madden], "I Was Wrong" [Madden, Lawrence], "No, No, Señor" [Marquis, chorus] (Jack Scholl, M. K. Jerome).
Working Title: *Studio Romance.*

The Story: Steve Stewart, talent scout for Apex Pictures, is on a publicity tour with a busload of chorus girls when he is stranded in a small town. There, he discovers singer Mary Brannigan and takes her to Hollywood. Mary flunks her screen test and alienates Apex stars Raymond Crane and Bernice Fox, but she starts to find success when Steve renames her Doris Pierce, glamorizes her image, and lands her *a spot at a prestigious benefit show. Steve promotes Crane and Mary in the movies as "the world's greatest love team," making Bernice jealous. Steve wants to marry Mary, only to realize her and Crane's affections are more than publicity.*

Stage Struck and Talent Scout constitute two-thirds of the career film output of Jeanne Madden, a wholesome young singer who landed a Warner Bros. contract and spent a few halcyon months in Hollywood before moving her life in a direction away from show business.

Madden (1917–1989) hailed from Scranton, Pennsylvania, where she excelled in local theatricals before coming under the tutelage of Metropolitan Opera diva Queena Mario. She landed some radio work on NBC and was noticed by studio head Jack L. Warner, who signed the 18-year-old in February 1936 and brought her to California for a pretty good gig: a featured role opposite Dick Powell and Joan Blondell in a Busby Berkeley–directed musical with an E.Y. Harburg–Harold Arlen score. The film, *Stage Struck*, wrapped in May. In July, Madden's father died back home, but that didn't deter Warner Bros. from holding the world premiere of *Stage Struck* in Scranton on August 28, designated "Jeanne Madden Day" in town.

That night, an estimated 6,000 people jammed downtown streets to welcome the hometown girl turned movie star, as the *Scranton Times-Tribune* recalled on the occasion of its 75th anniversary:

> Spotlights illuminated the street, and anticipation filled the air. The crowds were orderly—until the star's car approached. Then their excitement gave way, and mayhem ensued.... Several women and children were crushed in the tight crowd, fainted and had to be carried inside the theater.... At the premiere, Miss Madden ... called Ms. Blondell "a peach" and described Mr. Powell as "a fine chap." Miss Madden thanked the crowd for its "wonderful reception home" and said that she "felt just the same" as when she graduated from Central High School, "only, if anything, a little more nervous."
>
> "I hope you all like the picture, and I hope you all get 'stage struck,'" she said, and bowed off the stage.[69]

In *Stage Struck*, the newcomer played a similarly motivated small-town miss who yearns to break into showbiz, as Ruth Williams, whose press clippings tout her as "The Spirit of East Weehaukeegan." Harried stage director George Randall (Powell) spends most of the film trying to dissuade her because he doesn't want her corrupted. This was no typical Berkeley effort—lacking the elaborate production numbers for which he was famous—and for him would be overshadowed by what happened away from the screen. After a night of drinking at a party in September 1935, Berkeley was involved in an auto crash that resulted in three deaths; the director implicated himself further by leaving the scene, and was charged with second-degree murder. He went on trial three times: The first two trials ended with hung juries; the third, which resulted in an acquittal, was completed a year later, during the national release of *Stage Struck*, which could have helped that film attract audiences.

Light on glitz, *Stage Struck* is more distinctive as screwball comedy than a musical, what with the welcome broad playing of Blondell as a Libby Holman/Peggy Hopkins Joyce professional celeb type, complete with canine retinue, and the pre-release cutting of the Harburg-Arlen tunes "Why Can't I Remember Your Name?" and "You'd Be Kinda Grandish." There are a couple of novelty numbers by the popular quartet Yacht Club Boys; one of them, "The Income Tax," verifies that not everyone liked the tax even when it was new. Anyone expecting an elaborate Berkeley-style climactic musical number must have been sorely disappointed. Warren William is also on hand as a Broadway impresario—but is severely wasted, and Warner Bros. was so inclined to misuse the highly paid contractee that, even as *Stage Struck* was shooting, William and his agent were negotiating the actor's exit from the studio.[70] The supporting part played by William was so unappealing that another Warners star, Pat O'Brien, took a suspension from the studio rather than accept the assignment.[71]

The most obvious flaw in the casting is Madden, who is acted off the screen by Blondell (1906–1979) and fails to show the pizzazz of a real would-be starlet, although she has a pleasant duet with Powell (1904–1963) on "Fancy Meeting You," in which their characters contemplate prior meetings in past lives while visiting a museum of natural history. (Powell's off-screen chemistry was with Blondell, whom he married just after the film's September 19, 1936, national premiere.) *Motion Picture Daily* lauded Madden's "splendid voice and ... charming personality."[72] But *New York Times* critic Frank S. Nugent offered little encouragement:

> Miss Madden, the newcomer of the picture, is a pert little ingénue with a slight but pleasant voice, but she speaks as though she is remembering every word her elocution teacher told her.... We seem to recall reading somewhere that tears were shed at the Powell-Blondell nuptials; it must have been by someone who had seen *Stage Struck*.[73]

Unfortunately, Madden's next assignment was *Talent Scout*, which gave her a little more to do but was firmly in the B-musical category, right down to its journeyman director (William Clemens), second-tier composing team (Jack Scholl and M.K. Jerome), and untried leads. Its young acting talent—Madden, Donald Woods, Fred Lawrence, and Rosalind Marquis—seemed to serve as much to promote higher-tier WB fare than appear in this lesser effort. As a warm-up of sorts for *Talent Scout*, the studio sent Madden, Lawrence, and Marquis on a nationwide airplane trip to promote the bigger-budget *Gold Diggers of 1937*.[74]

The *Talent Scout* script was pretty routine, too. Cocky studio talent finder Woods—who boasts, "I sent Kay Francis, Dick Powell, and Pat O'Brien to

Young Warner Bros. stars Rosalind Marquis (left), Fred Lawrence, and Jeanne Madden are featured in the low-budget *Talent Scout* (1937).

movieland!"—falls for his latest tank-town discovery (Madden), then gives her up when he realizes she loves her leading man. That leading man is played by Lawrence (1909–1983), a former Ben Bernie band vocalist known as Frank Prince when he appeared in *Shoot the Works* [q.v.]. This would be by far his biggest role in a movie. Woods (1906–1998) played plenty of leads in smaller pictures such as this before transitioning into character parts over a long career.

Over 62 minutes of watchable but thoroughly routine entertainment, there are bickering studio moguls (played by old pros Joseph Crehan and Charles Halton), frustrated screenwriters, and an intentionally wretched number, "In the Silent Picture Days," that sinks Madden's character's screen test. Madden contributes her pertness and well-trained voice, but not much else in what *Variety* dismissed as "affable entertainment ... a kindly afterthought for the nabes"— meaning neighborhood theaters.[75] The script was co-penned by George R. Bilson, the writer-producer who fathered Emmy-winning director Bruce Bilson (*Get Smart, The Odd Couple*) and was the great-grandfather of actress Rachel Bilson (TV's *The O.C.*). Oh, and Joan Blondell was also in *Talent Scout*, but her appearance—a split-second view in archival footage depicting a "star-studded" Hollywood party—points up the difference in status between this film and *Stage Struck*.

Madden was on her way out at Warner Bros.; she would make only one more film, an adventure drama at low-rent Republic Pictures called *Sea Racketeers* (1938) opposite Clark Gable lookalike Weldon Heyburn. After a brief time on the stage—she starred on Broadway in 1938–39 in the original production of *Knickerbocker Holiday*—Madden would find more lasting contentment as a wife and mother. She married an artist, Keith Martin, in 1938 and soon retired from performing to raise a family of three sons and work in the hotel business back in Pennsylvania, bringing her life full circle.

Ready, Willing and Able
(Warner Bros.; March 6, 1937)

Director: Ray Enright. Dialogue Director: Gene Lewis. Screenplay: Jerry Wald, Sig Herzig, Warren Duff, based on the *Saturday Evening Post* story by Richard Macaulay. Additional Dialogue: Pat C. Flick, Maurice Leo. Contributors to Treatment: Ben Markson, Mary McCall. Photography: Sol Polito. Editing: Doug Gould. Musical Director: Leo F. Forbstein. Orchestral Arrangements: Ray Heindorf. Dance Director: Bobby Connolly. Art Director: Carl Jules Weyl. 93 minutes.

Cast: Ruby Keeler (Jane Clarke); Lee Dixon (Pinky Blair); Allen Jenkins (Van Courtland); Louise Fazenda (Clara Heineman); Ross Alexander (Barry Granville); Carol Hughes (Angie); Hugh O'Connell (Truman Hardy); Wini Shaw (Jane Clarke); Teddy Hart (Yip Nolan); Addison Richards (Edward McNeil); [Al] Shaw and [Sam] Lee (moving men); E. E. Clive (Sir Samuel Buffington); Jane Wyman (Dot); May Boley (Mrs. Beadle); Charles Halton (Brockman); Adrian Rosley (Angelo); Lillian Kemble Cooper (Mrs. Buffington); Barnett Parker (waiter); Dickie Jones (kid); Myrtle Stedman (mother); Thomas Pogue (captain); Milt Kibbee (steward); Ferdinand Schumann-Heink (purser); Ferdinand Munier (Mr. Twittingham); George Andre Beranger, Bobby Watson, Al Herman (actors); Dennis Moore, Carlyle Moore, Jr. (reporters); James Newill (voice double for Ross Alexander).

Songs: "Handy With Your Feet" [Keeler, chorus], "Just a Quiet Evening" [Alexander, danced by Keeler, Dixon, reprised by Alexander], "Sentimental and Melancholy" [Shaw], "There's a Little Old House" [Dixon, Alexander, Rosley], "Too Marvelous for Words" [spoken by Alexander, reprised by Alexander, Keeler, then by Alexander, Shaw, Keeler, Dixon, chorus], "The World Is My Apple" [Dixon, Alexander; reprised as dance by Shaw and Lee] (Johnny Mercer, Richard A. Whiting).

Academy Award Nomination: Best Dance Direction (Bobby Connolly).
Home Video: Warner Archive DVD.

The Story: Struggling screenwriters Barry Granville and Pinky Blair get Amalgamated Studios interested in their new musical, "Fair Lady," but only if they can get English actress Jane Clarke to play the lead. A young American woman named Jane

Clarke pretends to be the actress to get the role; she is an accomplished dancer but cannot sing like the "real" Jane, and her reluctance holds up rehearsals. Jane admits her deception, which causes a rift with Barry, who loves her, and the real Jane threatens to sue the studio. The English Jane arrives in New York but is exposed by Barry and Pinky's agent, Van, as an imposter herself. A dispute with the studio threatens the show's opening, but Truman Hardy, the American Jane's fiancé, bankrolls the production, which goes on as slated with Jane and Barry in the leads ... but which Jane? The answer might be found in the climactic "Too Marvelous for Words" number.

Who is the male lead in *Ready, Willing and Able*? If you watch this routine backstager, you would likely conclude that Ross Alexander should share top billing with Ruby Keeler. However, the actual credits point to rubber-legged hoofer Lee Dixon, a heretofore supporting player who received his best billing in a feature. Dixon would soon leave Hollywood, originate a memorable role in one of Broadway's greatest musicals—and then endure a too-short existence.

In *Ready, Willing and Able*, Dixon and Alexander portray a screenwriting,

Ruby Keeler and Lee Dixon received top billing in *Ready, Willing and Able* (1937), but Dixon's prominence was short-lived.

composing, and producing duo so impoverished they can't afford to get their pants from the cleaners, and must sit around their apartment performing their latest tune in their boxer shorts. Alexander's character falls for an American woman (Keeler) posing as the British star the boys need to put across their new show, although it is Dixon who dances the memorable climactic number, "Too Marvelous for Words," with Keeler—atop giant typewriter keys. Still, Alexander, a rising star at Warner Bros., ends up with the girl, and Dixon, a stage import in his second feature film, is the best friend throughout. So why do the opening credits pair Keeler and Dixon, with Alexander placed fifth among the supporting players?

Well, Warner Bros.—when it debuted *Ready, Willing and Able* in March 1937—figured that audiences might avoid a film in which the leading man was deceased. Ross Alexander shot himself in the head on January 3, 1937, shortly after completing the filming of *Ready, Willing and Able*. He was 29 and said to be grieving over the suicide of his wife, actress Aleta Freel, a year earlier. Alexander left behind another wife (Warner contract actress Anne Nagel); whispers (mainly retroactive) about his possible bisexuality; and a quandary for his studio as it promoted his final film. This decision to downplay Alexander's participation was reached quickly, as multiple trade publications reported Dixon's elevation to second billing barely a week after the actor's demise.[76] A two-page ad spread put by Warner Bros. in select trades not long after reflected the move, including photos of Keeler, Dixon, and comic relief Louise Fazenda, Wini Shaw, Allen Jenkins, and Carol Hughes ... but no Alexander. The pressbook distributed to theaters leave no doubt as to the promotable starring pair; it was filled with doctored photos showing Keeler together with Dixon, the "rangy, young eccentric hoofer ... whom the Warners lured from the Broadway stage."[77]

Rated as "lethargic" and "lightweight" by *Variety*, *Ready, Willing and Able* was the finale for Ruby Keeler at Warner Bros.[78] The co-star of *42nd Street*, *Dames*, and *Footlight Parade* signed with RKO to make at least two films at a cool $40,000 per; the lone result was a non-musical, *Mother Carey's Chickens* (1938), which famously was the film Katharine Hepburn had refused to do, leading to her departure from the studio. After one more film, the 1941 Columbia musical *Sweetheart of the Campus*, Keeler (1910–1993) settled into retirement. The "Too Marvelous for Words" number—which earned an Oscar nomination for Bobby Connolly's dance direction—was a decent way for her to go out in *Ready, Willing and Able*.

"Too Marvelous for Words" lyricist Johnny Mercer and composer Richard Whiting were teamed for five films at Warner Bros. before the latter's death from a heart attack in 1938. One of the duo's biggest challenges was the "Words" number, which was to show Alexander's character dictating a letter to his sweetie—and then the sweetie reading the missive out loud. Mercer was asked to write different lyrics for each chorus, rather than repeating words. As Richard Whiting's daughter Margaret recalled in Gene Lees' biography of Mercer:

> Daddy said, "How're we going to write a song describing all the words that she is? We're going to have to go through the damn dictionary." He and Johnny were going through the dictionary together, and laughing about it. Mercer said, "I'll probably go for every word in the dictionary. She's beautiful, she's wonderful, she's glorious." Eventually they came up with the title "Too Marvelous for Words."[79]

This solved the lyrical problem, for the song related to the singer not finding enough words to describe his love—"no vocabulary swell enough." Not only did the title create a national catchphrase, but "Too Wonderful for Words" also became a big hit, most notably for Bing Crosby. Mercer and Whiting greatly benefited from the success of "Too Marvelous for Words," which, Mercer said, made them "secure enough to sit around (Mercer's) poolside and throw rocks at the blackbirds."[80] In the film, to cover for his lack of musical talent, Alexander is shown speaking some of the lyrics; when he sings, he's dubbed by James Newill. But the real attraction is the typewriter motif—and those long-legged dancing girls joining Keeler and Dixon on the keyboard.

Even if it makes us bide our time until its finale, *Ready, Willing and Able* offers pleasantly diverting supporting players such as Jenkins, Fazenda, Hugh O'Connell, and pint-sized comedian Teddy Hart (younger brother of famed lyricist Lorenz Hart). Jane Wyman can be glimpsed as a secretary in one of her scores of small roles on the long road to stardom. The vaudeville team of Shaw and Lee appears briefly to reacquaint viewers with its familiar piano-moving act. But one also comes away wondering about Lee Dixon.

A Brooklyn kid, Dixon (1910–1953) got his first break as a Broadway chorister in the short-lived *America's Sweetheart* in 1931, this during and after stints as a bank clerk, an accountant, a nightclub emcee, and a meter reader for the Brooklyn Edison Company. A bigger boost was delivered by Rudy Vallee, who saw Dixon dancing at the Cocoanut Grove in New York, and helped him hook up with Warner Bros. in Hollywood with a $400-per-week contract. "When I got the first salary check," Dixon reminisced to his hometown newspaper in a chatty 1943 interview, "I had it cashed all in ten-dollar bills and just sat and counted it all day."[81]

Dixon spent about 18 months on the West Coast, with a memorable movie debut in the Busby Berkeley-created "All's Fair in Love and War" number in *Gold Diggers of 1937*, in which he was billed fifth as Dick Powell's sidekick. This was followed by *Ready, Willing and Able* and then more support for Powell in *The Singing Marine*, in which Dixon was third-billed, and *Varsity Show*, in which he is seen having little to do besides looking halfway convincing as a college kid. As part of the Hollywood publicity machine, Dixon and fellow *Ready, Willing and Able* player Carol Hughes posed for a nationally distributed newspaper photo series titled "Do You Know How to Kiss"—oh, the grind of stardom!

Warner Bros. touted Dixon as a carefree, quirky sort—kind of an ADHD sufferer before anyone had heard of that medical term—who always had to be moving when music came to his ears. "I stay away from weddings and funerals because I'm afraid of what I'd do when the orchestra strikes up Lohengrin or a dirge," went the studio pressbook puffery for *Ready, Willing and Able*.

> I've been thrown out of every place we've ever lived in Hollywood. I never turn on the radio myself, but some neighbor in the next room or apartment is bound to get a jazz number going, and ... I can't stop until the music does. I don't blame my neighbors for complaining, because it must be annoying to have someone always tap dancing over your head.[82]

In the wake of *Ready, Willing and Able*, Dixon was announced for a featured role opposite Ginger Rogers in Warners' adaptation of the Broadway musical *On Your Toes*; the movie got made in 1939, but with neither performer. After a spell with the Municipal Opera of St. Louis, Dixon returned to New York to appear in the 1940 Broadway musical *Higher and Higher* and make one more Warners film, the '40 two-reeler *Double or Nothing*. The rest of his movie career would consist of a two-reel Technicolor musical, *Double Rhythm* (Paramount, 1946), and the 1947 John Wayne Western *Angel and the Badman*, in which he had a prominent supporting role. By then, Dixon had married twice—to singer-model Alicia Quigley, with whom he eloped in 1938, and former Ziegfeld dancer Eileen Shirley, in 1944. He opened a short-lived "tap academy" in New York City and acted on radio and then-experimental television shows.

He also had played the part that would make his name in musical history—cowhand Will Parker in the original Broadway cast of *Oklahoma!* The landmark Richard Rodgers–Oscar Hammerstein II production debuted on March 31, 1943, with Dixon having created some of his own choreography, especially in the "Kansas City" number. The strong response to the show's premiere had Dixon exultant backstage: "We're up to our armpits in charm. We'll run forever!"[83] *Oklahoma!* seemingly has run forever, but its cheerful cowboy was all too mortal—hampered by an alcohol problem. Elaine Steinbeck, the original *Oklahoma!* stage manager, recounted to author Max Wilk the company's troubles with "Dixie":

> We adored him, and the audiences loved him—Oscar said he'd written the part of Will Parker for Lee, but it was difficult having him. We would always keep his understudy ... ready to go in for Dixie, every day that first year, because he just sometimes wouldn't show up. He always delivered when he went on, and the audiences adored him, he was a wonderful performer, but it was a losing battle.[84]

Celeste Holm, who played Will's sweetheart, Ado Annie, and went to Hollywood to pursue a film career, hinted to Wilk about Dixon's post–*Oklahoma!*

troubles: "When I got to California, I met Lee—after he'd left the show. He wasn't well at all, had some awful things wrong, and he said to me, 'Oh, God, Celeste, I wish I were back in *Oklahoma!* again.'"[85]

Dixon may have had to keep moving, but his career seemed to be standing still. He died in a New York City hospital on January 8, 1953, after what a *New York Times* report teamed as "a brief illness."[86] He was 42 years old.

3. Slumming with the Songsters

On the set of an RKO musical comedy called *Music for Madame* in 1937, a pretty 19-year-old blonde named Joan Fontaine was not looking happy. The producer Pandro S. Berman, who was visiting the set, asked her why she was so glum.

> "Why, Mr. Berman, I have to sing and play with Nino Martini in this picture," she said, referring to the famous tenor, "and you know I can't do either well."
> "Hmmm," replied Berman. "Can you dance?"
> "Well, not very…"
> "That gives me an idea," said Berman. "I think I'll put you in Fred Astaire's next picture." And that was no joke.[1]

Just as, say, one doesn't have to look scary or scream loudly to be in a horror movie, one need not be able to sing or dance well to be part of a musical. But a tone-deaf actor didn't have to like being part of the scenery, even in a genre that was so popular in 1930s Hollywood. Contract players were cattle, subject to the studio assignments. This was the case with Spencer Tracy, recruited as a tough-guy alternative to singer John Boles in Fox's *Bottoms Up*, and Humphrey Bogart, who vowed not to appear in the hick tale *Swing Your Lady* until backed into a corner by Warner Bros. Not surprisingly, neither man was forced to vocalize. Joan Fontaine wasn't old enough or bankable enough to have a say in what she was making in 1937, but that would change as her stardom rose. Other luminaries—among them Gloria Swanson, Claudette Colbert, and Joan Crawford—could sing and were more than willing to demonstrate their hidden talents. They did all right, too!

In this chapter are recaps of select 1930s movie musicals that showcased established actors not known for melodic talents, or included performers who were on the way to stardom, whether or not they could sing or dance. We can derive some satisfaction from the fact that none of the below were as bad as

Clint Eastwood in *Paint Your Wagon*—although Bogie could've given Clint a run for his money.

Torch Singer
(Paramount; September 8, 1933)

Directors: Alexander Hall, George Somnes. Producer: Albert Lewis. Screenplay: Lenore Coffee, Lynn Starling, based on the *Liberty* magazine story *Mike* by Grace Perkins. Photography: Karl Struss. Editor: Eda Warren. Sound: Harold C. Lewis. Costumes: Travis Banton. Running Time: 72 minutes.
Cast: Claudette Colbert (Sally Trent aka Mimi Benton); Ricardo Cortez (Tony Cummings); David Manners (Michael Gardner); Lyda Roberti (Dora Nichols); Baby LeRoy (Bobbie, age 1); Charley Grapewin (Andrew Judson); Sam Godfrey (announcer); Florence Roberts (Mother Angelica); Virginia Hammond (Julia Judson); Mildred Washington (Carrie); Cora Sue Collins (Sally, age 5); Helen Jerome Eddy (Miss Spaulding); Albert Conti (Carlotti); Ethel Griffies (Agatha Alden); Shirley Ann Christensen (Baby Sally); Davison Clark (Seymour); William B. Davidson (Jarrett); Bobbe Arnst, Toby Wing (girls in Mimi's apartment); Eddie Phillips (man in Mimi's apartment); Edward LeSaint (doctor); Lester Dorr (man in radio station); James Burke (taxi driver); Edward Cooper (butler); Jerry Tucker (kid listener); Walton Trout (baby).
Songs [all performed by Colbert]: "Don't Be a Cry Baby," "Give Me Liberty or Give Me Love," "It's a Long Dark Night" (Leo Robin, Ralph Rainger); "The Slumber Boat" ("Sail, Baby, Sail") (Jessie L. Gaynor, Alice C.D. Riley).
Alternate Title: *Broadway Singer*.
Home Video: Universal DVD.

The Story: In a charity ward, unwed chorus girl and mother-to-be Sally Trent meets recently widowed Dora Nichols. Both women give birth, Sally to a girl, also named Sally, and Dora to a boy, Bobbie. The two women pool their resources and live together, but Dora loses her job and leaves to get married, and Sally cannot find work. Sally asks Agatha Alden—the moneyed aunt of the baby's father, Michael Gardner, who doesn't know about the baby because he is traveling in China—to take care of her daughter, but Agatha declines. Sally gives up her baby for adoption. Told she hasn't suffered enough to be a great singer, Sally hardens her image to become a successful nightclub performer and, renamed Mimi Benton, attracts the attention—and affection—of radio producer Tony Cummings. Her career takes an unexpected turn when she fills in for the narrator of a children's radio program and becomes a listener favorite as "Aunt Jenny." Michael returns from abroad and searches for Sally as she begins a quest to find her daughter—even if it means giving up her program.

Paramount had an interesting strategy to make Claudette Colbert into a siren: Star her in a musical. *Torch Singer*—the story of an unwed mother who becomes a nightclub singer and then, unexpectedly, a children's radio host—definitely had pre–Production Code leanings, so this plan somehow made sense.

"Claudette Colbert will be 'the wickedest woman in town.' ... *Torch Singer* ... is Paramount's answer to the popular demand that Miss Colbert be given 'bad-girl' roles," vowed studio publicity stories disseminated to the nation's newspapers in the fall of 1933. Although she'd vocalized a little in a couple of musicals (*The Big Pond*, *The Smiling Lieutenant*), Colbert was known neither as a Mae West/Marlene Dietrich type nor certainly as a pop singer. But she becomes both in *Torch Singer*, an underrated film that has only come to light in recent years.

Colbert (1903–1996) was in a fruitful part of her career, and despite rumors she would jump to another studio, she signed a new contract with Paramount that allowed her to work via loanout for other studios. *Torch Singer* was one in a string of successes that also included Cecil B. DeMille's *Cleopatra* and *Four Frightened People*, John M. Stahl's *Imitation of Life* (for Universal), and Frank Capra's *It Happened One Night*, the last (made while on loan to Columbia) bringing the actress a 1934 Academy Award. For *Torch Singer*, she initially was paired with Paramount up-and-comer Cary Grant, who, a trade-mag report indicated, was to perform three songs.[2] But he was replaced in the cast by Ricardo Cortez, in what turned out to be a routine role as a radio mogul, and Grant never did get to co-star with Colbert. The songs were supplied by Leo Robin and Ralph Rainger, who had some experience in this area; Rainger was the composer of the ultimate "torch song": the Libby Holman standard "Moanin' Low." Alexander Hall (later known for *Here Comes Mr. Jordan*) and George Somnes, who months before had been supervising Paramount's dramatic school, shared directorial duties of a screenplay based on Grace Perkins' *Liberty* magazine story *Mike*.

The *Torch Singer* role may not seem in Colbert's wheelhouse, but she pulls it off with effective transitions between toughness and tenderness. The gowns by Travis Banton add to the scenery. Particularly effective is a scene in which her character, singer Mimi Benton, is halfheartedly at the microphone as kiddie host "Aunt Jenny" while hoisting a drink and a smoke not in a studio but in her own apartment. Suddenly she must sing a lullaby—the familiar "The Slumber Boat"—that, as she performs it, begins to remind her of her lost child, and Colbert plays the moment with admirable subtlety and conviction.[3] When the father of Mimi's baby does show up—as played by David Manners in little more than a walk-on—he complains about his "new" ex-girlfriend: "You've changed all right! You're selfish ... hard." Her reply, courtesy of the Lenore Coffee-Lynn Starling screenplay: "Sure I am, just like glass. So hard; nothing'll cut it but diamonds. Come around some day with a fistful. Maybe we can get together."

In *Torch Singer* (1933), an unlikely children's radio host (Claudette Colbert) charms a sponsor (Charley Grapewin) in the presence of her boss and boyfriend (Ricardo Cortez).

Colbert didn't need to worry if she could out-act Manners—this was one of the decorative parts he loathed playing—but she outlasts others who might have stolen the show. Blonde, Polish-born comedienne Lyda Roberti appears as Mimi's friend and roommate, but she and her offbeat accent—with language manglings such as "You snake in the bush!"—disappear from the story early on. (Roberti would make similar but bigger impacts in other movies before dying young.) Cora Sue Collins, at age 6 a highly-in-demand child performer, appears briefly as Colbert's "grown-up" daughter shortly before being surpassed by Shirley Temple as Hollywood's cutest little girl.[4] In a similarly small role, but with more audience attention, is Baby LeRoy, barely past his first birthday. In a couple of minutes of conspicuous screen time as Roberti's son, he grabs Colbert's nose and makes a face at her singing! The tyke had made an impact, at seven months of age, in the Maurice Chevalier comedy *A Bedtime Story*. Now, as reputedly the youngest person signed to a long-time studio contract, he had more upstaging ahead, most notably of W.C. Fields. Even Clark Gable, in *It Happened One Night*, wouldn't be as distracting a co-star to Colbert as little Ronald LeRoy Overacker (1932–2001).

Colbert's contralto is more than suitable in *Torch Singer*'s four songs, three written by Robin and Rainger. The reviewer from the fan magazine *Silver Screen* was among the many impressed:

> The worst woman in New York—and the best torch singer! That's Claudette Colbert in her new picture. And why didn't someone tell us that she could sing before? Naughty old Paramount for holding out on us like that. Why, that gal can put over everything from a honky-tonk song to the most sensational torch song of the year, "Give Me Liberty or Give Me Love."[5]

Mimi's credo is articulated in a "conversation" with her baby daughter: "Don't ever let any man make a sucker out of you. Make him know what you're worth. Anything they get for nothing is always cheap." This is a woman who is going to succeed on her own terms, no matter how fortunate she was to be handed a big break. No wonder this proto-feminist film has aged well, and *Torch Singer* was deservedly revived in 2009 for a Universal DVD set titled "The Pre-Code Hollywood Collection." In 1933, *The Film Daily* praised the film as a "good feminine sob drama with plenty that will interest the men as well."[6] More than 80 years later, the same goes.

Let's Fall in Love
(Columbia; December 26, 1933)

Director: David Burton. Associate Producer: Felix Young. Story/Screenplay: Herbert Fields. Photography: Benjamin Kline. Editor: Gene Milford. Sound: George Cooper. Musical Director: [Constantin] Bakaleinikoff. Art Direction: Stephen Goosson. Costumes: Robert Kalloch. Running Time: 67 minutes.

Cast: Edmund Lowe (Ken Lane); Ann Sothern (Jean Kendall aka Sigrid Lund); Miriam Jordan (Gerry); Gregory Ratoff (Max Hopper); Greta Meyer (Lisa Bjorkman); Betty Furness (Linda); Art Jarrett (composer); Anderson Lawler (Allen Foster); Tala Birell (Hedwig Forsell); Ruth Warren (Nellie); Marjorie Gateson (Agatha Holmes); Kane Richmond (Ray); John Qualen (Svente Bjorkman); Niles Welch (Archie Frost); Ethel Clayton (actress); Lorin Raker (secretary); Selmer Jackson (Barton); Charles Giblyn (Garland); Michael Visaroff (Trent); Edwin Stanley (Roland Markwell); Consuelo Baker (Mildred); Sven Hugo Borg (Eric); Samuel S. Hinds (New York executive); Eddie Featherstone (stagehand).

Songs: "Let's Fall in Love" [Jarrett, chorus, reprised by Sothern, twice], "Love Is Love Anywhere" [Sothern, Qualen, chorus, reprised by Jarrett] (Ted Koehler, Harold Arlen).

Disc: Victor 24467 ("Let's Fall in Love," Harold Arlen).

The Story: Hedwig Forsell, the hot-tempered Swedish star discovery of director Ken Lane, quits Lane's latest picture in a huff and goes back to her native land. Not wanting the film to be canceled, Ken promises Premiere Pictures chief Max Hopper that he will find a replacement. A contest to find the next great Swedish star fails to yield the favored result, but Ken is entranced after a chance meeting with carnival worker Jean Kendall, and asks her to pretend to be Swedish. Ken re-dubs Jean as "Sigrid Lund" and has her tutored by a Swedish couple, the Bjorkmans. Jean falls in love with Ken even though he is engaged to Gerry. Jean's impersonation succeeds in fooling Max, who signs her to star in the picture. A jealous Gerry and her friends Linda and Allen figure out that Jean is an imposter, and Gerry announces the deception at a party. Ken resigns from the studio, and Jean disappears, but the resulting publicity as "the girl who fooled Hollywood" works in the studio's favor. Ken finds Jean back at the carnival, and they are happily reunited.

A movie about a young woman becoming a movie star was a movie in which a young woman became a movie star. In art, the young woman was Jean Kendall, formerly a circus sideshow employee. In life, she was Ann Sothern, a Hollywood washout turned Broadway star. The movie was *Let's Fall in Love*.

Confused? It's not so complicated. Before she was named Ann Sothern, the young woman was Harriette Lake. She was born in Idaho, raised in Minnesota, and attended the University of Washington. While visiting her mother, a vocal coach at Warner Bros. in Los Angeles, Lake landed a small role as part of a "sister act" in the 1929 studio revue *The Show of Shows*.[7] After a few bit parts for Warners and MGM, she fled for the East Coast in frustration. But while in Hollywood, she had met famous showman Florenz Ziegfeld at a party, and she tested for, and won, the second lead in his 1931 musical, *Smiles*, although she was forced out of the show by its jealous star, Marilyn Miller, before it opened in New York. Not to be deterred, Lake made it to Broadway in a succession of shows—*America's Sweetheart, Everybody's Welcome, Of Thee I Sing*—before being called by Columbia Pictures mogul Harry Cohn. Cohn, seeking an ingénue for an upcoming musical film, gave her the name under which she became famous.

Sothern (1909–2001) recounted the circumstances in a 1987 TV interview. She recalled that Cohn, citing Arthur and Alice Lake as examples, said: "'Well, we can't have your name Lake because there are too many Lakes.'"

> He made out a list and he called me in. On the list there were a lot of names.... E.H. Sothern's name was there. I admired him because he was a very fine Shakespearean actor, so I took Sothern. My mother's name was Annette, so I took Ann. And that's how I became Ann Sothern.[8]

Written by former Broadway librettist Herbert Fields and directed by David Burton, *Let's Fall in Love* found Sothern playing the girl chosen by her own Harry Cohn—a big-shot director played by Edmund Lowe—to play in his next big musical for the Cohn-like boss played by Gregory Ratoff. The catch for this all-American girl: She had to pretend to be Swedish, for she was replacing a temperamental (but now AWOL) Scandinavian star. Anyone who watched the film in 1933 knew this was a parody of the mystique of Greta Garbo, as every studio spent much time looking for (and never finding) the "next Garbo." Although her fakery is exposed in the final reel, the ingénue in the film charms her colleagues—and the nation—by singing the title song, which became a real-world hit thanks to recordings by Eddy Duchin and others.

Let's Fall in Love was one of the few early sound musicals produced by Columbia, but the "minor major" studio was improving its product and its star power, employing such big acting names as John Barrymore, Carole Lombard, Claudette Colbert, and Clark Gable for its 1933–34 releases. The upgrade included the signing, to write songs for *Let's Fall in Love*, of the team of lyricist Ted Koehler and composer Harold Arlen, who had fashioned such radio and stage hits as "Get Happy" and "Stormy Weather." Columbia apparently had tall ambitions for the film as a full-blooded musical, and one trade publication reported that this was to be a "spectacular musical production along the lines of Ziegfeld and [Earl] Carroll shows."[9]

Arlen and Koehler penned five tunes for *Let's Fall in Love*, but Columbia

Ann Sothern (née Harriette Lake) shows off ample charm in her breakthrough film role in Columbia's *Let's Fall in Love* (1933).

left only two in the final version. The catchy "Let's Fall in Love" is pushed repeatedly: by vocalist Art Jarrett (within the first two of the 67 minutes), then twice by Sothern, besides frequent use in underscoring. "Love Is Love Anywhere," represented as a Swedish-type folk song in the narrative, is performed twice; the encore, by Jarrett, is turned into a pop ballad. But "Breakfast Ball," promoted with the film in radio broadcasts shortly before its release, was dropped. So were two more sophisticated numbers. According to Arlen biographer Edward Jablonski:

> Considering the primordial state of the film musical in 1933, the two extended, integrated plot sequences [Arlen and Koehler] wrote were quite advanced for the time. One was a quartet in which Ratoff rejects Sothern as the substitute Swedish star, "She's Not the Type"; the other is the climactic "The Swede Is Not a Swede," when she is revealed ... as an imposter.... Columbia was not ready for such invention.[10]

Arlen and Koehler would enjoy better Hollywood experiences than *Let's Fall in Love*, and so would Sothern, but she would never forget hers.

> Ann Sothern saw herself on the screen for the first time in Columbia's *Let's Fall in Love*, and laughed that she certainly couldn't ever fall in love with herself! In fact, she couldn't believe it was herself up there on the screen. Her appearance was that of a total stranger; her voice was far different than she had expected; and since they had changed her name from Harriet [sic] Lake to Ann Sothern, she simply said, "Well, I guess I'll just have to take your word for it that it's me!"[11]

One wishes for a little more song variety in *Let's Fall in Love*, but it puts to good use what it has, and the story moves briskly in what *The Film Daily* called "an unusually efficient script.... Ann Sothern, who recently changed her name from Harriet [sic] Lake, emerges as a new screen find."[12] Harry Cohn already knew that: He had signed Sothern to a long-term contract after watching a preview.

Sothern and Lowe (1890–1971) were paired again in Columbia's *Grand Exit* (1935), but Sothern would find better roles, and longer-term employment, at MGM. *Let's Fall in Love* was remade by Columbia for 1949 release of *Slightly French* with Dorothy Lamour and Don Ameche; by then, a certain star had left the first Ann Sothern movie far behind. She would make other musicals—among them *Lady Be Good*, *Panama Hattie*, and *Words and Music*—but none are as charming as her first with her new name.

Moulin Rouge
(20th Century/United Artists; January 19, 1934)

Director: Sidney Lanfield. Producer: Darryl F. Zanuck. Associate Producers: William Goetz, Raymond Griffith. Screenplay: Nunnally Johnson, Henry Lehrman. Story: Nunnally Johnson. Photography: Charles Rosher. Editor: Lloyd Nosler. Dance Direc-

tor: Russell Markert. Musical Director: Alfred Newman. Art Directors: Richard Day, Joseph Wright. Costumes: Gwen Wakeling. Running Time: 70 minutes.
Cast: Constance Bennett (Helen Hall/Raquel); Franchot Tone (Douglas Hall); Tullio Carminati (Victor Le Maire); Helen Westley (Mrs. Morris); Andrew Tombes (McBride); Russ Brown (Joe); Hobart Cavanaugh (drunk); Georges Renavent (Frenchman); Fuzzy Knight (Eddie); Ivan Lebedeff (Ramon); The Boswell Sisters (themselves); Russ Columbo (himself); Richard Carle (man in "Boulevard of Broken Dreams" number); Lucille Ball (showgirl).
Songs: "The Boulevard of Broken Dreams" [Bennett, reprised by Bennett, chorus], "Coffee in the Morning and Kisses in the Night" [Bennett, reprised by Bennett, Columbo, Boswell Sisters, chorus], "Song of Surrender" [Carminati] (Al Dubin, Harry Warren).
Disc: Brunswick 6733 ("Coffee in the Morning and Kisses in the Night"/"Song of Surrender," Boswell Sisters).

The Story: Broadway tunesmith Douglas Hall and his wife, Helen, quarrel over her wanting to resume her stage career. When the French star Raquel ("The Girl From the Moulin Rouge") is signed by producer Victor Le Maire for his and Douglas' latest show, Helen recognizes Raquel as her former vaudeville partner. With Raquel's blessing, Helen poses as the French star during rehearsals so Douglas will recognize her talents. When both Douglas and Victor fall for "Raquel," Helen decides to test her husband's fidelity.

In 1933, Constance Bennett was one of the most highly paid actresses in Hollywood, making $7,000 weekly, but she had a problem: People thought she took herself too seriously. Savvy at the bargaining table, blunt with interviewers, and newly married into nobility (the French producer Henri de la Falaise), she hadn't had much levity in her choice of pictures. The woman who had made her initial mark in Hollywood as a comedienne, in *Sally, Irene and Mary* (1926), was now known for dramas such as *Rockabye, Two Against the World, What Price Hollywood?*—and *Bought!*, the 1931 Warner Bros. film for which she was reportedly paid a lofty $30,000 per week. "I'm human enough to want to be liked by people," Bennett was quoted in a rare interview by the fan magazine *Movie Classic* in a 1933 story meant to soften her image. "But my definition of people does not include jellyfish. And neither does it include posers. Any person who lacks the courage to stand up for his own convictions is a very pitiable object."[13]

Bennett (1904–1965) was making comedies again in 1933, notably the bawdy *Bed of Roses* at RKO, but when she signed with Darryl F. Zanuck's 20th Century Pictures for one of its first productions, the musical comedy *Moulin Rouge*, it was big news because it was such a departure for her. The film wasn't that unusual in premise. The script, by Nunnally Johnson and Henry Lehrman, about a woman who tests her spouse's loyalty by disguising herself as someone else had overtones of the famous Ferenc Molnar play *The Guardsman* (a Alfred Lunt-Lynn Fontanne vehicle with a gender switch), not to mention Shakespeare, although it was more or less a remake of the 1925 silent film *Her Sister From Paris*. It also had a capable, young leading man—Franchot Tone, borrowed from MGM, although Zanuck initially sought to use Robert Montgomery from that studio.[14]

Pop music stars Russ Columbo and the Boswell Sisters provided box-office insurance, and there was a trio of songs from Al Dubin and Harry Warren, whose tunes had made Zanuck and the mogul's former studio, Warner Bros., a lot of money with *42nd Street*. But could Connie sing and dance? Well enough. Touted a 20th Century trade ad for *Moulin Rouge*: "What, Connie Bennett in a musical? Nothing else but. We don't have to tell the world about her acting. This picture will tell plenty about how she can sing ... and dance!"

Moulin Rouge is a straight comedy for all but the final 15 or so of its compact 70 minutes, but then it gives itself over to music with two elaborate production number. "Coffee in the Morning and Kisses at Night" is a duet by Bennett and Columbo (in his lone segment) that is followed by the Boswells' bluesy spin, then by a reprise in a schoolyard that warns that too many kisses equals too many kiddies. Capping the film is the 8½-minute "Boulevard of Broken Dreams," in which a fallen woman (Bennett) recalls better days in a Paris where a gigolo and gigolette (among the latter, recognizable if you look fast, is Lucille Ball) can take "a kiss without regret."[15] Only then does Broadway composer Douglas Hall (Tone) realizes that his brunette wife and the blonde bombshell to whom he's been mysteriously attracted are one and the same.

Connie Bennett is no Sophie Tucker—or, as a dancer, even Ruby Keeler—but she acquits herself well. And even if it strains credibility for her character to be mistaken for a French revue star in a two-sided love triangle, the same disbelief must be suspended to buy the fact that Franchot Tone can't spend any amount of time with a disguised spouse and not know it's her. *Photoplay*'s scribe echoed the feelings of most reviewers: "Gorgeous clothes, hot-cha dances, smart dialogue, and splendid performances by Constance Bennett and Franchot Tone put this film in the A-1 class."[16] As his character struggles with his affections, Tone (1905–1968) is particularly good as he tries to explain why he should be content with being happy at home over going French: "Bermuda—who wants to see Bermuda? Why, I can see Bermuda anytime I want. I don't have to ... you see what I mean?" Bob Montgomery could hardly have done better.

Zanuck liked the finished product so much, he rewarded director Sidney Lanfield with a five-year contract.[17] The Boswell Sisters made a radio hit out of "Coffee in the Morning," and "Boulevard of Broken Dreams" was covered by many artists, among them Bing Crosby, Connee Boswell, and the Hal Kemp and Ted Weems orchestras, and most popularly by Jan Garber and His Orchestra. "Boulevard" eventually became associated with Tony Bennett, who successfully revived it in the 1950s.

In promoting *42nd Street*, Zanuck had concocted a popular rail tour nationwide, the "42nd Street Special," filled with contract talent—Bette Davis, Lyle Talbot, Claire Dodd, and others—who did not appear in the film. He did the same with the "Moulin Rouge Caravan," although 20th Century did not have the advantage of a lengthy list of contract players. Thus, second- and third-tier stars like Jack Mulhall, Roscoe Ates, Nancy Welford, and Mary Carlisle were joined by faded silent-era notables Anna Q. Nilsson, Ben Turpin, Creighton Hale, and Antonio Moreno, plus lovelies said to be chorines from the picture. The announced intent was to start in the East and work across the continent—there was even a politico-filled luncheon in Washington, D.C. In Hartford, Connecticut, at least, fans didn't seem to care that the travelers were dimming stars. On February 8, 1934, the troupe arrived in that city via police escort to be greeted by some 6,000 people, mainly females, in zero-degree weather. The hubbub resulted in the smashing of glass poster cases in the lobby of the Capitol Theater and the tearing off of buttons and badges from the lawmen on hand.[18] The caravan didn't quite proceed as intended—its journey petered out in Kansas City after 28 days.[19]

Constance Bennett had no need to participate in any pandemonium. She was too busy reigning in Hollywood.

Bottoms Up
(Fox; March 22, 1934)

Director: David Butler. Producer: B.G. De Sylva. Story/Screenplay: B.G. De Sylva, David Butler, Sid Silvers. Photography: Arthur Miller. Editor: Irene Morra. Sound: Joseph E. Aiken. Dance Director: Harold Hecht. Musical Director: Constantin Bakaleinikoff. Art Director: Gordon Wiles. Costumes: Russell Patterson. Running Time: 85 minutes.

Cast: Spencer Tracy (Smoothie King); Pat Paterson (Wanda Gale aka Wanda Brock); John Boles (Hal Reid); Sid Silvers (Spud Mosco); Herbert Mundin (Limey aka Mr. Brock); Harry Green (Louis Wolf); Thelma Todd (Judith Marlowe); Robert Emmett O'Connor (Rooney); Dell Henderson (Lane Worthing); Suzanne Kaaren (Wolf's secretary); Douglas Wood (John Baldwin); Johnny Boyle (dance specialty); Sammy Glasser (harmonica player); Walter Hartwig (waiter); David Field (reporter); Samuel E. Hines (bellboy); Mariska Aldrich (opera singer); Ernest Wood (hotel clerk); John T. Murray (radio announcer); Frank O'Connor (director); Larry Steers (party guest); Lucille Ball, Lynn Bari, Barbara Pepper (chorines).

Songs: "I'm Throwing My Love Away" [Paterson], "Little Did I Dream" [Boles], "Turn on the Moon" [Boles, reprised by Silvers] (Harold Adamson, Burton Lane); "Is I in Love? I Is" [Paterson] (Mercer Cook, J. Russel Robinson); "Waitin' at the Gate for Katy" [Boles, chorus] (Gus Kahn, Richard A. Whiting).

The Story: Vagabond con artists Smoothie, Spud, and Limey meet homeless movie extra Wanda Gale and scheme to get her—and her pleasant voice—into picture stardom. They circulate rumors that Limey and Wanda are "Lord Brocklehurst" and his daughter, visitors from England. With Smoothie as their press agent, the "Brocks" catch the attention of matinee idol Hal Reid and his co-star Judith Marlowe. Smoothie boosts Wanda's career by cozying up to 4 Star Film executive Louis Wolf and studio president Baldwin. Limey attempts to blackmail Wolf, so the studio signs Wanda, Smoothie, and Spud to contracts to keep matters quiet. Limey forges a note ordering a large role for Wanda in Hal's new picture. Hal and Wanda become an off-screen couple as the film's premiere approaches, but how long can Smoothie's ruse last?

Before moving to MGM for decades of top stardom, two Academy Awards, and a lasting association with Katharine Hepburn, Spencer Tracy spent five unhappy years as a contract leading man at Fox. Between 1930 and 1935, he made 19 movies at Fox, most of which lost money, and the actor's unreliability due to his alcoholism made matters worse. One of the oddest—and least revived—of those Fox features is what would be the only musical of Tracy's career, *Bottoms Up*. Fortunately, or perhaps unfortunately for some, Tracy (1900–1967) does not sing in the film, which doesn't give him a bad role but illustrates how he was misused at his first home studio.

Bottoms Up was the creation of two key members of the team that brought Fox its first great musical hit, 1929's *Sunnyside Up*: producer-screenwriter B.G. "Buddy" De Sylva and director-screenwriter David Butler. Butler directed *Sunnyside Up*, for which De Sylva wrote the script and score with his then-songwriting partners Lew Brown and Ray Henderson. Lifted by the appeal of co-stars Janet Gaynor and Charles Farrell, *Sunnyside Up* was a huge box office success; the off-camera unit's 1930 follow-up, *Just Imagine*, not so much. After De Sylva, Brown, and Henderson broke up as a team, De Sylva and Butler collaborated on a 1933 Fox musical, *My Weakness*, in which comic Sid Silvers played a supporting role. Silvers joined De Sylva and Butler in writing *Bottoms Up*—and in finding a cast for their 1934 sendup of Hollywood and its personalities.

De Sylva, Butler, and Silvers sought Lilian Harvey, the German-imported star of *My Weakness*, for the new film, but after signing for the role, Harvey was released to appear in another Fox musical, *Lottery Lover* [q.v.].[20] Her replacement, English actress Pat Paterson, was newly imported to Hollywood by Fox chief Winifred Sheehan. Early publicity for *Bottoms Up* linked her off screen with fellow cast member Tracy, who was not only married but also already whispered to be an item with fellow star Loretta Young. "If the off-set scenes of Pat Paterson ... and Spencer Tracy were put into one picture, you might see the beginning of a romance," wrote powerful columnist Louella Parsons:

> The two are in the same picture, but that doesn't necessitate lunching together, talking together, and seeing each other at every possible moment. Maybe Spence is just trying to make Loretta Young jealous, or maybe it's a lovers' quarrel, but all the Fox studio

is agog over his attentions to Pat Paterson, who is as blond[e] as Loretta and the same type.[21]

Paterson (1910–1978) would prove no catch for Tracy, for she met romantic star Charles Boyer on the Fox lot, married him three weeks later (in February 1934), and stayed with him until her death.[22] In the case of *Bottoms Up*, art would imitate life to a degree, as Peterson played an aspiring actress whose career buildup is connected to her relationship to her leading man, a musical star played by John Boles (1895–1969). In the film, the affection between the two is genuine, to the disappointment of the con artist—"Smoothie" King, played by Tracy—who has schemed with his friends to make her a star.

The similarities between Boles' Hal Reid and Tracy had to have not been lost on the latter. Reid is drunken and cynical, dismissive of his work as "the most stupendous ... piece of junk I've ever seen." When Paterson's character, Wanda Gale, asks Reid for an autograph in the first reel of *Bottoms Up* with an encouraging "I think you're wonderful!" his sad reply is "I wish I did." Tired of one-dimensional hero roles and unmoved by worldwide adulation, Reid is the

John Boles (left) and Harry Green portray some of the Hollywood types in *Bottoms Up* (1934).

film's most interesting character—he's actually the most honest figure in a cast full of folks posing as people they're not. He doesn't care that he's been deceived by Wanda because he knows everyone in Hollywood is a phony. Boles' performance is fine enough—especially in the film's big production number, "Waitin' at the Gate for Katy"—but how different would *Bottoms Up* have been with Tracy as Hal … had Tracy been able to supply the requisite baritone?

The "Katy" finale is typically pre–Code, a Hicksville parody in which rural swains wait and whistle outside the windows of a girls' school in which the students are in various degrees of undress, as photographic effects enable the boys to appear and disappear from view. It's worth the wait, but the preceding material is more than filler, and a potent attack on the movie machine. There's the boorish, semi-literate talent chief of the 4 Star Film Company (played by the stereotypically Jewish Harry Green) who knows the company's real power lies with the money-man president, whom Smoothie wisely attempts to smooze: "You make 52 pictures a year, don't-cha, but only 12 of them are hits, Now, my idea is to only make the 12 good ones!" There are the studio security chief (Robert Emmett O'Connor) who wants to keep trouble in house so the real authorities don't get involved; the pretentious starlet who brags that kissing total strangers on screen is "part of my art"; and the fan-magazine writer who yearns to be an opera singer. This wasn't mere exaggeration. As he convinces his co-conspirators to become movieland imposters, Smoothie refers to a couple of real-life inspirations: a phony count (Michael Romanoff, who ran a Hollywood restaurant and was a technical adviser on many films) and "this little girl who came out here from Iowa" and pretended to be an Englishwoman to get a part in *Cavalcade*. (She would become Margaret Lindsay.) In what to him is just another racket, Smoothie is careful not to do anything that's actually illegal, all to earn more perks from his new, publicity-conscious co-conspirators, who know that everything's a façade.

Not surprisingly, *Bottoms Up* ran into censorship problems pre-release. The Hays Office suggested modification of certain song and dance numbers, but Fox appealed the decision and a special three-man jury—consisting of studio chiefs Harry Cohn of Columbia, Emanuel Cohen of Paramount, and Jack Warner of Warner Bros.—was convened in March 1934. They decided that the numbers in questions were "a bit warm in spots," but recommended the picture be released as is.[23] Fox decided to do retakes anyway, which might explain the removal of the production number for the title song. The number was included in the print shown at previews in February, but was absent after the film was cut from 96 minutes to 85 minutes before release. A *Hollywood Reporter* account (February 28, 1934) described the "Bottoms Up" number as Pat Paterson "singing away the depression and gathering after her a hot, laughing, jazzy parade of social leaders, chorus girls, bankers, and brokers."[24] Sounds tantalizing.

Thelma Todd's appearance as a conniving female star is welcome—especially when her character meets the con men and pretends to know who's who—and Herbert Mundin has some amusing moments as a pretend nobleman whose talents as a forger come in handy. In-jokes abound even in the bit-part casting: Mariska Aldrich, who appears as the fan-magazine writer who unsuccessfully sings during a Hollywood party, was a real operatic soprano, and Walter Hartwig, who appears briefly as part of a joke regarding Sid Silvers' character's nose, was a Broadway producer who was cast because of the shape of his proboscis.[25] No wonder *New York Times* reviewer Mordaunt Hall, usually not easily impressed, described *Bottoms Up* as "a neat, carefree piece of work ... an artless little tale, which like many of its ilk proves to be thoroughly entertaining," and *Variety*'s Abel Green lauded it as "good cinematic fare from every angle, particularly the elements of comedy and plot, of which aspects most filmusicals are singularly devoid."[26]

However, *Bottoms Up* was a lukewarm performer at the box office, and it didn't do much for Spencer Tracy, whose best films were not being made at Fox but while on loan—at Warner Bros. in *20,000 Years in Sing Sing*, at Columbia in *Man's Castle*, and, most recently, at MGM in *The Show Off*. But people were beginning to take notice, even if Tracy might have thought his career was stalling. In a front-page column written while *Bottoms Up* was in production, influential *Hollywood Reporter* Editor and Publisher W. R. Wilkerson stood up for the under-exploited actor:

> We have never seen Tracy giving anything resembling a bad performance, and we have seen him in some pictures that were so bad that standout ability ... was almost impossible.... And it's a damned shame that he has to be tied to a studio whose production intelligence does not approach his fine talents.... Give Tracy two or three GOOD pictures, one after the other, and there is not a male star (or female) who would top him in selling tickets, for he has everything that any audience wants in a screen performer.... Something ought to be done in this business that would give relief to such a sterling artist....[27]

Coincidentally, as *Bottoms Up* was playing at Radio City Music Hall in New York City, Tracy was competing against himself nearby in *The Show Off*. Within a year or so, Tracy would be in the fold for good at Metro, and Fox would rue the lost opportunity.

Music in the Air
(Fox; December 13, 1934)

Director: Joe May. Producer: Erich Pommer. Screenplay: Howard I. Young, Billie [Billy] Wilder, based on the musical play by Jerome Kern and Oscar Hammerstein II (New York opening, November 8, 1932; 342 performances). Continuity: Robert Liebmann.

Musical Adaptation: Franz Waxman. Photography: Ernest Palmer. Sound: A. L. Von Kirbach. Dance Director: Jack Donahue. Musical Director: Louis De Francesco. Art Director: William Darling. Running Time: 83 minutes.

Cast: Gloria Swanson (Frieda Hatzfeld); John Boles (Bruno Mahler); Douglass Montgomery (Karl Roder); Jane Lang (Sieglinde Lessing); Al Shean (Dr. Walter Lessing); Reginald Owen (Ernst Weber); Joseph Cawthorn (Hans Lippmann); Hobart Bosworth (Cornelius); Sara Haden (Martha); Roger Imhof (burgomaster); Jed Prouty (Kirschner); Christian Rub (Zipfelhuber); Fuzzy Knight (Nick); Marjorie Main (Anna); George Chandler (stagehand); Ferdinand Munier (innkeeper); Grace Hayle (innkeeper's wife); Otto Fries (butcher); Torben Meyer (pharmacist); Otis Harlan (baker); Herbert Heywood (fire captain); Lee Kohlmar (priest); Ann Howard (Elsa); Betty Jane Graham (Marguerita); George Ernest, Henry Hanna (children); Adolph Dorr, Frank Austin (peasants); Perry Ivins (radio engineer); Dave O'Brien (voice double for Douglass Montgomery); Betty Heistand (voice double for June Lang).

Songs: "I'm Alone" [Swanson, twice], "I'm Coming Home" [Boles], "I Am So Eager" [Swanson, Boles, chorus, reprised by Lang, Boles, then by Swanson], "I've Told Every Little Star" [Montgomery, Lang, twice, reprised by orchestra, then by Boles, Swanson, Montgomery, Lang, chorus], "Melodies of May" [Lang, chorus], "Night Flies By" [Swanson], "One More Dance" [Boles], "Prayer" [Montgomery, children], "There's a Hill Beyond a Hill" [male chorus], "We Belong Together" [Montgomery, reprised by Montgomery, Lang, Boles, Swanson, company] (Jerome Kern, Oscar Hammerstein II).

The Story: In a Bavarian village, Dr. Walter Lessing and schoolteacher Karl Roder write "I've Told Every Little Star" for a town festival. The townspeople fund their journey to Munich with Sieglinde, the doctor's daughter and the teacher's sweetheart, to get the song published by Walter's old friend, Ernst Weber. In Ernst's office, Karl meets temperamental prima donna Frieda Hatzfeld and librettist Bruno Mahler, who is writing an operetta to star Frieda and himself and wants to add "I've Told Every Little Star" to the production. Frieda becomes infatuated with Karl, and Bruno is enamored with Sieglinde, whom he wants to make the lead in the show. Karl pleads with Sieglinde to return home, but she stays in Munich. The three villagers are disgraced when changes are made in the operetta—but the show must go on, as broadcast via radio back to the appreciative village.

Music in the Air was no asset to the career of Gloria Swanson in 1934, when the Broadway-imported modern-dress operetta failed to make much of an impact on film. But it forged a relationship that would become crucial 16 years later in the rebuilding of a stardom that movies like this one helped to dim.

This was the first—and only—musical for Swanson (1899–1983), but she had proved she could sing on the screen. She delivered a few incidental songs in her first three talkies—*The Trespasser* (1929), *What a Widow!* (1930), and *Indiscreet* (1931)—in a pleasing soprano, and in *Tonight or Never* (1931), she played an opera singer although she did not sing. Swanson nearly became a reluctant party to the glut of early sound songfests in 1930, when plans were made (and swiftly dropped) to refashion her aborted silent melodrama *Queen*

Kelly into an operetta; the film was released, but only internationally, without music. By 1934, the superstar of the silents was working before the camera less frequently—about to dump her fourth husband, she was still in the gossip columns—in favor of personal appearances in which she performed excerpts from *The Trespasser* and other works. Her films were losing punch at the box office, and she was without a studio affiliation.

Swanson signed a contract with MGM in January and was announced to co-star in *Riffraff* opposite Clark Gable, and maybe for a remake of Elinor Glyn's *Three Weeks*. She agreed to appear in Samuel Goldwyn's *Barbary Coast* but then backed out, claiming a scheduling problem. In June, a writer for the fan magazine *Modern Screen* joined those fretting over Swanson's future: "Ever since M-G-M announced that it had signed Gloria Swanson to a long-term contract, people have been asking, "Will she be able to come back?" This same studio signed Colleen Moore on a year's contract and nothing sensational resulted. Will Gloria be defeated in the same manner? Should she even try again?"[28]

She did try again, but not at Metro-Goldwyn-Mayer. Instead, Swanson was borrowed by Fox to star in *Music in the Air*, a prestige project based on the Jerome Kern–Oscar Hammerstein II Broadway show.[29] This would allow her not only to sing such romantic melodies as "I've Told Every Little Star" and "We Belong Together" but also to reunite her with John Boles, her co-star in 1927's *The Love of Sunya*, for which Swanson was credited with getting Boles into the flickers. The juvenile leads were less known—Douglass Montgomery (formerly known as Kent Douglass) had lately made an impression in *Little Man, What Now?*, but his counterpart (neé June Vlasek) was not only new as a co-star, but also new as June Lang. Most of the stage score was kept for the screen—as was comedian Al Shean, formerly of the famed vaudeville duo Gallagher and Shean. Unfortunately, two fine numbers, "The Song Is You" and "In Egern on the Tegern See," were left out of the vocalizing. "The Song Is You" is only heard instrumentally over the opening credits—it was filmed for Boles to sing, then cut—and "Tegern See" is reduced to underscoring and a few notes played on a piano.

The producer of *Music in the Air*, Erich Pommer, was in charge of European production for Fox, for which he produced *Liliom* (1934) in France with Charles Boyer. The studio's original intent was also to make *Music in the Air* in France, and in multiple-language versions, but the German-born Pommer, who made his name at his home-country UFA studio before working briefly at Paramount and MGM in the late 1920s, returned to Hollywood when the project was relocated. The director, Joe May, and co-screenwriter, Billie (aka Billy) Wilder, were German émigrés as well; the screenplay was Wilder's first for an American film. According to Swanson's autobiography, Pommer enthusiastically recruited her for *Music in the Air*:

John Boles and Gloria Swanson sing with gusto in Fox's failed-but-interesting *Music in the Air* (1934).

"There's a terrific screenplay," Mr. Pommer was saying.... "It's perfectly suited to you, or I wouldn't be calling." ... The next day, Mr. Pommer agreed to all my conditions, and we signed a contract. Only then could I uncross my fingers and take over a sumptuous star bungalow on the Fox lot for the duration of the picture.[30]

The bungalow was just the start of Fox's spending on its new leading lady. The studio built a Bavarian village and reproductions of the Munich zoo and opera house on its lot for Swanson's film, and Dr. P. Mario Marafioti, Enrico Caruso's former voice coach with whom she had worked off and on since *The Trespasser*, helped her prepare for her role as a high-class singer.[31]

When it opened at year's end in 1934, *Music in the Air* earned many positive reviews, including the one by *The New York Times*' Andre Sennwald, who called it "a skillfully photographed work ... among the superior musical pictures."[32] Indeed, the film holds up well 70-plus years later, with plenty of effective comedy, much of it stemming from the bickering of the egotistical theater luminaries played with gusto by Swanson and Boles. They duet whimsically on "One

More Dance"/"Night Flies By," in which diva and lyricist offer their preferred versions of the same melody. Another entertaining number for Swanson and Boles is "I'm Coming Home"/"I'm Alone," during which they describe the scenario of their new operetta seemingly on the fly, and with an unexpected chorus joining in at the end. For the sake of the comedy, the big-city show people are depicted as contentious and self-centered—"You're too wonderful for words!" is the Swanson character's favorite greeting, which drips with insincerity—but the rural townspeople can battle and bicker with the best.

There really is music in the air in a film in which compositions are created in record time: Shean's Bavarian village doctor composes "I've Told Every Little Star" within moments after hearing a bird chirp.[33] *Music in the Air* began a successful, if too short, film career for half of the legendary vaudeville team of Gallagher and Shean. The backup leads (whose singing was dubbed) play more naturalistically. Although Montgomery (1907–1966) is adequate, the pretty but colorless Lang is the film's weakest link, especially in contrast to Swanson's vivaciousness. In a post-career interview published in *Classic Images*, Lang (1917–2005) stated that Swanson was "very aloof" to her, possibly because Lang's role ended up being the larger of the two.[34]

Fox's trade ads for *Music in the Air* sought to capture exhibitors with offers of "*Melody* to keep your audiences singing gayly for a year … *merriment* to keep them smiling happily for months … *magnificence* to keep a sparkle in their eyes for days!" But audiences more inclined toward gritty Depression-minded fare didn't go for Teutonic escapism. "Poor and fair have been the reports—mainly poor," was the reading on *Music in the Air* of *Harrison's Reports*, the publication tailored for independent exhibitors, by mid–1935.[35] Bridgeport, Connecticut, may have been 50 miles from New York City, but its audiences were different in taste, as a local movie house owner complained, unfortunately using the Swanson film as an example:

> Thanks to the publicity departments, the fan magazines, the syndicates, the radio and Dame Rumor, fans know more about pictures before they open than do the gentlemen who buy them—and pay good money for them. "I played *Music in the Air*," complained Joe Exhibitor. "What a nose dive I took! The people just wouldn't come in to see it. Who told them? After all, I put out 5,000 heralds, took lots of ad space, had some names to sell in Swanson, Boles and Montgomery—and still it was a flop. I give up!"[36]

Swanson conveyed her disappointment in her autobiography: "We all felt fairly certain of success during the shooting, but the picture flopped. Hollywood producers learned once again that the taste of New York and Broadway during the darkest days of the Depression was no barometer for the rest of the nation…."[37] *Music in the Air* was the year's biggest box-office loser for Fox, at a sizable deficit of $389,000.[38]

Swanson did not make *Three Weeks* at Metro, nor any other film at any other place, until the 1941 RKO comedy *Father Takes a Wife*, but her next movie jump-started the comeback some people had been expecting for 15 years. When Wilder and producer Charles Brackett hired Swanson to play Norma Desmond in *Sunset Blvd.* (1950), she was practically out of the picture business and Wilder was one of the hottest writer-directors in Hollywood. He wanted her to make a screen test; she balked (considering her star status) but relented, and the rest was a chapter in cinema history in which *Music in the Air* was a mere footnote.

Under the Pampas Moon
(Fox; June 1, 1935)
and *Paddy O'Day*
(20th Century–Fox; December 25, 1935)

Under the Pampas Moon

Director: James Tinling. Producer: B.G. De Sylva. Screenplay: Ernest Pascal, Bradley King. Story: Gordon Morris. Additional Dialogue: Henry Johnson. Photography: Chester Lyons. Editing: Alfred DeGaetano. Sound: A.L. Von Kirbach. Musical Director: Arthur Lange. Dance Director: Jack Donohue. Art Director: William Darling. Costumes: René Hubert. Running Time: 80 minutes.

Cast: Warner Baxter (Cesar Campo); Ketti Gallian (Yvonne La Marr); Veloz and Yolanda (dancers in café); John Miljan (Gregory Scott); J. Carrol Naish (Tito); Soledad Jiménez (Mama Pepita); Jack La Rue (Bazan); George Irving (Don Bennett); Blanca Vischer (Elena); Rita Cansino [Rita Hayworth] (Carmen); Armida (Rosa); Ann Codee (Madame La Marr); Philip Cooper (Little Jose); Paul Porcasi (Pierre); Max Wagner (Big José); Chris-Pin Martin (Pietro); Tito Guizar (singer in café); Hector Sarno (farmer); T. Armandi (gaucho); Harry J. Vejar (blacksmith); Sam Appel (bartender); Arthur Stone (Rosa's father); David Penn (singer); George Lewis (aviator); Maurice Black (waiter); Bobby Rose (jockey).

Songs: "The Gaucho" [Baxter, chorus] (Buddy G. De Sylva, Walter G. Samuels); "Je t'adore" [Gallian] (Bernie Grossman, Harry Akst); "Veredita" [Guizar] (Miguel de Zarraga, Cyril J. Mockridge); "Zamba" [chorus, danced by Hayworth] (Miguel de Zarraga, Arthur Wynter-Smith); "Cobra Tango" [danced by Veloz and Yolanda, Baxter, Jimenez] (authorship undetermined).

Working Titles: *The Gaucho. Gaucho Lover.*

The Story: In Argentina, Cesar Campo loses his heart to a French singer, Yvonne LaMarr, after her plane is forced to land on the pampas during a trip to a cabaret engagement with her manager, Gregory Scott. Cesar loses his prized horse, Chico Lindo, when the steed is stolen by fellow gaucho Bazan on behalf of Scott, whose offer to buy Chico Lindo had been refused by Cesar. With help from dancer Carmen, Cesar takes his search for the animal to Buenos Aires—where he reunites with

Yvonne, who is singing there—and he gets in trouble for his unrefined manner, even after unexpected funds allow him and his mother to enjoy a fancy night out. Scott puts big money on Chico Lindo in an important race, but Cesar throws his bola to knock the jockey off his old horse to lose the race. Cesar reclaims the horse—and returns home with his Mama ... and Yvonne.

Paddy O'Day

Director: Lewis Seiler. Producer: Sol Wurtzel. Screenplay: Lou Breslow, Edward Eliscu. Photography: Arthur Miller. Editing: Alfred DeGaetano. Sound: Alfred Bruzlin. Musical Director: Samuel Kaylin. Dance Director: Fanchon. Art Directors: Duncan Cramer, Lewis Creber. Running Time: 76 minutes.

Cast: Jane Withers (Paddy O'Day); Pinky Tomlin (Roy Ford); Rita Cansino [Rita Hayworth] (Tamara Petrovitch); Jane Darwell (Dora); George Givot (Mischa); Francis Ford (Tom McGuire); Vera Lewis (Aunt Flora); Louise Carter (Aunt Jane); Russell Simpson (Benton); Michael Visaroff (Popushka Petrovitch); Nina Visaroff (Momushka Petrovitch); Pat O'Malley (Wilson); Robert Dudley (chauffeur); Selmer Jackson, Ruth Clifford, Larry Steers (first-class passengers); Jessie Pringle, Evelyn Selbie (immigrants); Myra Marsh (matron); Jane Keckley (maid); Tommy Bupp, Sherwood Bailey, Harry Watson (street boys); Russ Clark (traffic cop); Larry Fisher (truck driver); Hal K. Dawson (motorist); Egon Brecher, Leonid Snegoff, Demetrios Alexis (Russian musicians); Clarence H. Wilson (Brewster); Richard Powell (taxi driver).

Songs: "I Like a Balalaika" [Withers, chorus], "Keep That Twinkle in Your Eye" [Withers, three times] (Edward Eliscu, Troy Sanders); "Changing My Ambitions" [Tomlin] (Pinky Tomlin, Coy Poe); "Which Is Which" [Cansino, chorus] (Sidney Clare, Harry Akst); "Sleep My Baby (Bauishka Bain)" [Cansino] (authorship undetermined).

Working Titles: *The Immigrant; Immigrants; The Little Immigrant.*

Disc: Brunswick 7594 ("Changing My Ambitions," Pinky Tomlin).

The Story: Paddy O'Day, an 8-year-old Irish girl, comes to New York by boat while eagerly awaiting a reunion with her mother, who works as a cook for a wealthy Ford family. On the ship, she befriends a Russian dancer, Tamara Petrovitch, and her family. Unfortunately, Paddy's mother died just before her daughter's arrival, and the girl must find a home. Roy Ford, from the family that employed Paddy's mother, is willing to take the girl in, but it is decided she will live with the Petroviches with Roy's support. With Roy's backing, the Russians open a café, and despite an effort by Roy's maiden aunts to deport Paddy, the girl is permitted to stay.

Under the Pampas Moon and Paddy O'Day came so early in Rita Hayworth's career that she wasn't even being called Rita Hayworth yet. The future superstar was billed as Rita Cansino in both 1935 Fox musicals—10th in *Under the Pampas Moon*, a Argentina-set Warner Baxter vehicle that brought the teenager her first screen role, and third in *Paddy O'Day*, a musical comedy with a much younger headliner, Jane Withers.

Born into the famous family of Spanish dancers, Margarita Carmen Cansino (1918–1987) performed with her clan from a young age, and gained a Fox contract in February 1935 as a solo when studio chief Winifred Sheehan spotted her dancing at the Mexican resort Agua Caliente. The studio considered changing her name to "Rita Rubio," but decided to let her keep her surname and put out stories grouping her with other young actresses Astrid Allwyn, June Lang, and Helen Wood as top bets to rise from minor parts to stardom in 1935. Cansino first played an unbilled bit as a ballroom dancer in the melodrama *Dante's Inferno*, but that film wasn't released until after her official debut in *Under the Pampas Moon*. In the latter, she is on screen less than two minutes, first for a brief dance sequence, then for a scene interacting with Baxter's character for talk about his lost horse.

"I was 15 years old," Hayworth told author John Kobal years later about her first day on the set." ... This was my first part in a film and I got there at 9 o'clock.

> I wasn't made up and the whole set was ready and they were waiting for me, I was rushed into the make-up, and ... somebody came in and screamed, "Don't you know when I say 9 o'clock you're supposed to be ready and made up!" So I got back on the set, trembling and shaking. I apologized to Mr. Baxter, I told him it was the first time I'd ever had a call and didn't know what it meant.... And this other man, not the

Young Rita Hayworth joins star Warner Baxter in her big scene in *Under the Pampas Moon* (1935).

director but some assistant, came back in and started screaming. I was supposed to say about 10 words and I couldn't get them out. I was so nervous. That was a terrible day. Mr. Baxter kept saying, "Just relax. Don't let them bother you."[39]

Appearing older than her years, and dancing the "Zamba" smartly, the youngster acquitted herself well enough to earn a mention in *Motion Picture Daily*'s May 1935 summation of the picture: "Rita Cansino, in a bit dance, suggests possibilities."[40] Fox publicity also credited Cansino for teaching Baxter the tango he performed in one of the musical numbers.

The rest of *Under the Pampas Moon* doesn't deliver much. It was a bid by Fox to recapture the popularity of Baxter's Cisco Kid role, for which the actor (1889–1951) had won an Oscar for *In Old Arizona* (1928). Latino stereotypes abound in a fish-out-of-water comedy-drama about a boastful gaucho seeking his stolen steed in the big city. Second-billed Katti Gallian, a French actress in a short Hollywood stay, sings one number and shows little else, even though she is billed above the title. Mexican tenor-guitarist Tito Guizar, touted as "Radio's Troubadour of Love," and the dance team of Veloz and Yolanda provide specialties that add to the film's bona fides as a musical. But viewers also must endure Baxter's havoc-wreaking with his hayseed mother (Soledad Jiménez) in a fancy cabaret—painful stuff even by 1935 standards, especially when the son reminds his mom that, to look good in the big city, she will have to get rid of her moustache! "This may amuse children," noted *Harrison's Reports*' astute reviewer, "but adults will be bored at the ridiculousness of the whole thing."[41]

Fox was already impressed enough by Cansino's work in *Dante's Inferno*—which patrons wouldn't see until its release that August—to give her a long-term contract. She was billed fourth as a native girl in *Charlie Chan in Egypt*, a June release that brought her another exotic part, and was announced as the lead in the Henry King–directed romantic drama *Ramona*—which would have been a big break—but Loretta Young ultimately was given the role. Instead, Cansino's fourth feature was *Paddy O'Day*, which began production in September and began its release at year's end. In her biggest role to date, she played another ethnic dancer, this one Russian, who befriends the titular Irish orphan (Withers) newly arrived in America.

Besides getting to dance, Rita sings a little, apparently dubbed (as she would nearly always be on the screen), and gets to enjoy a romance with the scholarly bird collector-cum-songwriter played by co-star Pinky Tomlin. Cansino and Tomlin, a singer-composer who had made a splash with the standard "The Object of My Affection," dated briefly for real, although their outings were studio-arranged. "There wasn't much for her to do and she didn't project like a hot potato ... but her beauty was already there. She was exceptional even then," Tomlin recalled to historian John Kobal.[42]

Withers (b. 1926) kept her career as Fox's scrappy second-string Shirley

Temple flourishing with programmers like this one, which the studio touted as an adventure of a girl "with a twinkle in her eye and a saucy Irish brogue in her song." Audiences liked Withers even though—or perhaps because—she was not as sugary as Temple, more like a "regular" child. The native of Atlanta came to prominence in support as a bratty alternative to Temple in the latter's *Bright Eyes* (1934), and Fox kept Withers busy in four and five features a year into the early '40s. By the time *Paddy O'Day* was ready for release, Withers (or her representatives) were holding out, the youngster threatening not to work unless her $150-per-week Fox contract wasn't raised to $1,000 per week. Fox saw the wisdom in the investment.

Besides Pinky Tomlin, future Oscar winner Jane Darwell and George Givot—the dialect comedian promoted as radio's "Greek ambassador"—supported the little star in *Paddy O'Day*, and it also added to the future Rita Hayworth's confidence before the camera. It wouldn't be until 1937, and a contract switch to Columbia, when the actress would acquire the surname under which she would achieve fame. By then, her appearance had become sleeker, more glamorous and more Anglicized, but Hayworth's former screen look can be seen by film watchers who seek out her earliest work.

Banjo on My Knee
(20th Century–Fox; December 4, 1936)

Director: John Cromwell. Associate Producer/Screenplay: Nunnally Johnson, based on the novel by Harry Hamilton. Photography: Ernest Palmer. Editor: Hanson Fritch. Sound: Edmund H. Hansen, E. Clayton Ward, Roger Heman. Musical Director: Arthur Lange. Art Director: Hans Peters. Set Decoration: Thomas Little. Running Time: 95 minutes.

Cast: Barbara Stanwyck (Pearl Elliott); Joel McCrea (Ernie Holley); Walter Brennan (Newt Holley); Buddy Ebsen (Buddy); Helen Westley (Grandma); Walter Catlett (Warfield Scott); Anthony [Tony] Martin (Chick Bean); Katherine DeMille (Leota Long); Victor Kilian (Slade); Minna Gombell (Ruby); Spencer Charters (Judge Tope); The Hall Johnson Choir (singers at dock); George Humbert (Jules); Hilda Vaughn (Gurtha); Cecil Weston (Hattie); Louis Mason (Eph); Tom Herbert (man in chair at Scott's); Russ Powell (bartender); James Dundee, Frank Marlowe, Milburn Stone (sailors); Nick De Ruiz (cook); Salty Holmes (jug blower); Eddy Waller (truck driver); Henry Otho, Ed Schaefer (police officers); Davison Clark, Tom Mahoney (police sergeants); Ben Hendricks (officer); Otto Fries (deputy); Jack Pennick (man in boat); Theresa Harris (blues singer).

Songs: "Banjo on My Knee" [Ebsen, Brennan, chorus, reprised by Ebsen, chorus], "There's Something in the Air" [Martin], "Where the Lazy River Goes By" [Stanwyck, reprised by Martin, Stanwyck] (Jimmy McHugh, Harold Adamson); "Oh! Susanna" [Brennan instrumentally], "Old Folks at Home" (aka "Swanee River") [Brennan instrumentally, danced by Ebsen, Stanwyck] (Stephen Foster); "St. Louis Blues" [Harris,

Hall Johnson Choir, plus numerous times instrumentally] (W. C. Handy); "Dixie" [Brennan instrumentally] (Daniel Decatur Emmett); "I'm Looking Over a Four Leaf Clover" [Brennan instrumentally] (Mort Dixon, Harry M. Woods).
Academy Award Nomination: Best Sound Recording (Edmund H. Hansen).
Disc: Brunswick 7782 ("There's Something in the Air"/"Where the Lazy River Goes By," Tony Martin).
Home Video: 20th Century–Fox DVD.

The Story: On a boat next to an island in the Mississippi River, native son Ernie Holley and Tennessee "land girl" Pearl Elliott are married. During the wedding-night festivities, and before the marriage is consummated, Ernie punches unwelcome visitor Slade, and, wrongly thinking he's killed the man, flees. Ernie tours the globe as a sailor for six months, returns to the island, and announces his intentions to take Pearl and his father, Newt, to Aruba. Pearl is angered and goes to New Orleans, where she works as a dishwasher in a café and meets singer Chick Bean. Newt reunites with Pearl and Chick for a performing act dubbed "The River Troubadours." Ernie reappears and incites another brawl; he is bailed from jail by island girl Leota, who carries a torch for him. Pearl goes to Chicago with Chick, but she returns to the island as Ernie is about to be united with Leota.

Barbara Stanwyck rarely got to show off her contralto in the movies, and it wasn't until seven years into her Hollywood career that she sang and danced for the first time in a real musical, 20th Century–Fox's *Banjo on My Knee*. Her presence was appreciated back in 1936, but this oh-so-folksy comedy-drama with songs doesn't have much more to recommend itself today.

Fox had high hopes for the film, based on a novel by Harry Hamilton about what studio publicity called "singing, dancing, brawling, foot-loose and happy Mississippi River folk."[43] Janet Gaynor, the studio's biggest adult female star, and newly rising Henry Fonda were initially cast as the leads—a loutish river man and his long-suffering sweetheart—but were replaced by Stanwyck and Joel McCrea before filming. (This was the second of Stanwyck and McCrea's six screen pairings, the first being 1934's *Gambling Lady*.) The originally announced screenwriter was author William Faulkner, in one of his occasional forays into motion pictures, but his script (forecast in early trade ads as a "rich-as-earth Southern tale") was rejected by Fox for its wordiness and too-literary quality. Nunnally Johnson, a longtime favorite of studio production chief Darryl F. Zanuck, penned the scenario instead for director John Cromwell, who listed the early talkie musicals *Close Harmony* and *The Dance of Life* (both 1929) among credits that more famously included RKO's 1934 version of Somerset Maugham's *Of Human Bondage*.

In a letter published as an advertisement in the Hollywood trades shortly before the release of *Banjo on My Knee* in late 1936, and signed by Fox President Sidney R. Kent, the studio touted the story's appeal "with all of the dramatic force of *Tobacco Road* and the mellowness of *Steamboat 'Round the Bend*, with a quality of its own ... a power that spells bigness." *Steamboat 'Round the Bend*, the posthumously released Will Rogers comedy of a few months before, was a Fox property that could safety be cited in studio advertising. *Tobacco Road*, the long-running Broadway play about poor, lazy Georgia farmers, was not attached to the studio, and the play's producers unsuccessfully sued Fox for using the play's name in its publicity *for Banjo on My Knee*, claiming that Fox was destroying the play's potential value as a motion picture.[44] Despite the "destruction," *Tobacco Road* came to the screen on its own in 1941.

Even if it didn't have that much "bigness," *Banjo on My Knee* earned mainly positive reviews, particularly for Walter Brennan's comic performance as the McCrea character's father, Newt Holley, a toothless yokel who delights in playing his homemade "contraption"—a portable one-man orchestra with banjo, kettle drum, cymbals, bottles, and more—and frets that his son won't provide him a grandchild. After years of small, often unbilled roles, Brennan (1894–1974) was just starting to emerge as a top character player; shortly after the release of this film, he won the first of his three Best Supporting Actor Academy Awards for *Come and Get It*. Brennan seemingly has more to do with Stanwyck than McCrea in *Banjo on My Knee*, for the story has the leads tediously parted for long periods of time, mainly because McCrea's Ernie Holley is such a hothead and must exit. Meanwhile, Katherine DeMille makes a shapely villainess, and city-slicker supporting player Walter Catlett's sole function is as a punching bag for multiple violence-prone characters.

One of the challenges faced by Fox was to make realistic-looking scenes of a storm strong enough to wreck a houseboat on the Mississippi River. The studio built a large moat, filled it with water, and subjected to it high-pressure pumps that created the faux turbulence. Six large spill buckets, each containing some 2,500 gallons of water, were dumped into the maelstrom, accompanied by flashes of lightning and peals of thunder to create a convincing effect for key junctures of the film.[45]

Three of the songs in *Banjo on My Knee* were created by composer Jimmy McHugh and lyricist Harold Adamson, newly paired in what would become a fruitful collaboration for many years. Their title song is sung by "shanty boat person" Buddy Ebsen as a tribute to laziness: "I never done a lick of work/I never even tried...." The Hall Johnson Choir—with an unbilled Theresa Harris singing lead—contributes a strong performance of "St. Louis Blues," which is heard throughout the picture because it's Newt's favorite song. But the musical chores are mainly handled by dancer Ebsen and singer Tony Martin (then billed as Anthony in a thankless second lead). Each has a number with Stanwyck, who acquits herself well twice on Adamson and McHugh's "Where the Lazy River Goes By," even with the traces of her New York accent in her vocalizing.

As *Variety*'s reviewer wrote, her "deep and throaty ... mike voice, is good enough ... to have her singing in plenty of pictures to come."[46] Stanwyck (1907–1990) would rarely sing in her own tones on screen; her most notable song vocals were in *Lady of Burlesque* (1944).

Interestingly for the time, Stanwyck's character in *Banjo on My Knee* is not reflexively loyal to her man over her own well-being, and this feminist slant was not lost on some commentators of the day, including British scholar E. W. Robson in his 1939 book, *The Film Answers Back: An Historical Appreciation of the Cinema*. Robson saw the desire of the bride to make her own life and not follow her husband abroad as indicative of "a new generation of vigorous young actresses capable of carrying serious dramatic roles of immediate social importance.

> ... Stanwyck portrays the bride as a woman of the people, forthright, independent, courageous, and hard-working.... The position of wives and fiancees whose fate is economically linked to that of their men folk has undergone a change of treatment in the American film ... showing the women's point of view.[47]

This would, of course, be exactly the kind of role for which Stanwyck would build her enduring reputation, and although *Banjo on My Knee* did not

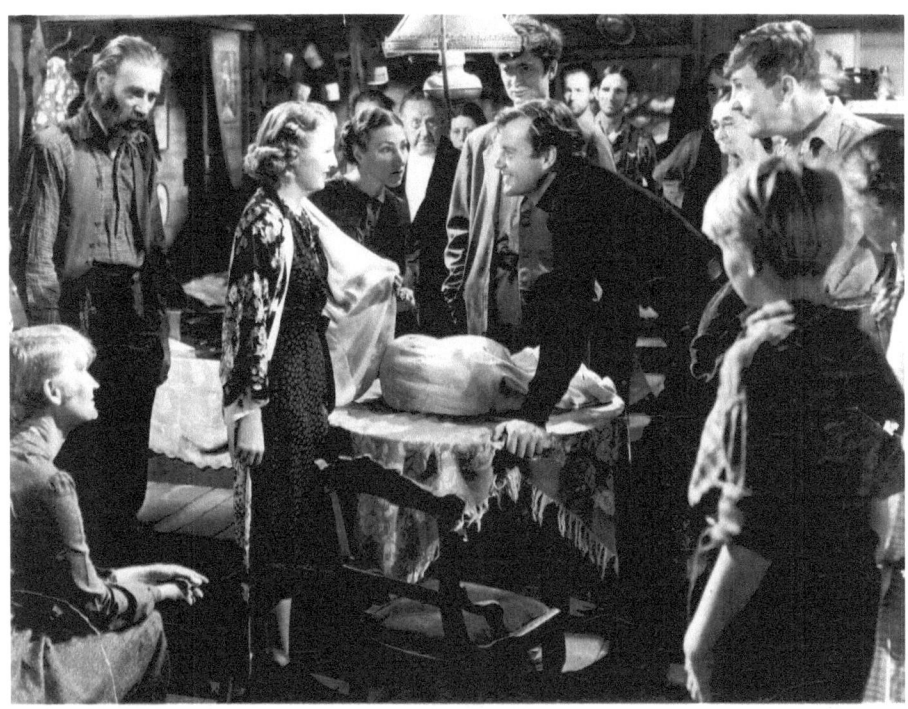

Barbara Stanwyck and Joel McCrea (center) play a bickering couple in *Banjo on My Knee* (1936).

make the impact Fox might have expected, her and Brennan's fine work make it palatable. It also led to better things for Stanwyck. She had told McCrea (1905–1990) how much she wanted to play the lead in *Stella Dallas*, and he lobbied with producer Samuel Goldwyn, who was filming it, to get Stanwyck cast.[48] The 1937 drama would bring Stanwyck the first of her four Oscar nominations.

Music for Madame
(RKO; October 8, 1937)

Director: John Blystone. Producer: Jesse L. Lasky. Screenplay: Gertrude Purcell, Robert Harari. Story: Robert Harari. Photography: Joseph H. August. Special Photographic Effects: Vernon L. Walker. Editor: Desmond Marquette. Sound: George D. Ellis. Art Director: Van Nest Polglase. Musical Director: Nathaniel Shilkret. Running Time: 81 minutes.

Cast: Nino Martini (Nino Maretti); Joan Fontaine (Jean Clemens); Alan Mowbray (Leon Rodowsky); Billy Gilbert (Krause); Alan Hale, Sr. (Flugelman); Grant Mitchell (Robinson); Erik Rhodes (Nadzio); Lee Patrick (Nora); Romo Vincent (truck driver); Frank Conroy (Harding); Bradley Page (Rollins); George Shelley (Barrett); Jack Carson (assistant director); Ward Bond (Violets); Barbara Pepper (blonde on bus); Edward H. Robins (William Goodwin); Alan Bruce (groom); Ada Leonard (Miss Goodwin); Grace Hayle (fat woman); Milburn Stone (detective); Stanley Blystone, Pat O'Malley (policemen); Robert Homans (desk sergeant); Jack Mulhall, Larry Steers (wedding guests); Myra McKinney (admirer); James Donlan (suspect with cold); Russ Powell (singing suspect); George Meeker (orchestra leader); Sam Hayes (radio announcer).

Songs: "I Want the World to Know" [Fontaine, reprised twice by Martini], "(My Sweet) Bambina" [Martini] (Gus Kahn, Rudolf Friml); "King of the Road" [Vincent] (Edward Cherkose, Nathaniel Shilkret); "Music for Madame" [Shelley, reprised by Martini] (Herb Magidson, Allie Wrubel); "Vesti la giubba" from *Pagliacci* [Martini, reprised by Rhodes, Martini] (Ruggero Leoncavallo); Overture from *Tannhäuser* [orchestra] (Richard Wagner).

The Story: On his way to Hollywood for "a fling" in the movies, aspiring opera singer Nino Maretti is noticed by two jewel thieves, Harding and Rollins, who employ the unsuspecting tenor in a scheme to rob film producer Goodwin. Nino attends a wedding reception for Goodwin's daughter. Also "crashing" the event is would-be operetta composer Jean Clemens, who intends to meet famous conductor Rodowsky. While Nino sings to charm the party guests, Harding and Rollins rob the Goodwins of a valuable pearl necklace. Detective Flugelman and district attorney Robinson grill potential "mystery tenors." Nino and Jean meet and get jobs as extras on a movie supervised by Rodowsky. She realizes his deception when he sings her composition "I Want the World to Know." To fund Jean's operetta, Nino confesses to the jewel theft so Jean's roommate, Nora, can claim the $25,000 reward. Nino *and Nadzio sing on a radio program so that Rodowsky can identify the "correct" tenor. The conductor refuses to identify Nino but gets him to sing at a concert at the Hollywood Bowl, where the crooks seek revenge.*

Primarily a vehicle for Italian-born operatic tenor Nino Martini, *Music for Madame* earns a place in this chapter because of the early-career appearance of second-billed Joan Fontaine (1917–2013). This was the fifth movie credit for the young actress; new to the RKO roster, she would have a busy 1937, even if wasn't terribly memorable for the quality of material. This wasn't even the only musical she made in '37—more fans recall the other one, *A Damsel in Distress*, because its co-stars were Fred Astaire, George Burns, and Gracie Allen. In her autobiography, *No Bed of Roses*, Fontaine dispensed with *Music for Madame* in a single then-I-was-in-this sentence. It's no classic, true, but this airy, comic musical deserves a little better.

But not for Fontaine, who makes scant impression in a typical ingénue role, this one as an extra singer and would-be composer who falls for Martini's wannabe singer. The real story is Martini—one of a bevy of opera singers who

Opera tenor Nino Martini and not-yet-famous starlet Joan Fontaine are awkwardly paired in RKO's *Music for Madame* (1937).

made bids for movie stardom in the mid–1930s. To studios buoyed by the Oscar-nominated success of America's own Grace Moore in Columbia's *One Night of Love* (1934) came Mary Ellis and Michael Bartlett, Marion Talley and Everett Marshall, Gladys Swarthout and Jan Kiepura, Lily Pons and James Melton (who actually crossed over from pop after he came to films). Even the great Lawrence Tibbett, who had made such a hit during the musicals' first wave with *The Rogue Song* in 1930, came back for two films at Fox, *Metropolitan* and *Under Your Spell*. They had novelty value, especially for big-city audiences, but most of their films failed to make money.

Martini, too, was an import from opera at the dawn of sound. He had debuted on the stage in his native land in 1925, and came to the United States initially at the behest of Paramount founder Jesse L. Lasky. At that studio, Martini (1905–1976) sang "Come Back to Sorrento" in the all-star revue *Paramount on Parade* (1930) and starred in a two-reeler, *Moonlight and Romance*.[49] He spent four years as a leading tenor at mid-decade with the Metropolitan Opera, and would garner much radio exposure.

Meanwhile, Lasky was ousted at Paramount in 1932, went bankrupt, and, for a spell aligned with Mary Pickford, reappeared as an independent producer at Fox, where he made flops such as *I Am Suzanne!* [q.v.] but reintroduced Martini to the screen with *Here's to Romance* (1935). Another musical comedy, *The Gay Desperado* (1936), a delightful United Artists release for standout director Rouben Mamoulian, followed; the female lead in the latter was the young Ida Lupino. Upon his and Lasky's move to RKO, Martini got an even younger, less experienced co-star for *Music for Madame*, which was shot in the summer of 1937.

Martini is a likable sort in the film, playing an Italian immigrant (hence, providing a reason for his lack of mastery of English) who is an unwitting accessory in jewel robbery, then becomes the "mystery tenor" for whom the authorities—and famed conductor Leon Rodowsky—are searching. Portrayed by Alan Mowbray, Rodowsky is a thinly failed caricature of superstar baton-wielder Leopold Stokowski, with mounds of conceit revealed in such pronouncements as "In America today, I am probably the only musician" and the description of his upcoming Hollywood Bowl concert as "an oasis in the desert of boredom." Between the not-too-frequent and not-too-operatic numbers, Mowbray makes the film worth watching, but RKO tossed in some comedy insurance with sneezing Billy Gilbert and frequent Astaire-and-Rogers foil Erik Rhodes. Rhodes (1906–1990) does his lame-brained-Italian act to effective if familiar effect, parodying Martini in speaking voice but hardly matching his soaring tones during a radio "duel" of "Vesti la giubba."

RKO reportedly spared no expense for the climactic Hollywood Bowl performance; it shot the performances on location by renting the bowl at $300 a day, hiring an 80-piece orchestra, and supplying 500 extras to sit in an audience for director John Blystone. The studio could have packed the place by simply advertising a Martini concert to the public, but rules prohibiting the use of non-extras in such situations prevented that from occurring.[50] Fontaine contributes a voice—which, studio publicity assured, was her own—to a section of Gus Kahn and Rudolf Friml's "I Want the World to Know," and some sound effects to "King of the Road," a novelty number in which a truck driver sings as Martini and Fontaine toot horns inside the trucker's cab. The driver is played by Romo Vincent, a corpulent singer-impressionist-comedian who had lately attracted moviedom's attention for his master-of-ceremonies work in the ballroom of the Biltmore, the famous L.A. hotel. *Music for Madame* was one of his first films; his long list of credits would extend to a 1977 episode of TV's *The Love Boat*.

At this juncture, Fontaine was known less for her acting talent than for being the younger sister of Olivia de Havilland. She'd debuted in pictures billed ninth, as Joan Burfield, in the 1935 MGM entry *No More Ladies*, then played roles of varying sizes in a few unremarkable films (*A Million to One, You Can't Beat Love, The Man Who Found Himself, Quality Street*) before ending up in *Music for Madame*. Foreshadowing the siblings' famous feud was publicity over a supposed clause in Fontaine's contract with Lasky that her connection with de Havilland, the Warner Bros. star, not be mentioned. "I'd rather wash dishes for a career than have it thought I was trading on my sister's success," Fontaine admonished a wire-service reporter during a 1937 interview. "…While I'm still under 20, which won't be long, I want to do unsophisticated parts. I hate slinky gowns, lots of lipstick and colored fingernails."[51] Ah, youth!

Released when audiences were beginning a backlash against all the opera in films, *Music for Madame* lost $375,000 at the box office.[52] Its main player came in for much of the criticism, but *Variety*'s "Flin" liked the young co-star: "Seems that Nino Martini just can't make the grade…. He has a personable and attractive way…. But Nino can't act…. Film also introduces a newcomer, Joan Fontaine, as leading woman. She has looks and youth and gets by with what is given her to do."[53]

Martini was all done at RKO—he made only one more film (*One Night With You*, in England, 10 years later). After another money-losing opera musical—*Hitting a New High*, with Lily Pons—Jesse Lasky was gone from that studio as well.

Swing Your Lady
(Warner Bros.; January 8, 1938)

Director: Ray Enright. Dialogue Director: Jo Graham. Screenplay: Joseph Schrank, Maurice Leo, based on the play by Kenyon Nicholson and Charles Robinson (New

York opening, October 18, 1936; 105 performances). Photography: Arthur Edeson. Editor: Jack Killifer. Sound: Charles Lang. Art Director: Esdras Hartley. Music: Adolph Deutsch. Musical Director: Leo F. Forbstein. Dance Director: Bobby Connolly. Running Time: 77 minutes.
Cast: Humphrey Bogart (Ed Hatch); Frank McHugh (Popeye); Louise Fazenda (Sadie); Nat Pendleton (Joe "Hercules" Skopapolous); Penny Singleton (Cookie); Allen Jenkins (Shiner); Leon Weaver (Waldo); Frank Weaver (Ollie Davis); Elviry Weaver (Mrs. Davis); Ronald Reagan (Jack Miller); Daniel Boone Savage (Noah); Hugh O'Connell (Smith); Tommy Bupp (Rufe); Sunny [Sonny] Bupp (Len); Joan Howard (Mattie); Sue Moore (Mabel); Olin Howland (hotel proprietor); Sammy White (specialty dancer); Victor Potel (Clem); Roger Gray, John "Skins" Miller, Foy Van Dolsen, Frank Pharr (hillbillies); Georgia Simmons (mountain woman); June Gittelson (waitress); Spec O'Donnell (kid in overalls).
Songs: "Dig Me a Grave in Missouri" [Weavers, band], "Hillbilly From Tenth Avenue" [Singleton, chorus], "Mountain Swingaroo" [Singleton, White, chorus], "The Old Apple Tree" [Weavers, chorus], "Swing Your Lady" [Singleton, chorus] (M. K. Jerome, Jack Scholl).
Home Video: Warner Archive DVD.

The Story: Promoter Ed Hatch arrives in the Ozarks while touring with his top client, wrestler Joe "Hercules" Skopapolous, and trainers Popeye and Shiner. Lacking a male foe in the sticks to match against Joe, Ed instead recruits a lady blacksmith, Sadie, as a ring opponent, although Ed's girlfriend, Cookie, objects. Not knowing they are to wrestle each other, Joe and Sadie meet and fall in love. When Sadie's longtime beau, Noah, shows up to claim his gal, Ed is inspired to put Joe and Noah in the ring instead, with the winner to claim Sadie in what gains national attention as the "Love Match of the Century." But Ed needs Joe to throw the match, lest he lose his meal ticket.

Humphrey Bogart top-billed in a musical? Nat Pendleton and Louise Fazenda as romantic leads? Professional wrestling and hillbillies? Ronald Reagan? No wonder *Swing Your Lady* is such an easy target. As early as the 1970s, alleged hipsters got hold of this dismal Warner Bros. comedy with songs, which was clowned as "a bomb all the way around" in Harry and Michael Medved's book *The 50 Worst Films of All Time*.[54] Bogart walks listlessly through a part—as a fast-talking wrestling promoter—that he didn't want, in a movie that he considered (and many of his biographers have agreed) to be his worst.[55] Even the vampiric mad doctor Bogie played in *The Return of Dr. X* (1939) couldn't compare.

Some context is needed, however. The film industry is a copycat business, and *Swing Your Lady* was Warners' response to a mini-fad for rural culture. Country, or "hillbilly," music gained mainstream exposure as rural audiences, especially those in the South, gained access to radios. Adapted from a short-lived Broadway "hillbilly" play, *Swing Your Lady* sought to capitalize on a trend that was cinematically exploited most successfully by Paramount in its 1937 hit *Mountain Music*, starring radio comedian Bob ("The Arkansas Traveler") Burns. Bogart, a few years away from A-list star status—and hardly the house-

Humphrey Bogart pretends to have fun as a wrestling promoter character who watches Nat Pendleton and Louise Fazenda square off in *Swing Your Lady* (1938).

hold name he would become—was unlucky enough to become attached to the project by his studio.

Not typically one to refuse a role, Bogart sent his representative, agent Leland Hayward, to ask WB execs Jack L. Warner and Hal Wallis to decline. The brass responded by giving the actor a $1,000-per-week salary boost if he'd make *Swing Your Lady*, and the financially insecure Bogart had to agree. According to Bogart biographers A.M. Sperber and Eric Lax: "The whole matter left him determined never to be financially muscled again, and he resolved to build up a cash reserve he later referred to as 'F-Y money.'"[56]

Bogart (1899–1957) wasn't the only unlucky one. Cast as the lady blacksmith who falls in love with her future 'rassling opponent was Louise Fazenda—aka Mrs. Hal Wallis. (The more Amazonian Hope Emerson played the role in the original Broadway production of *Swing Your Lady*.) Here's an example of her romantic byplay with Pendleton:

> JOE (Pendleton): "I like big girls!"
> SADIE (Fazenda): "You ain't so puny yourself.... Say, mister! Who in the name of Jerusalem are ye, anyway?"

JOE: "Joe Skopapolous."
SADIE: "Huh?"
JOE (pointing out his name on the back of his shirt): "Skopapolous! Skopapolous!"
SADIE: "What are ye? Eye-talian?"
JOE: "Naw, I'm of Greek accent!"

A scene in which Fazenda's character wrestles Bogart's to the ground had to have been even more amusing to the studio bosses. At least Nat Pendleton wasn't miscast—he was a former Olympic wrestler, only not stupid like the dopey "Hercules" in the film. Ronald Reagan wasn't either: In a small role in his third movie, the former radio announcer/future U.S. president plays an Associated Press newspaper reporter who says journalistic things like "Our readers want to know" and (to Bogart) "I'll write the story; you just give me the facts." Fortunately for a small-part player like Reagan, he was on the set for only five days.

With Bogart unenthusiastic about spreading the word on *Swing Your Lady*, Warner Bros. was left to fabricate newspaper stories that allegedly quoted the actor as admitting he was ill-fitted for portrayal in a movie about wrestling:

> "Why," moaned Bogart, "does it always have to happen to me? I've never been to a wrestling match in my life. I think it's the dullest sport in the world. And here I am, not only watching 'em but almost having to take part in 'em. I guess I don't live right. Or maybe I'd better in for numerology or change my name or something."[57]

The brunt of the actual publicity chores was left to Fazenda (1895–1962), who embarked on a national tour tied to openings in key cities in early 1938. Among the stops was one in Washington, D.C., for a White House lunch date with Eleanor Roosevelt.[58] Theater owners, as always, had to do their part in promoting their bookings, although more effort was expended in audience-friendly areas. For example, in the burg of Winchester, Kentucky, one W.A. Sandefur, manager of the Leeds and Colonial Theatres, marked the local opening of *Swing Your Lady* by constructing a bar, six feet wide and eight feet long, to entirely cover his box office space. Using cutout cartoons, painted catchphrases were printed on all four sides, reading such as "Mountain Musick Yes Sir-EE!" and "Spechul Notice ... it's a humdinger."[59] The intentional misspellings probably didn't keep anyone away.

Bubbly Penny Singleton, soon to be typecast forever as Hollywood's version of Blondie, was signed by Warner Bros. for *Swing Your Lady* after an impressive second-lead part in MGM's *After the Thin Man*. With her name recently changed from the original, Dorothy McNulty, she was given the role after Joan Blondell, after reading the script, chose to serve a four-week suspension over doing the film. Singleton (1908–2003) sings and dances in *Swing*

Your Lady, but Warners' real answer to Bob Burns is the novelty act the Weaver Brothers and Elviry, a Missouri-bred family trio direct from vaudeville with down-home melodies and homemade instruments. The mix of music and mirth—from Bogie, there wasn't much good of the first and precious little of any of the latter—in what folks then called "the grunt-and-groan game" of wrestling garnered opinions all over the map.[60] *Variety*'s reviewer lauded it as "a rollicking, considerably different laugh-piece which should do from average to good business everywhere," but the highbrow *New York Times* more thoughtfully saw the film as "vulgar," "ludicrous," and "irresponsible," yet an "anthropologically valuable study of Americana."[61]

"Anthropologically valuable"?

Swing Your Lady actually made a small profit, according to Sperber and Lax, countering the Medveds' claim that it was a money-loser—but Warner Bros. was more comfortable mining an urban vein, and the Weavers moved to Republic for a series of low-budget comedies produced through 1943. By then, their erstwhile colleague Bogart was doing better for himself.

The Ice Follies of 1939
(Metro-Goldwyn-Mayer; March 3, 1939)

Director: Reinhold Schünzel. Assistant Director: Edward Woehler. Producer: Harry Rapf. Screenplay: Leonard Praskins, Florence Ryerson, Edgar Allan Woolf. Story: Leonard Praskins. Photography: Joseph Ruttenberg, Oliver T. Marsh. Editor: W. Donn Hayes. Art Director: Cedric Gibbons. Set Decoration: Edwin B. Willis. Sound: Douglas Shearer. Music Directors: Franz Waxman, Georgie Stoll. Orchestral and Vocal Arrangements: Leo Arnaud, George Bassman. Skating Choreography: Frances Claudet, Val Raset. Scenic Effects for "Cinderella" Finale: Merrill Pye. Ice Follies Ensembles: Dolly Tree. Costumes: Adrian. Running Time: 82 minutes. Technicolor sequence.

Cast: Joan Crawford (Mary McKay aka Sandra Lee); James Stewart (Larry Hall); Lew Ayres (Eddie Burgess); Lewis Stone (Douglas Tolliver, Jr.); Bess Ehrhardt (Kitty Sherman); Lionel Stander (Mort Hodges); Charles D. Brown (Barney); Truman Bradley (Paul Rodney); The International Ice Follies, with Eddie Shipstad, Roy Shipstad, Oscar Johnson (ice follies dancers); Marie Blake (Effie Lane); Wade Boteler (policeman); James Flavin (doorman); Arthur Loft (director); Joe Manz (Tolliver's chauffeur); Hal K. Dawson (publicity man); Charles Judels (makeup man); Louis Adlon (dress designer); Adolph Hebert, Larry Jackson (skating horse); Harrison Greene (agent); Libby Taylor (maid); William Tannen (doorman); Eddie Kane, James McNamara (dinner guests); Edward Earle (man).

Songs: "It's All So New to Me" [Crawford, chorus] (Bernice Petkere, Marty Symes); "Blackbirds" [chorus, danced by Ice Follies], "Cinderella Reel" [danced by Ice Follies] (Roger Edens, Franz Waxman); "Loveland in the Wintertime" [danced by Ice Follies] (Cliff Friend, Dave Franklin); "The Bonnie Banks o' Loch Lomond" [danced by Ice

Follies] (trad.); "Comin' Thro' the Rye" [danced by Ice Follies] (Robert Burns, trad.); "The Fountain in the Park" [aka "While Strolling Through the Park One Day" [danced by Ice Follies] (Ed Haley); "There Is a Tavern in the Town" [danced by Ice Follies] (trad.).
Working Title: *Ice Follies*.
Disc: Victor 26205 ("It's All So New to Me," Joan Crawford).
Home Video: Warner Archive DVD.

The Story: Professional skater Larry Hall falls for a cigarette girl, Mary McKay, and includes her in his act with ice partner Eddie Burgess although she can't skate well. Larry's career suffers, but he and Mary elope, and he longs to produce his own ice extravaganza. Mary convinces Monarch Studios producer Douglas Tolliver, Jr., to offer her a contract as an actress. However, under the terms of the pact, Mary cannot marry without the studio's permission, so she and Larry must keep their union secret. As the rechristened Sandra Lee, Mary becomes a star with her first picture, further straining the marriage. Larry reunites with Eddie and convinces producer Mort Hodges to fund his "Ice Follies" show, which becomes a smash hit and attracts interest from Tolliver. Can Larry and Mary reconcile personally as well as professionally?

Maybe it didn't seem so bad all those years ago, the only star pairing of Joan Crawford and James Stewart—and in a figure skating musical, besides. But *The Ice Follies of 1939* was no plus for MGM, and we are left to shake our heads at how it got made at all.

One might blame popular culture. Sonja Henie had parlayed multiple Olympic gold medals and national tours into screen success at 20th Century–Fox, and Metro wanted a piece of that. Crawford (1904–1977) thought herself a singer—she'd sung a little early in her talkie career and had even begun to study opera—and wanted to participate in musicals. And she owed a debt of gratitude to *Ice Follies* producer Harry Rapf, who had launched Crawford's Hollywood career by signing her to a Metro contract in 1924.[62] Crawford was promised (and recorded) at least three songs—a sufficient showcase for her voice, and enough, perhaps, to quell her concerns about the project, and the lately flagging box office returns of her movies—as filming commenced.

As a newcomer at MGM, Stewart (1908–1997) played a secondary part in the 1936 Crawford vehicle *The Gorgeous Hussy*, but he had come a long way since. (The below-the-title billing in the opening credits read: "Starring Joan Crawford with James Stewart," which was much more favorable to Stewart than it would have been a year or so before.) Still, he was already accustomed to better material. Largely untried behind an American camera—making only his second U.S. picture—was director Reinhold Schünzel, who wrote and directed the German film *Viktor and Victoria* (1933), which became the basis for the 1980s Hollywood musical *Victor/Victoria*. The studio drew attention to *Ice Fol-*

lies in advance by issuing a one-reel "MGM Miniatures" short, *Ice Antics*, which involved trick skaters and included scenes from the Crawford picture.

Ice Follies was hardly MGM's most important 1939 release, but the studio supplied its trademark gloss by showing off Crawford in trademark gowns by Adrian and importing the touring International Ice Follies company, which had been launched in 1936 by brothers Eddie and Roy Shipstad with Oscar Johnson to capitalize on the skating boom. All three men appear in the film, as does young "Sweetheart of the Ice" Bess Ehrhardt. Hollywood scribes attempted to build Ehrhardt as an all-American rival to the Swedish Henie. Part of its push was to hold *Ice Follies'* world premiere in Ehrhardt's hometown of Superior, Wisconsin, where it was reported as "the greatest event in local theatrical history.

> The highlight ... was a phone call from Miss Ehrhardt on tour, the call amplified so that the audience, sidewalk crowds and those listening to the (radio) broadcast at home could hear the message. Following the premiere, a special midnight show was put on to accommodate the waiting crowds, and other events publicized later included a "Bess Ehrhardt Day" sponsored by the high school which she had attended, the student body attending special performance.[63]

Despite the effort, Ehrhardt's film career ended here; the wife of Roy Shipstad, she returned to touring with the International Ice Follies.

If patrons were led to believe the leads of *Ice Follies of 1939* would both skate and sing, they would be disappointed. MGM handed out publicity shots of Crawford, Stewart, and Lew Ayres on skates together, but they glided on the ice for nary a second on screen. This is a too-standard story—hampered by the lack of sparks generated by the two stars—about the strained marriage of a movie star and a wannabe impresario, until it blossoms with an impressive 15-minute Technicolor finale featuring the International Ice Follies. Unfortunately for Crawford, almost all of her singing was cut—whether for length or quality; all that remains is a chorus or so of Bernice Petkere and Marty Symes' "It's All So New to Me" in the climactic "Cinderella" sequence.[64] Based on the existing recording, her rendition of Arthur Freed and Nacio Herb Brown's "Something's Gotta Happen Soon" seems a real loss. Another Crawford number announced, then cut, was "Here I Go Falling in Love Again."

Even with the lessened musical content, trade ads promised "A New Idea in Musical Drama" and "A Thrilling 'Great Ziegfeld' on Ice." *The Film Daily* promised exhibitors that *Ice Follies of 1939* was a "sure-fire pop spectacle that can't miss anywhere."[65] But whispers over the quality of the film began in sneak previews, and movie-goers watched with displeasure or stayed away from the product once in release. A theater owner in Kansas reflected the views of many about Crawford: "She is still poison at my box office.... James Stewart should go places with someone, but not with Joan"—and in Ontario, another theater owner called it "our folly in 1939 for playing it. Didn't do business."[66]

James Stewart (left), Joan Crawford, and Lew Ayres couldn't skate—and didn't—in *The Ice Follies of 1939*, but MGM publicity photographs had viewers thinking otherwise.

When asked, late in life, her impressions of *Ice Follies of 1939*, Crawford didn't mince words: "Everyone was out of their collective minds when they made *Ice Follies*. Me, Jimmy Stewart, and Lew Ayres as skaters—preposterous. A dancer I am, a skater I'm not.... Nice music and costumes, and the Shipstad ice people helped, but it was a catastrophe. The public thought so, too."[67] Indeed, the film lost more than $300,000 at the paybox.

The public's memories proved short, however. Crawford rebounded with a strong part among the ensemble in *The Women*, and Stewart was soon enthralling fans in his first Oscar-nominated performance, in *Mr. Smith Goes to Washington*. *The Ice Follies of 1939* was left to chill in obscurity ... and to be recalled in books like this.

4. Big Ideas, Bigger Casts ... and Some Oddities

We know that bigger is not always better when it comes to the movies, so why have the makers of the Hollywood musical so blatantly devalued such advice?

Right from the start, studios sought to fill the screen with not necessarily better performers, songs, and production numbers than seen before, but at least with more of them. As the talkies dawned, MGM began the trend toward musical extravaganza by exhausting its roster with *The Hollywood Revue of 1929*. The company known for "more stars than there are in heaven" employed all of such—save for the foreign-accented Ramon Novarro and Greta Garbo and the perennially mysterious Lon Chaney—and sometimes to actual exhaustion, with occasional middle-of-the-night shooting of specialties for stars already busy with daytime projects. The whole thing culminated with a rendition of the new song "Singin' in the Rain" by many of the film's 30 acts dressed in raincoats before a huge replica of Noah's ark. Metro followed that first revue with an even-bigger production, *The March of Time*, spending $750,000 on it before halting production early in 1930 over concerns about its non-story entertainment value. It was never released, although some of its production sequences appeared as color specialties in unrelated MGM features and shorts.

Not to be outdone, Warner Bros. responded with its own company pastiche, *The Show of Shows* (1929), with John Barrymore's declamation from *Henry VI* adding class to a film with an even-more-jaw-dropping finale, the seemingly endless "Lady Luck." *Paramount on Parade* and Fox's *Happy Days* added to the studio excesses, and so did the best of this early-revue bunch, Universal's all-Technicolor *King of Jazz*, a huge financial flop that survives in retrospect as an amazing achievement, with Broadway showman John Murray Anderson's distinctive direction, Paul Whiteman and His Orchestra's rendition of "Rhapsody in Blue," and America's first true exposure to Bing Crosby.

The influence of vaudeville and the competitive threat of radio kept moviemakers trying to top themselves even after musicals endured their 1931–32 slump, and we're not just talking about the big-big-big-budgeted Busby Berkeley or Sam Goldwyn fare. If Hollywood types weren't trying to be impressive through sheer volumes of talent—as with *International House* and *Moonlight and Pretzels*—they were trying to attract viewers with unusual presentation styles—see *Melody Cruise*—and over-the-top stories—as with *I Am Suzanne!* Or, as perhaps could be conceived only by the budget-busting impresario Lou Brock, all of the above, as shown in such oddities as *Down to Their Last Yacht* and *Top of the Town* [all titles in this paragraph q.v.].

Need to be convinced? Read on.

International House
(Paramount; May 25, 1933)

Director: Edward Sutherland. Screenplay: Francis Martin, Walter De Leon. Story: Neil Brant, Louis E. Heifetz. Photography: Ernest Haller. Costumes: Travis Banton. Running Time: 68 minutes.

Cast: Peggy Hopkins Joyce (herself); W.C. Fields (Professor Henry R. Quail); Rudy Vallee (himself); Stuart Erwin (Tommy Nash); George Burns (Dr. Burns), Gracie Allen (Nurse Allen); Sari Maritza (Carol Fortescue); Colonel Stoopnagle and Budd (themselves); Cab Calloway and His Orchestra (themselves); Bela Lugosi (General Petronovich); Baby Rose Marie (herself); Franklin Pangborn (hotel manager); Edmund Breese (Dr. Wong); Lumsden Hare (Sir Mortimer Fortescue); Sterling Holloway (chorus king); Lona Andre (chorus queen); Harrison Greene (Herr Von Baden); Henry Sedley (Serge Borsky); James Wang (Inspector Sun); Ernest Wood (newsreel reporter); Edwin Stanley (Rollins); Cyril Ring (Mr. Brown); Clem Beauchamp, Jerry Drew (cameramen); Norman Ainsley (ticket agent); Bo-Ling (cigar counter girl); Bo-Ching (female bellhop); The Girls in Cellophane.

Songs: "My Bluebird's Singing the Blues" [Baby Rose Marie], "She Was a China Teacup and He Was Just a Mug" [male vocalist, danced by Holloway, Andre, Girls in Cellophane], "Thank Heaven for You" [Vallee] (Leo Robin, Ralph Rainger); "Reefer Man" [Calloway and orchestra] (Andy Razaf, J. Russel Robinson).

Disc: Brunswick 6340, Melotone 12887, Oriole 2823, Romeo 2196 ("Reefer Man," Cab Calloway Orchestra); Brunswick 6570, Melotone 12852, Oriole 2800, Perfect 12960 ("My Bluebird's Singing the Blues," Baby Rose Marie).

Home Video: Universal DVD/VHS.

The Story: Dr. Wong has invented the radioscope, which can broadcast sound and pictures from anywhere on the globe, and is taking bids on its rights at the International House hotel in Wu Hu, China. Tommy Nash, who represents the American Electric Company, is delayed, first by bad weather—which forces him to make the trip to Wu Hu with famed beauty Peggy Hopkins Joyce—and then by the mistaken impression that he has the measles and must be quarantined. Also among the bidders are General Petronovich, who is Peggy's ex-husband, and Sir Mortimer Fortesque,

4. Big Ideas, Bigger Casts ... and Some Oddities   129

who is accompanied to the conference by Tommy's estranged fiancée, Carol. Off-course autogyro pilot Professor Henry Quail arrives in Wu Hu and is mistaken for the American representative. Wong shows broadcasts of Rudy Vallee, Colonel Stoopnagle and Budd, Baby Rose Marie, and Cab Calloway and his orchestra. Quail and Peggy are paired and Tommy, who has won the bid for his company, and Carol are reunited. They fly off in Quail's "The Spirit of Brooklyn" air vehicle.

Upon its release in the spring of 1933, *International House* was described by *The Hollywood Reporter* as "a curious hodge-podge of gags, girls, slapstick comedy and an impressive array of radio, stage and screen names—with Peggy Hopkins Joyce thrown in for fair measure."[1] The review failed to mention the science-fiction angle, but the summation was otherwise accurate. In retrospect, we think of this as a W.C. Fields vehicle—its success earned him a lucrative contract that cemented his status as a leading Paramount player. So why was it Peggy Hopkins Joyce who was billed first in an all-star film touted as "the *Grand Hotel* of comedy"? And why didn't *International House* make it to DVD as part of a Peggy Hopkins Joyce collection? Some explanation is in order.

Joyce (1892–1957) was the biggest pure celebrity in the *International House* cast, but not for any discernible performing talent. She was, however, the world's most famous gold digger—in the tradition of "material girls" such as Madonna or the Kardashians. A sometime actress, dancer, writer, model, and writer, she married six times and lived most of her life in high style, even when her financial condition couldn't support it. She was thought to be the inspiration for Lorelei Lee, the ambitious flapper created by Anita Loos for magazine short stories and, later, for the stage musical and movie *Gentlemen Prefer Blondes*. Joyce came to prominence in 1917 when she debuted on the Broadway stage in the *Ziegfeld Follies*. She soon became prominent in pop culture for her constant need for publicity and the ease with which she could be joked about or even quoted in song lyrics—but she was past her prime as the '30s dawned. *International House* was her first stab at talkies after a handful of silent-film credits, and in December 1932 when she was signed to play (essentially) herself, it made more headlines than Fields' presence.

Hollywood wags wondered why Joyce, at age 39, was taking another stab at movies, even as she prepped for her assignment by appearing in a sketch to show off her husky voice and fancy wardrobe in a sketch at the Paramount Theater in New York. Some figured she was coming West to look for a new husband, as she was stalled at four at the time. Or she was looking for showbiz fodder for a book to follow her recently published first novel, *Transatlantic Wives*. Or she needed the money, for in the fall of '32 many of her cherished jewels and gowns had been seized by U.S. customs officials. Reason No. 3 made the most sense, given her reputation. According to an industry report, Joyce was guaranteed $1,250 per week for a minimum of four weeks, a small sum compared to Fields' four weeks at $3,000 per.[2] Joyce's own account of her career move—under her byline for the International News Service and published in newspapers nationwide in January 1933—shed little light on her reasoning. It did, however, show a good sense of self-awareness.

Paramount promoted *International House* (1933) co-star Peggy Hopkins Joyce with this caricature alluding to the professional celebrity's elegance.

4. Big Ideas, Bigger Casts ... and Some Oddities

When I left New York for Hollywood, my mother cried, as though she thought I was going away forever. She doesn't seem to mind my trips to Europe, but apparently she thought Hollywood was full of Indians.... They're still asking me when I'm going to get married. It's all so silly, because a lot of women have been married oftener than I. And, anyway, why don't they give me a chance to get acquainted—after all, I've been here only four days."[3]

Paramount ate this kind of stuff up, touting Joyce in early trade ads as a "space grabber de luxe." The studio must've loved the breathless gossip that Joyce already was dating actor Jack Oakie (thus giving that proletarian funnyman's image a touch of class) and that she was judging a fashion contest as between Lilyan Tashman and Hedda Hopper at Agua Caliente. *International House* was filmed in February and March 1933 for its premiere in May and general release in June. Planted concurrently for further fan enjoyment were almost certainly apocryphal magazine items like this one:

> Bela (Dracula) Lugosi was beaming. "Certainly glad to get away from a horror picture," he grinned. "I have no horror part in this new picture, *International House*."
> "What part do you play?" W.C. Fields asked.
> "Oh, I'm a former husband of Peggy Hopkins Joyce," Bela said.
> "Well," drawled Fields, "I suppose it's all in what you mean by 'horror part.'"[4]

Joyce had to have had a thick skin, or a strong sense of pragmatism, given how much she would be lambasted on screen in *International House*. After the shy hypochondriac played by Stuart Erwin (1903–1967) is forced to travel across the Chinese desert with PHJ in tow, his fiancée (Sari Maritza) is dumbfounded: "You were perfectly platonic with Peggy Hopkins Joyce?" "Didn't I get a divorce from you in Paris?" Joyce later asks her Russian ex-husband (Lugosi), but then walks off with him upon learning of his financial prospects. When Erwin's character gets to the point: "You mean you're going to marry a millionaire?" Joyce replies, "I never marry anything else!" At least Joyce got to traipse around in an array of gowns by Paramount fashion master Travis Banton.

The fictionalized Joyce thinks that millionaire is Professor Henry Quail, an eccentric autogyro pilot who is neither a million-dollar man nor the presumed American representative slated to arrive at the titular Chinese hotel to cash in on the much-coveted, television-like "radioscope" invention. Joyce plays straight woman to everyone in the picture, but especially Fields, who got away with a line about Joyce sitting on "a pussy"—as in cat—despite much balking from the Hays Office. A cleverly staged scene in which Fields and Joyce end up in the same hotel bed made it into the film, but another touchy sequence, Cab Calloway and orchestra's rendition of "Reefer Man," was trimmed from many prints, and thus from decades of television showings, before being restored in time for the home-video era. "The gags are very funny ... and the lines are funny, too—and plenty blue," opined a laudatory *Hollywood Reporter* review.[5]

Calloway's appearance—as well as specialties by Rudy Vallee (serenading his megaphone with "Thank Heaven for You"), kid singer Baby Rose Marie, and radio comedy duo Colonel Stoopnagle and Budd—was filmed by director Edward Sutherland at Paramount's former studio at Astoria, New York, for logistical reasons. Shown as "radioscope" broadcasts, they were extraneous to the plot, as was a dance number, "She Was a China Tea-cup and He Was Just a Mug," led by Sterling Holloway, Lona Andre, and a bevy of beauties clad only in cellophane. Reports were that Paramount brass had to sweet-talk (and adequately compensate) crooning king Vallee to appear even so briefly—they initially wanted him for a lead role. But an act like Stoopnagle and Budd was more willing to provide visuals for its airwaves schtick—in this case, the duo's typically dry but "peachy" chatter concerned a group of outlandish inventions. George Burns and Gracie Allen, plus Franklin Pangborn (as a fidgety hotel manager), provided longer-lasting comic punch in what was essentially a follow-up to Paramount's radio-oriented hit *The Big Broadcast*.

Interviewed by the author in 1992 about these early ether-inspired Paramounts, the then-96-year-old George Burns had positive, if jokey, memories:

> Everybody who was in radio was in those movies.... Movies are very easy to do, because you could do most of them sitting down. Now at my age, it's better to do something when I'm sitting down. I pay somebody to sit down for me.[6]

Fields (1880–1946) and Joyce weren't required to sing in *International House*, which had differing impacts on their respective careers. Fields landed the $100,000-per-movie, three-films-a-year, three-year Paramount contract that prompted a half-page ad in the *Hollywood Reporter* that read "W.C. FIELDS/ THE NEW DEAL/Giving the Suckers a Break." After being largely misused in silents (for which he couldn't show off his distinctive voice) and in early talkies such as the Marilyn Miller operetta *Her Majesty, Love*, Fields was having fun in pictures. The *International House* writing team of Francis Martin and Walter DeLeon, both former vaudevillians, tailored their script to Fields so obviously that Fields biographer James Curtis said "it could only be described as a stacked deck."[7] He was king of the set. A well-known piece of film shows Fields calmly directing people to safety during what was purported to be the real earthquake that hit the Los Angeles area on March 10, 1933. The clip played in theaters nationwide as part of Paramount News coverage, but *International House* director Edward Sutherland disclosed years later that it was made after the quake as a joke.

Meanwhile, having played second fiddle to a man for possibly the first time, Peggy Hopkins Joyce never acted in another film. She agreed to a role in *Broadway Thru a Keyhole* [q.v.] but allegedly took ill after one day and left the project; scuttlebutt was that she was uncomfortable with the man-eating character she was to play. In 1934, authorities threatened to repossess Joyce's villa in Italy; columnist Louella Parsons later reported that Joyce had agreed to appear in the Paramount musical *Collegiate*, but dropped out because her part was too small.[8] Maybe she decided she didn't need the money this time.

Melody Cruise
(RKO; June 22, 1933)

Director: Mark Sandrich. Executive Producer: Merian C. Cooper. Associate Producer: Lou Brock. Screenplay: Ben Holmes, Mark Sandrich. Additional Dialogue: Allen Rivkin, P. J. Wolfson. Photography: Bert Glennon. Editing: Jack Kitchin. Special Effects: Vernon L. Walker, Linwood G. Dunn. Musical Director: Max Steiner. Dance Director: Dave Gould. Art Directors: Van Nest Polgalse, Carroll Clark. Sound: Hugh McDowell, Jr. Synchronization and Sound Effects: Murray Spivack, George Marsh. Running Time: 75 minutes.

Cast: Charles Ruggles (Pete Wells); Phil Harris (Alan Chandler); Helen Mack (Laurie Marlowe); Greta Nissen (Elsa Von Rader); Chick Chandler (Hickey); June Brewster (Zoe); Shirley Chambers (Vera); Florence Roberts (Miss Potts); Marjorie Gateson (Grace Wells); Betty Grable, Marion Byron (stewardesses); Nat Carr (travel agency customer); Harry C. Bradley (passenger); Eddie Borden (onlooker at dock); Tudor Williams (singer); Nora Cecil (gossipy woman).

Songs: "He's Not the Marrying Kind" [female chorus, "danced" by Chandler], "Isn't This a Night for Love?" [Harris, chorus; reprised instrumentally for ice ballet], "This Is the Hour" [Harris, Nissen] (Val Burton, Will Jason).

Working Titles: *Maiden Cruise*; *Maiden Voyage*.

Home Video: Turner Home Entertainment VHS.

The Story: In New York City, playboy Alan Chandler and his businessman friend Pete Wells board a winter cruise ship bound for their native California. To keep from becoming too attached to his girlfriend, Elsa Von Rader, a drunken Alan writes a letter detailing Pete's many affairs, and has it sent to Pete's wife, Grace, with instructions it be opened only if Alan marries; that way, Pete will be a willing "chaperone." After attending a bon voyage party, Zoe and Vera sleep too late in Pete's stateroom and remain on board after the ship has sailed, so Pete bribes steward Hickey to keep the matter quiet, then asks him to keep Alan and Elsa apart. Alan romances fellow passenger Laurie, but she thinks he and Elsa are still an item. As the ship nears Los Angeles, Grace now has reason to suspect her husband. In California, Alan tries to win Laurie back ... but there's still the matter of that letter.

Best known for its early use of rhythmic dialogue and imaginative camera effects, *Melody Cruise* was touted by RKO as "the first musical movie conforming to screen rather than stage standards." It was not, as the studio implied, the usual tired backstager in which the action would stop dead for a singer with a theme song, or for a chorus line kicking in lockstep. Instead, it played almost like a cartoon, with kaleidoscopic cinematography, fantasy elements, fast pacing, quick cutting, sly comedy—but with the required feminine pulchritude. It wasn't the first of the movie musicals that moved to the new beat—music and dialogue were as closely aligned in two earlier American releases, Paramount's even-more-sophisticated *Love Me Tonight* and United Artists' *Hallelujah, I'm a Bum*, not to mention René Clair's 1931 French films *Le Million* and *À Nous la Liberté*. But *Melody Cruise* was unusual enough to attract plenty of attention upon its release in the summer of 1933.

This excursion had benefited from a dry run. In January 1933, RKO issued a three-reel musical comedy titled *So This Is Harris!*—the "Harris" being Phil Harris, the bandleader and vocalist in his fourth year at Los Angeles' Cocoanut Grove nightclub and heard on radio nationwide. Director/co-screenwriter Mark Sandrich, making his second sound feature after having cut his teeth on comic two-reelers since 1927, and producer Lou Brock, head of RKO's short subjects department, dreamed up a tale about a golfer who discovers his new-found links partner, played by the real Harris, is the syncopated rival for his wife's affections. *So This Is Harris!* would go on to win the Academy Award for best short subject. It affirmed RKO's reputation, under Brock's supervision, for entertaining short films with unusually high production values, with such promising directors as George Marshall and future Oscar winner George Stevens and cinematographers Nicholas Musuraca and Ted McCord.

The audience for *So This Is Harris!* would prompt a feature project by the same creative team. That team nearly did not include Phil Harris, as Ben Lyon and Nelson Eddy were originally linked to Harris' role in *Melody Cruise*, but Brock convinced studio brass that Harris—who'd not made a film before *So This Is Harris!*—could handle the part, especially another one as a chick magnet. *Melody Cruise* was shot in March and April 1933 as *Maiden Cruise*; a legal despite prompted a change to the final title just as shooting ended.[9] A publicity campaign was devised through a tie with the Cunard steamship line, whose ads assured readers that its excursions to Panama, South America, Havana, and elsewhere matched the gaiety and romance seen in *Melody Cruise*. As the June premiere approached, RKO threw a party on behalf of the film aboard the Aquitania, docked at Pier 54 in New York City, that aired on NBC radio's red network.

Throughout, Harris kept up regular gigs with his band. "Phil Harris is the busiest man in Hollywood," reported *The Film Daily*.

> He is on the *Maiden Cruise* set from 9 a.m. to 8 p.m., then rushes to the Cocoanut Grove, where he leads the orchestra and warbles over the radio until 1:30 a.m. This is followed by a combination dinner and breakfast. He then retires at 3 a.m., arises at 7 a.m. to make-up and be on the set again at 9 a.m.[10]

4. Big Ideas, Bigger Casts ... and Some Oddities 135

Charlie Ruggles, Paramount's dependable light comedian, was signed to team with neophyte actor Harris in the long-form venture, and the older man pretty much walks away with the film. Harris plays a socialite who, during a winter voyage from New York to California by way of Panama, converts his pal's infidelities into an insurance policy of sorts against marriage, but the scheme backfires when the playboy falls for a small-town-girl passenger (Helen

Playboy Phil Harris is tamed by Helen Mack in RKO's lively and innovative *Melody Cruise* (1933).

Mack). Ruggles' character spends most of the 75 minutes fretting over being found out—especially when two beauties are found half-clothed in his stateroom after a wild party. Says Ruggles: "How am I going to explain two women in my room?" Harris: "You know how to explain one woman in your room, don't you? ... Double it."

The creative plotting is nicely supplemented by a quartet of song numbers in which spoken dialogue functions as song lyrics, as opposed to other sections when what ought to be dialogue is sung. In "He's Not the Marrying Kind," a chorus of anonymous ladies waxes semi-poetic mooning over Harris' romantic reluctance, and the ship's crew swabs the deck in time to the melody. Even better is "Isn't This a Night for Love?"—which supplements Harris' serenade to Mack with a chorus of steerage passengers singing in foreign tongues, and is capped by the starry sky forming a shimmering design right out of a page of sheet music. Sandrich keeps things moving with a succession of creative wipes and dissolves, then uses a climactic special effect to illustrate the state of Ruggles' marriage as the contents of an incriminating letter are revealed. The inventiveness is apparent from the start, as sounds created by snowbound New Yorkers—a newsboy blowing on his hands, Wall Street stock tickers, a train whistle and chugging—establish a rhythm of sorts that make the balmy cruise to follow all the more appealing.

Despite the pretense of art, the film refuses to take itself seriously, with a series of laughably artificial back projections—filmed at Santa Barbara, Yosemite National Park, and elsewhere shown as Harris pursues Mack all over California, where she turns him down in a variety of settings.[11] A final-reel ice ballet sequence is disappointingly dull for a film meant to be so unconventional, although many reviewers in 1933 thought it one of the highlights of *Melody Cruise*. Mordaunt Hall of *The New York Times* liked all the singing and clowning, as did most critics, but he knew where the film's real distinction was: "... the imaginative direction of Mark Sandrich, who is alert in seizing any opportunity for cinematic stunts.... There are moments when it has a foreign aspect.... The characters in the beginning choose to talk in rhyme, but later they decide to discard the doggerel and converse more or less like ordinary human beings."[12]

Providing able support as an amorously curious steward, Chick Chandler was name-checked by Hall and many others. New to film after years on the stage, he was being built up by RKO in *Melody Cruise* publicity as "a new type of comedian who can deliver the 'mad Marxian humor.'"[13] It turned out he was no Groucho or Harpo, but he went on to a long movie career. Mack (1913–1986) and Greta Nissen (1905–1988) make appealing romantic options for the leading man. Mack had just made her first impact, in a dramatic role in *Sweepings* (1933), when cast in *Melody Cruise*, and she would be seen more widely within a few months in the mega-sequel *The Son of Kong*. The Norwegian-born Nissen impresses here in a rare sound-era role to showcase her talents, but her accent dimmed her career after the advent of sound.

Despite a lack of star power exemplified by Harris' lack of screen magnetism, *Melody Cruise* was liked enough by audiences to earn $150,000 at the box office.[14] RKO entrusted Brock with producing another travelogue musical: *Flying Down to Rio* (1933), which contained many of the same comedic and technical novelties as *Melody Cruise* but would become more notable as the first Fred Astaire–Ginger Rogers pairing. Less impressively, Brock would also be responsible for RKO's 1934 flop *Down to Their Last Yacht* [q.v.]. Sandrich helmed five of the nine Astaire-Rogers collaborations at RKO and was filming the Bing Crosby vehicle *Blue Skies* when he died in 1945 after a heart attack.

Harris (1904–1995) had a more spotty film resume. Music and radio celebrity—notably as a vain, jive-talking version of himself on ether shows with Jack Benny and future wife Alice Faye—would consume more of his career. However, his obituaries would be headlined by his crowning cinematic achievement: the voicing of Baloo the Bear in Walt Disney's *The Jungle Book* (1967).

Moonlight and Pretzels
(Universal; August 3, 1933)

Director: Karl Freund. Dialogue Director: Monte Brice. Producers: William Rowland, Monte Brice. Associate Producer: Stanley Bergerman. Screenplay: Monte Brice, Sig Herzig. Story: Monte Brice, Arthur Jarrett, Sr. Photography: William Miller. Editing: Robert Snody. Musical Director: Jay Gorney. Dance Director: Bobby Connolly. Sound: Frank MacKenzie. Running Time: 84 minutes.

Cast: Leo Carrillo (Nick Pappacropolis); Mary Brian (Sally Upton); Roger Pryor (George Dwight); Lillian Miles (Elsie Warren); William Frawley (Mac); Bobby Watson (Bertie); Herbert Rawlinson (Sport Powell); Jack Denny and His Orchestra, Frank and Milt Britton Band, Alexander Gray, Bernice Claire, The Eton Boys, The Girlfriend Trio, John Hundley, Doris Carson, Richard Keene (themselves); Len Mence, Louis Sorin (Hobart brothers); Alexander Campbell, Robert Conness (Wentworth and Jones, producers); James B. Carson, Max Stamm (beer drinkers); Donald MacBride (Hobarts' associate); Paul White (kid); Geraldine Dvorak (party guest); Doro Merande [Dora Matthews] (hymn singer); Mary Lange; "Fifty of New York's Famous Show Girls."

Songs: "Ah, But Is It Love?" [Pryor, Miles, Claire, Hundley, Miles, Eton Boys, Girlfriend Trio, chorus], "Baby in Your Hat" [Pryor], "Dusty Shoes" [Gray, Miles, chorus, Denny orchestra], "I Don't Need It Anymore" [Miles], "Let's Make Love Like the Crocodiles" [Pryor], "Moonlight and Pretzels" [Carson, Stamm, chorus, Brittons band] (E.Y. Harburg, Jay Gorney); "There's a Little Bit of You (In Every Love Song)" [Pryor, reprised by Brian] (E.Y. Harburg, Sammy Fain); "Are You Making Any Money?" [Miles], "I Gotta Get Up and Go to Work" [Keene, Carson, chorus] (Herman Hupfeld).

Working Title: *Shoot the Works*.

The Story: Stranded in a small town, songwriter George Dwight goes to work in Sally Upton's music store. After receiving a nominal royalty check for one of his tunes, he goes to New York City, signs with Hobart & Hobart Publishers, and becomes famous by writing tunes for musical comedy star Elsie Warren. George leaves the Hobarts in a dispute and decides to self-produce his next show, "Moonlight and Pretzels." Sally goes to visit George, who initially is too busy to notice her, and gets a job in the chorus. The new producers threaten to sell their controlling interest to the Hobarts, who sense a hit and want to own the production, so George teams with gambler Nick Poppacropolis to raise the needed funds. Nick's rival, Sport Powell, who wants to star Sally instead of Elsie, takes control of the show, but Sally flips a coin with him to win "Moonlight and Pretzels" on the eve of its premiere.

Universal's swift response to *42nd Street* was *Moonlight and Pretzels*, an independently produced, New York–filmed quickie that became one of the biggest movie musical hits of 1933. Seldom cited today as part of the vanguard of second-wave song films, it ought to be—upon its release, *The New York Times* called it "among the screen's most successful invasions of the musical comedy world."[15] The film features an energetic, if cinematically unheralded, cast and some entertaining production numbers—one of which, particularly topical in the depths of the Depression, remains especially impressive.

Moonlight and Pretzels was the brainchild of producers William Rowland and Monte Brice, whose company had been making a series of "Radio Shorts" for Universal, starring singers Art Jarrett and Arthur "The Street Singer" Tracy and newspaperman/poet Nick Kenny.[16] Brice knew East Coast talent well, as producer-director of one- and two-reelers in New York for Paramount since the dawn of sound. In March 1933, just as Warner Bros.' *42nd Street* was rejuvenating the genre across the country, Rowland and Bruce signed to produce a musical feature with backing by Universal and the Exhibitors Reliance Corporation. Universal hadn't made a musical since the financial flop *King of Jazz* in 1930, but the timing was right. Filming of *Moonlight and Pretzels* commenced on May 27, 1933, at the Eastern Service Studio, the former Paramount East Coast facility in Astoria, New York. Shooting at that Queens site was finished a month later, and the film was in theaters barely a month after that. According to historian Richard Koszarski, whose book *Hollywood on the Hudson* details the film's production history, *Moonlight and Pretzels*, which was produced for just over $139,000, went on to become Universal's most profitable film of the year by returning five times its negative cost.[17]

Using nearby—and, by Hollywood standards, inexpensive—talent kept the costs in check. The male lead, Roger Pryor (1901–1974), was a Broadway juvenile who had never made a feature; he landed a role initially announced for Lew Ayres and then Wallace Ford and went on to a moderately successful film career. The son of famous bandleader Arthur Pryor, he was behind top-billed character actor Leo Carrillo in the credits, presumably on name value. If Pryor in *Moonlight and Pretzels* reminded audiences of the rat-a-tat-tat style of Lee Tracy, it was no fluke: When Tracy was on stage in New York in *The Front Page*, Pryor was playing the same role in Chicago. And in the comedy *Blessed Event*, Pryor created the stage role that was played by Tracy on the screen.

The top female in the cast, Mary Brian (1906–2002), was an established Hollywood personality, but had been dropped by Paramount after nearly a decade as a contract player and was now free-lancing. Co-star Lillian Miles (1907–1972), a spunky blonde who had appeared in only one film, was a protégé of composer-pianist Al Siegel, who had helped develop Ethel Merman's nascent career. Supporting actor William Frawley, whose first feature this was, was straight out of vaudeville and Broadway; Herbert Rawlinson, cast as the heavy, was a declining leading man of the silents who came at no great cost from the stage. New York-based guest stars from radio and the stage—Bernice Claire, Alexander Gray, the Eton Boys, and the Jack Denny and Frank/Milt Britton bands—were booked for musical specialties, the dances for which were supervised on the stage of the Casino Theater by Bobby Connolly, a top choreogra-

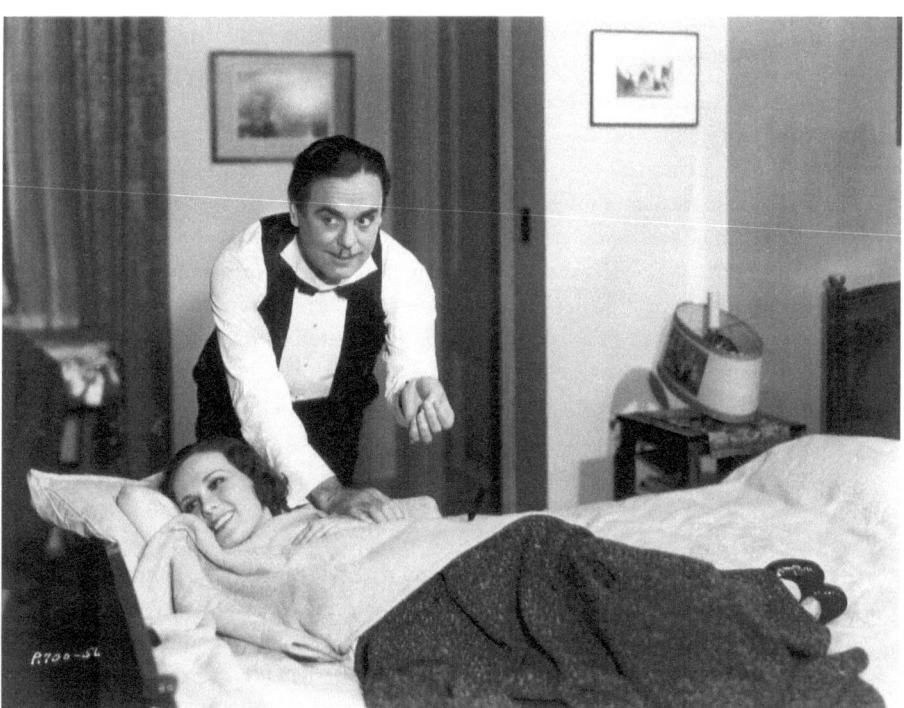

A gambler (Leo Carrillo) tries to get in good with a starlet (Mary Brian) in Universal's underrated *Moonlight and Pretzels* (1933).

pher whose credits included multiple editions of the *Ziegfeld Follies*. Alexander Gray and Bernice Claire were a well-known team in early sound operettas at Warner Bros., but their appearances in *Moonlight and Pretzels* were separate.

Studio-planted newspaper stories boasted of the film's use of 50 of "Broadway's most perfect show girls," hand-picked by "feminine beauty experts" from the chorus lines of *The Gay Divorce*, *Strike Me Pink*, and *Take a Chance*. The director of *Moonlight and Pretzels* was Karl Freund, Universal's top cameraman, who had worked in German silent and early Hollywood talkies—most notably on *The Last Laugh*, *Metropolis*, and *Dracula*—but had supervised only one film (*The Mummy*, 1932). He was promoted because studio mogul Carl Laemmle thought Freund could become the next great German filmmaker.[18] Laemmle dispatched his brother-in-law, producer Stanley Bergerman, to the East to keep a handle on the whole thing.

Brice's functional-enough screenplay concerns an egotistical songwriter turned Broadway producer and his battle against greedy financiers to mount his big show. Pryor's George Dwight boasts to would-be producers that he's written "279 songs here just to start with…. I got weather songs, moon songs, river songs, baby and mammy songs." Dismissively asked to leave until he's written a song about a crocodile, Dwight goes to the piano to play one already in his files. However, Dwight is perceptive and unselfish enough to warn the gambler (Rawlinson) who has seized control of the show and installed Sally, the untrained newcomer played by Brian, as its star: "You and I can't make stars … the people sitting out here do that," meaning the audience. Dwight loves the girl and doesn't want her tarnished by showbiz heartbreak. A seasoned pro goes on instead in this variation of the rising-star story in *42nd Street*: Sally doesn't win applause in the Ruby Keeler way, but she does triumph for non-performance reasons.

Dwight's stage production in *Moonlight and Pretzels* includes a lively beer garden number that bears the show's title; it's capped by over-the-top slapstick violence from the Frank and Milt Britton Band. The other songs are little remembered. "Ah, But Is It Love?" is sung by Bernice Claire, John Hundley, and the Eton Boys, among scores of others. "I Gotta Get Up and Go to Work," a domestic duet for guest singers Richard Keene and Doris Carson, and "Are You Making Any Money?," a suggestive Miles solo, were contributions from composer Herman Hupfeld, who would become much more famous for writing "As Time Goes By." Unfortunately, Miles would enjoy only a short movie career. She sang "The Continental" in the 1934 Astaire-Rogers musical *The Gay Divorcee* but became better known for her performance as a crazed, piano-playing drug addict in the exploitation film *Reefer Madness*.

The songs in *Moonlight and Pretzels* are catchy enough—"Ah, But is It Love?" was a radio success for Paul Whiteman—but narratively, such a prosaic tunesmith as Dwight would seem an unlikely source for the downbeat on-stage finale. Actually penned by lyricist E.Y. Harburg and composer Jay Gorney, "Dusty Shoes" presents baritone Alexander Gray in an eight-minute mini-epic touted by Universal as "a dramatic cavalcade of American life from 1928 to 1933." With the generous use of stock footage, and a giant stock market-modeled set with girls dancing atop rolls of ticker tape, the sequence takes us from Gray singing, amid a chorus of hoboes, of a future when his dusty shoes "will pound the street again," to a mournful reprise by Miles recounting the onset of the market crash, to Gray promising that his people will "tramp, tramp, tramp" to find work and forget the Depression blues. At the end, Gray is back in a business suit, and the hoboes are re-dressed for success.

The similarities of *Moonlight and Pretzels* to the new, bigger Warner Bros. musicals were not lost on reviewers in 1933. It really didn't seem to matter to *Photoplay*'s: "It keeps as close to *42nd Street* as it can. But you won't mind that a bit, because it's *fun*, put over by an excellent cast from stage and screen ... [in] a show well worth anybody's time."[19] The theme of "Dusty Shoes" was similar to that of Harburg and Gorney's 1930 song "Brother, Can You Spare a Dime?," which was heard in the stage musical *Americana* and as a radio hit, and to the Al Dubin and Harry Warren–written "Remember My Forgotten Man" number from Warner Bros.' *Gold Diggers of 1933*, which opened just before *Moonlight and Pretzels* began production, and historians dismiss the lower-budget variation. Richard Barrios has opined that the "Dusty Shoes" choreography was "quite deliberately stolen" from *Gold Diggers of 1933*.[20] The numbers aren't exactly the same — the more famous one is told from a female's point of view, and is a good bit less optimistic — and in a copycat industry like American cinema, "stolen" is a relative term.

Whatever its inspirational sources, *Moonlight and Pretzels* deserves to be something more than a footnote in the history of the early American film musical. It did not, however, lead to bigger and better things for the Rowland-Brice partnership. The two producers did not repeat their success with two more Astoria-shot musicals. "They said *Moonlight and Pretzels* was an accident!" went ads for the first, *Take a Chance* (Paramount, 1933); maybe "they" were right, for the result was a disappointing adaptation of the Broadway show, even with the talents of James Dunn, Buddy Rogers, Lillian Roth, and June Knight. The follow-up, *Sweet Surrender* (Universal, 1935, apparently now lost), failed despite the rare cinematic appearance of popular tenor Frank Parker and dancer-singer Tamara.

I Am Suzanne!
(Fox; December 21, 1933)

Director: Rowland V. Lee. Producer: Jesse L. Lasky. Story/Screenplay: Rowland V. Lee, Edwin Justus Mayer. Photography: Lee Garmes. Editing: Harold Schuster. Musical

Director: Louis De Francesco. Dance Director: Sammy Lee. St. Moritz Puppet Revue and Inferno Revue: Yale Puppeteers. Art Director: Max Parker. Sound: E. C. Ward. Running Time: 99 minutes.

Cast: Lilian Harvey (Suzanne); Gene Raymond (Tony Malatini); Leslie Banks (Baron aka Adolph Herring); Georgia Caine (Mama); Murray Kinnell (Luigi Malatini); Geneva Mitchell (Fifi); Halliwell Hobbes (Dr. Lorenzo); Edward Keane (Georges Valdon); Lionel Belmore (Satan); Scotty Beckett, Jane Withers (children in hospital); Edward Peil (reporter); Michael Mark, Tom Ricketts (puppeteers); Harry Semels (audience member); Podrecca's Piccoli Marionettes.

Songs: "Esk-i-O-Lay Li-O-Mo" [Harvey, chorus, reprised by Harvey, puppets], "Just a Little Garrett" [Harvey, Raymond], "Oh How I've Sinned," "One Word," "Rainy Day," "St. Moritz Waltz" [chorus], "Wooden Woman" (Forman Brown, Frederick Hollander).

Working Titles: *Marionettes*; *Puppet Show*.

The Story: Suzanne is a popular dancer in a Paris revue but is unhappy over being dominated by her manager, "The Baron." Tony Malatini, who owns a nearby puppet theater, watches Suzanne perform and is smitten; he wants to sketch her to create a puppet in her image. Conflicted between her loyalty to the Baron and her growing affection for Tony, Suzanne is injured during a performance and told she may never dance again. Suzanne joins the marionettes troupe as she recuperates, and Tony and his father create a successful show with puppets modeled on celebrities. Tony celebrates by having his puppets announce he and Suzanne are to be married, but she runs away—claiming "I am Suzanne! ... I will not be a puppet any longer!"— and shoots a gun at her puppet. She returns to the Baron and the revue, but her heart and mind aren't in her dancing. Impresario Georges Valdon puts the troupe, and Suzanne, under contract in competing shows. An anguished Suzanne dreams that the puppets put her on trial as an unbeliever and sentence her to be strangled in a spider's web. Encouraged by Tony, who admits his love for her as a human more than a puppet, Suzanne finally triumphs on stage.

For every Maurice Chevalier, Marlene Dietrich, or Charles Boyer who parlayed stardom in foreign-language films into Hollywood triumph, there were one or more like Lilian Harvey. The internationally famous star of light operettas spent two years making movies in America—none with the results she, nor audiences, desired. Her Hollywood career lasted four films, including the bizarre fantasy musical *I Am Suzanne!*—which seemed to portend a stateside breakthrough but only hastened Harvey's return to Europe.

The London-born, Berlin-bred daughter of a British mother and German father, Harvey built her movie career at the German company UFA, for which she made *Congress Dances* (1931), the musical that brought her a contract from Fox in 1933. That studio immediately set to work on promoting her to the American masses; it helped that Harvey had an elfin quality that reminded some of Fox's reigning queen, Janet Gaynor, only with Eurocentric elegance and a trained singing voice. Harvey (1906–1968) was, a fan magazine reported, "one star who can wear marabou and ostrich feathers and spangles and never look overdressed."²¹ Fox put Harvey in two musical comedies: *My Lips Betray*, opposite John Boles (and, for box office insurance, low comic El Brendel), and *My Weakness*, with Lew Ayres. The former was delayed in release, then rapidly disappeared. The latter, a *Pygmalion*-type tale from the creative team that produced the studio's *Sunnyside Up*, was savaged by critics.²²

By the third quarter of 1933, the Harvey experiment was not working, despite Fox's fervent attempts to promote her, even concocting romances with the likes of Gary Cooper, as *The Hollywood Reporter's* "Low-Down" column sarcastically reported:

> The Fox publicity department must be having one terrible struggle getting Lilian Harvey's name LINKED with that of some famous male star—for publicity purposes, of course, regardless of what the star herself may have in mind. It's getting so that every time a famous he-star sets foot upon the Fox lot, or finds himself saying so much as "Hello" to Miss Harvey, there or anywhere else, some studio photographer jumps upon them from nowhere, and requests them to pose for a picture. We happen to know that the Harvey-Cooper "romance" was only a press agent's dream.... Then they picked on Gene Raymond, and stories were printed that he was deluging the Harvey with orchids. Neither Gene nor Gary has petted Miss Harvey with so much as a daisy—but Gene could not, being a chivalrous lad, get out of posing with her on the studio lot, even though he sensed the yarn that would probably go with the picture. Maybe they'll get tired of it before long and print some photos of Miss Harvey with Willy Fritsch who, after all, IS supposed to be her husband, y'know.²³

Fritsch, Harvey's frequent co-star in Germany—and linked with her off-screen—was in Europe, but Raymond (1908–1998) was the male lead in Harvey's third Hollywood film, *I Am Suzanne!* Its filming in the fall of 1933 was a memorable experience for the star, but not for the right reasons. A mishap during an adagio number—reportedly the result of a chorister losing his hold on Harvey—left her black and blue, and an errant snowball thrown from the chorus during another number made her nose bleed. But the worst hurt was the broken left foot she suffered after a fall from a tightrope. Bailed up by bandages and tape, she finished the picture anyway. Her *Suzanne* character didn't have it so good, either, in what Fox touted as "a love story that lives and throbs against the world's strangest background." It was directed and co-written by the underrated filmmaker Rowland V. Lee, who had already demonstrated a talent for fantasy-tinged dramas with the sensitive *Zoo in Budapest* (1933), and produced by recent Paramount exile Jesse L. Lasky.²⁴ *I Am Suzanne!* is simultaneously a kiddie show filled with cute marionettes and a borderline-creepy examination of an artist's search for self-identity.

Suzanne (who doesn't seem to have a last name) is fought over, passive-aggressively, by her martinet theatrical manager (Leslie Banks, 1890–1952), a

A troubled dancer (Lilian Harvey) shows off her dance skills to a puppeteer (Gene Raymond) in the bizarre Fox musical *I Am Suzanne!* (1933).

fake count, and young puppeteer Tony (Raymond, perhaps miscast), who wavers between loving the real girl and the marionette he has created in her image. Both men claim their control by exclaiming "I am Suzanne!" yet attempt to grant her romantic freedom with the knowledge she cannot accept it. Even the ending is ambiguous: Tony seems to have won out, and Suzanne conquers her temporary fear of dance, but the count remains in her life. Suzanne's anguish is portrayed in a strange dream sequence in which she is put on trial by the marionette community and sentenced to be strangled in a spider's web as the puppet court cries "Choke her, hang her … kill, kill, kill!" This is followed by a finale in which a Satanic figure "pulls the strings" on humanity by exiling to hell a mother-in-law, a cross-dresser, and other undesirables, as Harvey materializes as if by magic from her marionette alter ego, only to be thrown around like a puppet. This definitely was daring, although a modern viewer might remark that *I Am Suzanne!* didn't trust its audience enough to delve deeper into its protagonist's psyche.

The puppets in the tale were from Italy's innovative Podrecca's Piccoli company. The prestigious, innovative troupe was known for its marionettes crafted in the guise of celebrities, and *Suzanne* offers a pleasing number with wooden versions of Charlie Chaplin, Garbo, the Marx Brothers, and, of course, Fox star Will Rogers. In another production number, "Esk-i-O-Lay Li-O-Mo," Harvey is guided down a tightrope to build a snowman, which comes to life only to melt at her feet. Fox reported that this sequence required a 300-foot-long winding slide built of plaster of paris and leading from high in the wings of a corner of a stage, around a miniature chalet and out into a supposed rink of ice, on a set designed by art director Max Parker. Lasky and his cohorts garnered publicity for the film by circulating a story about his insuring a chorus of 60 girls for $20,000 a head—a hefty sum for such an endeavor.

No matter the promotion, the entertainment value of *I Am Suzanne!* was high enough to bring positive early reviews. Mordaunt Hall's *New York Times* review saluted the Podrecca marionettes as much as Harvey, however: "*I Am Suzanne!* ... succeeds in being quite a fascinating diversion. If its story is inconsequential, the frailties are forgotten when the puppets strut their stuff."[25] Columnist Edwin Schallert of the *Los Angeles Times* praised the picture as "easily one of the most imaginative, and beautiful yet conceived for the talking screen."[26] Arthur Forde, the correspondent for England's *Hollywood Filmograph*, who had seen much of Harvey's European work, predicted a bright future for her in America: "Recent rumors about Lilian Harvey's popularity have all been settled now that Fox Films gave her such a fine and interesting production as the whimsical *I Am Suzanne*. It will not only establish her as a great favorite in these United States, but will increase her great drawing power with her myriad admirers in European countries."[27]

The "great favorite" prediction never happened. *I Am Suzanne!* did good business in major markets and made *The Film Daily's* "Roll of Honor" for 1934, but it underachieved outside the big markets. A complaint aired multiple times in trade reports from smaller cities concerned the length of the puppet sequences. In the wake of the disappointment, Harvey turned down—or was rejected for, depending on who is to be believed—a co-starring role in Fox's *George White's Scandals* (1934), thus opening the door to newcomer Alice Faye.[28] Harvey was announced for a reteaming with Lew Ayres for *Lottery Lover* [q.v.], which was temporarily shelved, and then assigned by Fox to *Serenade*, a Viennese story. To complicate matters, Harvey was now romantically involved with her protégé, German filmmaker Paul Martin. She aired her career grievances to *Picture Play* magazine in an interview headlined "Last Try for Lilian":

> Somehow, so far, I haven't jelled! ... Whose fault it's been, I don't know. All I can say is that I've tried my best and I believe the fault has been poor stories.... I shan't go on acting here in Hollywood if I'm given mediocre roles. I'd rather not take money I don't earn.[29]

By the time readers digested that article, Harvey was gone from Fox, her contract "torn up" by mutual consent, and new star Pat Paterson replaced her for *Lottery Lover* and *Serenade*. After one more U.S. production, the 1935 Columbia romantic comedy *Let's Love Tonight* (in which she sang only once), Harvey resigned with UFA and went back to Germany. The press there had gloated over her lack of success in Hollywood, but her return was greeted with open arms. Harvey made movies in Germany until her support of Third Reich enemies hastened her departure in 1939. She spent much of the '40s in the U.S., but her career in films was over, and *I Am Suzanne!* was on its way to being mainly overlooked.[30]

Down to Their Last Yacht
(RKO; August 25, 1934)

Director: Paul Sloane. Producer: Lou Brock. Screenplay: Marion Dix, Lynn Starling. Story: Herbert Fields, Lou Brock. Photography: Edward Cronjager. Special Effects: Vernon Walker. Editing: Arthur Roberts. Musical Director: Max Steiner. Dance Director: Dave Gould. Art Directors: Van Nest Polglase, Carroll Clark. Sound: Hugh McDowell, Jr., P. J. Faulkner, Jr. Running Time: 64 minutes.

Cast: Mary Boland (Queen of Molakamokalu); Polly Moran (Nella Fitzgerald); Ned Sparks (Captain "Sunny Jim" Roberts); Sidney Fox (Linda Colt-Stratton); Sidney Blackmer (Michael Forbes); Sterling Holloway (Freddy Finn); Marjorie Gateson (Mrs. Colt-Stratton); Irene Franklin (Mrs, Gilhooley); Charles Coleman (Sir Guy); Ramsey Hill (Geoffrey Colt-Stratton); Tom Kennedy (Joe "Uncle Ed" Schultz); Gigi Parrish (Patricia Gilhooley); Hazel Forbes (Corinne Palmer); Maurice Black (Joe Spilatti); Martin Cichy (Mr. Kussnagel); Dot Farley (Mrs. Kilpatrick); Phil Dunham (Mr. Weems); Betty Farrington (Mrs. Weems); Felix Knight (island singer); Crauford Kent (saxophone player); Al Kikume (native messenger); Virginia Reid [Lynne Carver], Helen Collins, Cynthia Hobart, Alice Moore, Harry Semels, Marie Wilson, Florence Wix (passengers); John David Horsley (youth); Tudor Williams.

Alternate Title: *Hawaiian Nights*.

Songs: "Beach Boy" [female vocalist, "native" chorus], "Funny Little World" [Fox, Gateson, Black, Farrington, Dunham, Franklin, chorus] (Ann Ronell); "South Sea Bolero" ["native" chorus] (Max Steiner, Ann Ronell); "There's Nothing Else to Do in Malakamokalu But Love" [Knight, chorus, twice] (Cliff Friend, Sidney Mitchell); "Tiny Little Finger on Your Hand" [Blackmer, chorus] (Val Burton, Will Jason).

The Story: Linda Colt-Stratton and her formerly wealthy parents are forced by the Depression to work at menial jobs and live on their yacht. Nella Fitzgerald charters the Colt-Strattons' yacht and hires them as "teachers" of social graces for a journey from the West Coast for newly rich commoners catered to by former bluebloods. Gambler Michael Forbes, who has fallen in love with Linda, sneaks on board to be with her. Captain "Sunny Jim" crashes the yacht aground on a South Sea island. On Malakamokalu, the "queen" forces the visitors to do her bidding, tries to decide who *will be her king, and the natives sing and dance. The queen grants her captives their freedom, but at the expense of their boat.*

Among aficionados of the 1930s movie musical, *Down to Their Last Yacht* is the *Heaven's Gate* of its day: a bloated flop that ruined the career of its producer, virtually ended the career of its lead ingénue, saw one of its supporting actors threatened with death, embarrassed its studio, and fully merited its oft-quoted panning by *The New York Times* as a "sorry mélange of Hollywood native dancing, theme-song singing, and preposterous comedy."[31] To that we say … yes!

This strange brew of Depression-period social satire and South Seas fantasy was the responsibility of Lou Brock (1892–1971), the former RKO short subjects department chief who had won the studio an Oscar for the three-reeler *So This Is Harris!* and graduated successfully to features with *Melody Cruise* [q.v.] and the inaugural Fred Astaire-Ginger Rogers musical, *Flying Down to Rio* (1933), the latter grossing an impressive $480,000.[32] Brock was relieved of his shorts duties and given free rein—sans Astaire and Rogers, who clicked despite being billed below official leads Dolores Del Rio and Gene Raymond on *Rio*. That film's aviation-minded stunt sequences marked an obvious attempt by Brock to out–Busby Warner Bros. master Berkeley. According to the studio's then-new production chief, Pandro S. Berman, Brock rebuffed an offer to oversee the first Astaire-Rogers starrer, *The Gay Divorcee*, with the comment: "I can blow better scripts out of my nose."[33]

Instead, Brock was announced to produce a self-penned musical, *Down to Their Last Yacht*, as well as two comedies, *The Great American Harem*, with Gloria Stuart and William Gargan, and *Cockeyed Cavaliers*, with the team of Bert Wheeler and Robert Woolsey.[34] "We haven't scratched the surface in screen musicals," the 42-year-old Brock told an Associated Press reporter in 1934.

> The backstage setting, so long a stand-by, is practically gone. The next step has been the "mechanical spectacle." Another cycle has been the screening of old and popular operettas. I believe things like those have had their day…, but for the screen of today we need novelty, new ideas, new stories, and departures in the manner of presenting them.[35]

For all his lofty visions of presentation, Brock tended to go light on guts, and that was certainly the case with *Down to Their Last Yacht*. The story, co-fashioned by Brock, mixed overly familiar themes of audience wish fulfillment—the monetarily rejuvenated masses being served by displaced bluebloods—and tropical isle class-culture comedy with roots not only in J.M. Barrie's play *The Admirable Crichton* but also in recent movies such as *Let's Go Native* (1930) and *We're Not Dressing*, the *Crichton* musical comedy adaptation filmed, and opened, by Paramount a few months ahead of Brock's film. Just as ominous of a warning sign was the *Yacht* cast, which was devoid of top-tier talent and relied on comedic players—Mary Boland, Polly Moran, Ned Sparks, and matronly vaudevillian Irene Franklin—more typically seen in support.

Even the romantic leads lacked sizzle. Sidney Fox (1907–1942), a coquettish brunette, was a former contract star at Universal (*Murders in the Rue Morgue*, *Once in a Lifetime*) who had stepped away to marry screenwriter Charles Beahan but now was ready to divorce her husband and jump-start her career. Her character of a rich girl turned poor mirrored her real-life experience as a native New Yorker. Sidney Blackmer (1895–1973), pushing 40, was a reliable second lead and heavy type who was on the upswing, newly signed to an RKO term pact. A more interesting ensemble player was Hazel Forbes (1910–1980), a blonde ex-showgirl who was making her screen debut after inheriting a reported $3 million estate from her recently deceased toothpaste heir husband.[36] In a story that broke nationally just after the filming, and before the release, of *Yacht*, Forbes was the victim of an attempted extortion scheme. She turned over to police two letters from an anonymous sender, demanding a total of $8,500 and

Producer Lou Brock, standing beneath the camera crane, oversees a tropical production number in his ill-fated *Down to Their Last Yacht* (1934) (courtesy University of Southern California Archives of the Cinematic Arts).

4. Big Ideas, Bigger Casts ... and Some Oddities 149

promising harm to her if she continued to act. But could she act? And could anybody in the cast sing?

With Paul Sloane, director of multiple Wheeler and Woolsey comedies at RKO among other films, at the helm, production on *Down to Their Last Yacht* began on the studio lot in April 1934 with a budget of $175,000; it grew by another $50,000 when RKO president B.B. Kahane approved extra funds in hopes of elevating the film to A-level status.[37] Brock used his burgeoning support to construct a massive island set that dazzled visitors such as the reporter from *International Photographer* magazine who described said island's artificial waterfall:

> "Can't" is an obsolete word in Hollywood.... On stages 8 and 9, in a space of 20,000 square feet, is this indoor pool. It is made of plaster to resemble granite and the water coming from a fire hose at full capacity falls 50 feet into this rock-bound pool. Around the edge of the pool are 50 cocoanut palms made of stuff by the artisans over in the trick department. On the synthetic bench of a lagoon is a 150 foot wrecked yacht. If you don't think this seems like the real thing, go and see *Down to Their Last Yacht*.[38]

Names linked in the trades to *Down to Their Last Yacht*—but unseen in the final 64-minute release—were pop singer Gene Austin, faded stars Molly O'Day and Wesley Barry, and comic Richard "Skeets" Gallagher. The production proceeded so slowly that Brock was forced to divide his unit into two: one headed by himself, one by Sloane.[39] The roster of extras grew, especially those for the film's capper—the tropical "South Sea Bolero"/"Beach Boy" dancing, drumming, and singing number. Increasingly temperamental, Brock began adding personnel; bosses at the studio, which was already in some turmoil after the resignation of short-term production chief Pandro S. Berman, were put on guard to make sure Brock asked for the proper in-house approval. For example, in a memo to Brock from Kahane, the producer was upbraided for his lack of economic oversight by using 56 dancers and 40 singers instead of the budgeted 21 dancers and 28 singers over a two-week period.[40] In a memo to another studio official, written as a strategy to attempt to reign in their spendthrift producer, Kahane complained, "We do not feel we can assign him more than one picture at a time.... This is far from an ideal way of proceeding with productions."[41]

Brock and Sloane finished shooting on July 5, but when the higher-ups saw what they had wrought, retakes of up to 25 percent of the film were demanded.[42] Sam White was brought in from directorial chores on RKO comedy shorts to helm the new scenes under Brock's supervision. Meanwhile, the studio's publicity machine was hard at work girding its potential audience for what it hoped would be an eager reception. A promotional contest landed one John David Horsley, 6 feet 2 with dark hair and blue eyes, with the title of "A Perfectly Desirable Man" by 5,000 American women; the honor won him a role in *Down to Their Last Yacht*, along with 23 other Adonises, for the island numbers.[43] Articles about Horsley failed to mention that he'd been in Hollywood for four years, mainly in bit parts, save for a featured role in the Poverty Row action drama *The Flaming Signal* (1933).

Advance text touted the "South Sea Bolero" dance finale as even better than the catchy "Carioca" of *Flying Down to Rio*, and "Beach Boy"—written by Ann Ronell, composer of "Who's Afraid of the Big Bad Wolf?" in Walt Disney's *Three Little Pigs* cartoon—garnered plenty of radio play after being recorded by Paul Whiteman and his orchestra. So was "There's Nothing Else to Do in Malakamokalu But Love," written by Cliff Friend and Sidney Mitchell. It was performed in the film by unbilled Felix Knight—who would be better known as Laurel and Hardy's co-star in the same year's *Babes in Toyland*—and a chorus of blacked-up island boys.

Then came the dawn. "Not a single drop of entertainment value can be wrung from this story," wrote the reviewer from *Photoplay*, and *The Film Daily* panned a "story of two-reel weight" that would satisfy an audience "that isn't too particular about rhyme or reason"[44] The fan magazine *Modern Screen* graded it with a "D": "It looks as if the studio planned to make a musical-to-end-all-musicals—and they succeeded in ending their own before the first reel was over. Such a jumbled-up mess deserves mention if for no other reason than to warn our good friends to save their money."[45] A column by Central Press correspondent James Aswell, who had just covered the Lindbergh baby murder trial for that Hearst Newspapers syndicate, used that reference in a particularly nasty evaluation: "If I were called upon to pick the 10 worst pictures of the year, I'd step down from the stand and proceed with the deadliness of a Hauptmann witness to tap the shoulder of *Down to Their Last Yacht* as a starter.... Or perhaps that would do for all 10."[46]

Why the venom? *Down to Their Last Yacht* begins somewhat promisingly, despite some shaky singing by the two Sidneys. The first half hour is social satire, as reverse class snobbery is mined for laughs—the *nouveau riche* are all gangsters, gamblers, tax cheats, and womanizers, and the cultured types are hard-working and noble on this boat ride containing, as the organizer played by Moran (1883–1952) puts it, "all the servants from the Social Register and all the passengers from the cash register!" Ronell's "Funny Little World," led off by Fox and picked up fragmentally by a succession of shipboard singers, sums up the situation nicely with its words of "topsy-turvy" times in which "he who once walked with a tootsie fair is a millionaire."

Where *Down to Their Last Yacht* runs aground is after the shipwreck on the oceanic dot of Malakamokalu, where the loudmouthed antics of the Caucasian monarch played by top-billed Boland (1880–1965) overpower the film. Some of the initially important characters all but disappear, and the final lengthy production number, definitely no Carioca (and no girls strapped to flying airplanes, as in *Rio*), stops the frenzied action in its tracks. "Perhaps the most that can be said for this musical potpourri is that it beats its competitors to the field by inaugurating the new tom-tom cycle," wrote the *Los Angeles Times* in a sarcastic tone.[47] The film ends on an oddly upbeat note: The island visitors, happy enough with their now-classless society, accept permanent captivity after the queen blows up their boat—but audiences must've been too tuned out to appreciate the message.

The result was that Brock's film was a $198,000 loser for RKO and would become known around the studio lot as the worst feature the company ever made.[48] Kahane observed reaction to it at two sneak previews and wrote to a studio colleague: "I never felt so sick at heart and disappointed at the reactions given any picture as was given *Down to Their Last Yacht*."[49] Brock was slated to make another "international" musical, *Adios, Argentina*, with Alice Faye and Tito Guizar and the dance team of Veloz and Yolanda, but that project was scrapped and the producer was let go in early November 1934. "Quietly and quickly shifting his affiliation," Brock moved over to 20th Century–Fox as an independent producer, in a move that "took the [film] colony by surprise," reported *Variety*.[50] Brock made no films at Fox, then went on to Universal, where he returned with 1937's *Top of the Town* [q.v.], but he never again wielded the clout he had in '34.

Sidney Fox fared even worse after *Down to Their Last Yacht*, which was the final film she made. (At bottom-rung Liberty Pictures, she appeared in *School for Girls*, a drama that was shot before *Yacht* but not released until 1935.) Fox endured her stormy marriage to Beahan until 1942, when she was found dead of what was officially called an "overdose of sleeping powders." She hadn't worked in three years.

Down to Their Last Yacht was shown frequently in late-late shows of the 1960s or thereabouts but is seen these days only in infrequent airings by Turner Classic Movies, from which modern audiences can decide if it's one of those so-bad-it's good novelties or one of contenders for the "worst movie of all time." After multiple watchings, we're still not certain.

Gift of Gab
(Universal; September 20, 1934)

Director: Karl Freund. Producer: Carl Laemmle, Jr. Associate Producer: Rian James. Screenplay: Rian James. Story: Jerry Wald, Philip G. Epstein. Adaptation: Lou Breslow. Photography: George Robinson. Special Photography: John P. Fulton. Editing: Raymond Curtiss. Musical Director: Edward Ward. Art Director: David S. Garber. Costumes: Vera West. Running Time: 70 minutes.

152   Unsung Hollywood Musicals of the Golden Era

Cast: Edmund Lowe (Phillip "Gift of Gab" Gabney); Gloria Stuart (Barbara Kelton); Ruth Etting, Ethel Waters, Phil Baker, Paul Lukas, Chester Morris, Roger Pryor, Binnie Barnes, [Boris] Karloff, Bela Lugosi, June Knight, The Downey Sisters, The Beale Street Boys, Graham McNamee, Gus Arnheim and His Orchestra, Gene Austin, Candy and Coco, Alexander Woollcott (themselves); Alice White (Margot); Victor Moore (Colonel Horatius Trivers); Hugh O'Connell (Patsy); Helen Vinson (nurse); Tom Hanlon (radio announcer); Douglas Fowley (Mac); Henry Armetta (janitor); Andy Devine (McDougal); Marion Byron (telephone girl); Sterling Holloway (sound effects man); Edwin Maxwell (Norton); Sid Walker, John "Skins" Miller, Jack Harling (stooges); Leighton Noble (orchestra leader); Maurice Black (auction shop owner); Tammany Young, Richard Cramer (mugs); James Flavin (alumni president); Warner Richmond (cop); Leonard Kibrick (freckled kid); Rian James.
Alternate Titles: *Let 'Em Rave*; *Smooth Gab.*
Songs: "Blue Sky Avenue" [Austin with Candy and Coco, twice], "I Ain't Gonna Sin No More" [Downey Sisters, Arnheim orchestra, reprised by Waters, Beale Street Boys, Arnheim orchestra, then again by Beale Street Boys], "Talking to Myself" [Etting, twice] (Herb Magidson, Con Conrad); "Don't Let This Waltz Mean Goodbye" [Noble, chorus] (Jack Meskill, Albert von Tilzer); "Somebody Looks Good" [Downey Sisters, Baker] (George Whiting, Albert von Tilzer); "Trivers Livers, I Love You" [Beale Street Boys] (authorship undetermined).
Disc: Columbia 2954-D ("Talking to Myself," Ruth Etting); Decca 141 ("I Ain't Gonna Sin No More," Ethel Waters); Victor 24725 ("Blue Sky Avenue," Gene Austin).

The Story: Phillip Gabney has "the gift of gab," but he talks himself in and out of various jobs. He is hired as master of ceremonies at radio station WGAB for a program sponsored by Trivers Chopped Chicken Livers company head Colonel Horatius Trivers. With help from program director Barbara Kelton and promotion by his friend Patsy, Gabney leads the "Trivers Livers Hour" to great success—and inflates his already outsized ego. "The Great Gabney" becomes a "radio reporter," but is barred from broadcasting a big football game after he punches a college official, so he broadcasts the game from the stands via a microphone in his lapel. A drunken Gabney awakens too late to attend a landing by a trans–Atlantic flier, so he fakes the broadcast without knowing the flier has been killed, then is fired. Barbara revives Gabney's reputation by sending him on a dangerous assignment to cover a plane crash in a remote area—into which he daringly parachutes. Gabney and Barbara are married on the air.

Gift of Gab was yet another radio revue, albeit with some interesting names and a meatier story than the usual upon which to hang the specialties. It attracted decent reviews, did so-so box office, disappeared into the Universal vaults—eventually to become coveted by fans of cinema icons who were both in the movie and not in the movie—and re-emerged after 65 years as not terribly worthy of all the attention.

The major attraction of *Gift of Gab* upon its release in the fall of 1934 was its top-billed player, Edmund Lowe, and a lineup of ether standouts headed by

Ruth Etting, Ethel Waters, Gene Austin (of "My Blue Heaven" fame), acerbic commentator Alexander Woollcott, Gus Arnheim and his orchestra, comedian-accordionist Phil Baker (doing his "absent-minded doctor" sketch), and Memphis-based newcomers The Beale Street Boys. The 70-minute film also featured a skit with Universal stars—among whom were horror masters Boris Karloff and Bela Lugosi—and a comedy act billed in ads as the Three Stooges. Given the fervor of the fan bases behind those performers, it's not hard to imagine why *Gift of Gab* was such a sought-after film for so long.

But first to 1934, when Rian James—the erstwhile newspaper columnist who was one of the writers on *42nd Street*—adapted a story co-written by radio wag Jerry Wald into a screenplay about a glib emcee/reporter and also functioned as the de facto producer on *Gift of Gab*. According to production records cited by historian Gregory William Mank, most of James' allotted $230,000 budget went to Lowe ($20,000) and the radio personalities.[51] Baker's $10,000 fee belied his latter-day obscurity in comparison to Etting, who was paid $7,000 to sing twice and appear in one other scene, and Waters, who got $2,500 to sing a number filmed in New York City.[52] Baker's segment wasn't filmed in the East, for he brought his "Armour Jester" radio troupe to Hollywood to do the show while he appeared in *Gift of Gab*. Etting, the renowned "Glorifier of American Song," never quite made it in the movies. Although she made many shorts, her feature-film appearances are sporadic and mainly limited to walk-on specialties, and *Gift of Gab* is one of the few full-length pictures in which she even has a smidge of dialogue.

Gift of Gab, helmed by Karl Freund and shot during July 1934, came at difficult times in the lives of Lowe and supporting player Victor Moore; Lowe had lost his wife, actress Lilyan Tashman, to cancer in March, and Moore's spouse, former actress Emma Littlefield, died in New York of post-operation complications on June 25. Lowe was a tad past his prime, but as a former headliner at Fox now free-lancing, he still had box-office clout. Gloria Stuart (1910–2010) was an appealing leading lady, and Alice White, Hugh O'Connell, and Sterling Holloway provided backing comedy. Universal promo ads made a big deal about Freund having directed the studio's *Moonlight and Pretzels* [q.v.], further verifying the earlier musical's hit status.

Although audiences did not turn out much for it, many reviewers liked *Gift of Gab* for its story as well as the name-novelty value. "Between dramatic suspense and the musical specialties there is never a dull moment," opined *The Film Daily*.[53] "Good music, swell dialogue, insanely amusing sequences; an appealing, if not original story, and grand performances throughout make this one of the best bets of the season," praised *The Hollywood Reporter*.[54] *The New York Times* dissented—saying, "It constitutes a minor miracle that the sum of so much talent should be such meagre entertainment"—as did *Variety*: "A hodge-podge of behind-the-mike goings-on ... cumbersome and never imports the realism that only an average technical supervision would have insured."[55]

Gift of Gab was soon forgotten as its release ran its course. But as decades passed, it became a tantalizingly "lost" film, especially as the only unavailable entry among the eight features in which Karloff and Lugosi both appeared. In 1999, a print turned up and was quickly circulated.[56] The results, to both horror mavens and Stoogephiles, were uniformly disappointing. The film verified documentation that the "Three Stooges" in *Gift of Gab* were not the Howard, Fine, and Howard seen in Universal's *Myrt and Marge* [q.v.] and countless Columbia shorts, but a knockoff threesome assembled (for one scene) when Universal could not acquire the services of the actual Stooges. Worse, the Karloff-Lugosi "teaming" was not precisely that: The "blood-curdling murder mystery" shown in the radio studio includes both men, but never on screen at the same time. Lugosi is seen standing in a closet as a gun-wielding tough for all of three seconds; Karloff, top-hatted and fright-wigged as the "Phantom," comes and goes

Bela Lugosi (far left) and Boris Karloff (sitting left) aren't seen on screen together in *Gift of Gab* (1934), but they are in this still, with Chester Morris, Douglass Montgomery (who didn't make the final cut), Roger Pryor, Paul Lukas, June Knight, and Binnie Barnes.

in about a minute. Binnie Barnes, June Knight, Chester Morris, Roger Pryor, and Paul Lukas join in the sketch, with Morris and Pryor portraying dimwitted detectives and Lukas reduced to playing a corpse![57]

It's pretty standard stuff, but at least we can see the sketch—and the rest of *Gift of Gab*—instead of just speculating about it.

Top of the Town
(Universal; March 26, 1937)

Director: Ralph Murphy. Executive Producer: Charles R. Rogers. Associate Producer: Lou Brock. Production Assistant: Sam White. Screenplay: Brown Holmes, Charles Grayson. Story: Lou Brock. Photography: Joseph Valentine. Special Effects: John P. Fulton. Editing: Maurice E. Wright. Dance Director: Gene Snyder. Production Designer: John Harkrider. Musical Director: Charles Previn. Vocal Arranger: Charles Henderson. Instrumental Arranger: Frank Skinner. Sound: William Hedgecock, Bernard Brown. Running Time: 86 minutes.

Cast: Doris Nolan (Diana Borden); George Murphy (Ted Lane); Ella Logan (Dorine); Hugh Herbert (Hubert); Gerald Oliver Smith (Borden executive); Mischa Auer (Hamlet); Gregory Ratoff (J. J. Stone); Peggy Ryan (Peggy); Jack Smart [J. Scott Smart] (Beaton); Ray Mayer (Roger), Henry Armetta (Baccigalluppi), Gertrude Niesen (Gilda Norman), The Three Sailors [Harry Blue, Bert Jason, Bob Robson]; The Original California Collegians; The Four Esquires; Claude Gillingwater (William Borden); Ernest Cossart (Augustus Borden); Samuel S. Hinds (Henry Borden); Richard Carle (Edwin Borden); Joyce Compton (Beulah); Verna Leslie [Frances Grant], Ethelreda Leopold (dancers); Willie Fung (prop man); Billy Wayne (painter); Sean Mor (elevator man); Alexander Melesh (designer); Harry Depp (secretary); Jack Chefe (waiter); Leonid Snegoff (Russian); Tom Herbert (comic waiter); Milton Shockley (porter); Lee Tong Foo (Chinese ambassador); Bud Flannigan [Dennis O'Keefe] (Frank); Zeffie Tilbury (club patron); Walter Byron; David Oliver.

Songs/Musical Numbers: "Blame It on the Rhumba" [Niesen], "Fireman Save My Child" [Herbert, chorus], "I Feel That Foolish Feeling Coming On" [Logan, chorus], "Jamboree" [Herbert, Logan, Collegians, Esquires, Niesen, Murphy, Ryan, company], "There Are No Two Ways About It" [Logan, Sailors, also danced by Ryan], "Top of the Town" [Murphy, Logan, Herbert, Smith, Auer, Ratoff, Ryan, Smart, Armetta, Mayer, Three Sailors, Niesen, reprised by male vocalist in Moonbeam Room], "Where Are You?" [Niesen] (Harold Adamson, Jimmy McHugh); "Anchors Aweigh" [danced by Three Sailors] (Alfred Hart Miles, Charles A. Zimmerman).

Disc: Brunswick 7818 ("Blame It on the Rhumba"/"Top of the Town," Gertrude Niesen); Brunswick 7837 ("Where Are You?"/"Jamboree," Gertrude Niesen).

The Story: Bandleader Ted Lane hires socialite Diana Borden for the chorus of his show at a supper club in New York. She is a showbiz neophyte who has just traveled to Russia and wants to bring "art" to nightclubs, but Ted hopes he can use her to convince her four uncles to hire him for the Moonbeam Room, a luxury club at the top of the 100-story skyscraper they own. Ted realizes that the uncles disapprove of Diana's new career and that she can't help him, but he falls in love instead of firing her. Ted gets the Moonbeam Room contract, but Diana learns of his original motive and leaves for Europe. Ted instead hires singer Gilda Norman, who carries a torch for him. Diana gains control of the Moonbeam Room and wants to open Ted's show ... but with a few high-minded changes.

After the triumphs of *Melody Cruise* [q.v.] and *Flying Down to Rio*, and then the catastrophe of *Down to Their Last Yacht* [q.v.], producer Lou Brock found himself in cinematic limbo for two years before he launched the second act of his career with another of his elaborate, oddball musicals. But *Top of the Town*, despite exhaustive studio promotion by the "new" Universal, ended up exhausting too-large amounts of cash—and, ultimately, the patience of too many who watched it.

In the wake of the *Yacht* crash in late 1934, Brock was let go by RKO, where he'd headed the shorts department before forging the Fred Astaire–Ginger Rogers partnership in *Rio*. He signed a six-month pact with Fox, where he sat idle despite talks with Cole Porter about a possible project and Alice Faye about an Argentina-set songfest, and complained "he could not find any story cooperation from officials."[58] He took the Porter and Argentina projects to Paramount in 1935, but with no more success. Brock finally connected at Universal for a "super-musical" titled *Everybody Sings*, and then retitled *Top of the Town*. This was not the cozy Carl Laemmle–led company, but the "new" Universal, acquired from foreclosure in 1936 after overspending on its production of *Show Boat*. Under new production head Charles Rogers, the budgets were mainly retightened. The company became solvent again on the strength of the screwball comedy *My Man Godfrey* and the Deanna Durbin vehicle *Three Smart Girls*—but Universal aimed for its first "million-dollar" musical to rival the extravaganzas at other studios.

Brock signed Bert Lahr to star in *Top of the Town*, but that fell through and Brock assembled a diverse cast headed by classy ingénue Doris Nolan (newly imported from Broadway) and happy hoofer George Murphy (from MGM), playing a heiress and bandleader who vie for artistic control of a luxury nightclub in New York City. Supporting them were radio singers Ella Logan and Gertrude Niesen, and 13-year-old dancer Peggy Ryan, all new to pictures; and a cavalcade of comics that included Hugh Herbert, Mischa Auer, Gregory Ratoff, Henry Armetta, Jack Smart, and "freak" contortionist act the Three Sailors.[59] Composer Jimmy McHugh and lyricist Harold Adamson supplied the songs, and Gene Snyder paused from directing New York's Radio City Music Hall Rockettes troupe to do the choreography. Walter Lang was tabbed to direct, but he was replaced—with illness the reported excuse—a month into shooting by Ralph Murphy. It really didn't matter who the director was—this was Brock's show, right down to his more-favorable billing on screen than the man behind the camera.

After many delays in a production initially slated to start in February

1936, *Top of the Town* was filmed between early September and December. Characteristic of Brock's style of supervision, there was a minimum of skimping. Except, perhaps, on the story, concocted by Brock—with unbilled help from famous humorist Robert Benchley—and scripted by Brown Holmes (*I Am a Fugitive From a Chain Gang*) and Charles Grayson, and the top of the cast, with promising but unproven Nolan (1916–1998) and Murphy (1902–1992).

The vaguely futuristic setting provided an excuse for production designer John Harkrider—a famous Ziegfeld show alumnus—to show off his Art Deco sets, the most gaudy of which was the 100th-floor "Moonbeam Room."[60] Reportedly 70 feet high, covering 40,500 square feet and able to accommodate 1,000, this set housed a climactic 17-minute sequence that must be seen to be believed. Nolan's high-minded heiress has transformed her former boyfriend's nightclub show into a somber ballet conducted by a mad–Italian maestro (Armetta, of course) featuring *Hamlet* recitations (by Auer), a blackface Greek chorus, and oppressed Russians toiling in a salt mine. With patrons sitting slack-jawed (as is the viewer), nodding off (maybe ditto), or getting up to leave, Murphy's bandleader revs up "Jamboree," a "bit of Harlem" swing number that gets the one-percenters up and dancing in their tuxes and gowns, abetted by members of Murphy's rejected troupe (Logan, Herbert, Ryan, et al.) who are conveniently on hand as hired help. At the fade-out, Murphy consoles a dejected Nolan, and the cast of a thousand is still dancing.

To promote a film it bragged was "mysteriously, magnificently mad," Universal distribution manager James R. Grainger promised what one report called "one of [the] most widespread national ad and exploitation drives in the history of [the] organization."[61] This included, among many examples, a stunt at the Motion Picture Theater Owners Association convention in Miami in which Grainger

> employed two very striking young blondes in the most abbreviated of bathing suits and had them hand out matches advertising *Top of the Town* to arriving delegates. Introduced by names, the conventionites reacted. A slant on the blondes makes the reason why understandable.[62]

The strategy seemed to be working. By late March, on the day of the New York premiere of *Top of the Town* at the Roxy Theatre, the studio reported an impressive 98 first-run bookings, 60 of which were to show the film on the national opening week of April 16.[63] That was the good news; the bad news was that meant people were about to see what *Variety* called "a bundle of mediocrity ... one of the greatest conglomerations of just fair talent any filmusical has offered."[64] *The Billboard* dismissed it as "just a series of variety turns strung together by a weak story," but *The Film Daily* countered with a differing view of "an admirable departure from the routine treatment of musicomedies."[65]

As was not infrequently the case, *The New York Times* (via Frank S. Nugent) was the most unforgiving:

> Through some unaccountable oversight, Universal omitted the kitchen sink, but it tossed practically everything else it could into its new musical colossus.... Everything, that is, except a sense of humor, a semblance of continuity and the veriest morsel of credibility.... Without them, the picture is just a big and dumb variety show....[66]

Whether or not it was "dumb," it was no surprise that *Top of the Town*'s exorbitant budget and non-matching box-office returns made it a big money-loser. The settings and production values are first-rate for 1937, but the plot is too thin. Perhaps the biggest problem is Doris Nolan, who comes off like Katharine Hepburn had The Great Kate been cast in a 1930s Universal musical. (Nolan played the sister of Hepburn's character in *Holiday* in 1938.) Without any sense of the comic timing needed in such a film, Nolan seems not to be in the same movie as the rest of the cast. We get a hint of this from the creatively staged opening credits, as each of the main actors sings a few words of the title song—except Nolan, who just stands there. In a 1990s interview with author Anthony Slide, Nolan aired her frustrations with the assignment:

> I read the script, and I said, "I can't do it. This is ghastly. Here I am, a dramatic actress, and you're having me waltz through as a rich society lady, doing nothing. I'm surrounded by singers and dancers. Nothing to do!" Universal said they had groomed me for stardom, that this was a big production, and I had to do it.
>
> I couldn't sing. I couldn't dance. I just wore these costumes, all these fancy clothes. I was surrounded by comedians, the equivalent of goons. I was beautifully photographed, but I had absolutely nothing to do except walk through it. The picture was a crashing failure ... a big flop.[67]

Nolan made only a few films in Hollywood before returning to the stage. She married Canadian actor Alexander Knox and moved to England after he was blacklisted from Hollywood in the 1950s.

Much better in *Top of the Town* are the secondary females, especially Ella Logan, a spunky Scot with a comic touch and a comfort with the camera that should've been used more often than it was in films. She's especially appealing while dressed as a sailor for the "There Are No Two Ways About It" number, which introduced the future standard. Little Peggy Ryan also shines after introducing herself as "an Eleanor Powell imitator"; this was actually true, as the real girl initially attracted moviedom's attention by a smash impersonation of the tap star at an Actors Fund benefit. Niesen gets to sing McHugh and Adamson's "Where Are You?," which became a standard as recorded by Mildred Bailey, Frank Sinatra, and, most recently, Bob Dylan (for his 2015 album, "Shadows in the Night").

Top of the Town is rarely seen nowadays, having last showed up in USA Network showings in the 1980s. By then, most of its principals were either long retired or long gone; among the latter was Lou Brock. After producing one more feature, the radio-themed melodrama *Behind the Mike* (1937), he was

Song-and-dance man George Murphy and miscast dramatic actress Doris Nolan duet in the Universal (and universal) flop *Top of the Town* (1937).

back at RKO heading the shorts unit, supervising, writing, and sometimes directing subjects starring Leon Errol, Edgar Kennedy, and cowboy singer Ray Whitley. He collaborated on the script of another full-length musical, *They Met in Argentina* (1941); it was so bad that co-star Maureen O'Hara pleaded with her agent not to have to do it, and, despite the inclusion of Rodgers and

Hart songs, it lost $270,000 for RKO.[68] After the last musical with which he would be entrusted, Brock was booted again from his original studio.

The decline from there proceeded more slowly. Brock finished his career as a producer or associate producer of low-budget features at Producers Releasing Corporation, Republic, and Monogram. Among his finales were the PRC "prestige" family-minded fantasy *The Enchanted Forest* (1945, filmed in Cinecolor) and two Monogram thrillers, *The Shadow Returns* (1945) and *Behind the Mask* (1946), based on radio's famous "Shadow" series. He produced a pair of exploitation-type pictures at Republic: *Flame of Youth* (1949), on juvenile delinquency, and *Prisoners in Petticoats* (1950), a women-in-prison drama. His last recorded credit was as a "segment producer" in the 1953 compilation film *Merry Mirthquakes*.

Brock died of a heart attack in Los Angeles in 1971. His obituary in *Variety* stated he'd been retired for 15 years, although his final reported vocation was as the night clerk at a Hollywood hotel.[69] Such would not have been a predicted end for this neglected figure in the history of the early Hollywood musical who torpedoed his career through artistic excesses and questionable decisions ... but that's entertainment.

New Faces of 1937
(RKO; July 1, 1937)

Director: Leigh Jason. Executive Producer: Samuel L. Briskin. Producer: Edward Small. Screenplay: Nat Perrin, Philip G. Epstein, Irving Brecher. Adaptation: Harold Kusell, Harry Clork, Howard J. Green, based on the story "Shoestring" by George Bradshaw and the sketch "A Day at the Brokers" by David Freedman. Photography: J. Roy Hunt. Special Effects: Vernon L. Walker. Editing: George Crone. Musical Director: Roy Webb. Dance Director: Sammy Lee. Vocal Arrangements: Charles Henderson. Art Director: Van Nest Polglase. Sound: John Tribby. Costumes: Edward Stevenson. Running Time: 100 minutes.

Cast: Joe Penner (Seymore Seymore); Milton Berle (Wallington Wedge); Parkyakarkus [Harry Einstein] (Parky); Harriet Hilliard (Patricia Harrington); William Brady (Jimmy Thompson); Jerome Cowan (Robert Hunt); Thelma Leeds (Elaine Dorset); Lorraine Krueger (Suzy); Tommy Mack (Judge Hugo Straight); Bert Gordon (Count Mischa Moody); Patricia Wilder (Hunt's secretary); Richard Lane (broker); Dudley Clements (stage manager); William Corson (assistant stage manager); George Rosener (doorman); Dewey Robinson (Joe Guzzola); Harry C. Bradley (Count Moody's secretary); Lowe, Hite, & Stanley, The Brian Sisters, Derry Deane, Eddie Rio and Brothers, The Loria Brothers, Ann Miller, The Three Chocolateers, The Four Playboys, Mary [Frances] Gifford, Mary Louise Smith, Betty Johnson, Harriett Brandon [Jan Wiley], Beatrice Schute [Hillary Brooke], Juanita Fields, Cynthia Westlake (themselves); Harry Bernard (bridge guard); Robert Emmett O'Connor (police officer at audition); Sidney Kibrick (kid at audition); Louise Carver (woman at audition); Jan Duggan (singer at audition); Skeets Herfurt (preacher in "Peckin'" number); Mil-

dred Boyd (maid in "Peckin'" number); Catherine Brent; Dorothy Roberts; Camille Soray [Julie Gibson]; Rene Stone; Diane Toy.
Songs: "If I Didn't Have You" [Hilliard, Brady], "It Goes to Your Feet" [Four Playboys, danced by Lowe, Hite & Stanley, Krueger, chorus], "Love Is Never Out of Season" [Brady, danced by Hilliard, Rio Brothers], "Our Penthouse on Third Avenue" [Hilliard, Brady] (Lew Brown, Sammy Fain); "New Faces" [Brian Sisters, chorus; danced by Miller, then sung by Hilliard, chorus] (Charles Henderson); "Peckin'" [Three Chocolateers, company] (Harry James, Ben Pollack, Edward Cherkose); "When the Berry Blossoms Bloom" [Penner] (Joe Penner, Hal Raynor); "The Widow in Lace" [Leeds, Loria Brothers, chorus] (Walter Bullock, Harold Spina).
Working Title: *Young People.*
Home Video: Warner Archive DVD.

The Story: Stage producer Robert Hunt puts on intentionally bad shows; he makes a killing on his flops by selling backers excessive percentages of the productions and pockets the extra funds; a successful show would leave him heavily in debt. Patricia Harrington, a chorus girl in Hunt's latest effort, complains when business manager Wallington Wedge announces the removal of one of the "good" numbers, and the show crashes. Patricia's boyfriend, Jimmy Thompson, has written a show called "New Faces" but can't get anyone to read it, so Patricia gives Hunt $15,000 to produce it. Hunt launches a national search for fresh talent for the show, then ignores all the good auditions in favor of mediocrities like Seymore Seymore. When leading lady Elaine learns of Hunt's scheme, he "disappears," leaving the inept Wallington in charge, Patricia as the new star, and Seymore out. Wallington learns of Hunt's plan for the show, loses all his money to a shady stockbroker and again oversells "New Faces"; Seymore is rehired, then fired again after Wallington wises up. At an Atlantic City preview, Seymore sneaks on stage to sing and clown, and the elaborate "Peckin'" number makes "New Faces" a hit. Jimmy talks the backers—three of whom each bought 85 percent of the show—into dividing the profits evenly.

"If vaudeville be dead, it's buried here," wrote a *New Yorker* critic of *New Faces of 1937*.[70] So much for RKO's promotional ads that promised "a hundred new faces and a thousand new ideas!" for a corpulent musicomedy that was just another excuse to drag in a bunch of radio personalities for flabby humor, overlong sketches, and so-so songs. It was somewhat telling that there was no cinematic *New Faces* of 1938 or 1939, but this film was a precursor of sorts to *The Producers* and helped to spawn Albert Brooks.

New Faces of 1937 was RKO's attempt to emulate the *Big Broadcast* films at Paramount. It was produced by Edward Small, who spent his four decades-plus career making movies, mainly as an independent. Among his most notable releases were *I Cover the Waterfront* (1933), *Brewster's Millions* (1945), *The Fuller Brush Man* (1948), and the noir classic *Kansas City Confidential* (1952). Meanwhile, stage producer Leonard Sillman had mounted Broadway revues with bona fide newcomers under the *New Faces* titles in 1934 (with Henry Fonda and

Imogene Coca) and 1936 (Coca and Van Johnson). RKO obtained permission from the Sillman show rights holders to use the title *New Faces of 1937*, which was announced in November 1936 as an attraction with all-new picture talent.[71]

Well, not all "new," at least depending on a strict definition of the word. Radio comics Joe Penner and Parkyakarkus had appearing in films fairly recently (Penner in Paramount's *College Rhythm* and *Collegiate*, Parkyakarkus in the Eddie Cantor musical *Strike Me Pink*). Parky (1904–1958) was the Cantor radio show's "Greek" comedian—he'd changed his stage name from Harry Einstein and adopted the new moniker—and the zany, simpering Penner (1904–1941) hosted his own radio show, on which he clowned with his famous "Wanna buy a duck?" catchphrase and exaggerated giggles. The third of the film's three key funnymen was brash, big-toothed Milton Berle (1908–2002), who had appeared in a few silent films as an uncredited child actor but who essentially was making his feature-film debut. Berle was a stage headliner, praised by *Variety* as "a major phenomena [sic] of post–Hoover Broadway" (Hoover being Herbert, not J. Edgar) and was already both celebrated and reviled for his freely admitted lifting of other people's gags.[72] During the shooting of *New Faces*, Berle brought *Community Sing*, his Sunday night CBS radio show, west with him, with supporting player Tommy ("Judge Hugo Straight") Mack and writer Irving Brecher joining him with the film.[73] Despite Berle's emerging career, his best years were ahead of him, of course.

Also in support: Bert Gordon, aka "The Mad Russian," another of Cantor's comics. The film's female lead—Harriet Hilliard (1909–1994), half of TV and radio's future Ozzie and Harriet—had just made a splash in her film debut opposite Fred Astaire in *Follow the Fleet*, and second lead Thelma Leeds (1910–2006) had come from the New York stage and appeared fleetingly in *Follow the Fleet*, so they were only fairly "new." But as this was *New Faces of 1937*, actual new faces had to be found. Tryouts for the film were highly publicized and heavily attended.[74]

In March 1937, a *Washington Post* reporter watched a *New Faces of 1937* tryout in Hollywood—a Depression-style *American Idol*–type cattle call. The story, headlined "Pathos, Bathos Blend During Search for New Talent Worthy Screen Place," revealed more desperation than ambition in the participants.

> [T]he amateurs were there, hundreds of them, young and middle-aged, beautiful and plain, talented and demented. Everyone thought he could do something.... Tenors, basses, contraltos and voices difficult to determine. Adolescent sopranos twitted into the microphone and lady sopranos with big bosoms sighed dismally for perfect lovers they never had.
>
> Everyone seemed nervous.... There was one man—he must have been almost 40.... He began an eccentric dance ... [b]ut he was so pathetic, in his eager, frightened

fashion, that the judges were touched; they politely applauded him.... Too late, for everyone realized the applause was a mistake. It encouraged the dancer to an encore.... He ran across the stage, circled and leaped in the air; he landed on his head. It was funny the first time, but he repeated it over and over again. In a moment it was painful. The judges looked at one another and stopped the pianist. The dancer ran to them, like a friendly dog, and bowed.[75]

Still, the search yielded the movie's romantic lead, William Brady, discovered singing in a New York nightclub; not long prior, he'd been Bill Brady, teen tenor from Washington, D.C. He plays a young librettist—and boyfriend of Hilliard's character—who seeks to get his *New Faces* produced, only to be thwarted by a producer (Jerome Cowan) whose racket is to make intentionally lousy shows and pocket the money from extra financial shares sold to unknowing backers. Berle and Parkyakarkus portray the producer's toadies; Penner is the spectacularly untalented comic who keeps getting hired and fired, depending on who is in charge and whether they're on the up and up.

Besides Brady (1913–2003), there are other new acts, some of which stuck around in movies after *New Faces* was filmed:

William Brady makes eyes at Harriet Hilliard (the future Harriet Nelson) in RKO's problematical *New Faces of 1937*.

- Lorraine Krueger, a pretty, blonde dancer from St. Louis, was cast as Joe Penner's girlfriend. She dances to the song "It Goes to Your Feet" in the film and appeared in movies until the mid '40s.
- The Loria Brothers were seven "Mexican jumping beans" discovered by an RKO talent scout singing on radio and in clubs in New York, but they actually were from Mexico. They can be seen in the first-reel "Widow in Lace" number.
- Lowe, Hite & Stanley were a vaude team consisting of a midget, a normal-sized man and a "giant" ranging in billed height from 3-foot-2 to 7-foot-9 (although the super-tall Henry Hite was probably closer to 7-6. They cut up with Joe Penner in a scene in an audition line, and dance to "It Goes to Your Feet."
- Derry Deane was a 4-year-old, violin-playing, curly haired Shirley Temple look-alike from Michigan who performs a brief instrumental solo.
- Eddie Rio, a New Yorker, does a skillful comic pantomime of a woman taking a bath (it was almost rejected for the film after PCA condemned it for "vulgarity"). He and his brothers dance with Hilliard in the "Love Is Never Out of Season" number.
- The Four Playboys, a singing and instrumental quartet from Minnesota, had been appearing on Ben Bernie's radio show. They perform "It Goes to Your Feet."
- The Brian Sisters, a vocal trio from Idaho with siblings aged 8, 10, and 12, are seen briefly in the final-reel "New Faces" number. They appeared to better advantage in an "Our Gang" comedy and in a few 20th Century–Fox musicals.
- Ann Miller, a lanky, 14-year-old dancer from Texas, was spotted in a San Francisco club by actor-writer Benny Rubin and brought to the attention of RKO.

Miller launched her lengthy Hollywood career in *New Faces of 1937* with a solo dance in the "New Faces" number. A segment showcasing showgirls yielded our first glimpses of future movie notables Frances Gifford, Hillary Brooke, and Jan Wiley. Other "new faces" signed for the film were so unlucky to not be seen at all, as their footage was cut.[76]

Another newly "discovered" act was The Three Chocolateers, an African-American trio from California who, according to RKO's official account, created the "dance sensation" that was the basis of the film's climactic number, "Peckin.'" Needing new material for their act, the three happened to pass a chicken farm and were enthralled by the birds' head-bobbing while eating.[77] They added the moves to their act at the San Francisco Cotton Club and gained the attention of bandleader Ben Pollack, whose cornetist Harry James met with the Chocolateers and helped set their dance to music that was interjected into *New Faces of 1937*. The number begins as the Chocolateers "peck" on a farm set, which transforms into a Harlem-style nightclub (where the trio serves chicken!), and then to a bridal boudoir—and the nuptials of Hilliard and Brady as the entire company thrusts heads at each other. This "new dance sensation" didn't do much for the Chocolateers in film, but it landed them spots with Duke Ellington and Tommy Dorsey and solo gigs at the prestigious Apollo Theatre in New York.

The sum total of this talent—new and old—was less than RKO hoped for. *New Faces of 1937* garnered mixed reviews, and lost $258,000 for the studio.[78] Edward Small severed his ties with RKO even before its release, and Harriet Hilliard was so unhappy with her assignments that she requested, and gained, her release. In mid–June, just before the film's July 1 debut, RKO announced—and trumpeted in trade ads—that it was planning a *New Faces of 1938*, based on positive response during previews for *New Faces of 1937*, but the studio eventually canceled what was envisioned as a series. *The Film Daily* thought the film "built for laughs ... one of the funniest pictures screened in many moons," but *Variety* blasted it as "a hodgepodge of vaudeville, night club and radio talent, unskillfully blended and rather inanely promulgated."[79]

What was the problem? It doesn't help that Brady lacks charisma; Hilliard's husband, bandleader Ozzie Nelson, might've been a better choice. Many reviewers declared the 100-minute film overlong by 20 or so, and RKO historians Richard Jewell and Vernon Harbin, citing studio records, targeted audience and theater owner hostility toward the Penner and Parky antics.[80] Berle's performance earned him a long-term contract at Radio (where he and Ann Miller would make *Radio City Revels* in 1938), but our thought is that there's too much of him. His sketch with Richard Lane as a shady stockbroker goes on for nearly 10 minutes and could've been easily excised—but many reviews praised the sketch (originally penned for vaudeville by former Eddie Cantor writer David Freedman) as the film's comedy highlight. So there weren't many easy answers for the *New Faces of 1937* problem, except that it wasn't very new and certainly not very good.

However, people do recall it now for its similarity to Mel Brooks' *The Producers* (1968), which also concerned intentionally bad productions but was much funnier; no plagiarism is likely, as schemes such as the ones in both movies stemmed from a longtime showbiz meme. What's lesser known is that, had not *New Faces of 1937* been made, we might not have been blessed with the talents of Oscar-nominated comedian-actor-writer Albert Brooks. His parents were Harry (Parkyakarkus) Einstein and Thelma Leeds, who married after meeting during pre-production of *New Faces of 1937*. Movies have had lesser legacies than that.

5. Dancing Down Poverty Row

If bigger musicals were better musicals, as so many moviemakers have believed (judging by the previous chapter), then wouldn't the term "Poverty Row musical" be an oxymoron? Well, no. The small independents made feature-length musicals, too—even in the economically challenging 1930s. The actors may have come cheaper, the production numbers (if there were production numbers) less elaborate, and the songwriting talent, as with the sets and equipment for many companies, often rented out or hired on a freelance basis. Many an actor or composer on the way up or the way down partook of the lower-rung songfests. And if audiences in the big cities may have turned up their noses, patrons in smaller towns or urban neighborhood theaters found these films suitable diversions. Of course, given the complicated (and sometimes haphazard) ways in which indie films were distributed by a series of exchanges around the country, some smaller movies were seen several months, or longer, after their initial releases—or, sometimes, not at all in some locales.

Not all of the Poverty Row outfits—and we use "Poverty Row" as much as a reference to the level of filmmaking as we do the geographical location that loosely inspired the term—produced musicals. Some, especially the smallest, preferred to concentrate on Westerns or other action-oriented stories, or perhaps society dramas, which could be cheaply made. Others dabbled in song— Tiffany-Stahl produced one of the very first sound musicals, *Lucky Boy* [q.v.], and Liberty, Monogram, Chesterfield, and Invincible took some stabs at the genre.

The early '30s saw many Poverty Row companies in the movie biz, as the major studios' restrictive policies regarding distribution beyond their established theater chains created the need for product at non-affiliated movie houses. However, the indie field narrowed significantly in 1935 with the formation of Republic Pictures. Behind the new concern was Herbert J. Yates, the president of the film processing laboratory Consolidated Film Industries, whose firm did work for many Poverty Row companies (and which frequently owed him money). Ambitious to become a studio boss himself, Yates forged the union of six small companies—Chesterfield, Invincible, Liberty, Majestic, Mascot, and Monogram—into Republic as a production and distribution entity. Yates built a credible roster of contracted performers, directors, and writers for his studio. He assumed artistic control to go with his financial power by nudging out Nat Levine, the former Mascot president who had been a reluctant partner, and forcing the former Monogram heads, W. Ray Johnston and Trem Carr, into departing to form a "new" Monogram.

Republic's first big successes were the Westerns of John Wayne and singing cowboy Gene Autry, but the company produced many conventional musicals. Among the company's initial releases were *Harmony Lane* (1935), a drab biopic of composer Stephen Foster, and *Follow Your Heart* (1936), for which the studio gained attention for its pairing of operatic luminaries Marion Talley and Michael Bartlett. But Yates would use the form to foster his ambition—and attempt to rival the majors—with Republic's 1937 productions of the bigger-budget musicals *The Hit Parade* and *Manhattan Merry-Go-Round* [both q.v.].

Of the former, the *Cleveland Plain Dealer* opined: "Maybe *The Hit Parade* didn't cost a million, but it looks like it—and best of all, it happens to be worth that much, anyway."[1] That was exactly what Herb Yates wanted to hear.

The Phantom Broadcast
(Monogram; April 15, 1933)

Director: Phil Rosen. Producer: William T. Lackey. Screenplay: Tristram Tupper, from his story "Phantom of the Air." Photography: Gilbert Warrenton. Editing: Carl Pierson. Art Director: E.R. Dickson. Sound: J.A. Stransky, Jr. Running Time: 72 minutes.

Cast: Ralph Forbes (Norman Wilder); Vivienne Osborne (Elsa Evans); Arnold Gray (Grant Murdock); Gail Patrick (Laura Hamilton); Paul Page (Dr. Robert Brooks); Pauline Garon (Nancy); Guinn "Big Boy" Williams (Sandy Higgins); Rockliffe Fellowes (Joe Maestro); Harland Tucker (program manager); Carl Miller (Lefty Morris); Mary MacLaren (Beth); George Nash (artist); Althea Henley (model); George ["Gabby"] Hayes (police lieutenant); Louise Beavers (Penny); Kit Guard (tough guy); Henry Hall (Thornton); Dick Rush (police officer).

Songs [all performed by Forbes/Gray/voice double]: "My Good-bye to You," "Out Where the Moonbeams Greet the Morning" [three times], "Tell Me Once More," "There's Nothing That Matters But Love" (George Waggner, Norman Spencer, Bernard B. Brown).

Working Title: *False Fronts.*
Also Known As: *Phantom of the Air.*
Home Video: Alpha DVD; Sinister Cinema DVD.

The Story: Radio singer Grant Murdock sends romantic notes to some of his female fans; among them is Elsa Evans, who vows she will marry the crooner. lsa's associate, gangster Joe Maestro, wants Elsa to seduce Murdock into signing a contract with him, but Murdock's manager and piano accompanist, Norman Wilder, a hunchback, is a roadblock to the deal. The reason: Wilder's is the actual voice over the air, and Murdock merely mouths the words before the studio audience. Laura Hamilton is tutored by Wilder, who tells her she must decide between the demands of a singing career and marriage to Robert, a ships' doctor. Wilder and Murdock argue over who is more valuable to their "act," and over their mutual attraction to Laura. Elsa accuses Murdock of being unfaithful. When Murdock is found dead in his apartment by Wilder, the hunchback removes Laura's vanity case from the scene and calls the police to confess to the murder. When Laura shows up, Wilder realizes she is not the killer, and sends her away. Police shoot a fleeing Wilder, who goes to the studio for the show to sing "My Good-bye to You" on the radio one final time—then dies in Laura's arms. Laura and Robert honeymoon on an ocean liner, while the real killer wonders why Wilder "took the rap."

The movie-going public's insatiable hunger for "inside radio" scenarios found some satisfaction with *The Phantom Broadcast*, a musical/mystery/borderline-horror thriller from the Monogram Pictures Corporation. Much praised at the time of its release for its originality, this downbeat indie was actually quite derivative, with overtones of *The Phantom of the Opera*, *Svengali*, *Cyrano de Bergerac*, and any number of gangster pictures. No matter, for its inspirations—and its ignoring of then-less-than-authoritative Production Code strictures—make it a bizarre little treat 80 years later.

Monogram, one of the higher-grade independent companies, was formed in February 1931 in a renaming of the Syndicate Film Exchange, which produced Westerns under the name Rayart Pictures (named for producer W. Ray Johnston), and Continental Talking Pictures, which specialized in melodramas. Johnston handled the finance end of Monogram, and his longtime business partner Trem Carr was in charge of production; the company was strong on distribution, boasting 89 percent of the U.S. in its network territory upon its founding.

On its face, *The Phantom Broadcast*—filmed in Hollywood in six days of February 1933 as *False Fronts*—didn't seem that much different than the typical crank-it-out Monogram drama. Busy cinematographer-turned-director Phil Rosen helmed such dependable talent as Ralph Forbes (1896–1951), a British actor recently in the news as the now-former Mr. Ruth Chatterton; second-tier femme fatale Vivienne Osborne (1896–1961); promising ingénue Gail Patrick (1911–1980), on loan from Paramount; and action perennials Guinn "Big Boy" Williams (1899–1962) and George "Gabby" Hayes (1885–1969). A few years before, Forbes was an up-and-comer—his Hollywood debut was in Paramount's 1926 hit *Beau Geste*. Now, he was a dependable supporting player in prestige pictures (*The Green Goddess*, *Christopher Strong*) and a top-liner in the likes of

The Phantom Broadcast. Osborne was making a career of playing shady ladies under a veneer of class, and this entry was no exception.

What was unusual about *The Phantom Broadcast* was the script, penned by Tristram Tupper, a novelist, magazine writer, and screensmith upon whose novel the 1928 Fox film *The River* was based.[2] The story capitalized on the public interest in the faces behind the voices heard in the ether, but with a twist: What if one of those voices wasn't who we thought it was? Forbes intelligently plays a singer, pianist, and personal manager, who—with his hunchback appearance a physical hindrance to fame—employs a front man to achieve radio stardom, mobster influence be damned. When the tall, handsome, womanizing figurehead is murdered, the manager fears that his pretty protégé (played by Patrick) is the guilty party, although given that the victim was such a heel, there is no shortage of candidates.

The Phantom Broadcast offers some nice touches, and not just in the abnormal concern Forbes' character has for his pupil, and his emphasis on the personal sacrifices she must make for a career. ("Music is a zealous master," he warns in a particularly Phantom-esque manner.) This unrequited love inspires the manager to fantasize he is normal—when he looks in a mirror, a handsome, upright version of himself looks back, but only for a few seconds. Even more heart-rending is the sequence of events after the manager discovers the body of the murder victim: After ridding the scene of potentially incriminating evidence against the girl and falsely confessing to the killing to the police, the crippled man realizes all he's done has been for naught. He dies not knowing the identity of the real killer, who (pre–Code enforcement) goes unpunished while wondering why.

English-born Ralph Forbes alternated between second leads in prestige pictures and top-billed roles in the likes of *The Phantom Broadcast* (1933).

The film's title refers to the exciting climax: the radiocast by a "dead man" at the stroke of the hour of air time; this was luridly advertised in the trades as "The Voice of Ether That Lured to Death"! The final song, "My Good-bye to You," was one of four lushly romantic tunes written for the movie by lyricist George Waggner—see *Girl o' My Dreams* and *Dizzy Dames* [both q.v.]—and composers Norman Spencer and Bernard Brown, whose future work for Warner

Bros, cartoons would include the delightful "I Love to Singa" and "My Green Fedora." Brown also was a sound engineer who headed the sound department at Universal and won an Oscar for that studio's *When Tomorrow Comes* (1940). Not so ironically, the voice heard singing in *The Phantom Broadcast* was almost certainly a double, unidentified all these decades.

The quality of Monogram's work did not go unrecognized. *Variety* praised *The Phantom Broadcast* as "a highly credible indie effort ... worth supporting."[3] The *Motion Picture Herald* urged its readers to see "an intensely interesting melodrama ... novel and modern ... a show that any theatre, big or little, can proudly offer its patrons."[4] *The Billboard* added that "Monogram's film of a musical Cyrano who creates something of a Frankenstein is definitely above-average screen entertainment. The screenplay ... and direction ... are excellent."[5] A writer from the *Hollywood Reporter*, aiming his comment at exhibitors, went even further:

> When this reviewer reports that *The Phantom Broadcast* is the best independent picture from every point of view that he has seen in many a day, there is hardly any better recommendation that can be given exhibitors. You will like this picture, as will your patrons, and ... that's the object of this business.[6]

Forbes' effort in *The Phantom Broadcast* led to another strong role at Monogram, as a retribution-minded attorney in the Tupper-written *The Avenger* (1933), a modern take on *The Count of Monte Cristo*. The London-born actor alternated between the stage, silver screen (*The Hound of the Baskervilles*, *The Private Lives of Elizabeth and Essex*, *Tower of London*), and even early television until his death at age 54 in New York City after what were reported as complications from a recent operation. By this time, *The Phantom Broadcast*, as an indie, was an early attraction on TV around the country.

Arnold Gray, who plays the pretend crooner in *The Phantom Broadcast*, met an even sadder end than Forbes. Recognizable to buffs for his acting role as the iceman in the W.C. Fields classic *The Dentist*, Gray became the regular stand-in for Joel McCrea and married Josephine Ramos, the stand-in for Dolores Del Rio. Ramos contracted tuberculosis and was taken by her husband in the spring of 1936 on what was to be a final cross-country trip in a medically equipped trailer financed by McCrea. At a TB camp near San Diego, Gray died of a heart attack on May 7, 1936, at age 37. His wife perished three days later.

Dance, Girl, Dance
(Invincible-Chesterfield; September 1, 1933)

Director: Frank R. Strayer. Presented by: Maury M. Cohen. Assistant Director: Melville Shyer. Screenplay/Dialogue: Robert Ellis. Photography: M. A. Anderson. Editing:

Roland Reed. Musical Director: Lee Zahler. Dance Director: Pearl Eaton. Art Director: Edward C. Jewell. Sound: L. E. Clark. Running Time: 67 minutes.
Cast: Alan Dinehart (Wade "Val" Valentine); Evalyn Knapp (Sally Patter aka Pat); Edward Nugent (Joe Pitt); Ada May (Claudette); Mae Busch (Lou Kendall); Theodore von Eltz (Phil Norton); Gloria Shea (Cleo Darville); George Grandee (Mozart); The Pearl Eaton Girls.
Songs: "I'm the Little Peanut Vendor's Little Missus" [May] (Eugene Conrad, Harry Carroll); "It Takes a Lot of Jack (To Make a Little Jill Say Yes)" [May] (J. Keirn Brennan, George Grandee); "Mother Goose" [Grandee] (authorship undetermined); "Seeing Is Believing" [Knapp, twice] (James Morley, Lee Zahler).
Also Known As: *Male and Female*.
Home Video: Alpha DVD.

The Story: Small-time vaudeville act Joe Pitt and Sally Patter break up—professionally and domestically—after Joe blames his new wife's showbiz inexperience for their lack of success. Joe pairs with Cleo Darville to dismal results, while agent Lou Kendall helps Sally get a job as a chorine with New York nightclub revue producer Wade Valentine. Sally becomes understudy to the show's temperamental star, Claudette, and is hit on by backer Phil Norton. Sally becomes ill during a show and has to drop out; she gives birth to Joe's child. Sally returns to New York, where Valentine outlines his new show for her to star in. Valentine proposes to Sally, but she puts him off. Joe, back in New York after his act with Cleo has broken up, visits Sally's apartment, apologizes for his past behavior, and sees his child for the first time. Joe gets a steady job as a soap salesman, but Lou encourages him to return to the stage. He flops until Sally shows up to save the act by singing her composition "Seeing Is Believing."

"Care-free, pleasure-mad revelers, they could not see the broken heart she screened behind her smiling face, and, so, they screamed madly from their ringside tables, 'Dance Girl Dance!'" Wow ... that ad copy wasn't quite what we saw in on screen in *Dance, Girl, Dance*. Still, this backstage drama, set in what its studio touted as "the dingy dressing rooms of four-a-day vaudeville theaters," has enough pre–Code leanings to be worth watching for a few minutes more than an hour.

One of the indies' first responses to the post–*42nd Street* musical revival, *Dance, Girl, Dance* was a co-production of the Invincible Motion Pictures Corporation and the Chesterfield Motion Picture Corporation. The two companies teamed for an 18-film program for 1933–34 with national distribution by First Division Pictures—among the other titles was the musical *Rainbow Over Broadway* [q.v.]. Directed by indie specialist Frank R. Strayer and penned by prolific actor-turned-prolific screenwriter Robert Ellis, *Dance, Girl, Dance* was shot at the Mack Sennett Studios in August 1933—but not for very much of that month.

Maury M. Cohen, Invincible's president, knew how to make something out of nothing, and this apparently extended to his publicity for *Dance, Girl,*

Dance. The result was this item, published by a newspaper wire service columnist:

> Maury Cohen has just made *Dance, Girl, Dance*, a musical production with songs, chorus girls, and all those trimmings, in five days. The average time spent on such films in the major studios is eight weeks.
> How is it done? Cohen ... says that everything is in the preparation. Most of the pictures turned out by major studios are started before the scripts are completed. Nobody knows exactly what will be done.
> There isn't a camera turned on one of Cohen's pictures until every little detail has been settled. Not a scene is shot that isn't essential, and every scene is carefully timed so that it will not run over the time allotted.[7]

Director Strayer was used to operating with limited time and resources. He had been making quickies for nearly a decade, in a variety of genres, although in retrospect he is most remembered in this period for horror chillers such as *The Vampire Bat* (Majestic Pictures, 1933); *The Ghost Walks* (Invincible Pictures, 1934); and *Condemned to Live* (Invincible, 1935). His *Manhattan Tower* (Remington Pictures, 1932) has been rediscovered and praised as a worthy variation on the *Grand Hotel* formula of multiple storylines within a single locale. Strayer made a more lasting home at Columbia, where he would go on to make most of the *Blondie* series.

For Strayer's supposed five days of filming, the patron of *Dance, Girl, Dance* got a variation on the *Burlesque/The Dance of Life* story about a married tank-town vaudeville team that splits up, with one partner attaining success but ultimately loving—and reuniting with—the other. Here, it is the female half—played by Evalyn Knapp—who is the doer; another difference is that, unbeknownst to her ex-partner (Edward Nugent), she is pregnant with his child. We never hear the word "pregnancy," of course, but we know what's happening even before we see the kid in his crib. Interestingly, unlike many pre–Code heroines who gave birth out of wedlock, Knapp keeps the baby throughout. Nugent's character is too enamored with himself to know what's going on; he's the kind of trouper who makes sure to leave his performing schedule with some open dates in case The Palace in New York City comes calling.

Knapp (1908–1981) debuted in early talkies at Warner Bros. She and Grant Withers were top-billed in 1930's *Sinners' Holiday*, in which James Cagney (in his movie debut) and Joan Blondell were second leads. By 1933, she was mainly doing action films, including the title role in the Universal serial *The Perils of Pauline*; in fact, some theaters paired chapters of the serial on the same program as *Dance, Girl, Dance*. If Knapp is remembered now, it's mainly as the leading lady in B-Westerns and other adventures with cowboys like Ken Maynard, Tim McCoy, Johnny Mack Brown, and Smith Ballew. (Her singing in *Dance, Girl, Dance* is likely dubbed.)

Eddie Nugent (1904–1995), who provided occasional leads and comedy support throughout the 1930s, makes a passable comic lead. Nugent, the everlasting juvenile type, was a welcome presence in scores of films with his boyishness and snap. "It's the psychological effect that keeps me young," Nugent was quoted by newspapers in a likely publicist-fed story that conformed to what movie watchers thought of the actor. "I'll be playing juveniles when I'm 50."[8] Change of plan: Nugent left pictures after 1937 to act on Broadway and, later, direct for the stage and television.

Actually, it is Alan Dinehart (1889–1944), playing a rare sympathetic role in a film career dominated by heavy parts, who is first-billed in *Dance, Girl, Dance* as the impresario whose love goes unrequited. Mae Busch (1891–1946), a silent-screen leading lady now known as a harridan in Laurel and Hardy comedies, earned frequent mention by reviewers for her role as a wisecracking theatrical agent. When Nugent's character tells her about a vaudeville performer who is "sawed in half," Busch's slyly shoots back: "I know which half you're after!" You wouldn't be hearing stuff like that after the Hays office put its foot down.

Also in the cast is George Grandee (1900–1985), a diminutive (5-foot-3½) actor/pianist/composer who made a few films. It was he, and not star Erich von Stroheim, who supposedly voiced Otto the ventriloquist's dummy in the 1929 musical melodrama *The Great Gabbo*. Grandee's droll, biting wit—which landed him on tour with Sophie Tucker and helped him become a confidante of Howard Hughes—is on ample display here. Grandee became a favorite at Hollywood parties and in Los Angeles–area nightclub engagements into the 1970s.

There isn't much else in *Dance, Girl, Dance* to recommend it, although it was saluted by *The Film Daily* as "a nice little number with excellent production values and very well directed."[9] Five days, huh? Maybe Maury Cohen really did know what he was doing.

Rainbow Over Broadway
(Chesterfield-First Division; December 1, 1933)

Director: Richard Thorpe. Producer: George A. Batcheller. Story: Carol Webster. Adaptation/Dialogue: Winifred Dunn. Photography: M.A. Anderson. Editor: Roland Reed. Musical Director: Edward Kay. Ensembles: Fanchon and Marco. Art Director: Edward C. Jewell. Sound: L.E. Clark. Running Time: 72 minutes.

Cast: Joan Marsh (Judy Chibbins); Frank Albertson (Don Hayes); Lucien Littlefield (Timothy Chibbins); Grace Hayes (Trixie Valleron); Gladys Blake (Nellie Vallerson); Glen Boles (Mickey Chibbins); Dell Henderson (Bowers); Nat Carr (Sanfield); Harry Myers (Berwisky); May Beatty (Queenie); George Grandee (Bob Chibbins); Aline Goodwin (singer); Maxine Lewis; The Foster Sisters; Fanchon Marco Girls.

Songs: "I Must Be in Love With Love" [Goodwin], "Look Up, Not Down" [Grandee,

reprised by Hayes, Marsh], "There Ain't No Substitute for Love" (Elizabeth Morgan, Albert von Tilzer); "Dance My Blues Away" [Hayes] (Neville Fleeson, Albert von Tilzer); "Let's Go Places and Do Things" [Albertson, Marsh] (Harry MacPherson, Albert von Tilzer); "While I'm in the Mood" [Hayes] (George Whiting, Albert von Tilzer).
Working Title: *Just Off Broadway*.
Home Video: Alpha DVD.

The Story: En route to New York, famous orchestra leader Don Hayes visits his former sweetheart, Judy Chibbins, and her dysfunctional family in Kansas City. The clan is in financial trouble, especially since their timid father, Timothy, got married to vain, washed-up stage singer Trixie Valleron. Judy and her songwriting brother, Bob, are stuck working in a music store. In New York, Don pitches Trixie to nightclub owner Sanfield as a novelty attraction, and pays for the family to come East. Judy and Bob supply the songs for Trixie's Gay Nineties-styled show, but Trixie is kept unaware of the show's tone to make sure she will perform the numbers. Trixie is talked by her jealous friend and vaudeville rival, Queenie, into leaving the show on the eve of its opening; she returns but then threatens to leave after finding out that her stepchildren are the songwriters. Trixie relents and takes the stage, and Judy is reconciled with Don.

Rainbow Over Broadway concerns the efforts of the younger members of a Midwestern family to convince a popular bandleader to give them a shot at Broadway despite the distraction of their selfish stepmother, a once-famous singer stuck in the past. The songs are passable, and what dance routines survive look fancier than the usual for Poverty Row. Fortunately, the stepmom is portrayed by longtime vaudeville headliner Grace Hayes, whose haughty performance gives this comedy-drama whatever kick it has.

At one point, the former Nellie Valleron fumes while her pretty stepdaughter—portrayed by Joan Marsh—plays a favorite song in a peppy style at odds with the balladic rendition previously offered by the older woman. This leads to the following exchange with the bandleader—played by Frank Albertson—in which Mrs. Timothy Chibbins is oblivious to her bitchiness:

> HAYES (referring to Marsh's song): "It's silly, that kind of stuff."
> ALBERTSON: "Oh, a lot of people like it, Mrs. Chibbins!"
> HAYES (sweetly but assertively): "Valleron.... Trixie Valleron, if you *don't* mind!"
> ALBERTSON (politely): "Not at all."
> HAYES: "Fancy my changing the beautiful name of Valleron to Chibbins."
> (Albertson blankly looks straight ahead, sensing a train wreck.)
> HAYES: "Have you ever been to New York?"
> ALBERTSON: "Why, yes, I spend most of my time there."
> HAYES: "Don't you just love it?"
> ALBERTSON: "Well, New York's all right."

HAYES: "I'll *say* it's all right, providing you know your New York. Do *you* know your New York?"
ALBERTSON (suddenly wanting to be in New York ... or anywhere else): "Well, slightly."

Somehow, Albertson's character is impressed enough to want to use the diva as a club performer, which gives the statuesque Hayes the excuse to do her Mae West imitation, delaying the suspense of bringing the romantic leads together and stretching *Rainbow Over Broadway* to a passable length. Filmed in the fall of 1933 at the Mack Sennett Studios by the Chesterfield Motion Pictures Corporation, this was part of the indies' first responses to the post–*42nd Street* musical revival. *Rainbow Over Broadway* was a co-production of the Invincible Motion Pictures Corporation and Chesterfield; the two companies teamed for an 18-film program for 1933–34 with national distribution by First Division Pictures—among the other titles was another musical, *Dance, Girl, Dance* [q.v.]. Maury M. Cohen, Invincible's president, knew how to grind out quickies like this one in a short production schedule and a tight budget.

Rainbow Over Broadway was praised by *Variety* as "excellent.... Script is intelligent and so is Richard Thorpe's direction.... Grace Hayes photographs handsomely. Always a class trouper, this performer ... might be used by other producers."[10] Thorpe, who by his mid–30s had directed dozens of low-rung productions, escaped the indies shortly thereafter for the major security of MGM, where he continued a filmmaking career (*Night Must Fall, The Prisoner of Zenda, Jailhouse Rock*) that lasted into the late 1960s.

Hayes (1895–1989) wasn't tremendously employable on the screen, mainly because of her age, but she had plenty to do here. She became a stage headliner in the late 1920s as the partner of pianist-composer Neville Fleeson. She attracted attention as an imitator of West, then gained more through her own radio show on NBC; the West angle was played up big in promotion for *Rainbow Over Broadway*. Among Hayes' other film credits are *King of Jazz* (1930), *Myrt and Marge* (1933) [q.v.], *Babes in Arms* (1939), and *Always Leave Them Laughing* (1949). Her son was the popular actor and comedian Peter Lind Hayes, with whom she performed frequently in vaudeville and in her popular Hollywood nightclub, the Grace Hayes Lodge. As her performing career ebbed, she owned and operated an even more popular club in Las Vegas, the Red Rooster.

Marsh (1913–2000) was a former child actress, a blonde WAMPAS "Baby Star" alumna, and the daughter of Academy Award–winning cinematographer Charles Rosher. She was making strides as an adult player by this time, especially as W.C. Fields' daughter in *You're Telling Me!* (1935), but she never made big stardom and her film career stalled after a temporary period of retirement following a 1936 marriage to screenwriter Charles Belden. Albertson (1909–1964) was a former Fox juvenile who spent many years playing wisecracking types who were supposed to be younger than his real age, and Glen Boles (1913–2009), who plays the younger of the two Chibbins brothers, was a screen and stage actor who gave up that career after World War II service to establish a practice as a psychotherapist for 50 years.

Also in *Rainbow Over Broadway* is George Grandee, the pint-sized actor, pianist, and composer who had appeared in *Dance, Girl, Dance*. Another interesting name connected to the film was composer Albert von Tilzer, who was best known for the standard "Take Me Out to the Ball Game." Von Tilzer co-wrote the songs for *Rainbow*, one of which, "Let's Go Places and Do Things," was considered a comeback for a tunesmith whose best days had come and gone.

Rainbow Over Broadway is difficult to evaluate, if only because existing prints, presumably chopped up for TV airing, run only about 50 minutes of a 70-minute original release. What's left suffers from a surplus of characters, undeveloped subplots, and abrupt continuity—but is that because of the script or the TV cutting? We're not sure, but we're inclined to give it the benefit of the doubt.

Girl o' My Dreams
(Monogram; November 17, 1934)
and *The Shadow of Silk Lennox*
(Commodore; November 1, 1935)

Girl o' My Dreams

Director: Ray McCarey. Producer: William T. Lackey. Story/Screenplay: George Waggner. Photography: Ira H. Morgan. Editing: Jack Oglivie. Musical Director: Edward Ward. Art Director: E.R. Dickson. Sound: J.A. Stransky, Jr. Running Time: 65 minutes.

Cast: Mary Carlisle (Gwen); Sterling Holloway (Spec Early); Edward Nugent (Larry Haines); Arthur Lake (Bobby Barnes); Creighton Chaney [Lon Chaney, Jr.] (Don Cooper); Tom Dugan (Joe Smiley); Gigi Parrish (Mary); Jeanie Roberts (Kittens); Lee Shumway (Coach); Harry Bowen (photographer); George Cleveland (newsreel man); Olaf Hytten (Professor E. Phlatt); The Crane Sisters [Betty Mae and Beverly Crane] (Nip and Tuck); The Three Lieutenants [Frank McKee, Herbert Hall, Jack Frost]; Ted Dahl and His Orchestra.

Also Known As: *Love Race*.

Songs: "Joe Senior" [Holloway, Lake, chorus], "Lucky Star" [Three Lieutenants, danced by Crane Sisters], "Thou Art My Baby" [Nugent, Carlisle, Chaney, Lake, Three Lieutenants; reprised by band at dance] (George Waggner, Edward Ward).

Home Video: Alpha DVD; Sinister Cinema DVD.

The Story: Larry Haines, a star track hurdler at Rawley College, thinks he's the big man on campus. To take Larry's ego down a peg, Larry's teammate, high jumper

Bobby Barnes, and the school newspaper editor, Spec Early, scheme to fix the "Joe Senior" most-popular contest so that Larry will lose. The beneficiary of the ballot box stuffing is shot putter Don Cooper, who starts paying attention to Larry's girlfriend, Gwen, at the expense of his girl, Mary. Mary retaliates by inviting Larry to the school dance, and the rivalry is on—with a big meet ahead.

The Shadow of Silk Lennox

Director/Producer: Ray Kirkwood. Screenplay: Norman Springer, based on his story "The Riot Squad." Photography: Robert E. Cline. Editing: Holbrook Todd. Art Director: Zarah Tazil. Orchestrations: Marion Madison. Running Time: 60 minutes.

Cast: Lon Chaney, Jr. (John Arthur "Silk" Lennox); Dean Benton (Jimmy Lambert); Marie Burton [Catherine Cotter] (Nola Travers); Jack Mulhall (Ferguson aka "Fingers" Farley); Eddie Gribbon (Lefty Sloan); Larry McGrath (police inspector); Allen Greer (Dutch); Theodore Lorch (Kennedy); Murdock MacQuarrie (Haskell); Hal Taliaferro [Wally Wales] (Swann); Ace Cain (Inspector Bull); Jules Cowles, Ray Turner (murder witnesses); Frank Niemann and His Orchestra.

Songs: "Congo" [Niemann band, danced by Burton], "Forgotten Melodies" [Benton, Niemann band], "Going Steady With Your Sis," "Love Is the Way" ["Bonnie and Her Boyfriends" vocal trio, Niemann band], "Walking in the Dark" [Benton, danced by Burton, reprised by Benton] (Dean Benton).

Working Title: *The Riot Squad.*
Home Video: Alpha DVD; Mill Creek DVD; Sinister Cinema DVD.

The Story: Underground kingpin John "Silk" Lennox runs a shady nightclub where the song-and-dance team of Jimmy Lambert and Nola Travers is the featured act. Silk tricks Jimmy into playing a telephone recording that provides him an alibi for a bank robbery. The authorities suspect Silk for the robbery and the ensuing death of one of his henchmen, so they infiltrate his mob with a government man posing as a safecracker. Silk menaces Jimmy, who initially implicates his boss, and Nola is imperiled when she threatens to take the recording to the police. Silk attempts to find the $50,000 from the robbery, which has been hidden away by one of his men, but he is killed in a gunfight by the G-man, who saves Jimmy and Nola.

"Chaney sings!" is the big news to a modern-day movie buff seeing *Girl o' My Dreams* for the first time. Indeed, watching an impossibly young Lon Chaney, Jr., croon is a surprise for those who know Hollywood's Wolf Man only for his Universal monster rallies of the 1940s. But in 1934, a viewer of this then-new college musical might have replied "So what?"—or perhaps "Who's Lon Chaney, Jr.?"

That's because Chaney (1906–1973) was billed with his birth name, Creighton Chaney, during the first few years after his world-famous film star father's death in 1930. Determined not to exploit his dad's fame for his own screen success, the younger Chaney spent the 1930s bouncing around the studios and alternating between bits in major pictures (*Bird of Paradise*), villainous roles in Westerns and other action programmers, and occasional leads in low-budget productions, such as the 1932 RKO serial *The Last Frontier*. When he was offered a contract by RKO in 1932, Chaney refused to sign it if he had to be billed as Lon, Jr., but the studio gave in to his demand. "I'm honestly grateful to them for giving me the chance to make good under my own steam as Creighton Chaney," was how the young man was quoted in a fan magazine. "I figure they must think I have something to offer on my own."[11]

There wasn't all that much to offer in Monogram's *Girl o' My Dreams*, which had Chaney billed fifth as a dull-witted track athlete in an ensemble that also included Mary Carlisle, Eddie Nugent, and Arthur Lake. Chaney gets to have some fun as a bruiser who suddenly begins reading charm books and wearing silk underwear after winning a rigged "most popular senior" campus contest at the expense of an insufferably self-centered teammate (Nugent). Girlfriend swapping ensues! Chaney also acquits himself reasonably well in singing part of George Waggner and Edward Ward's song "Thou Art My Baby," which begins as a classroom "lecture" by Nugent but is hijacked by his more burly co-star, who lays atop a piano a la Helen Morgan.

A movie vet whose career extended from a bit acting role in Valentino's *The Sheik* to directing the '60s *Batman* TV series, Waggner wrote the screenplay and lyrics for *Girl o' My Dreams*, but his association with Chaney was only beginning. He directed Chaney in his two breakout horror films at Universal: *Man Made Monster* and *The Wolf Man* (both 1941), and produced Chaney's *The Ghost of Frankenstein* (1942) and *Frankenstein Meets the Wolf Man* (1943). According to Hollywood lore—or at least a story that appeared in print in 1941—Waggner was impressed enough by Chaney's performance in *Girl o' My Dreams* that he told the actor, "Some day, I'm going to direct you in a picture which will offer you some real 'character work.'"[12] And so he did.

Before he attained stardom as the Wolf Man, Lon Chaney, Jr., was a handsome would-be contract player trying to find his footing in the movies.

Monogram touted *Girl o' My Dreams* as a successor to its hit college musical comedy *The Sweetheart of Sigma*

Chi (1933), also starring perennial "B" leading lady Carlisle (b. 1914). The *Film Daily* reviewer correctly noted that Sterling Holloway, cast as the editor of the college rag (as in newspaper), "steals the show ... with his swell eccentric comedy." "This one will have little appeal to the sophisticated and more serious ... but it is likely, cheery fare for the younger element," the writer added.[13] Still, *Girl o' My Dreams* wasn't going to drum up any more singing roles for Chaney, who in an interview years later recalled the frustration of his early years in Hollywood:

> I was in a new picture practically every two weeks, always as a heavy. I'll swear I spoke the line "So you won't talk, eh?" at least 50 times, and I'd rather not think about how often I had to say, "Don't shoot him now—I have a better plan!" ... Now I knew what Dad meant when he said, "I've taken the bumps." Well, I'd taken them. I did every possible tough bit in pictures."[14]

The actor might have thought his "tough bits" were past him in 1935 when—now under the name Lon Chaney, Jr.—he signed a contract with independent producer Ray Kirkwood to star in what were announced as 24 "action melodramas," eight pictures a year for three years, for release by New York City-based Commodore Pictures.[15] Commodore was better known for churning out B-Westerns, including, in 1935, vehicles for Bob Steele, Tom Tyler, and Jack Perrin. The first Chaney to be issued under the company aegis was a gangster thriller with songs, *The Shadow of Silk Lennox*, in which Chaney traded in his baritone for a non-singing role as the titular crime king uttering much of the same menacing dialogue he deplored. ("You dirty little rat!" he yells as his slaps around one of his adversaries with the fury of Jimmy Cagney.)

By this time, Chaney, Jr., had practically been starved into living off his father's reputation. Publicity for his first Commodore pictures, *The Shadow of Silk Lennox* and *A Scream in the Night* (aka *Scream in the Dark*, 1936)—in the latter, he played a dual role as a clean-cut police detective and a one-eyed derelict—freely traded on the father's "Man of a Thousand Faces" mystery. Syndicated newspaper columnist Robbin Coons noted such in a 1935 story about the younger Chaney's Commodore films:

> Like his father, Lon Jr. is his own make-up man. He is studying the art intensively, devoting three hours daily to practice in transforming his personality through the use of make-up and character study....
>
> It was last year that Creighton Chaney, who was in the water heater business before he came into pictures as a character juvenile, was persuaded to assume the name of Lon Chaney Jr. and attempt characterizations like those of his father. From the beginning, he had preferred character work to "straight juveniles" although he could qualify for those too.[16]

The Shadow of Silk Lennox, one of those states-rights' productions that was so obscure that none of the major trade publications reviewed it, is 60 minutes by the clock, but seems twice as long with its draggy pace and poor acting.

The hero of the story, a G-man who brings down Lennox, is played, none too convincingly, by Jack Mulhall (1887–1979), a former leading man of silents. The story of Mulhall, who had acted with the senior Chaney (in 1922's *Flesh and Blood*), could have served as a cautionary tale to an aspiring star like Lon, Jr. Mulhall was constantly considered to be on and off the comeback trail in 1930s news media. He was still popular enough, columnist Jimmie Fidler reported, for Hollywood audiences to applaud whenever he showed up on screen even in minor roles, but 1935 wasn't a great year for Mulhall—he separated from his wife and declared bankruptcy after stating he'd had only 30 years of work in the prior six months.[17] Still, he would act in movies as late as 1959 and took better care of himself than Chaney, Jr., outliving him by six years.

Joining the junior Chaney at the other end of the career spectrum from Mulhall was 21-year-old Dean Benton, who played the juvenile lead in *Silk Lennox*, and wrote the words and music for the film's five songs. Playing a song-and-dance man in Lennox's nightclub, Benton is romantically paired with actress-dancer Marie Burton in one of her few film roles of any size. Benton (1914–1996) broke into Hollywood as a Universal contract player. He appeared in nearly two dozen films but in only a handful of credited roles. Among the latter was in the Bela Lugosi serial *The Return of Chandu* (1934). *Silk Lennox* appears to have been his only crack at singing and songwriting for the screen.

There isn't much subtlety in Chaney's too-brutish performance in *The Shadow of Silk Lennox* in what could've been an interesting, ambiguous good/bad guy role. The crummy script and dialogue don't help, but Chaney was never known for subtlety. Unfortunately, the pact with Kirkwood/Commodore did little besides give him some experience, as *Silk Lennox* and *A Scream in the Night* were all that were made out of the 24 films announced. Chaney had to wait until the very end of the '30s—and his breakout performance as Lenny on the big screen's *Of Mice and Men*—to clear a path toward the stardom for which he'd so long toiled. Not surprisingly, in the early '40s, *The Shadow of Silk Lennox* was hauled out of whatever vault it was in and put back into circulation as fodder for fans of its now heavily exploited leading man.

Dizzy Dames
(Liberty; May 15, 1935)
and *The Old Homestead*
(Liberty/Republic; August 1, 1935)

Dizzy Dames

Director: William Nigh. Producer: M.H. Hoffman. Story/Continuity/Dialogue: George Waggner. Suggested by the story "The Watch Dog" (aka "Love Me, Love My Dog") by P.G. Wodehouse. Photography: Harry Neumann. Editing: Mildred Johnston. Production Manager: Rudolph Flothow. Musical Director: Howard Jackson. Dance Director: Maurice Kosloff. Sound: L.E. Clark. Running Time: 68 minutes.

Cast: Marjorie Rambeau (Lillian Bennett/Marlowe); Florine McKinney (Helen Bennett); Lawrence Gray (Terry Ramsey); Inez Courtney (Arlette); Berton Churchill (Dad Hackett); Fuzzy Knight (Buzz); Kitty Kelly (La Vere); Lillian Miles (Gloria); John Warburton (Rodney Stokes); Mary Forbes (Mrs. Stokes); Paul Irving (Mr. Stokes); Christine Marston (rhumba dancer).

Songs "I Was Taken by Storm" [Gray, McKinney, twice] (Edward Heyman, Louis Alter); "Let's Be Frivolous" [Gray, reprised in dance by Knight, Courtney, chorus] (George Waggner, Howard Jackson); "Love Is the Thing" [Knight] (Harry Tobias, Neil Moret); "The Martinique" [Miles, danced by Marston, chorus] (George Waggner, Louis Alter).

The Story: Lillian Bennett, a once-acclaimed actress, runs a New York boarding house for show people (and a trained seal). Lillian's daughter, Helen, wants to come home after years away at finishing school, but Lil, who fears Helen will catch the show-business bug, never has told her child about her former fame. Among Lil's roomers are Terry, a struggling songwriter and tenor; La Vere, who owns the seal; song-and-dance duo Arlette and Buzz; and aged trouper Pop Hackett. After making her tenants promise not to tell Helen they're in show business, Lil is visited by Helen, who takes a mutual liking to Terry although she is engaged to socialite Rodney Stokes. Rodney invites Helen and her new friends to his family home, where Terry is hired to write a Junior League revue to star Helen, Rodney, and the jealous Gloria. Helen learns of her mother's past, but Lil makes her promise to choose the security of marriage to Rodney over an uncertain career. The revue is a success, however, landing Terry a new job—and Helen.

The Old Homestead

Director: William Nigh. Producer: M.H. Hoffman. Story/Continuity/Dialogue: W. Scott Darling, based on the novel *Denman Thompson's The Old Homestead* by John Russell Corvell. Photography: Harry Neumann. Editing: Mildred Johnston. Production Manager: Rudolph Flothow. Musical Director: Howard Jackson. Sound: Harold Bumbaugh. Running Time: 71 minutes.

Cast: Mary Carlisle (Nancy Abbott); Lawrence Gray (Bob Shackleforth); Dorothy Lee (Elsie Wilson); Willard Robertson (Uncle Jed); Edward Nugent (Rudy Nash); Lillian Miles (Peggy); Fuzzy Knight (Lem); Eddie Kane (Wertheimer); Harry Conley (J. Wilberforce Platt); The Sons of the Pioneers: Vern [Tim] Spencer, Bob Nolan, Len Slye [Roy Rogers], Hugh Farr (singing farmhands); Gayne Whitman (radio executive); George Lloyd (irate husband); Sally Sweet (singer).

Songs: "Happy Cowboy" [Miles, Knight, Sons of the Pioneers], "That Old White Mule of Mine" [Knight, Sons of the Pioneers], "Way Out There" [Sons of the Pioneers] (Bob Nolan); "Harlem Nasty Man" [Sweet] (George Waggner, Howard Jackson); "Honey Dat I Love So Well" [Knight, Sons of the Pioneers] (Harry Freeman); "Love Me Ever" [Miles] (George Waggner, Howard Jackson, Jack Bennett); "Moonlight in

Heaven" [Gray, Sons of the Pioneers, reprised by Gray] (Jack Scholl, Louis Alter); "Old Rover" [Sons of the Pioneers] (Tim Spencer); "Plow Boy" [Gray, Sons of the Pioneers, four times] (J. Keirn Brennan, Ted Snyder); "Somehow I Knew" [Lee] (Harry Tobias, Neil Moret, Charles Rosoff); "When Our Old Age Pension Check Comes to Our Door" [Knight, Sons of the Pioneers] (Manny Stone); "Tiger Rag (Hold That Tiger)" [Knight, Sons of the Pioneers] (The Original Dixieland Jazz Band); "Deep River" [female vocalist] (trad.).
Home Video: Sinister Cinema DVD.

The Story: Thanks to recommendation letters written by his sweetheart, Nancy, Missouri farmer Bob Shackleforth lands a contract to sing on a New York radio program along with his friend Lem and a "hillbilly" quartet of hired hands. With Uncle Jed as emcee, "The Old Homestead" show is a big hit, but Bob allows fame to go to his head after he is given his own program. He ignores Nancy by stepping out with singer Elsie Wilson, and Elsie's bandleader boyfriend, Rudy Nash, takes a liking to Nancy. Uncle Jed falls for nightclub owner Peggy, whom the boys suspect is a gold digger. Disillusioned by city life, Jed and the boys resume their broadcasts back home on the farm, where Bob returns to the fold.

Dizzy Dames and *The Old Homestead* are by no means the best films discussed in these pages, but they do hold some interest, if only because they brought back one of the early Hollywood musical's most prolific performers, albeit with much fewer of the resources he was used to back in 1929–30.

Lawrence Gray was among the busiest male leads of the early Hollywood musical days. He was paired with Marion Davies (*Marianne, The Florodora Girl*); the Duncan Sisters (*It's a Great Life*); and Marilyn Miller (*Sunny*). He also functioned in an ensemble (*Spring Is Here*) and even was top-billed himself (*Children of Pleasure*). He had a jaunty presence—but one not threatening to his bigger-name co-stars—plus a flair for comedy and a more-than-functional tenor. Unlike many who hit big during the advent of sound, Gray (1898–1970) was not a direct import from the theater—he'd been a juvenile at Paramount during the 1920s. When musicals temporarily went out of style, he had no important legit work to fall back on, and his career opportunities grew as fallow as they had been directly before *The Jazz Singer*. After appearing in six 1930 picture releases, Gray was seen twice in 1931 and 1933, not at all in 1932, and in one 1934 film.

In 1932 and '33, Gray tried vaudeville with an act in which he sang songs from some of his movies and some of his favorite tunes ("Isn't It Romantic?" among the latter). Trade reviewers were OK with the presentation—which included an excerpt of the performer singing to Marion Davies in *Marianne*—but weren't overwhelmed. "He got a light reception ... and closed to heavy hand.... Gray has a pleasant and affable personality that is not particularly impressive, but which, nevertheless, fits in with the singing of popular songs," commented *The Billboard*.[18] "May not rate much as a b.o. draw ... but as an act shapes up as okay," was the tepid response from *Variety*.[19] When little Liberty Pictures, and its president, M.H. Hoffman, came calling in late 1934, it was much appreciated. "M.H. Hoffman is bringing Lawrence Gray back to the screen," wrote columnist Louella Parsons." ... He has a very appealing voice and a very nice personality. But the boy couldn't get a job until Hoffman gave him the lead in *Dizzy Dames*."[20]

Gray was not first-billed in *Dizzy Dames*—the above-the-title distinction went to respected dramatic star Marjorie Rambeau (1889–1970). MGM contract player Florine McKinney (1909–1975)—lately in the cast of that company's prestigious *David Copperfield*—took the female romantic lead. Most of the rest of the cast came from musical comedy: Fuzzy Knight, Kitty Kelly, Lillian Miles, and another very pleasing circa '30 movie musical player in peppy Inez Courtney (1908–1975), whose nimble dancing and comedic charm brought her to Hollywood in a string of support roles (including one alongside Gray in *Spring Is Here*). William Nigh, an action specialist who helmed Metro's *Lord*

Piano man Lawrence Gray romances pretty Florine McKinney in Liberty Pictures' *Dizzy Dames* (1935).

Byron of Broadway [q.v.], directed the *Dizzy Dames* menagerie through a script by George Waggner that was inspired by a magazine story by P.G. Wodehouse. *Dizzy Dames* was filmed in January 1935 at the RKO Pathe Studios in Culver City, with *The Old Homestead* following a month later. The latter was released shortly after Liberty's assimilation into the newly formed Republic, and went out as a Republic release.

No matter one's opinion of the songs and dances, your inclination to like *Dizzy Dames* may be reliant upon a difficult supposition: not only that the retired Broadway star played by Rambeau has kept her 20-something daughter oblivious to her background, but also that the mom could ask the boarders at her home for show people to keep their own interests secret while the daughter visits. If you can suspend disbelief enough on the above, you might enjoy the scene in which a trained seal bathes in the rooming house's communal tub. ("He's the only one working" is the rationale of the seal's owner, one of the titular dizzy dames.) Or the one in which a tenant recounting the death of her plumber boyfriend in a flood asks Courtney if she believes in reincarnation. "No," she replies with a limited frame of reference, "but we played Joplin once and it rained all week." A big problem is that performers like Courtney and Kelly are underused as the romantic subplot dominates the film's second half, although Knight at least gets an number to himself, "Love Is the Thing," that displays the eccentric piano playing talents that made him a vaudeville standout long before the talkies came in.

Dizzy Dames had high enough production values that two of its songs, "I Was Taken by Storm" and "The Martinique," earned promotion for some time before the film's release to most of the country. *Dizzy Dames* played in small markets as early as May 1935 but didn't open in New York—and earn a tepid *Variety* review—until July 1936. By then, Helen Morgan and the Hal Kemp Orchestra had gotten mileage out of their respective cover recordings of "Storm," but the movie followed too slowly in many locales to fully capitalize. The exotic "The Martinique" is the climactic number, sung by Lillian Miles in a style reminiscent of her more famous introduction of "The Continental" in *The Gay Divorcee* (1934). Miles was a blonde in the earlier film—and in 1933's *Moonlight and Pretzels* [q.v.]—as well as the exploitation classic *Reefer Madness* (aka *Tell Your Children*, 1936). Miles, rhumba dancer Christine Marston, and a chorus of dancing waiters do most of the heavy lifting in a *Dizzy Dames* sequence impressively choreographed by Maurice Kosloff, but Gray gets the last chorus as his character wins the girl.

Gray also experienced a last-reel happy ending in *The Old Homestead*—a comic modernization of a famous 1880s rural play—but the citified actor was not so effectively cast. As a mopey Missouri farmer who would rather tend his land than develop his voice, he is rightly chided by co-star Mary Carlisle:

"You're not a cowboy; you're a singer!" Still, the farmer gets to New York radio as the front man of an ensemble of his hired hands. Four of such were more-genuine cowboys—portrayed by the members of the well-known country-Western group the Sons of the Pioneers. This was the first feature film for the "hillbilly" quartet best known for creating and recording "Tumbling Tumbleweeds," and the Sons are pretty much why anyone other than Lawrence Gray fans would bother to remember *The Old Homestead*.[21] Specifically, they remember the group's rhythm guitarist and sometime vocalist, Leonard (Len) Slye (incorrectly billed on screen as "Sly"), who left the act in 1938 to become legendary cowboy star Roy Rogers (1911–1998).

Sometimes with the help of supporting player Fuzzy Knight (who would go on to scores of Westerns as a perennial "B" sidekick), the Sons of the Pioneers provide a variety of sounds to *The Old Homestead*. Their original compositions include a yodeling number ("Way Out There"); they harmonize to "Tiger Rag"; and they provide backup for Gray's mellower tones on the plug songs "Plow Boy" (performed four times in not much over an hour) and "Moonlight in Heaven" (twice). As welcome a presence here as she is in *Dizzy Dames*, Lillian Miles sings "Happy Cowboy"—composed by Sons co-founder/vocalist Bob Nolan—with the group as her character romantically pursues Gray's Uncle Jed (Willard Robertson). There's no lack of talent in the cast, but Eddie Nugent and Dorothy Lee are wasted in parts smaller than filmgoers were accustomed to seeing them in. *The Old Homestead* qualifies as a Western in a broad sense because of the style of most of its songs, but only the first and last few minutes take place outside the nominally more civilized showbiz hubbub of New York City.

The year 1935 was particularly notable for Lawrence Gray, and not because his film work was on the rebound. In August, just as *The Old Homestead* was starting to be seen, he and Mexican actress Mary Louisa Figueroa were married; newspaper reports indicated that they were brought together by a mutual friend, actress Dolores Del Rio. After a few more quickies, but no more musicals, Gray left the movies, and he focused on radio opportunities as emcee of the Mutual program "Morning Matinee." "He has mastered lyrics in seven languages," wrote one reporter, "and would rather be known as a good baritone than a matinee idol."[22]

The singing didn't last a whole lot longer: By early 1941, Gray was working as a representative of the controversial Clayton Knight Committee, an organization that supported U.S. intervention in World War II, for which he visited cities nationwide recruiting Americans to join the Canadian and Royal Air Force as pilots or in other civilian positions.[23] Gray and his wife eventually moved to Mexico City, where he functioned as a liaison between the Mexican film industry and Hollywood before his death.

Frankie and Johnnie
(Republic; May 1, 1936)

Director: Chester Erskine. Producer: William Saal. Screenplay: Moss Hart, based on the play by Jack Kirkland. Additional Dialogue: Lou Goldberg. Photography: Joseph Ruttenberg. Editor: William Thompson. Musical Director: Victor Young. Art Director: Samuel Corso. Sound: Earl Wolcott. Running Time: 66 minutes.

Cast: Helen Morgan (Frankie); Chester Morris (Johnnie Drew); Lilyan Tashman (Nellie Bly); Florence Reed (Lou); Walter Kingsford (Timothy); William Harrigan (Curley); John Larkin (Andy); Cora Witherspoon (Mrs. Lumpy Thornton); Montagu Love (Brinn); Pedro de Cordoba (opera house actor); Jack Hazzard (sheriff).

Songs: "Get Rhythm in Your Feet" [black chorus], "If You Want My Heart" [Morgan, chorus], "It's You I Adore" [Morgan] (J. Russel Robinson, William Livingston), "Give Me a Heart to Sing To" [Morgan] (Ned Washington, Victor Young); "De Camptown Races" [male vocalist, "waiters" quartet] (Stephen Foster).

The Story: Bound for St. Louis in 1870, card shark Johnnie Drew fleeces a group of riverboat gamblers of $13,000 by pretending to be a rube. In the city, he is charmed by good-hearted music hall singer Frankie, who is about to be married to Curley, and attracts the attention of Frankie's rival, Nellie Bly. The gamblers attempt to take revenge against Johnnie, but the music hall's owner, Lou, signals to her aide, Timothy, to protect him from harm. Frankie and Johnnie are married, but having lost his bankroll, he plans to go to New Orleans to get a new stake—while beginning an affair with Nellie. Frankie borrows money from Lou so Johnnie won't leave town without her, but Johnnie takes the money and slips away from Frankie during a night at the opera house to ask Nellie to go off with him instead. Frankie goes to Nellie's home to confront Johnnie with a pistol in hand, but this time Lou signals Timothy to shoot Johnnie. Curley offers to take Johnnie away from her sorrow.

Neither a full-fledged musical nor a "Poverty Row" production, at least not in intent, *Frankie and Johnnie* is of interest as one of the lesser-acknowledged casualties of the Hays Office's enforcement of the Production Code. An independent production forced into distribution limbo just after its initial completion by the censorship transitions of 1934, it was shunned by major companies before being issued by Republic in a recut, toned-down version in 1936. If they weren't already bored by the dullness of the final cut, audiences were reminded of the film's troubles by the presence of a major cast member who had been dead for two years.

This dreary adaptation of the bawdy ballad of bygone days about a jealous woman who shoots her lover because he "done her wrong" already may have been questionable movie material for mainstream America.[24] *Her Man*, a 1930 Pathé movie inspired by the song, encountered censorship problems, and that same year, *Frankie and Johnnie*, a play by Jack Kirkland (future author of *Tobacco Road*), was raided and closed down by New York authorities.[25] Mae West, no shrinking violet, made ample use of the song in her 1933 movie *She Done Him*

Wrong and her play *Diamond Lil*. Although talk of a Code crackdown was brewing in Hollywood, producer-director Chester Erskine embarked on a production of *Frankie and Johnnie* in February 1934 at the recently reopened Biograph Studios in New York City, where such notables as Mary Pickford and D.W. Griffith had started in pictures.[26]

Erskine, the 30-year-old director of the stage successes *The Criminal Code* and *The Last Mile*, had just shot a drama, *Midnight* (with a young Humphrey Bogart), in New York. *Frankie and Johnnie* was to be the next in a series of film productions by the All Star Productions company showcasing East Coast stage talent and resources. As Erskine told newspaper correspondent Irene Kuhn shortly after shooting commenced:

> It is not our intention to show Hollywood how to make pictures. We are interested only in making good pictures.... To that end, naturally, we are following new ideas. My own thought is that the making of pictures should be more personalized. Hollywood grinds them out the way a factory does pins. It hires theater stars ... then ... they fit those stars into the Hollywood pattern, oftentimes wasting rich talent and robbing the name of its expensive lustre.[27]

Erskine had Broadway author Moss Hart, then best known for the hit comedy *Once in a Lifetime*, to adapt Kirkland's story, and he wanted established theatrical names Helen Morgan and Tallulah Bankhead to join Hollywood star Chester Morris (1901–1970) atop his cast. He got Morgan (1900–1941), the famed torch singer, to play Frankie, but Bankhead was replaced due to a reported "illness" just before filming and replaced by Lilyan Tashman as the story's notorious hussy, Nellie Bly.[28] Tashman, wife of actor Edmund Lowe, was well known as "The Screen's Best Dressed Woman." Other roles were announced for such legit-trained players as Florence Reed, Walter Kingsford, William Harrigan, veteran comedians Jack Hazzard and Percy Helton, and even radio musicologist Dr. Sigmund Spaeth.

Erskine finished the film by early March, having taken less than a month (as he had promised to Irene Kuhn in her account), with a tale including the traditional climax in which Johnnie is shot by Frankie. A fan magazine reporter who visited the set described the emotions for Morgan during the shooting of the scene and, in an article that appeared in July 1934, must have whetted fan appetites for a powerful piece of entertainment to come:

> When the time came for her to play it she couldn't cry. Erskin [sic] resorted to all the known studio tricks but no tears. Helen sent her maid for an onion but before she returned, the spirit of the thing came over Helen and she played the scene perfectly ... hysterically.... Johnnie's "blood" on her face and hands ... trembling and sobbing in anguish ... and for half an hour afterwards she could not stop crying.[29]

Because of this and other aspects of the story, *Frankie and Johnnie* came under immediate scrutiny from the newly empowered Production Code Administration. The PCA ordered that the 75-minute movie be shelved, forcing United Artists to drop out of a tentative distribution deal. PCA director Joseph Breen insisted in the fall of 1934 that the song "Frankie and Johnnie" be eliminated, that the source play by Kirkland not be mentioned, that the film did not specify Frankie's love for Johnnie as "illicit ... immoral behavior," and that no references to the saloon in which Frankie sings characterize it as a brothel, with its "attendant evidences of prostitution."[30] "The whole flavor and atmosphere of the story is such to support its almost complete unfitness for public exhibition before mixed audiences," Breen also wrote.[31]

The movie's new producer, William Saal of Select Productions, assured the censors that reshoots would be made; they were—in early 1935—but on the West Coast and without Erskine's participation. John H. Auer, uncredited, stepped in to direct, with original cameraman Joseph Ruttenberg.[32] Another non-participant in the retakes was Tashman, who had died on March 21, 1934, of abdominal cancer, and the new film had to be fashioned around footage of her incomplete performance. In June 1935, a 70-minute version—now tied to RKO—was reviewed in *The Film Daily*, which praised it as "pleasing entertainment with good cast and efficient handling" but mentioned only Tashman's death as the reason for the revamping.[33] Still, *Frankie and Johnnie* would not be released until Republic—whose founder, Herbert Yates, had helped bankroll the film as treasurer of Biograph Studios—announced in January 1936 it would do so.[34]

Reviewed at 66 minutes and advertised as "The Romeo & Juliet of a Roaring Age," the "final" *Frankie and Johnnie* strongly hints at the pre-release tampering, especially with a climax incongruent with the song: Johnnie is shot not by this overly kind-hearted Frankie but by a third party—so no Helen Morgan hysterics. The "Frankie and Johnnie" ballad isn't sung at all—so as not to remind viewers of the offending words—but is heard only in instrumental underscoring. Morgan is saddled with a one-dimensional character (thanks, no doubt, to the toning-down), and her limited acting skills are showcased at the expense of her singing voice. She sings only three songs—perhaps proving she was better in smaller screen doses, as in *Show Boat* (1936).[35] Too much is wasted on an incidental number set at an African-American wedding that lends nothing to the story, which moves in fits and starts, leaving one to speculate over what is missing.

Frankie and Johnnie suffers from an identity problem: At times it's a musical, a melodrama, even a parody (when Victor Young's background score becomes overly grim)—and succeeds as none. Who knows what it was supposed to be as conceived by Erskine and Hart? Many of the announced cast members are barely seen or absent entirely. Tashman wasn't billed at all, and the final print had no writing credit. The most tangible asset is Florence Reed's assertive per-

A gambler (Chester Morris) and a singer (Helen Morgan) envision wedded bliss in the troubled production *Frankie and Johnnie* (1936).

formance as Frankie's saloon-keeper boss. Reed, a star of silent films two decades before, was best known for originating the role of brothel queen "Mother Goddam" in the controversial play *The Shanghai Gesture* in 1926.

Not surprisingly, the box office for *Frankie and Johnnie* was indifferent and the critical response not even that good. "Unusually slovenly entertainment ... without any of the spicy trimmings," was the lament of *Variety*, which acknowledged the film's Hays Office "dehydration."; "ineffectual ... moving at a laggard pace," decreed *Motion Picture Daily*.[36] *The New York Times* chose to review the film in a single paragraph, written by Frank Nugent, that took too long to get to its punch line but summed up the whole sad affair:

> Slightly more lachrymose and off-key than a whiskey tenor.... Two years have passed since the picture was filmed in the Bronx, and those two years have seen the censors grow mightily in power and authority. What they have done to the picture is more than we can imagine. Even without their scissoring, however, it still must have been pretty bad. It done us wrong.[37]

The ill-fated love story inspired two more movies titled *Frankie and Johnny*, in 1966 with Elvis Presley and Donna Douglas and 1991 with Al Pacino and

Michelle Pfeiffer. The latter was directly derived from the Terrence McNally play *Frankie and Johnny in the Clair de Lune*.

The Hit Parade
(Republic; April 26, 1937)
and *Manhattan Merry-Go-Round*
(Republic; November 26, 1937)

The Hit Parade

Director: Gus Meins. Producer: Nat Levine. Associate Producer: Colbert Clark. Assistant Director: George Sherman. Screenplay: Bradford Ropes, Samuel Ornitz. Story: Bradford Ropes. Additional Dialogue: Harry Ruskin. Photography: Ernest Miller. Editing: Ernest Nims, Lester Orlebeck. Music Supervisor: Harry Grey. Musical Director: Alberto Colombo. Art Director: John Ducasse Schulze. Visual Effects: John T. Coyle. Sound: Terry Kellum. Running Time: 83 minutes.

Cast: Frances Langford (Ruth Allison); Phil Regan (Pete Garland); Louise Henry (Monica Barrett); Pert Kelton (Eadie White); Edward Brophy (Mulrooney); Max Terhune (Rusty Callahan); Inez Courtney (Tillie); Monroe Owsley (Teddy Leeds); Pierre Watkin (J.B. Hawley); J. Farrell MacDonald (O'Hara); William Demarest (parole officer); George Givot (Nick); Sammy White (Sammy); Duke Ellington and His Orchestra with Ivie Anderson, Eddy Duchin and His Orchestra, Carl Hoff and the Hit Parade Orchestra (themselves); The Gentle Maniacs [Paul "Mousie" Garner, Sam Wolfe, Richard Hakins] (themselves); Tic Toc Girls [Yvonne Manoff, Mildred Winston, Barbara Johnston] (themselves); Pick and Pat [Pick Malone, Pat Padgett aka Molasses and January] (themselves); Al Pearce and His Gang [Lord Bilgewater, The Human Chatterbox] (themselves); The Voice of Experience [Marion Sayle Taylor], Ed Thorgersen, Oscar and Elmer, Roy Smeck (themselves); Johnny Arthur (success story teller); Stanley Fields (bedtime story man); Kathleen Howard (Mrs. Barrett); Rita La Roy (ex-convict); William Newell (Burt Ambrose); Harvey Clark (Mr. Barrett); Otto Fries (major domo); Emmett Vogan (news commentator); Eddie Kane (Tony); Grace Hayle (cooking expert); Princess Luana, Galante and Leonarda (dancers); Jack Egan, Carleton Young (announcers).

Songs: "I'll Reach for a Star" [Langford], "Last Night I Dreamed of You" [Langford], "Was It Rain?" [Langford] (Walter Hirsch, Lou Handman); "If It Wasn't for Pete" [White, chorus], "Sweet Heartache" [Regan, reprised by Langford, then by Regan, Langford] (Ned Washington, Sam H. Stept); "Hail Alma Mater" [chorus] (Sam H. Stept); "The Glory Beyond" [danced by Langford, Kelton] (Alberto Colombo); "Happy Days Are Here Again" [Hoff orchestra] (Jack Yellen, Milton Ager); "I've Got to Be a Rug Cutter" [Ellington orchestra with Anderson] (Duke Ellington); "Love Is Good for Anything That Ails You" [Tic Toc Girls, Ellington orchestra, Duchin orchestra, Hoff orchestra, chorus] (Cliff Friend, Matty Malneck); "Geschichten aus dem Wienerwald/Wiener Blut" [Duchin orchestra, danced by Galante and Leonarda] (Johann Strauss II).

Also Known As: *We're on the Air*.

Reissue/Television Title: *I'll Reach for a Star.*
Disc: Brunswick 7864 ("Was It Rain?"/"Last Night I Dreamed of You," Phil Regan); Brunswick 7869 ("Sweet Heartache," Phil Regan); Brunswick 7989, Master 101 ("I've Got to Be a Rug Cutter," Duke Ellington Orchestra); Decca 1202 ("Was It Rain?"/"Sweet Heartache," Frances Langford).
Home Video: Alpha DVD.

The Story: Agent Pete Garland negotiates a new radio contract for high-class singer Monica Barrett, but she fires him because her adviser, attorney Teddy Leeds, thinks the work is beneath her. While scouting new talent, Pete and his ventriloquist friend Rusty discover singer Ruth Allison and her stage partner, Eadie. Pete wants to make Ruth a star, and she falls in love with him, but she hasn't told him she is an ex-convict who has jumped her parole. Ruth becomes a success on Manhattan's WBR and lands her own program. A jealous Monica, who has been fired from her show, exposes Ruth's past to the press. Ruth stays away from her next broadcast, but a lineup of guest stars appears instead on her behalf. Pete wins back Ruth by singing "Sweet Heartache," and the public is won over as well.

Manhattan Merry-Go-Round

Director: Charles F. Reisner. Associate Producer: Harry Sauber. Screenplay: Harry Sauber, based on the NBC Radio musical revue by Frank Hummert. Photography: Jack Marta. Editors: Murray Seldeen, Ernest Nims. Musical Supervisor: Harry Grey. Musical Director: Albert Colombo. Art Director: John Victor Mackay. Running Time: 87 minutes.

Cast: Phil Regan (Jerry Hart); Leo Carrillo (Tony Gordoni); Ann Dvorak (Ann Rogers); Tamara Geva (Charlizzini); James Gleason (Danny the Duck); Gene Autry, Ted Lewis and His Orchestra, Cab Calloway and His Cotton Club Orchestra, Kay Thompson and Her Ensemble (aka Her Radio Choir), Joe DiMaggio, Max Terhune, Smiley Burnette, Louis Prima and His Band (themselves); Henry Armetta (Spadoni); Luis Alberni (Martinetti); Selmer Jackson (J. Henry Thorne); Eddie Kane (McMurray); Moroni Olsen (Jonathan); Nellie V. Nichols (Momma Gordoni); Gennaro Curci (Michael Angelo); Sam Finn (Speed); Al Herman (Blackie); Robert E. Perry (Baldy); Jack Adair (Eddie); Thelma Wunder (Dorothy); Anna Demetrio (Charlizzini's maid); Neal Dodd (minister); Ralph Edwards (radio man); Gertrude Short (Danny's date); Joe King (chief detective); Stanley Blystone (detective); Jack Jenney and His Orchestra; Rosalean and Seville [The Lathrops].

Songs: "All Over Nothing at All" [Thompson and ensemble], "Have You Ever Been in Heaven?" [opening chorus, reprised by DiMaggio, then by Lewis band and Regan, then by Regan with Autry band], "I Owe You" [Regan, Prima band, reprised by Thompson and ensemble] (Jack Lawrence, Peter Tinturin); "I'm a Musical Magical Man" [Lewis and band], "Manhattan Merry-Go-Round" [opening chorus] (Sammy Kahn, Saul Chaplin); "It's Roundup Time in Reno" [Autry, Regan, Burnette, band] (Jack Lawrence, Jack M. Owens, Gene Autry); "Mama, I Wanna Make Rhythm" [Calloway and band, dancers, reprised by Regan] (Walter Kent, Jerome Jerome, Richard Byron); "When My Baby Smiles at Me" [Lewis band] (Ted Lewis, Andrew B. Sterling, Bill Munro).

Also Known As: *Manhattan Music Box.*
Academy Award Nomination: Best Art Direction (John Victor Mackay).
Home Video: Alpha DVD.

The Story: New York mobster Tony Gordoni takes over the Associated Recording Company, which rehires talented but hot-tempered tenor Jerry Hart through the intervention of receptionist Ann Rogers, who is Jerry's sweetheart. Gordoni signs up radio stars Ted Lewis, Cab Calloway, and Kay Thompson, but his mother complains that the opera star Charlizzini is not under contract. Gordoni orders Jerry—who is about to marry Ann—to romance the temperamental diva into entering the fold. Charlizzini agrees to record with ARC, but her demands on Jerry's time prevent him from explaining the situation to Ann. Impresario Martinetti forbids Charlizzini from recording, so Gordoni concocts a phony kidnapping of the diva to force Martinetti to change his mind. When the hoax is exposed, Jerry goes into hiding at Gene Autry's ranch, but he emerges after Autry records "It's Roundup Time in Reno" for ARC. Gordoni and Charlizzini pair up, Gordoni's henchman Danny finds a mate, and Jerry and Ann are reconciled.

Although Republic had been making modestly budgeted musicals in the two years since its creation, 1937's *The Hit Parade* and *Manhattan Merry-Go-Round* represented significant upgrades in investment—and echoes of the success of Paramount's "Big Broadcast" series. Now easily the biggest entity among the independent companies, and edging closer to "minor" majors such as Columbia and Universal, Republic was still making plenty of Westerns, serials and other action films, but with upgraded story variety and bigger-name talent. In 1937, the studio could boast current and upcoming releases with such known acting commodities as Lew Ayres, James Dunn, Ramon Novarro (making a brief comeback after two years away from the screen), Grant Withers, Paul Kelly, Lyle Talbot, Mary Brian, and the soon-to-ascend John Wayne. Republic's two breakout musicals—both with titular tie-ins to real-life radio shows—relied heavily on guest stars while featuring the studio's biggest non-cowboy musical lead, Phil Regan.

Regan (1906–1996) had flexed his tenor at Republic in *Happy Go Lucky* and the aptly titled (given Regan's ethnicity) *Laughing Irish Eyes*—but he cut his teeth elsewhere, and not in the usual way. A former police detective in his native Brooklyn, Regan parlayed a radio stint as "The Singing Cop" into a contract with Warner Bros.[38] There, he played supporting roles in features and leads in Vitaphone shorts—a second-string status that prompted his departure for Republic. While *The Hit Parade*—the first of Republic's two "super"-musicals—was being filmed in late 1936, the big news for Regan was the revelation that the 30-year-old actor not only was married, he also was the father of four children—the oldest already age 12.

Regan and his wife—who had married at 17 (and would stay married for

Republic's *Manhattan Merry-Go-Round* (1937) showcases the talents of (from left) Phil Regan, Ann Dvorak, Leo Carrillo, and Tamara Geva.

70 years)—decided to keep his marital status a secret for three years as the family made a home in Pasadena, out of the Hollywood spotlight. Mrs. Regan later 'fessed up to a newspaper reporter:

> Phil and I went everywhere.... I was "the girl friend." Phil would introduce me as, "Miss Josephine Dwyer, whom I hope someday to introduce as Mrs. Regan." It was true, too. Then a columnist came to us with a letter written from Brooklyn, in which the writer accused Phil of deserting his wife and four kids there, leaving them to starve while he posed as a bachelor. It certainly made me mad. So we announced our marriage.[39]

Fortunately, Regan's powerful voice seemed to matter more than his social eligibility, and Republic budgeted *The Hit Parade*—the title inspired by the very popular NBC/Lucky Strike program *Your Hit Parade*—at a reported $500,000, the company's most expensive film to date. (In contrast, a typical Republic B-Western at this time might cost $30,000 to $60,000.) Nat Levine, outgoing president of Republic, made the film his final project at the studio—his departure was said to be voluntary, but he was being bought out by Herbert Yates for $2 million.[40] Levine brought in a credible roster of radio celebs—the orchestras of Duke Ellington, Eddy Duchin, and (from the *Parade* radio show) Carl

Hoff; comedy acts Oscar and Elmer and Al Pearce and His Gang; and blackface duo Pick and Pat.[41] Also from the airwaves was Regan's romantic counterpart, pop singer Frances Langford (1913–2005), who introduced her signature song, "I'm in the Mood for Love," in Paramount's *Every Night at Eight* (1935).

In the *Hit Parade* film scenario, Langford played a golden-voiced ex-convict hiding her past from her showbiz mentor-turned-sweetheart (Regan) and the rest of the world until—at a pivotal point in the story—being exposed ... but ultimately embraced, literally by her co-star and professionally by her audience. The film was well received—lauded even by *The New York Times*, with a readership not quite on Republic's demographic radar, gave it faint praise as "a kind of amateur hour put on by professionals ... fairly amusing, fairly clever ... in a state of comfortable mediocrity."[42]

Directed by Gus Meins, a veteran of Laurel and Hardy and Our Gang comedies, *The Hit Parade* continues to play well. Its song lineup is led by the ballad "Sweet Heartache" and the Ellington novelty "I Want to Be a Rug Cutter," plus the ambitious finale, "Love Is Good for Anything That Ails You," in which a variety of acts—starting with Ellington and his band—chronicle the roots of a hit song, from the "jungle swing" of Africa to the waltzes of Europe to America's shores. "Was It Rain?" was a third "plug" song from the movie. There's also pleasing work by Max Terhune, a cowboy ventriloquist and impressionist summoned from Republic's B-Westerns unit to be seen and heard in a variety of disguises and voices. Unfortunately, the *Hit Parade* we see today is a 1950s theatrical reissue of 66 minutes, nearly two reels shorter than the original. The absent material is mostly radio specialties—including rare appearances by the ether's "Voice of Experience" and "The Human Chatterbox," plus novelty guitarist Roy Smeck. The current version, retitled *I'll Reach for a Star*, also is confusing as to the nature of the female lead's transgressions, and we're guessing some of that exposition is what's also missing.

Bolstered by the success of *The Hit Parade*, Republic designated *Manhattan Merry-Go-Round*—filmed in the late summer of 1937 and based on another NBC Radio series—as one of its 1937–38 "Anniversary Specials" targeted at top-level theaters. The formula was the same, but the lineup of attractions was even more diverse, even bordering on bizarre or wacky. Joining Regan was his new co-star, fellow Warner Bros. refugee Ann Dvorak. Regan had left that studio because of how he was used, and Dvorak (1911–1979) departed because of how she was paid. After a promising start for Howard Hughes in *Scarface* (1932) and at Warners in *Three on a Match* (1932), she spent much of the mid–1930s in WB's doghouse over salary disputes, and the quality of her scripts diminished until she moved on as a free-lancer.

Also featured were the Ted Lewis, Cab Calloway, and Louis Prima orchestras; uptown singer Kay Thompson (with her "Radio Choir"); reliable comic trouper James Gleason; and a noisy lineup of dialect actors in Leo Carrillo, Henry Armetta, Luis Alberni, and Nellie V. Nichols. Veteran director Charles F. Reisner knew how to juggle a lot of balls, given his work on MGM's star-filled *The Hollywood Revue of 1929* and *Hollywood Party*.

The real curveball in *Manhattan Merry-Go-Round*, however, was the appearance of Joe DiMaggio, the New York Yankees star made to sing a snatch of the film's showcase song, "Have You Ever Been in Heaven?" while somehow being mistaken for a crooner by Armetta. In his three-minute bit, DiMaggio reminds the excitable maestro that he's not a tenor or baritone, "I'm a centerfielder." DiMaggio's voiceover narration of a newsreel clip of his home run against the New York Giants in baseball's 1937 World Series hammers home the point. "No one bothered to make a test of him," commented a fan magazine of the DiMaggio stunt, "because no matter how terrible he was, he would draw a large part of the male population of the country to the box office."[43] DiMaggio's footage was shot at the Biograph Studios in New York—as were the all the guest-star acts for *Manhattan Merry-Go-Round* and *The Hit Parade*. The experience wasn't all bad: He met his first wife, dancer Dorothy Arnold, an extra in a nightclub number, on the set.

In Harry Sauber's script, Carrillo (1881–1961) plays a genial mobster who muscles into control of a recording company, then has to rely upon dreamy crooner Regan to win the favor of the opera star (portrayed by Broadway's Tamara Geva, a dancer not called upon to dance here) whom the crook's overtly Italian mother has badgered him into attempting to sign. Like so many other musicals of the era, *Manhattan Merry-Go-Round* makes fun of the high- and low-culture conflict between segments of the music-loving public, summed up here in "Mama, I Wanna Make Rhythm," sung by Calloway about a child-prodigy violinist who would rather "get hotcha." Geva's character shares that thought: She'd rather sings a pop ditty than an aria. The film's nod to current trends even extends to a brief demonstration of television!

Still, to remind us that this is Republic product, Max Terhune appears in a cameo, again searching for a job. And the cowboys come to the rescue, as the studio's biggest name, Gene Autry, shows up in the final reel to reunite the romantic leads. Considering how weird this seems, Gene and his bandsmen might as well have been space aliens. In this collision of sagebrush-hero purity and backstage sass, Autry (1907–1998) provides the biggest laugh. Having watched three sets of couples in the cast launch into passionate embraces at the drop of a song in a recording studio, he wonders aloud: "Hey, what kind of a place is this?" Almost as strange was his billing in the opening credits, in which the studio felt the need to identify him to its new crossover audiences with the subtitle "Introducing that cowboy singing star, Gene Autry."

Noted a Kansas City newspaper reviewer upon viewing *Manhattan Merry-*

Go-Round: "If you search long enough, you will find the kitchen sink among the properties."[44] The trade pubs more or less agreed: "The show will make dough for it has all the elements of mass entertainment," wrote *The Film Daily*, and *Motion Picture Daily* lauded a film "that has everything—well-woven story, good music, brisk comedy...—treated by distinct novelty in filmusical plots and variety of marquee names ... [in] musical numbers that run from opera to hi-de-ho."[45] From this corner, the film continues to hold up well.

The Hit Parade and *Manhattan Merry-Go-Round*, however sparing in budget compared to the biggest songfests at MGM, Paramount or Warner Bros., verified that musicals large as well as small would be staples at Republic, either with Phil Regan or without. The company made four more *Hit Parade* films alone, for 1941, 1943, 1947, and 1951. Like the 1937 picture, the '41, '43, and '47 editions were retitled for theatrical reissues and television airings—as, respectively, *Romance and Rhythm*, *Change of Heart*, and *High and Happy*. But, really, weren't they all high and happy?

Chapter Notes

Chapter 1

1. Courtney Ryley Cooper (1886–1940) was a prolific writer of short stories, biographies, and screenplays who was lauded by J. Edgar Hoover as "the best informed man on crime in the U.S." Cooper committed suicide while supposedly attempting to alert the FBI to German activities in Mexico; some believed he'd been murdered.

2. Steven Bingen, *Warner Bros.: Hollywood's Ultimate Backlot* (Lanham, Md.: Rowman & Littlefield, 2014), p. 17.

3. *Sound Waves*, November 15, 1928.

4. "The Screen: The Jailbird's Song," *The New York Times*, January 25, 1929.

5. "Film Reviews: *Weary River*," *Variety*, January 30, 1929.

6. "The Truth About Voice Doubling," *Photoplay*, July 1929.

7. "Sunday Movies—A Question That Must Be in Chillicothe," *Chillicothe (Mo.) Constitution-Tribune*, August 3, 1929.

8. Memo from April 26, 1929; Motion Picture Producers and Distributors of America digital archive entry on *Weary River*, Flinders Institute for Research in the Humanities: http://mppda.flinders.edu.au/records/620.

9. Walter Wagner, *You Must Remember This* (New York: Putnam, 1975), pp. 89–90.

10. "Jessel Gives In," *Exhibitors Daily Review*, October 15, 1928.

11. Three other notable names from *The War Song*—which opened in September 1928 and closed in December—were Gene Raymond (billed under his actual name of Raymond Guion), Lola Lane, and future Oscar winner Shirley Booth, who was the female lead. They do not appear in the surviving version of *Lucky Boy*, nor were they credited for appearing in it. (There is an actress playing a music store clerk in the film who looks a little like Booth in long shot, but....)

12. "The World's Worst in Acts Located," *Variety*, November 14, 1928.

13. "Loew's Takes *Lucky Boy*," *Variety*, January 23, 1929; "*Lucky Boy* Tie-Ups," *The Film Daily*, January 29, 1929.

14. "George Jessel in *Lucky Boy*," *The Film Daily*, January 6, 1929. The Jolson comparison extended as far away as Paris; when Tiffany-Stahl arranged a booking there, it was canceled after four days because of complaints from viewers who "appeared to resent the Jessel picture as a copy." "*Lucky Boy* Pulled in Paris After 4 Days," *Variety*, November 20, 1929.

15. "Fox Buys George Jessel's Tiffany-Stahl Contract," *Motion Picture News*, March 23, 1929. Jessel's only starring feature at Fox was *Love, Live and Laugh* (1929); he also appeared in a cameo in that studio's 1930 all-star musical, *Happy Days*.

16. "Film Reviews: *Battle of Paris*," *Variety*, February 12, 1930.

17. Robert Florey, *Hollywood d'hier et d'aujourd'hui* (Paris: Editions Prisma, 1948), pp. 158–159; Brian Taves, *Robert Florey: The French Expressionist* (Metuchen, N.J.: Scarecrow, 1987), p. 106.

18. Taves, *Robert Florey*, p. 118.

19. The numbers on Paramount's film output in Astoria come from *Exhibitors Herald-World*, July 20, 1929. Of the major studios, Paramount was the most devoted to making feature-length films in New York, as opposed to simply short subjects using stage talent.

20. "Gay Miss Lawrence: English Actress Is Engrossed With a New Talking Picture," *The New York Times*, July 7, 1929. The story verifies what was reported in the trades: *The Battle of Paris* had two directors on set, the other being John Meehan, who handled at least some of the dialogue sequences here, as he had with Paramount's earlier *The Lady Lies*. Meehan received no on-screen credit for *Battle of Paris*.

21. "War Scenes of *Great Lady* Are Made," *Hollywood Filmograph*, July 13, 1929.

22. "Over the Teacups," *Picture Play*, October 1929.

23. An item in *The Billboard* from July 20, 1929, "To Re-Do Scenes for *Gay Lady*, Toning It

Down," makes one wonder about the intended tone of the film. The article indicated that some scenes were to be retaken "due to the feeling that the picture is a little too 'daring' in certain spots" and that actor Walter Huston was coming East to appear in the retakes. Huston was not found in the final cut.

24. "Pictures in New York: *Battle of Paris*," *The Billboard*, February 15, 1930.

25. Sheridan Morley, *Gertrude Lawrence* (New York: McGraw Hill, 1981), p. 71.

26. Haines and Love were tied to *Lord Byron* per a February 1929 item "Last Minute News," in *Motion Picture Classic*; King was mentioned by *The Film Daily* April 14, "Charles King Starred," and June 18, 1929, "40 Talkers and 7 Silents Slated for M-G-M Release."

27. "Marion Harris in Talker," *Variety*, July 10, 1929; "Marion Needs Weight," *Variety*, July 31, 1929.

28. "Ethelind Terry With M-G-M," *Los Angeles Times*, August 28, 1929.

29. Newspaper Enterprise Association syndicated story, November 6, 1929.

30. The real estate man whom Terry would marry in 1928, and divorce in 1941 after an 11-year separation, was Benjamin Bogeaus from Chicago, who would be better known in the 1940s and '50s as the film producer Benedict Bogeaus.

31. "A Little From Lots," *The Film Daily*, September 15, 1929.

32. Kaley's late-'20s marital life is described in "More Hit and Run Marriages Lead to Chicago's Divorce Mill," *Variety*, February 29, 1928.

33. "*Byron's* Ending," *Variety*, October 23, 1929. Marion Shilling's role was initially announced for Shannon Day, a former Hollywood ingénue for whom *Lord Byron* would have ended a three-year drought in features. The production delays also may have cost Kaley the lead in MGM's filming of the Broadway musical *Good News* "Kaley Out—Hall In," *Variety*, January 23, 1930, although by the time that film began shooting, MGM already had passed on renewing Kaley's contract.

34. Marion Shilling Cook letter to author, January 12, 1993. Quoted in Edwin M. Bradley, *The First Hollywood Musicals: A Critical Filmography of 171 Features, 1927 Through 1932* (Jefferson, N.C.: McFarland, 1996), p. 226.

35. Cook letter to author, January 29, 1993. Quoted in Bradley, *First Hollywood Musicals*, pp. 226–227.

36. "The Screen: The Ungrateful Songwriter," *The New York Times*, March 8, 1930.

37. "*Lord Byron of Broadway*," *The Film Daily*, March 9, 1930.

38. "Film Reviews: *Lord Byron of Broadway*," *Variety*, March 12, 1930.

39. Richard Barrios, *A Song in the Dark: The Birth of the Musical Film* (New York: Oxford University Press, 2006), p. 197. I don't disagree, but the more one learns about the off-screen Terry, the "unfathomable hauteur" part seems to become more fathomable.

40. MGM thought enough of the two *Lord Byron* color sequences to include them as filler in otherwise black-and-white comedy two-reelers later on. "The Woman in the Shoe" can be seen in the 1933 Ted Healy and His (Three) Stooges short *Nertsery Rhymes*; "Blue Daughter of Heaven" is an insert in 1934's *Roast Beef and Movies*, with then-solo Stooge Jerome "Curly" Howard.

41. "Talker Stars for a Day," *Variety*, July 21, 1931.

42. Kaley's obituary is in the *Los Angeles Times*, September 9, 1965.

43. Terry is billed behind only Ritter on some lobby cards for *Arizona Days* and was mentioned prominently in newspaper publicity, but she is not listed in the on-screen credits, nor does she sing in surviving prints, in which she is briefly seen with only a couple lines of dialogue. It seems likely that her part was bigger but was cut down at some point, perhaps in the editing of the film for television.

44. "The Memory Shift," *Variety*, March 10, 1943.

45. Josephine Sanders took the stage surname of Delroy by combining the first three letters of the first names of her parents (Della and Royal). For more on the actress and her family, see the website of the McLean County (Illinois) Museum: mchistory.org/old/find/delroy_sanders_finding _aid.html#history

46. "Critic Designates Irene Delroy, Actress, 'Typical Girl of '30,'" *The Pantagraph* (Bloomington, Ill.), February 22, 1931. The item in Delroy's hometown newspaper quotes a feature story written about Delroy by the *Los Angeles Sunday Telegram*.

47. "Thirty Famous Unknowns," *Motion Picture Classic*, May 1929. Another fan-mag story, "Are the Stars Good Parents?" (*Picture Play*, May 1930), describes the Kings' concerns over moving Mrs. King and their kids from New York City, where they stayed during Charles' first few months of film stardom, to Los Angeles.

48. "Along the Coast," *Variety*, March 26, 1930.

49. Temporary, too, was the status of *Oh, Sailor, Behave!* as a Technicolor feature. It was initially announced as a color production but was made in black-and-white.

50. "Stage Revue at WB Hollywood Is Doubling All-Sound Grosses," *Variety*, July 16, 1930.

51. *Photoplay*, September 1930.

52. In 1930, Tiffany was back to being Tiffany Productions after a period in which it was called

Tiffany-Stahl. The retirement of producer John M. Stahl from the company board restored the studio to the name it had held in the days of the silents.
53. "Press Agent Puffs," *Motion Picture News*, May 31, 1930.
54. "*Paradise Island* Star Saw Cataline Scenery Only on the Curves," *New York Amsterdam News*, August 6, 1930.
55. "Paradise Island," *The Film Daily*, July 20, 1930; "Paradise Island," *Motion Picture News*, July 5, 1930; "Film Reviews: Paradise Island," *Variety*, August 13, 1930.
56. "Short Shots From New York Studios," *The Film Daily*, February 5, 1930. Items such as this declined to mention that Rogers was married to—and already estranged from—ex-stage partner Jack Pepper.
57. "Just Chit-Chat...," *Hollywood Filmograph*, March 8, 1930.
58. "Filming Scenes in *Queen High*," *The New York Times*, March 30, 1930.
59. "How to Hide 'Mike' Big Problem With Sound Man," *The Film Daily*, March 30, 1930.
60. "The Screen: Turning the Tables," *The New York Times*, August 9, 1930.
61. "Short Shots From New York Studios," *The Film Daily*, April 18, 1930.
62. "Stanley Smith In," *Variety*, June 20, 1933; "Awaiting Dick Powell's Recovery for *Parade*," *Variety*, July 11, 1933.

Chapter 2

1. "Tradeviews," *The Hollywood Reporter*, February 23, 1933.
2. "I Speak for Myself," *Radio Mirror*, July 1934.
3. Harry Medved and Michael Medved, *The Hollywood Hall of Shame: The Most Expensive Flops in Movie History* (New York: Perigee, 1984), p. 71.
4. Richard K. Hayes, *Kate Smith: A Biography, With a Discography, Filmography and List of Stage Appearances* (Jefferson, N.C.: McFarland, 1995), pp. 31, 34.
5. Medved, *Hollywood Hall of Shame*, p. 71.
6. "Para's Hello Everybody All Kate Smith and Songs," *The Hollywood Reporter*, January 4, 1933.
7. "Kate Smith in *Hello Everybody*," *The Film Daily*, January 28, 1933.
8. Hayes, *Kate Smith*, p. 34.
9. Gary Giddins, *Bing Crosby: A Pocketful of Dreams: The Early Years, 1903–1940* (New York: Little, Brown, 2001), pp. 265–266.
10. Joseph Lanza and Dennis Penna, *Russ Columbo and the Crooner Mystique* (Los Angeles: Feral House, 2002), p. 5.

11. "Along the Rialto," *The Film Daily*, July 26, 1933.
12. "Zanuck Tells Jolson to Wait and See If He Was Insulted," *The Billboard*, August 5, 1933.
13. "Actors Who Made 'Breaks' Good," *Photoplay*, January 1934.
14. Ball said she did not remember her appearance in *Broadway Thru a Keyhole* until she saw the movie many years later.
15. Neal Gabler, *Winchell: Gossip, Power and the Culture of Celebrity* (New York: Knopf, 1995), p. 179.
16. Ibid., p. 180.
17. "Film Reviews: *Broadway Thru a Keyhole*," *Variety*, November 7, 1933.
18. Lanza and Penna, *Russ Columbo*, p. 195.
19. Ibid., p. 230.
20. "A Musical Without Surprises," *The New York Times*, October 11, 1934.
21. Miles Kreuger, *Show Boat: The Story of a Classic American Musical* (New York: Oxford University Press, 1977), p. 111.
22. "Behind the Microphone," *Broadcasting*, December 1, 1932.
23. Jeff Lenberg, with Joan Howard Maurer and Greg Lenberg, *The Three Stooges Scrapbook* (Secaucus, N.J.: Citadel, 1999), p. 65.
24. *The Hollywood Reporter*, July 10, 1933.
25. "Myrt and Marge Starts New Cycle," *Universal Weekly*, January 27, 1934. The Love Life of a Crooner became the Columbo feature *Wake Up and Dream*. [q.v.]
26. Marion "Bonnie" Bonnell (1905–1964) was a minor player in the Three Stooges saga. When she was working with Ted Healy and His Stooges, she was rumored to be linked to Healy off screen, but the two were never married. In a bizarre 1935 incident that hit newspapers nationwide, Bonnell accused Healy of forcing his way into her Hollywood apartment and setting fire to bundles of her clothing and pieces of furniture. Healy responded by claiming Bonnell had fired a gun at him, and she dropped arson charges reportedly after deciding Healy was merely playing a joke according to a United Press syndicated article, December 26, 1935, and "News From the Dailies—Coast," *Variety*, January 8, 1936. Not long after, Bonnell married and then faded into obscurity and poverty, according to research by modern historian Bill Cappello. She died, possibly from the effects of alcoholism, in Santa Monica, California.
27. "Myrt and Marge," *The Film Daily*, January 16, 1934.
28. "Film Reviews: *Myrt and Marge*," *Variety*, January 23, 1934.
29. "Looking 'Em Over: *Myrt and Marge*," *Motion Picture Daily*, November 27, 1933.
30. Reviews quoted in *The Hollywood Reporter*, January 25, 1934.
31. "Hal LeRoy, Dancer in Clubs, Musicals

and Several Movies," *The New York Times*, May 4, 1985.
32. Associated Press syndicated column, published as "Hollywood Notebook," *Emporia* (Kansas) *Gazette*, January 2, 1934.
33. "A Little from 'Lots,'" *The Film Daily*, January 12, 1934.
34. Associated Press report, July 26, 1935, published as "Suit Is Settled by Stage 'Hoofer,'" *The Evening Independent* (Massillon, Ohio).
35. "Film Reviews: *Harold Teen*," *Variety*, June 5, 1934.
36. "*Harold* with Music Weak," *The Hollywood Reporter*, February 15, 1934.
37. From the start, censors protested the adaptation of *The Great Magoo* into a film. In a letter to Paramount, Joseph Breen and Will Hays protested the use of "questionable material" and "lowtime carnival atmosphere" from the play, and threatened the film "will have to be rejected." Letter from March 28, 1934; Motion Picture Producers and Distributors of America digital archive entry on *The Great Magoo* (aka *Shoot the Works*), Flinders Institute for Research in the Humanities: http://mppda.flinders.edu.au/records/975
38. If *The Great Magoo* is remembered at all now, it's for including the first version of the song standard "It's Only a Paper Moon," under the title "If You Believed in Me."
39. "The Screen: *Shoot the Works*, a Laundered Version of *The Great Magoo*, at the Paramount," *The New York Times*, July 7, 1934.
40. The makers of *Shoot the Works* reportedly tried to get the real Walter Winchell to play the Walter Winchell type; see "*Great Magoo* Will Not Have Winchell," *Variety*, February 22, 1934.
41. "In Review: *Wharf Angel*," *Picture Play*, July 1934.
42. Shirley Temple Black, *Child Star: An Autobiography* (New York: McGraw Hill, 1988), p. 44.
43. "Announcing the Monthly Broadcast of Hollywood Goings-On!" *Photoplay*, September 1934. The death on March 21, 1934, of screen actress Lilyan Tashman from abdominal cancer was linked to the deaths of Dorothy Dell and Lew Cody as fulfilling the superstition that tragedy happens "in threes."
44. Black, *Child Star*, p. 65.
45. Six songs were listed in trade ads and the program for *Shoot the Works*. Two, "In the Good Old Winter Time" and "Take a Lesson From the Lark," are only heard in currently existing prints as played instrumentally by the band during nightclub scenes. But they are played—and sung by Bernie and band—in a one-reeler, *Hark Ye Hark!*, released by Paramount in 1935. The similarity of costumes between the feature and short hint that the full-fledged numbers may have been filmed for *Shoot the Works* but were cut before its release.
46. "Blushing Lark," *Picture Play*, February 1935.
47. "The Guide to New Pictures: *One Hour Late*," *Hollywood*, March 1935.
48. "The Screen: *Love in Bloom*," *The New York Times*, April 20, 1935.
49. "Morrison Bankrupt," *Variety*, February 5, 1936.
50. "Vaudeville Reviews: Palomar, Seattle," *Billboard*, October 14, 1950.
51. "Know Clothes, and You'll Know Success—Peggy Fears," *Motion Picture*, December 1934.
52. Kevin Lally, *Wilder Times: The Life of Billy Wilder* (New York: Henry Holt, 1996), p. 66.
53. "Ten Fox Players Being Groomed for Stardom," *The Film Daily*, February 10, 1934. Fears actually flirted with Hollywood as early as 1926, when a trade publication reported that she had signed a contract with Warner Bros.: "Peggy Fears Signs With Warner Brothers," *Motion Picture News*, March 27, 1926, but nothing apparently came of it.
54. "Know Clothes…," *Motion Picture*, December 1934.
55. Ibid.
56. "Reviews of New Features: *Lottery Lover*," *The Film Daily*, February 5, 1935.
57. *Harrison's Reports*, January 12, 1935, and May 4, 1935; "The Shadow Stage: *Lottery Lover*," *Photoplay*, March 1935.
58. "Fox Goes All American; No Foreign Film," *Motion Picture Daily*, June 1, 1934; "Fox in Settlement of Rockett Contract," *Motion Picture Daily*, January 22, 1935.
59. "Three's the Party," Newspaper Enterprise Association syndicated column, February 1935, cited in *The Indiana Gazette* (Indiana, Pa.), February 13, 1935.
60. "Good News," *Modern Screen*, July 1935.
61. "In New York," Associated Press syndicated column, October 1938.
62. Anthony Slide, *The Encyclopedia of Vaudeville* (Westport, Conn.: Greenwood, 1994), p. 417.
63. "A Little from 'Lots,'" *The Film Daily*, December 16, 1935.
64. Bill Crow, *From Birdland to Broadway: Scenes from a Jazz Life* (New York: Oxford University Press, 1993), p. 62.
65. *New York Herald Tribune*, February 22, 1936.
66. "Red Hodgson Suing Riley-Farley Over 'Music Goes 'Round,'" *Variety*, February 19, 1936; "Music Goes Round, But Riley and Farley Going Separate Ways," *Variety*, December 9, 1936.
67. "Notes for the Record on *Music Goes 'Round*, at the Capitol," *The New York Times*, February 22, 1936.

68. Thomas C. Hischak, *The Tin Pan Alley Song Encyclopedia* (Westport, Conn.: Greenwood, 2002), p. 250.
69. "Hometown Star of Silver Screen Returns for Premiere," *Scranton (Pa.) Times-Tribune*, August 14, 2011.
70. John Stangeland, *Warren William: Magnificent Scoundrel of Pre-Code Hollywood* (Jefferson, N.C.: McFarland, 2010), p. 164.
71. "O'Brien Suspended," *Motion Picture Daily*, March 6, 1936; "O'Brien to Resume Work on Warner Lot," *Motion Picture Daily*, March 18, 1936.
72. "Stagestruck," *Motion Picture Daily*, August 7, 1936.
73. "The Screen: The Strand Presents Another Backstage Musical, *Stage Struck*, With Blondell and Powell," *The New York Times*, September 28, 1936.
74. "*Gold Diggers* Trip Gets Tremendous," *Motion Picture Daily*, November 17, 1936.
75. "Film Reviews: *Talent Scout*," *Variety*, August 25, 1937.
76. "Meredith Re-Signed," *Motion Picture Daily*, January 11, 1937; "Anne Nagel in Steel; Lee Dixon in Spot," *Variety*, January 12, 1937.
77. Pressbook for *Ready, Willing and Able*, Wisconsin Center for Film and Theater Research.
78. "Film Reviews: *Ready, Willing and Able*," *Variety*, March 17, 1937.
79. Gene Lees, *Portrait of Johnny: The Life of John Herndon Mercer* (New York: Knopf Doubleday, 2009).
80. Philip Furia, *Skylark: The Life and Times of Johnny Mercer* (New York: Macmillan, 2004).
81. "They Needed a Big, Dumb, Comic Cowboy," *Brooklyn Eagle*, October 10, 1943.
82. *Ready, Willing and Able* pressbook, WCFTR.
83. "Broadway Opening: *Oklahoma!*" *The Billboard*, June 9, 1951.
84. Max Wilk, *OK! The Story of "Oklahoma!" A Celebration of America's Most Loved Musical* (New York: Applause Books, 2002), p. 252.
85. Ibid.
86. "Lee Dixon," *The New York Times*, January 11, 1953.

Chapter 3

1. "With Astaire," United Press story quoted from *Charleston (W.Va.) Daily Mail*, June 30, 1937.
2. "Cary Grant Warbling," *Variety*, May 9, 1933.
3. According to the pressbook for *Torch Singer*, Bing Crosby became a technical adviser for a day and coached Colbert on how to sing the lullaby.
4. Cora Sue Collins (b. 1927) is little remembered, but indicative of her popularity was a poll in the summer of 1933 by the Iris Theater in Hollywood, which asked child attendees of its frequent kiddie matinees about their favorite young actors. Collins edged Baby Le Roy at the top of the balloting, and Shirley Temple, then appearing in "Baby Burlesks" shorts for Educational Pictures and in small roles in features, was in a distant third place. "Theater Polls Youngsters on Child Players; Cora Sue Collins Leads in Hollywood Vote," *Chicago Tribune*, September 24, 1933. Of course, that result would have been much different a year or so later. Collins, with credits that included *Smilin' Through* (1932), *The Scarlet Letter* (1934), and *Treasure Island* (1934), retired from the screen in the mid–1940s.
5. "Reviews of Recent Pictures: *Torch Singer*," *Silver Screen*, November 1933.
6. "Claudette Colbert in *Torch Singer*," *The Film Daily*, October 7, 1933.
7. In a musical number called "Meet My Sister," which included a series of real-life and imagined siblings representing various countries, Sothern was paired with the unrelated Marion Byron in Spanish garb.
8. American Movie Classics interview from 1987, quoted from Margie Schultz, *Ann Sothern: A Bio-Bibliography* (Westport, Conn.: Greenwood, 1990), p. 4.
9. "Musical for Columbia," *The Film Daily*, June 16, 1933.
10. Edward Jablonski, *Harold Arlen: Rhythm, Rainbows, and Blues* (Boston: Northeastern University Press, 1996), p. 77.
11. "Heavens! Is That Me?" *Screenland*, April 1937.
12. "Let's Fall in Love," *The Film Daily*, January 20, 1934.
13. "'I'd Like to Be Human—for a Change!' Says Connie Bennett," *Movie Classic*, July 1933.
14. Robert Montgomery was borrowed for *Moulin Rouge* from MGM in August 1933, according to trade reports, but Metro recalled him two weeks later because of a supposed scheduling problem, as he was assigned to a project with Clark Gable that would conflict with the *Moulin Rouge* shoot. "A Little From 'Lots,'" *The Film Daily*, September 8, 1933.
15. Music historian Lenny Kaye observes that publicity for *Moulin Rouge* indicates that the Dubin-Warren tune "Song of Surrender" was to be sung by Connee Boswell to Russ Columbo. Such a rendition apparently did not show up in the film as released, but "Song of Surrender" is sung by co-star Tullio Carminati as a sort of aphrodisiac for a Tone-Bennett love scene. See Kaye, *You Call It Madness: The Sensuous Song of the Croon* (New York: Villard, 2004), p. 321.
16. "Brief Reviews of Current Pictures," *Photoplay*, March 1934.

17. "Lanfield Gets 5-Year Contract," *The Film Daily*, November 6, 1933.
18. Eugene R. Gaddis, *Magician of the Modern: Chick Austin and the Transformation of the Arts in America* (New York: Knopf Doubleday, 2000). The appearance of the *Moulin Rouge* caravan in Hartford came the same evening as the world premiere of *Four Saints in Three Acts*, an opera written by Virgil Thomson and Gertrude Stein that debuted at the Wadsworth Atheneum, across the street from the Capitol Theater. Arthur Everett "Chick" Austin was the nationally innovative director of the Atheneum.
19. "Caravan Breaks Up," *Motion Picture Daily*, March 1, 1934.
20. "Rockett Casts Harvey," *Motion Picture Daily*, November 8, 1933.
21. Universal Service syndicated column, January 1934.
22. Charles Boyer committed suicide two days after the death of his wife in 1978.
23. "*Bottoms Up* Lacks Class But Registers Fairly Well," *The Hollywood Reporter*, February 20, 1934; "*Bottoms Up* in Final Form Is Praised by Reviewer," *The Hollywood Reporter*, February 28, 1934.
24. "Hotcha Scenes OK, Hays Nix Overruled," *Variety*, March 6, 1934; "Retakes for *Bottoms* Despite O.K. Verdict," *Variety*, March 6, 1934.
25. "Nose Fits Role," *Motion Picture Daily*, January 18, 1934, et al. Walter Hartwig was a former executive director of the New York Drama League who pioneered the "little theater" movement in America.
26. "The Screen: A Farcical Affair About Hollywood…," *The New York Times*, March 23, 1934; "Film Reviews: *Bottoms Up*," *Variety*, March 27, 1934.
27. "Trade Views," *The Hollywood Reporter*, January 23, 1934.
28. "Will Gloria Come Back Again?" *Modern Screen*, June 1934.
29. Columbia initially sought to make a screen version of *Music in the Air*. Once Fox acquired the property, it sought to borrow Irene Dunne from RKO before bringing in Swanson.
30. Gloria Swanson, *Swanson on Swanson: An Autobiography* (New York: Random House, 1980), p. 435.
31. *Ibid.*, pp. 435–436.
32. "The Screen: The Music Hall Presents a Screen Edition of the Kern-Hammerstein Show…," *The New York Times*, December 14, 1934.
33. "I've Told Every Little Star" was a hit for Jack Denny and His Orchestra in 1932 and was oft-revived, but for future generations, the most memorable version was teenager Linda Scott's pepped-up, million-selling smash of 1961.

34. Gordon Hunter, "June Lang: Meet the Girl," *Classic Images*, March 2009.
35. "Box-Office Performances…," *Harrison's Reports*, May 4, 1935.
36. *Bridgeport Sunday Herald* article excerpted in "The Public's 'Grape Vine' Method of Learning About Pictures," *Harrison's Reports*, March 9, 1935.
37. Swanson, *Swanson on Swanson*, p. 436.
38. Aubrey Solomon, *The Fox Film Corporation, 1915–1935: A History and Filmography* (Jefferson, N.C.: McFarland, 2011), p. 202.
39. John Kobal, *Rita Hayworth: The Time, the Place and the Woman* (New York: Norton, 1978), p. 62.
40. "*Under the Pampas Moon*," *Motion Picture Daily*, May 21, 1935.
41. "*Under the Pampas Moon*," *Harrison's Reports*, June 8, 1935.
42. Kobal, *Rita Hayworth*, p. 65.
43. *The Film Daily*, November 30, 1936.
44. "20th Cent–Fox Wins First Clash With Play Producer," *The Film Daily*, December 22, 1936.
45. W.T. Strohm, "Special Engineering Problems in a Motion Picture Studio," *Journal of the Society of Motion Picture Engineers*, August 1937.
46. "Film Reviews: *Banjo on My Knee*," *Variety*, November 28, 1936.
47. E.W. Robson, *The Film Answers Back: An Historical Appreciation of the Cinema* (London: John Lane the Bodley Head, 1939), pp. 299–300.
48. Dan Callahan, *Barbara Stanwyck: The Miracle Woman* (Jackson: University of Mississippi Press, 2012), p. 84.
49. Filmed in two-strip Technicolor, Martini's number in *Paramount on Parade* was missing for many years from extant black-and-white prints, in which he was glimpsed only briefly. The song was restored, as were most of the film's other color sequences, by the UCLA Film and Television Archive in the 1990s.
50. "Studios Stars and Stooges," *The Times* (Hammond, Ind.), August 17, 1937.
51. Associated Press syndicated column, February 1937.
52. Marsha Lynn Beeman, *Joan Fontaine: A Bio-Bibliography* (Westport, Conn.: Greenwood, 1994), p. 10; Richard B. Jewell, *RKO Radio Pictures: A Titan Is Born* (Berkeley: University of California Press, 2012), p. 143.
53. "Film Reviews: *Music for Madame*," *Variety*, September 15, 1937.
54. Harry Medved with Randy Dreyfuss and Michael Medved, *The 50 Worst Films of All Time (and How They Got That Way)* (New York: Warner, 1978), p. 238.
55. *Swing Your Lady* opened in Los Angeles in January 1938 as part of a double bill with Warners' *The Invisible Menace*, a dismal mystery-

comedy that headliner Boris Karloff—who was neither invisible nor menacing—considered to be one of *his* worst movies.
  56. A.M. Sperber and Eric Lax, *Bogart* (New York: Morrow, 1997), p. 88.
  57. "Bogart's Patience Tested," *Brooklyn Daily Eagle*, January 9, 1938.
  58. "Louise Fazenda Will Be Guest of Mrs. Roosevelt," *The Film Daily*, January 27, 1938.
  59. "Round Table in Pictures," *Motion Picture Herald*, March 26, 1938.
  60. Bogart's only other credit in a musical feature was the Warners all-star revue *Thank Your Lucky Stars* (1943), in which he had a non-singing cameo.
  61. "Film Reviews: *Swing Your Lady*," *Variety*, January 26, 1938; "The Screen: ... The Strand Brings in *Swing Your Lady*," *The New York Times*, January 27, 1938.
  62. Lawrence J. Quirk and William Schoell, *Joan Crawford: The Essential Biography* (Lexington, Ky.: University Press of Kentucky, 2002), p. 98.
  63. "Carlson Secures *Follies* Premiere in Honor of Star," *Motion Picture Herald*, April 29, 1939.
  64. Another casualty was a scene involving "Our Gang" regulars Carl "Alfalfa" Switzer and Darla Hood, who were then under contract to MGM.
  65. "Reviews of New Films: *Ice Follies of 1939*," *The Film Daily*, March 7, 1939.
  66. "What the Picture Did for Me," *Motion Picture Herald*, June 3, 1939; December 2, 1939. More bad news for Crawford: Her marriage to actor Franchot Tone was ending; the two divorced while *Ice Follies of 1939* was in theaters.
  67. Roy Newquist, *Conversations with Joan Crawford* (New York: Citadel Press, 1980), p. 84. When it brought *The Ice Follies of 1939* to DVD in 2009, the folks at Warner Archive—apparently having found few positive quotes about the film—used only Crawford's first sentence in this quote to misleadingly promote the disc on the case. More trivia: In the 1981 film *Mommie Dearest*, the infamous account of Crawford's family life, *Ice Follies of 1939* is the picture that the actress (played by Faye Dunaway) is preparing to film in the opening sequences.

Chapter 4

  1. "*International House* Fast and Funny Film 'Burlecue,'" *The Hollywood Reporter*, May 5, 1933.
  2. *The Hollywood Reporter*, December 12, 1932; Ronald J. Fields, *W.C. Fields: A Life on Film* (New York: St. Martin's, 1984), p. 109.
  3. International News Service syndicated feature, January 25, 1933.
  4. "Cal York's Monthly Broadcast From Hollywood," *Photoplay*, June 1933.
  5. "*International House* Fast and Funny...," *The Hollywood Reporter*, see above.
  6. George Burns interview with author, September 29, 1992, for Flint (Mich.) *Journal* article of September 30, 1992.
  7. James Curtis, *W.C. Fields: A Biography* (New York: Knopf, 2003), p. 257.
  8. Universal Service syndicated column, September 10, 1935.
  9. "Radio Alters Title," *The Hollywood Reporter*, April 11, 1933. The title change followed a lawsuit against RKO by the author of a novel called *Maiden Voyage*.
  10. "Four Hours' Sleep," *The Film Daily*, April 11, 1933.
  11. Back-projection aside, the special effects team behind *Melody Cruise* also was responsible for the stellar *King Kong* at around the same time.
  12. "The Screen: Charles Ruggles and Phil Harris in a Combination of Pleasant Nonsense and Agreeable Melody," *The New York Times*, June 23, 1933.
  13. "New Vogue in Comedians Set by Marx Brothers," *The Film Daily*, April 18, 1933.
  14. The $150,000 figure is from Jewell, *A Titan Is Born*, p. 75. RKO's yen for transportation-minded musicals may have been influenced by the fact that its head of production, Merian C. Cooper, was a former U.S. Army pilot who was a founding member of the board of directors of Pan American Airways.
  15. "The Screen: Melody and Cheer," *The New York Times*, August 23, 1933.
  16. Rowland and Brice sought the famous nightclub owner Texas Guinan to make one of their shorts in 1933, but her death, shortly after making *Hollywood Thru a Keyhole* [q.v.], ruined that plan.
  17. Richard Koszarski, *Hollywood on the Hudson: Film and Television in New York From Griffith to Sarnoff* (New Brunswick, N. J.: Rutgers University Press, 2009), p. 277.
  18. Koszarski, *Hollywood on the Hudson*, p. 275. *Moonlight and Pretzels* also represents an early collaboration of Freund with supporting actor William Frawley. Freund and Frawley would more auspiciously be connected to the classic 1950s TV sitcom *I Love Lucy*, for which Freund was the cinematographer and Frawley played his trademark role as Fred Mertz.
  19. "The Shadow Stage: *Moonlight and Pretzels*," *Photoplay*, November 1933.
  20. Barrios, *A Song in the Dark*, p. 380. The motif of humanity's hands outstretched to the singer is common to the "Remember My Forgotten Man" and "Dusty Shoes" numbers, for example.
  21. *Modern Screen*, January 1934.

22. *My Lips Betray* may have been delayed because of Fox's precarious finances, and also perhaps because Buddy DeSylva, producer of *My Weakness*, complained to the studio that the earlier film was not an adequate debut for Harvey and would damage the outlook for his production ("DeSylva Questions Lilian Harvey's Myth Pic Tale," *Variety*, June 27, 1933). *My Lips Betray* and *My Weakness* are said to exist only in prints at the UCLA Film and Television Archive, the former in incomplete form.

23. "The Low Down," *The Hollywood Reporter*, June 7, 1933.

24. A report in *Motion Picture Daily* ("Lasky After Holman," October 5, 1933) indicated that Lasky was trying to hire infamous singer Libby Holman "to sing a torch song" in *I Am Suzanne!* Holman had lately endured a court fight over her alleged role in the death of her husband, tobacco heir Zachary Smith Reynolds.

25. "Lilian Harvey and Podrecca's Marionettes in the Present Picture at the Radio City Music Hall," *The New York Times*, January 19, 1934.

26. "*I Am Suzanne* Gains Signal Honor," *Los Angeles Times*, December 18, 1933.

27. "*I Am Suzanne* Is Fox Hit With Lilian Harvey," *Hollywood Filmograph*, December 23, 1933.

28. The oft-told story is that Harvey rejected the *George White's Scandals* role because it was too small, but *The Hollywood Reporter* ("The Low Down," February 12, 1934) asserted that producer White turned her down.

29. "Last Try for Lilian," *Picture Play*, August 1934.

30. Harvey received an unexpected reference in Quentin Tarantino's 2009 film, *Inglourious Basterds*, in which a duet with her and Willy Fritsch from the 1936 film *Glückskinder* is heard, followed by an order by an actor playing Nazi propaganda chief Josef Goebbels not to mention her name in his presence. The mention was tied to Harvey falling out of favor with the Third Reich.

31. "The Screen: South Seas Fantasy," *The New York Times*, September 24, 1934.

32. Richard Jewell, "RKO Film Grosses: 1931–1951," *Historical Journal of Film, Radio and Television*, Vol. 14, No. 1, 1994, p. 43.

33. Bob Thomas, *Astaire: The Man, the Dancer, the Life of Fred Astaire* (New York: St. Martin's, 1984), p. 94.

34. Brock made *Cockeyed Cavaliers* with director Mark Sandrich just before *Down to Their Last Yacht*. He also supervised *The Great American Harem*, retitled *Bachelor Bait*, with Stuart Erwin and Rochelle Hudson instead of Gargan and Stuart, and directed by George Stevens.

35. Associated Press syndicated story, November 1934.

36. Hazel Forbes' movie career after *Down to Their Last Yacht* consisted of a bit part in an RKO comedy, *Bachelor Bait*, and a supporting role in a comedy short, *Trailing Along* (both 1934). She was married to singer Harry Richman, star of *The Music Goes 'Round* [q.v.], from 1938 to 1942. For more on her *Yacht* troubles, see "Extortion Notes Threaten Death to Hazel Forbes," Associated Press story taken from the *Chicago Tribune*, June 21, 1934, among numerous other reports.

37. Jewell, *A Titan Is Born*, p. 85.

38. "Earl Theisen's Hollywood Note Book," *International Photographer*, May 1934.

39. "Two Units for *Yacht*," *The Hollywood Reporter*, April 25, 1934.

40. Jewell, *A Titan Is Born*, p. 90, quoting a studio memo from July 14, 1934.

41. *Ibid.*, p. 86, quoting a studio memo from March 22, 1934.

42. *Daily Variety*, August 2, 1934.

43. United Press syndicated story, June 21, 1934.

44. "The Shadow Stage: *Down to Their Last Yacht*," *Photoplay*, November 1934; "Reviews of the New Features and Shorts: *Down to Their Last Yacht*," *The Film Daily*, September 22, 1934.

45. "Reviews—A Tour of Today's Talkies: *Down to Their Last Yacht*," *Modern Screen*, November 1934.

46. Central Press syndicated column, October 1934.

47. "Tropics Background for Musical Film," *Los Angeles Times*, August 27, 1934.

48. Jewell, *A Titan Is Born*, p. 90.

49. *Ibid.*

50. "Inside Stuff—Pictures," *Variety*, November 6, 1934.

51. Gregory William Mank, *Bela Lugosi and Boris Karloff: The Expanded Story of a Haunting Collaboration* (Jefferson, N.C.: McFarland, 2009), pp. 207–208.

52. In the surviving print of *Gift of Gab*, Etting sings "Talking to Myself." She also may have performed "Tomorrow, Who Cares?," which was mentioned in newspaper ads for theatrical engagements during the film's release, and whose songwriters are in the opening credits. However, there is no rendition of that by her in the 70-minute version presently circulating. (The 70 minutes matches the running time listed for the film in 1934.) Etting recorded "Tomorrow, Who Cares?" along with "Talking to Myself" for Columbia as *Gift of Gab* was going into release.

53. "Reviews of the New Features: *Gift of Gab*," *The Film Daily*, September 25, 1934.

54. *The Hollywood Reporter*, September 1934. Quoted from *Universal Weekly*, September 29, 1934.

55. "The Screen: Big Cast," *The New York*

Times, September 26, 1934; "Film Reviews: *Gift of Gab*," *Variety*, October 2, 1934.

56. Mank, *Bela Lugosi and Boris Karloff*, p. 205.

57. Douglass Montgomery appears in publicity photos of the murder sketch, but his participation apparently was deleted, as was a separate bit by Billy Barty playing Lowe's character as a baby. Wini Shaw was credited on some cast lists in 1934 as a cabaret singer, but she is nowhere to be seen in the surviving version. According to Gregory William Mank, Karloff was paid $500 for his time and Lugosi got $250.

58. "Inside Stuff—Pictures," *Variety*, November 6, 1934; "Alice Faye's Fox Filmusical," *Variety*, March 20, 1935; "Lou Brock Has His Studio Woes," *Variety*, March 27, 1935.

59. The comedy quotient would've been even higher had Edgar Kennedy and Charles Winninger, who were connected to the project in pre-production, appeared in the finished product.

60. Promotional articles for *Top of the Town* indicated a 1960 setting, but the film doesn't specify a time.

61. "U Going to Town on *Top of the Town* Ads," *Variety*, January 27, 1937.

62. "Moon Over Miami," *Motion Picture Daily*, March 18, 1937.

63. "*Top of Town* Booked," *Motion Picture Daily*, March 26, 1937.

64. "Film Reviews: *Top of the Town*," *Variety*, March 31, 1937.

65. "Motion Pictures: *Top of the Town*," *The Billboard*, April 10, 1937; "Reviews of New Films: *Top of the Town*," *The Film Daily*, March 27, 1937.

66. "The Screen: Universal Unveils Its Elaborate Revue, *Top of the Town*...," *The New York Times*, March 27, 1937.

67. Anthony Slide, *Actors on Red Alert: Career Interviews With Five Actors and Actresses Affected by the Blacklist* (Lanham, Md.: Scarecrow, 1999), p. 94.

68. Jewell, *A Titan Is Born*, p. 222.

69. "Obituaries," *Variety*, April 21, 1971. The report that Brock was a hotel clerk is from Arlene Croce, *The Fred Astaire and Ginger Rogers Book* (New York: Galahad Books, 1972), p. 38.

70. *The New Yorker*, July 10, 1937.

71. Sillman produced *New Faces* revues periodically through 1968. His 1952 Broadway version was remade for the screen with future notables Eartha Kitt, Paul Lynde, Carol Lawrence, Alice Ghostley, Ronny Graham, and Robert Clary.

72. "House Reviews: Paramount, N.Y.," *Variety*, February 6, 1933. Milton Berle's first film under that name was a 1934 Educational two-reeler, *Poppin' the Cork*.

73. According to Hal Erickson, *From Radio to the Big Screen: Hollywood Films Featuring Broadcast Personalities and Programs* (Jefferson, N.C.: McFarland, 2014), when producers Edward Small and Sam Briskin decreed that the first script for *New Faces of 1937* was inadequate, Irving Brecher did a rewrite with Nat Perrin and Philip G. Epstein (p. 43).

74. To illustrate the low odds of anyone getting to Hollywood as a performer from scratch, *Variety* compiled information from four majors—MGM, Paramount, RKO, and 20th Century-Fox—and reported that among them, of 52,000 people interviewed for studio contracts, only 56 made it to the West Coast for employment. Of that last number, 25 were hired by RKO, so *New Faces of 1937* could have skewed the percentage ("56 of 52,000 OK for Pix," *Variety*, December 29, 1937).

75. "Pathos, Bathos Blend During Search for New Talent Worthy Screen Place," *The Washington Post*, March 28, 1937.

76. At least one performer whose footage was cut from the general release prints ended up in the movie anyway, thanks to a crusade by his hometown. When Rene Stone, a young singer, landed a role in the film, his town of Purcell, Oklahoma, was bombarded by studio publicity about his participation. The local Chamber of Commerce set aside a day to honor Stone—only to see that he had been left out of the final version. Purcell residents sent telegrams and letters of protest to RKO, which responded by sending prints of *New Faces of 1937* to theaters throughout Oklahoma with Stone's scenes reinserted ("Oklahoma Youth Put Back in *New Faces*," *Motion Picture Daily*, August 23, 1937, and story syndicated to newspapers including the *Fitchburg* (Mass.) *Sentinel*, November 27, 1937).

77. *The Brooklyn Daily Eagle*, July 11, 1937. This was likely taken from an RKO press release distributed to newspapers nationwide.

78. Jewell, "RKO Film Grosses, 1931–1951," p. 57.

79. "Reviews of the New Films: *New Faces of 1937*," *The Film Daily*, June 29, 1937; "Film Reviews: *New Faces of 1937*," *Variety*, July 7, 1937.

80. Richard Jewell and Vernon Harbin, *The RKO Story* (New York: Octopus Books, 1982), p. 108.

Chapter 5

1. *Cleveland Plain Dealer*, quoted in "What the Newspaper Critics Say," *Independent Exhibitors Film Bulletin*, May 1, 1937.

2. Tristram Tupper (1885–1954) was a frequent contributor to *The Saturday Evening Post*. He also was the brother-in-law of General George C. Marshall, U.S. Army chief of staff during World War II and secretary of state and defense under President Harry S Truman. Tupper

was an Army brigadier general who served in both world wars.

3. "Film Reviews: *The Phantom Broadcast*," *Variety*, August 1, 1933.

4. "Showmen's Reviews: *Phantom Broadcast*," *Motion Picture Herald*, April 8, 1933.

5. "Motion Pictures: *The Phantom Broadcast*," *The Billboard*, August 5, 1933.

6. "*Phantom Broadcast* Good; Chevalier Picture Weak," *The Hollywood Reporter*, April 4, 1933.

7. Newspaper Enterprise Association syndicated column by Dan Thomas, September 1933.

8. "Veteran Player in Juvenile Role," *Waco* (Texas) *Tribune-Herald*, August 13, 1933.

9. "Reviews of the New Features: *Dance, Girl, Dance*," *The Film Daily*, October 26, 1933.

10. "Film Reviews: *Rainbow Over Broadway*," *Variety*, December 26, 1933.

11. "Is Lon Chaney's Son Fated to Suffer for Films, Too?" *Movie Classic*, January 1933.

12. "Director Foretold Chaney's Success," *Portsmouth* (Ohio) *Daily Times*, January 19, 1941. Source unidentified; likely a wire service story or studio press release.

13. "Reviews of the New Films: *Girl o' My Dreams*," *The Film Daily*, November 6, 1934.

14. Calvin Thomas Beck, *Heroes of the Horrors* (New York: Collier, 1975), p. 231.

15. "Chaney, Jr., Starts Series," *The Film Daily*, June 21, 1935. Ray Kirkwood is credited on screen as the sole director of *The Shadow of Silk Lennox*, although production charts from *The Hollywood Reporter* list Jack Nelson, a formerly prolific director of B-Westerns, as co-director.

16. Associated Press syndicated column by Robbin Coons, cited from *Moberly* (Missouri) *Monitor-Index*, November 2, 1935.

17. "Jim Fidler in Hollywood," McNaught Syndicate column, taken from *Wilkes-Barre* (Pa.) *Record*, November 27, 1936; "Jack Mulhall Files Bankruptcy Petition," United Press story, taken from *Nevada State Journal* (Reno, Nev.), April 17, 1935.

18. "New Acts: Lawrence Gray," *The Billboard*, August 6, 1932.

19. "New Acts," *Variety*, February 21, 1933.

20. Syndicated newspaper column, December 1934.

21. The Sons of the Pioneers also can be seen in a 1935 Patsy Kelly–Thelma Todd short, *Slightly Static*, made by the Hal Roach Studio for MGM release. It seems to have debuted just after *The Old Homestead*, but many viewers of the time may have seen the two-reeler first.

22. "Radio Dial Log: Radiography of Lawrence Gray," *Brooklyn Daily Eagle*, January 12, 1937.

23. "Actor to Meet With Aviators," *Ogden* (Utah) *Standard-Examiner*, January 5, 1941; "California Man Will Aid Youths in Canada Work,"

Helena (Montana) *Independent Record*, January 8, 1941.

24. Dudley Murphy, an often-experimental filmmaker, directed actress Gilda Gray in *He Was Her Man*, a 1931 Paramount short inspired by "Frankie and Johnnie."

25. Some believed the song "Frankie and Johnnie" to have been inspired by the shooting of a man by a prostitute named Frankie Baker in St. Louis in 1899. Baker escaped prison due to a self-defense finding in court. She unsuccessfully sued the respective makers of *She Done Him Wrong* and *Frankie and Johnnie*, claiming defamation, before her death in 1952.

26. The makers of *Frankie and Johnnie* used Pickford to promote the film when the actress returned to the scene of her early cinematic triumphs by "turning a camera crank" at the remodeled Biograph facility as the cast and crew watched. See "Mary Pickford 'Christens' Remodeled Biograph Studio," *Motion Picture Herald*, March 3, 1934, among other accounts.

27. Syndicated newspaper story, cited here from *The Pittsburgh Press*, "Old Biograph Plant Filming *Frankie and Johnnie*," March 3, 1934.

28. Bankhead was linked to *Frankie and Johnnie* in *Motion Picture Herald* (December 30, 1933), *Motion Picture Daily* (January 3, 1934), and *Modern Screen* (March 1934). Stage names Clifton Webb and Helen Broderick were listed as likely cast members in *The Hollywood Reporter* (January 17, 1934), but neither appeared.

29. "Frankie and Johnnie: He Was Her Man, But He Done Her Wrong," *Movies*, July 1934.

30. Letter from Breen, Production Code Administration files, October 8, 1934, cited in Peter Stanfield, *Body and Soul: Jazz and Blues in American Film, 1927–63* (Champaign: University of Illinois Press, 2005), p. 192.

31. Letter from Breen, Production Code Administration files, cited in Koszarski, *Hollywood on the Hudson*, p. 299.

32. "Frankie Unit Shooting in South," *The Film Daily*, February 16, 1935; "Short Shots From Eastern Studios," *The Film Daily*, March 18, 1935. Erskine eventually revived his movie career by directing, writing, and producing the 1947 hit comedy *The Egg and I*.

33. "Reviews of the New Films: *Frankie and Johnnie*," *The Film Daily*, June 25, 1935.

34. "Republic to Release *Frankie and Johnnie*," *Motion Picture Daily*, January 27, 1936.

35. A song sung by Morgan, "It's You I Adore," is missing from circulating prints, but it was in the film at least early in release.

36. "Film Reviews: *Frankie and Johnnie*," *Variety*, May 27, 1936; "Looking 'Em Over: *Frankie and Johnnie*," *Motion Picture Daily*, May 19, 1936.

37. "*Frankie and Johnnie* at Globe," *The New York Times*, May 25, 1936.

38. In the 1970s, former policeman Regan would be on the other side of the law, sentenced to a year in federal prison for bribery.

39. "'Unattached' Mr. Regan of Films Turns out to be Family Man," *Chicago Tribune*, February 14, 1937.

40. Jon Tuska, *The Vanishing Legion: A History of Mascot Pictures 1927–1935* (Jefferson, N.C.: McFarland, 1982), p. 185.

41. A *Variety* item, "Rep. Adds Maestros," January 27, 1937, reported the signing of Benny Goodman and his band for the film, but they did not appear.

42. "The Screen: Holiday Reports on *The Hit Parade*, a Radio Revue...," *The New York Times*, May 31, 1937.

43. "They Say in New York: Matinee Idol for Men," *Picture Play*, November 1937.

44. "Let's Go to the Movies," *The Kansas City Star*, December 12, 1937.

45. "Reviews of the New Films: *Manhattan Merry-Go-Round*," *The Film Daily*, November 11, 1937; "*Manhattan Merry-Go-Round*," *Motion Picture Daily*, November 8, 1937.

Bibliography

The American Film Institute Catalog of Motion Pictures: Feature Films, 1921–30. New York: Bowker, 1971.
The American Film Institute Catalog of Motion Pictures: Feature Films, 1931–40. New York: Bowker, 1993.
Ascheid, Antje. *Hitler's Heroines: Stardom & Womanhood in Nazi Germany*. Philadelphia: Temple University Press, 2003.
Barrios, Richard. *A Song in the Dark: The Birth of the Musical Film*. New York: Oxford University Press, 2006.
Beck, Calvin Thomas. *Heroes of the Horrors*. New York: Collier Books, 1975.
Beeman, Marsha Lynn. *Joan Fontaine: A Bio-Bibliography*. Westport, Conn.: Greenwood, 1994.
Bingen, Steven. *Warner Bros.: Hollywood's Ultimate Backlot*. Lanham, Md.: Rowman & Littlefield, 2014.
Black, Shirley Temple. *Child Star: An Autobiography*. New York: McGraw-Hill, 1988.
Bradley, Edwin M. *The First Hollywood Musicals: A Critical Filmography of 171 Features, 1927 Through 1932*. Jefferson, N.C.: McFarland, 1996.
_____. *The First Hollywood Sound Shorts, 1926–31*. Jefferson, N.C.: McFarland, 2005.
Burton, Jack. *The Blue Book of Hollywood Musicals*. Watkins Glen, N.Y.: Century House, 1953.
Callahan, Dan. *Barbara Stanwyck: The Miracle Woman*. Jackson: University of Mississippi Press, 2012.
Coffin, Lesley L. *Lew Ayres: Hollywood's Conscientious Objector*. Jackson: University of Mississippi Press, 2012.
Croce, Arlene. *The Fred Astaire and Ginger Rogers Book*. New York: Galahad Books, 1972.
Crow, Bill. *From Birdland to Broadway: Scenes from a Jazz Life*. New York: Oxford University Press, 1993.
Curtis, James. *Spencer Tracy: A Biography*. New York: Knopf, 2011.
_____. *W.C. Fields: A Biography*. New York: Knopf, 2003.
De La Hoz, Cindy. *Lucy at the Movies*. Philadelphia: Running Press, 2007.
Erickson, Hal. *From Radio to the Big Screen: Hollywood Films Featuring Broadcast Personalities and Programs*. Jefferson, N.C.: McFarland, 2014.
Fields, Ronald J. *W.C. Fields: A Life on Film*. New York: St. Martin's, 1984.
Florey, Robert. *Hollywood d'hier et d'aujourd'hui*. Paris: Editions Prisma, 1948.
Furia, Philip. *Slylark: The Life and Times of Johnny Mercer*. New York: Macmillan, 2004.
Gabler, Neal. *Winchell: Gossip, Power and the Culture of Celebrity*. New York: Knopf, 1995.
Gaddis, Eugene R. *Magician of the Modern: Chick Austin and the Transformation of the Arts in America*. New York: Knopf Doubleday, 2000.
Giddins, Gary. *Bing Crosby: A Pocketful of Dreams: The Early Years, 1903–1940*. New York: Little, Brown, 2001.
Hayes, Richard K. *Kate Smith: A Biography, with a Discography, Filmography and List of Stage Appearances*. Jefferson, N.C.: McFarland, 1995.
Hilmes, Michele. *Radio Voices: American Broadcasting, 1922–1952*. Minneapolis: University of Minnesota Press, 1997.
Hirschhorn, Clive. *The Hollywood Musical*. New York: Crown, 1981.

_____. *The Warner Bros. Story.* New York: Crown, 1979.
Hischak, Thomas C. *The Tin Pan Alley Song Encyclopedia.* Westport, Conn.: Greenwood, 2002.
Jablonski, Edward. *Harold Arlen: Rhythm, Rainbows, and Blues.* Boston: Northeastern University Press, 1996.
Jasen, David A. *Tin Pan Alley: The Composers, the Songs, the Performers and Their Times.* New York: Donald I. Fine, 1988.
Jewell, Richard B. *RKO Radio Pictures: A Titan Is Born.* Berkeley: University of California Press, 2012.
_____, with Vernon Harbin. *The RKO Story.* New York: Octopus Books, 1982.
Kaye, Lenny. *You Call It Madness: The Sensuous Song of the Croon.* New York: Villard, 2004.
Kennedy, Matthew. *Joan Blondell: A Life Between Takes.* Oxford: University of Mississippi Press, 2009.
Kobal. John. *Rita Hayworth: The Time, the Place and the Woman.* New York: Norton, 1978.
Koszarski, Richard. *Hollywood on the Hudson: Film and Television in New York From Griffith to Sarnoff.* New Brunswick, N.J.: Rutgers University Press, 2009.
Kreuger, Miles. *Show Boat: The Story of a Classic American Musical.* New York: Oxford University Press, 1977.
_____, ed. *The Movie Musical from Vitaphone to 42nd Street, as Reported in a Great Fan Magazine.* New York: Dover, 1975.
Lally, Kevin. *Wilder Times: The Life of Billy Wilder.* New York: Henry Holt, 1996.
Lanza, Joseph, and Dennis Penna. *Russ Columbo and the Crooner Mystique.* Los Angeles: Feral House, 2002.
Lees, Gene. *Portrait of Johnny: The Life of John Herndon Mercer.* New York: Knopf Doubleday, 2009.
Lenberg, Jeff, with Joan Howard Maurer and Greg Lenberg. *The Three Stooges Scrapbook.* Secaucus, N.J.: Citadel, 1999.
Liebman, Roy. *Vitaphone Films: A Catalogue of the Features and Shorts.* Jefferson, N.C.: McFarland, 2003.
Madsen, Axel. *Stanwyck.* New York: HarperCollins, 1994.
Maltin, Leonard. *The Great Movie Shorts.* New York: Bonanza, 1972.
_____. *Movie Comedy Teams.* New York: Plume, 1970.
Mank, Gregory William. *Bela Lugosi and Boris Karloff: The Expanded Story of a Haunting Collaboration.* Jefferson, N.C.: McFarland, 2009.
_____. *Women in Horror Films, 1930s.* Jefferson, N.C.: McFarland, 1999.
Medved, Harry, and Michael Medved. *The Hollywood Hall of Shame: The Most Expensive Flops in Movie History.* New York: Perigee, 1984.
_____, and Randy Dreyfuss. *The 50 Worst Films of All Time (and How They Got That Way).* New York: Warner, 1984.
Morley, Sheridan. *Gertrude Lawrence.* New York: McGraw-Hill, 1981.
Newquist, Roy. *Conversations with Joan Crawford.* New York: Citadel Press, 1980.
Pitts, Michael R. *Kate Smith: A Bio-Bibliography.* Westport, Conn.: Greenwood, 1988.
Quirk, Lawrence J., and William Schoell. *Joan Crawford: The Essential Biography.* Lexington, Ky.: University Press of Kentucky, 2002.
_____. *Poverty Row Studios, 1929–1940.* Jefferson, N.C.: McFarland, 1997.
Robson, E.W. *The Film Answers Back: An Historical Appreciation of the Cinema.* London: John Lane the Bodley Head, 1939.
Rust, Brian. *The American Dance Band Discography, 1917–1942* (Vols. 1 and 2). New Rochelle, N.Y.: Arlington House, 1975.
_____, with Allen G. Debus. *The Complete Entertainment Discography, From the mid–1890s to 1942.* New Rochelle, N.Y.: Arlington House, 1973.
Schultz, Margie. *Ann Sothern: A Bio-Bibliography.* Westport, Conn.: Greenwood, 1990.
Schwartz, Rosalie. *Flying Down to Rio: Hollywood, Tourists, and Yankee Clippers.* College Station: Texas A&M University Press, 2004.
Slide, Anthony. *Actors on Red Alert: Career Interviews With Five Actors and Actresses Affected by the Blacklist.* Lanham, Md.: Scarecrow, 1999.
_____. *The Encyclopedia of Vaudeville.* Westport, Conn.: Greenwood, 1994.
Smith, Don G. *Lon Chaney Jr.: Horror Film Star, 1906–1973.* Jefferson, N.C.: McFarland, 1996.

Solomon, Aubrey. *The Fox Film Corporation, 1915–1935: A History and Filmography*. Jefferson, N.C.: McFarland, 2011.
Sperber, A.M., and Eric Lax. *Bogart*. New York: Morrow, 1997.
Stanfield, Peter. *Body and Soul: Jazz and Blues in American Film, 1927–63*. Champaign: University of Illinois Press, 2005.
Stangeland, John. *Warren William: Magnificent Scoundrel of Pre-Code Hollywood*. Jefferson, N.C.: McFarland, 2010.
Swanson, Gloria. *Swanson on Swanson: An Autobiography*. New York: Random House, 1980.
Taves, Brian. *Robert Florey: The French Expressionist*. Metuchen, N.J.: Scarecrow, 1987.
Thomas, Bob. *Astaire: The Man, the Dancer, the Life of Fred Astaire*. New York: St. Martin's, 1984.
Turner, George E., and Michael H. Price. *Forgotten Horrors: The Definitive Edition*. Baltimore: Midnight Marquee Press, 1999.
Tuska, Jon. *The Vanishing Legion: A History of Mascot Pictures 1927–1935*. Jefferson, N.C.: McFarland, 1982.
Wagner, Walter. *You Must Remember This*. New York: Putnam, 1975.
Wilk, Max. *OK! The Story of "Oklahoma!" A Celebration of America's Most Loved Musical*. New York: Applause Books, 2002.

(Magazine and newspaper articles are listed under their pertinent chapter notes.)

Index

Unless otherwise indicated, titles in *italics* are films, and titles in "quotes" are music compositions/musical numbers. Numbers in ***bold italics*** refer to pages with photographs. Entries marked with an asterisk (*) are for the 50 films featured in this book.

Adamson, Harold 113, 156, 158
The Admirable Crichton (play) 147
Adrian 124
After the Thin Man (1936) 121
"Ah, But Is It Love?" 140
Al Jolson in a Plantation Act (1926) 13
Al Pearce and His Gang 194
Alberni, Luis 195
Albertson, Frank 174, 175
Aldrich, Mariska 102
Alexander, Ross 83, 84, 85
Alice in Wonderland (1933) 49
All Star Productions 187
Allen, Gracie 38, 53, 65, 66, 67, 116, 132
Allen, Judith 65
"All's Fair in Love and War" 85
Allwyn, Astrid 109
Allyson, June 55
Always Leave Them Laughing (1949) 175
Ameche, Don 95
Americana (play) 141
America's Sweetheart (play) 85, 93
Anderson, John Murray 127
Andre, Lona 132
Andrews, Julie 63
Angel and the Badman (1947) 86
"Archie" (comic strip) 55
"Are You Making Any Money?" 140
Arizona Days (1937) 25
Arlen, Harold 79, 80, 94, 95
Arlen, Richard 23
Armetta, Henry 49, 156, 157, 195
Arnheim, Gus (and His Orchestra) 45, 153
Arnold, Dorothy 195
"As Time Goes By" 140
Astaire, Fred 1, 70, 116, 137, 140, 147, 156, 162
Aswell, James 150
Ates, Roscoe 98

Athey, Ted 14, 15
Atkinson, Brooks 56
Auer, John H. 188
Auer, Mischa 156, 157
Austin, Gene 10, 149, 153
Autry, Gene 65, 167, 195
The Avenger (1933) 170
Ayres, Lew 69, 70, ***71***, 72, 73, 124, ***125***, 126, 138, 143, 145, 192

Babes in Arms (1939) 175
Babes in Toyland (1934) 150
Baby LeRoy 91
Baby Rose Marie 16, 132
Baby Rose Marie, the Child Wonder (1929) 16
Baby Take a Bow (1934) 62
Bachelor Bait (1934) 147
Back Street (novel) 41
Baer, Abel 14, 15
Bailey, Mildred 158
Baker, Phil 153
Ball, Lucille 48, 63, 97
Ballew, Smith 172
Banjo on My Knee (1936) 111–115, ***114***
Bankhead, Tallulah 187
Banks, Leslie 143
Banton, Travis 90, 131
Banyard, Beatrice 52
Barbary Coast (1935) 104
Barnes, Binnie ***154***, 155
Barrie, J.M. 147
Barrios, Richard 24, 141
Barry, Wesley 149
Barrymore, John 13, 94, 127
Barthelmess, Richard ***8***, 8–11, 65, 66
Bartlett, Michael 76, 117, 167
Batman (TV series) 178
The Battle of Paris (1929) 16–20, 34

Bauer, Ralph S. 11
Baxter, Warner 108, 109, *109*, 110
"Beach Boy" 149, 150
Beahan, Charles 148, 151
The Beale Street Boys 153
Beau Geste (1926) 168
Beaumont, Harry 23
The Beauties (1930) 25
Bed of Roses (1933) 96
A Bedtime Story (1933) 91
Beery, Noah 28
Behind the Mask (1945) 160
Behind the Mike (1937) 158
Belden, Charles 175
Benchley, Robert 157
Bennett, Belle 15
Bennett, Constance 49, 96–98
Bennett, Tony 97
Benny, Jack 66, 137
Benton, Dean 180
Bergerman, Stanley 140
Berkeley, Busby 1, 24, 54, 79, 80, 85, 128, 147
Berle, Milton 68, 162, 163, 165
Berlin, Irving 68, 74
Berman, Pandro S. 88, 147, 149
Bernard, Sam 15
Bernie, Ben 59, 60, 61, 63, 164
The Big Broadcast (1932) 38, 41, 132
The Big Broadcast of 1936 (1935) 68
The Big Pond (1930) 90
The Billboard (magazine) 68, 157, 170, 183
Bilson, Bruce 81
Bilson, George R. 81
Bilson, Rachel 81
Bing, Herman 76
Biograph Studios 188
Bird of Paradise (1932) 178
Blackmer, Sidney 148, 150
Blane, Sally 42, 46
Blessed Event (play) 139
Blondell, Joan 79, 80, 81, 121, 172
Blood Money (1933) 48
Bloom, Ken 20
"Blue Daughter of Heaven" 24
Blue, Monte 41
Blue Skies (1946) 137
Blumenthal, A.C. 69, 72
Blystone, John 118
Boasberg, Al 52
Bogart, Humphrey 88, 89, 119–122, *120*, 187
Boland, Mary 148, 150
Boles, Glen 176
Boles, John 88, *100*, 100–101, 104–106, *105*, 143
Bonnell, Bonnie 52
Booth, Doris Hilda 32
Bordoni, Irene 5
Boswell, Connee 97
The Boswell Sisters 97
*Bottoms Up (1934) 88, 98–102, *100*

"Bottoms Up" 101
Bought! (1931) 96
"The Boulevard of Broken Dreams" 97
Boyd, Betty 31
Boyer, Charles 73, 100, 104, 142
Brackett, Charles 107
Bradley, Grace 55
Brady, William 163, *163*, 165
"Breakfast Ball" 95
Brecher, Irving 162
Breen, Joseph 188
Brendel, El 143
Brennan, Walter 113, 115
Brewster's Millions (1945) 161
Brian, Mary 46, *139*, 139, 140, 192
The Brian Sisters 164
Brice, Monte 138, 140, 141
Bright Eyes (1934) 111
Bright Lights (1935) 25
Britton, Frank 139, 140
Britton, Milt 139, 140
The Broadway Melody (1929) 21, 24, 27
*Broadway Thru a Keyhole (1933) 43–49, *47*, 132
Brock, Lou 1, 128, 134, 137, 147, *148*, 149, 151, 156, 157, 158–160
Brooke, Hillary 164
Brooks, Albert 161, 165
Brooks, Mel 165
"Brother, Can You Spare a Dime?" 141
"Brother, Just Laugh It Off!" 36
Brown, Bernard 169, 170
Brown, Joe E. 15
Brown, Johnny Mack 172
Brown, Lansing 49
Brown, Lew 99
Brown, Nacio Herb 21, 24, 124
Brown, Tom 36
Burke, Joe 27, 29
Burlesque (play) 139
Burns, Bob 119, 122
Burns, George 3, 38, 65, 67, 116, 132
Burton, David 93
Burton, Marie 180
Burton, Val 31
Busch, Mae 173
Butler, David 99

Caged (1950) 36
Cagney, James 11, 56, 172, 179
Call Northside 777 (1948) 36
Calloway, Cab (and His Orchestra) 131, 194, 195
Cameron, Rudolph 36
Cansino, Rita *see* Hayworth, Rita
Cantor, Eddie 1, 162, 165
"Carioca" 150
Carlisle, Mary 98, 178, 179, 184
Carr, Trem 167, 168
Carrillo, Leo *139*, 139, *193*, 195

Carrington, Helen 36
Carroll, Earl 23, 94
Carroll, Nancy 17
Carson, Doris 140
Caruso, Enrico 105
Catlett, Walter 113
Cavalcade (1933) 101
CBS 51, 162
Ceballos, Larry 28
Chandler, Chick 58, 136
Chaney, Lon 30, 127
Chaney, Lon, Jr. 177–180, **178**
Change of Heart see *Hit Parade of 1943*
Chaplin, Charlie 145
Charlie Chan in Egypt (1935) 110
Chasing Rainbows (1930) 21, 27
Chatterton, Ruth 168
Chesterfield Motion Picture Corporation 166, 167, 171, 175
Chevalier, Maurice 91, 142
Children of Pleasure (1930) 182
Christopher Strong (1933) 168
Churchill, Frank 10
Clair, René 134
Claire, Bernice 139, 140
Clarke, Grant 9
Classic Images (newspaper) 106
Clemens, William 80
Cleopatra (1934) 90
Cleveland Plain Dealer (newsletter) 167
Close Harmony (1929) 17, 112
Coca, Imogene 162
Cockeyed Cavaliers (1934) 147
The Cocoanuts (1929) 18
Cody, Lew 62
Coffee, Lenore 90
"Coffee in the Morning and Kisses in the Night" 49, 97
Cohen, Emanuel 101
Cohen, Jeff 11
Cohen, Maury M. 171, 172, 173, 175
Cohn, Al 56
Cohn, Harry 93, 95, 101
Colbert, Claudette 88, 89–92, **91**, 94
College Rhythm (1934) 162
Collegiate (1936) 133, 162
"Collegiate Wedding" 57
Collier's (magazine) 9
Collins, Cora Sue 91
Collins, Ted 41
Colonel Stoopnagle and Budd 132
Columbia Pictures 30, 53, 55, 62, 74, 75, 76, 77, 84, 90, 93, 94, 95, 101, 102, 111, 117, 146, 172, 192
Columbo, Russ 39, 45–46, 48–50, **50**, 52, 62, 97
Come and Get It (1936) 113
"Come Back to Sorrento" 117
Commodore Pictures 179, 180
Community Sing (radio show) 162

Como, Perry 46
Compson, Betty 10
Condemned to Live (1935) 172
Congress Dances (1931) 142
Connolly, Bobby 84, 139
Connolly, Walter 74
Conrad, Con 45
Consolidated Film Industries 166
"The Continental" 140, 184
Continental Talking Pictures 168
Coons, Robbin 179
Cooper, Courtney Ryley 9
Cooper, Gary 143
Cortez, Ricardo 15, 90, **91**
Coslow, Sam 42
Costello, Johnny "Irish" 46
The Count of Monte Cristo (novel) 170
Courtney, Inez 183, 184
Cowan, Jerome 163
Crabbe, Larry "Buster" 62
Crawford, Joan 88, 123–126, **125**
Crehan, Joseph 81
The Criminal Code (play) 187
Cromwell, John 112
Crosby, Bing 1, 38, 39, 45, 46, 61, 65, 66, 67, 85, 97, 127, 137
"Crosby, Columbo, and Vallee" 45
The Cuckoos (1930) 28
Cummings, Constance 46, **47**, 49
Curtis, James 132
Curtis, Tony 63
Cyrano de Bergerac (play) 168

"Daddy's Little Girl" 68
Damerel, Donna see *Myrt and Marge*
Dames (1934) 84
Damita, Lili 72
Damone, Vic 46
A Damsel in Distress (1937) 116
*Dance, Girl, Dance (1933) 170–173, 175, 176
The Dance of Life (1929) 112, 172
Dante's Inferno (1935) 109, 110
Dare, Dorothy 55
Darwell, Jane 111
David Copperfield (1935) 183
Davies, Marion 182
Davis, Bette 56, 98
Day, Marceline 30, 31, **32**
Deane, Derry 164
de Havilland, Olivia 118
de la Falaise, Henri 96
DeLeon, Walter 132
Dell, Dorothy 1, 39, 46, 59–63, **60**
Del Rio, Dolores 147, 170, 185
Delroy, Irene 26–29
DeMille, Cecil B. 90
DeMille, Katherine 113
Dempsey, Jack 23
Denny, Jack 139
Denny, Reginald 69, 72

The Dentist (1932) 170
The Desert Song (play) 34
De Sylva, B.G. 99
Diamond Lil (play) 187
Dietrich, Marlene 90, 142
Dietz, Howard 19
DiMaggio, Joe 195
"Dinah" 42
Dinehart, Alan 70, 173
Disney, Walt 137, 150
The Divine Lady (1929) 10
Dixon, Lee 1, **83**, 83–87
Dizzy Dames (1935) 169, 180–184, **183**
Dodd, Betty 56
Dodd, Claire 98
"The Doll Dance" 24
Don Juan (1926) 13
Dorsey, Tommy 77, 165
Double or Nothing (1940) 86
Double Rhythm (1946) 86
Doucet, Catherine 49
Douglas, Donna 189
Dowling, Eddie 41
Down to Their Last Yacht (1934) 2, **6**, 128, 137, 146–151, **148**, 156
Downey, Morton 5, 17
Dracula (1931) 140
Dressler, Marie 52
"Drinking Song" 32
Drums Along the Mohawk (1939) 30
Dubin, Al 27, 29, 97, 141
DuBois, Gladys 19
Duchin, Eddy 94, 193
Dumbrille, Douglass 58
The Duncan Sisters 182
Dunn, James 141, 192
Dupont, Max 30
Durbin, Deanna 1, 156
"Dusty Shoes" 141
Dvorak, Ann **193**, 194
Dwyer, Josephine 193
Dylan, Bob 158
Dynamite (1929) 45

Eastwood, Clint 89
Ebsen, Buddy 113
Ed, Carl 55, 56
Eddy, Nelson 1, 134
Edwards, Cliff 23, 24, 25
Ehrhardt, Bess 124
Ellington, Duke 165, 193, 194
Ellis, Mary 117
Ellis, Patricia 56
Ellis, Robert 171
Emerson, Hope 120
The Enchanted Forest (1945) 160
The Encyclopedia of Vaudeville (book) 74
Errol, Leon 159
Erskine, Chester 187, 188
Erwin, Stuart 131

"Esk-i-O-Lay Li-O-Mo" 145
The Eton Boys 139, 140
Etting, Ruth 52, 153
Every Night at Eight (1935) 194
Everybody's Welcome (play) 93
Exhibitors Reliance Corporation 138

Fain, Sammy 56, 57
"Fancy Meeting You" 80
Farley, Edward 76
Farnum, William 31
Farrell, Charles 99
Farrell, Glenda 14
Father Takes a Wife (1941) 107
Faulkner, William 112
Faye, Alice 1, 39, 70, 137, 145, 151, 156
Fazenda, Louise 84, 85, 119, 120, **120**, 121
FBO (Film Booking Offices of America) 11
Fears, Peggy 1, 69–73, **71**
Fidler, Jimmie 180
Fields, Herbert 93
Fields, W.C. 1, 65, 91, 129, 130, 131, 132, 170, 175
Fiesta de Santa Barbara, La (1935) 68
Fifty Million Frenchmen (1931) 29
50 Worst Films of All Time (book) 119
Figueroa, Mary Louisa 185
The Film Answers Back: An Historical Appreciation of the Cinema (book) 114
The Film Daily (publication) 15, 24, 32, 43, 46, 54, 71, 95, 124, 134, 145, 150, 153, 157, 165, 173, 179, 188, 196
Fine, Larry *see* The Three Stooges
First Division Pictures 171, 175
The First Hollywood Musicals (book) 2, 5
The First Hollywood Sound Shorts (book) 1
First National Pictures 8, 9, 10, 25, 55, 72
Fitzgerald, Ella 77
The Five Pennies (1959) 77
Flame of Youth (1949) 160
The Flaming Signal (1933) 150
Fleeson, Neville 175
Flesh and Blood (1922) 180
Florey, Robert 17, 18
The Florodora Girl (1930) 182
Flothow, Rudolph 14
Flying Down to Rio (1933) 137, 147, 150, 151, 156
Flying High (play) 41
Follow the Boys (1944) 72
Follow the Fleet (1936) 162
Follow the Leader (1930) 37
Follow Thru (1930) 34
Follow Thru (play) 26, 34, 37
Follow Your Heart (1936) 167
Fonda, Henry 112, 161
Fontaine, Joan 88, 116, **116**, 118
Fontanne, Lynn 96
Footlight Parade (1933) 36, 84
Foran, Dick 69, 70

Index

Forbes, Hazel 148–149
Forbes, Ralph 168–170, *169*
Ford, Henry 15
Ford, Wallace 138
Forde, Arthur 145
40 Pounds of Trouble (1962) 63
42nd Street (1933) 5, 48, 55, 56, 84, 97, 98, 138, 140, 141, 153, 171, 175
Foster, Stephen 167
Four Frightened People (1934) 90
Four Hours to Kill (1935) 66
The Four Playboys 164
Fowler, Gene 60
Fox, Sidney 148, 150, 151
Fox Film Corporation/20th Century Fox 2, 10, 13, 14, 16, 34, 37, 46, 61, 62, 67, 69, 70, 72, 88, 99, 100, 101, 104, 105, 106, 108, 109, 110, 111, 112, 113, 115, 117, 123, 127, 142, 143, 144, 145, 146, 151, 153, 156, 164, 169
Foy, Bryan 52
Foy, Eddie 15
Foy, Eddie, Jr. 52, 54
Foy Productions 52
Francis, Kay 80
Frank and Milt Britton Band 139, 140
Frankenstein Meets the Wolf Man (1943) 178
"Frankie and Johnnie" 188
*Frankie and Johnnie (1936) 48, 186–190, *189*
Frankie and Johnnie (play) 186
Frankie and Johnny (1966) 189
Frankie and Johnny (1991) 189
Frankie and Johnny in the Clair de Lune (play) 190
Franklin, Irene 148
Franklin, Joe 43
Frawley, William 61, 139
Freed, Arthur 21, 24, 124
Freedman, David 165
Freel, Aleta 84
Freund, Karl 140, 153
Friend, Cliff 150
Friganza, Trixie 52
Friml, Rudolf 118
Fritsch, Willy 143
The Front Page (play) 139
The Fuller Brush Man (1948) 161
"Funny Little World" 150

Gable, Clark 82, 91, 94, 104
Gabler, Neal 48
Gallagher, Richard "Skeets" 149
Gallagher and Shean 104, 106
Gallian, Ketti 110
Gambling Lady (1934) 56, 112
Gang War (1928) 11, 30
The Gang's All Here (play) 55
Garber, Jan 97
Garbo, Greta 93, 127, 145
Garde, Betty 36
"The Garden of Proserpine" (poem) 9

Gargan, William 14, 147
Garland, Judy 1
The Gay Desperado (1936) 117
The Gay Divorce (play) 140
The Gay Divorcee (1934) 140, 147, 184
The Gay Lady see *The Battle of Paris*
Gaynor, Janet 99, 112, 142
Gentlemen of the Press (1929) 19
Gentlemen Prefer Blondes (1928) 129
George Jessel in a Theatrical Booking Office (1926) 13
George Washington Cohen (1928) 13
George White's 1935 Scandals (1935) 37
George White's Scandals (1934) 145
Gershwin, George 17
Gershwin, Ira 17
"Get Happy" 94
Get Smart (TV series) 81
Geva, Tamara *193*, 195
The Ghetto see *Lucky Boy*
The Ghost of Frankenstein (1942) 178
The Ghost Walks (1934) 172
Giddens, Gary 46
Gifford, Frances 164
*Gift of Gab (1934) 151–155, *154*
Gilbert, Billy 117
Girl Crazy (play) 37
*Girl o' My Dreams (1934) 169, 176–179
Girl of the Port (1930) 30
"Give Me Liberty or Give Me Love" 92
Givot, George 111
Glamour (1934) 49
The Glass Menagerie (play) 20
Gleason, James 195
Glennon, Bert 30, 31
Glyn, Elinor 104
"God Bless America" 43
Gold Diggers of 1933 (1933) 141
Gold Diggers of 1937 (1936) 80, 85
Gold Dust Gertie (1931) 29
Golden Dawn (1930) 70
Goldwyn, Samuel 104, 115, 128
Good News (1930) 34, 57
Good News (play) 34
Gordon, Bert 162
Gordon, Mack 46, 66
Gordon, Susan 77
The Gorgeous Hussy (1936) 123
Gorney, Jay 19, 69, 72, 141
"Got Me Doin' Things!" 67
Grainger, James R. 157
Grand Exit (1935) 95
Grand Hotel (1932) 172
Grandee, George 173, 176
Grant, Cary 49, 90
Grapewin, Charley 41–42, *91*
Gray, Alexander 61, 139, 140, 141
Gray, Arnold 170
Gray, Lawrence 1, 182–185, *183*
Grayson, Charles 157

Index

Great American Harem see *Bachelor Bait*
The Great Gabbo (1929) 173
The Great Magoo (play) 60, 63
Green, Abel 102
The Green Goddess (1930) 168
Green, Harry *100*, 101
The Greenwich Village Follies (play) 26
Grey, Zane 66
Griffith, Corinne 10
Griffith, D.W. 8, 187
The Guardsman (play) 96
Guinan, Texas 47, 48
Guizar, Tito 110, 151

Haines, William 21, 29
Hal Kemp (and His Orchestra) 77, 97, 184
Hale, Creighton 98
Hall, Alexander 90
Hall, Mordaunt 24, 102, 136, 145
The Hall Johnson Choir 113
Hallelujah, I'm a Bum (1933) 134
Halton, Charles 81
Hamilton, Harry 112
Hamlet (play) 157
Hammerstein, Oscar II 86, 104
"Happy Cowboy" 185
Happy Days (1930) 127
Happy Go Lucky (1936) 192
Harbach, Otto 29
Harbin, Vernon 165
Harburg, E.Y. 79, 80, 141
Harkrider, John 157
Harlan, Kenneth 30–32, *32*
Harmony Lane (1935) 167
"Harold Teen" (comic strip) 55
*Harold Teen (1934) 54–58, *57*
Harrigan, William 187
Harris, Marion 21
Harris, Phil 134–137, *135*
Harris, Theresa 113
Harrison's Reports (publication) 72, 106, 110
Hart, Lorenz 85, 159–160
Hart, Moss 187, 188
Hart, Teddy 85
Hartman, Don 69, 72
Hartwig, Walter 102
Harvey, Lilian 69, 99, 142–146, *144*
"Have You Ever Been in Heaven?" 195
Hayes, George "Gabby" 168
Hayes, Grace 52, 174, 175
Hayes, Peter Lind 175
Hayward, Leland 120
Hayworth, Rita 108–111, *109*
Hazzard, Jack 187
Healy, Ted 51–54
Hecht, Ben 60
Hedge, Ray 52, 53
A Hell of a Life (book) 74
**Hello, Everybody!* (1933) 38, 39–43, *40*
Hellzapoppin' (1941) 29

Helton, Percy 187
Henderson, Ray 99
Henie, Sonja 123, 124
Henry V (play) 127
Hepburn, Katharine 84, 99, 158
Her Majesty, Love (1931) 132
Her Man (1930) 186
Her Sister from Paris (1925) 97
Herbert, Hugh 156, 157
Here Comes Mr. Jordan (1941) 90
"Here I Go Falling in Love Again" 124
Here's to Romance (1935) 117
"He's Not the Marrying Kind" 136
Heyburn, Weldon 82
High and Happy see *Hit Parade of 1947*
Higher and Higher (play) 86
"Highway to Heaven" 29
Hilliard, Harriet (Harriet Nelson) 162, *163*, 164, 165
Hischak, Thomas C. 77
*The Hit Parade (1937) 167, 190–196
Hit Parade of 1941 (1940) 196
Hit Parade of 1943 (1943) 196
Hit Parade of 1947 (1947) 196
Hit Parade of 1951 (1950) 196
Hit the Deck (play) 27, 41
Hitchy Koo (play) 26
Hite, Henry see Lowe, Hite & Stanley
Hitting a New High (1937) 118
Hodgson, William "Red" 76
Hoff, Carl 193
Hoffman, M.H. 183
Holden, William 10
The Hole in the Wall (1929) 17
Holiday (1938) 158
Holloway, Sterling 69, 132, 153, 179
Hollywood (publication) 66
Hollywood Filmograph (publication) 145
The Hollywood Hall of Shame (book) 42
Hollywood Newsreel (1934) 56
Hollywood on the Hudson (book) 138
Hollywood Party (1934) 195
Hollywood Party (1937) 68
The Hollywood Reporter (periodical) 38, 43, 101, 102, 129, 131, 132, 143, 153, 170
The Hollywood Revue of 1929 (1929) 27, 127, 195
Holm, Celeste 86
Holman, Libby 90
Holmes, Brown 157
Home on the Range (1935) 66
Honey (1930) 34
Honeymoon Lane (play) 41
Honor Among Lovers (1931) 37
Hoover, Herbert 162
Hoover, J. Edgar 162
Hope, Bob 1, 63, 74
Hopper, Hedda 131
Horsley, John David 149–150
The Hound of the Baskervilles (1939) 170

"How Do I Know It's Sunday?" 57
Howard, Curly see The Three Stooges
Howard, Moe see The Three Stooges
Howard, Shemp 52
Hudson, Rochelle 57, 58, 74, **75**
Hughes, Carol 84, 85
Hughes, Howard 173, 194
The Human Chatterbox 194
Hundley, John 140
Hupfeld, Herman 140
Hurst, Fannie 41
Hurst, Paul 31
Hutchinson, Ron 16
Hutton, Betty 55

I Am a Fugitive from a Chain Gang (1932) 157
I Am Suzanne!* (1933) 117, 128, 141–146, **144
I Cover the Waterfront (1933) 162
"I Gotta Get Up and Go to Work" 140
"I Love a Girl in My Own Peculiar Way" 36
"I Love to Singa" 170
"I Love You Prince Pizzicato" 46
"I Want the World to Know" 118
"I Want to Be a Rug Cutter" 194
Ice Antics (1939) 124
The Ice Follies of 1939* (1939) 122–126, **125
I'll Reach for a Star see *The Hit Parade*
"I'm Alone" 106
"I'm Coming Home" 106
"I'm in the Mood for Love" 194
Imitation of Life (1934) 90
Imitation of Life (novel) 41
"In Egern on the Tegern See" 104
"In My Bouquet of Memories" 15
In Old Arizona (1928) 110
"In the Silent Picture Days" 81
"The Income Tax" 80
Indiscreet (1931) 103
International House* (1933) 1, 128–133, **130
International Photographer (publication) 149
Invincible Pictures Corporation 166, 167, 171, 172, 175
"Isn't It Romantic?" 182
"Isn't This a Night for Love?" 136
"It Goes to Your Feet" 164
It Happened One Night (1934) 90, 91
"It Was So Beautiful" 41
It's a Great Life (1929) 182
It's a Great Life (1935) 67
"It's All So New to Me" 124
It's Great to Be Alive (1933) 2
"I've Got a Girl in Every Port" 32
"I've Told Every Little Star" 104, 106

Jablonski, Edward 95
Jailhouse Rock (1957) 175
"Jamboree" 157
James, Gladden 31
James, Harry 164
James, Rian 153

Jan Garber and His Orchestra 97
"The Japanese Sandman" 24
Jarrett, Art 95, 138
Jason, Will 31–32
The Jazz Singer (1927) 5, 10, 12, 13, 182
Jenkins, Allen 84, 85
Jerome, Edwin 14
Jerome, M.K. 80
Jessel, George 12–16, **14**
Jewell, Richard 165
Jiménez, Soledad 110
Jimmy the Gent (1934) 56
Johnson, Chic 26–29, **28**
Johnson, Nunnally 96, 112
Johnson, Oscar 124
Johnson, Van 162
Johnston, Arthur 42
Johnston, W. Ray 167, 168
Jolson, Al 1, 5, 7, 10, 11, 12, 13, 46, 47, 48, 56, 74
Joyce, Peggy Hopkins 1, 47, 129–133, **130**
Judels, Charles 28
Judge, Arline 61, 66
The Jungle Book (1967) 137

Kahal, Irving 56, 57
Kahane, B.B. 149, 151
Kahn, Gus 118
Kaley, Charles **22**, 23–25
Kane, Helen 34
"Kansas City" 86
Kansas City Confidential (1952) 161
Karloff, Boris 153, 154, **154**
Karns, Roscoe 60
Kate Smith, the Songbird of the South (1929) 41
Kaye, Danny 77
Keaton, Buster 30
Keeler, Ruby 1, 46, 47, 83, **83**, 84, 85, 97, 140
Keene, Richard 140
Kelly, Kitty 183, 184
Kelly, Paul 46, 47, **47**, 60, 192
Kemp, Hal (and His Orchestra) 77, 97, 184
Kennedy, Edgar 29, 159
Kenny, Nick 138
Kent, Sidney R. 112
Kern, Jerome 29, 104
Kibbee, Guy 58
Kicking the Moon Around (1938) 77
Kid Boots (play) 22
Kiepura, Jan 117
King, Bradley 9
King, Charles 21, 26–29
King, Henry 110
King, Walter [Woolf] 70
The King and I (play) 20
King of Jazz (1930) 34, 127, 138, 175
"King of the Road" 118
Kingsford, Walter 187
Kirkland, Jack 186, 187, 188
Kirkwood, Ray 179, 180
Knapp, Evalyn 172

Knickerbocker Holiday (play) 82
Knight, Felix 150
Knight, Fuzzy 183, 184, 185
Knight, June 49, **50**, 141, **154**, 155
Knox, Alexander 158
Kobal, John 109, 110
Koehler, Ted 94, 95
Kohlmar, Lee 67
Kosloff, Maurice 184
Koszarski, Richard 138
Krueger, Lorraine 164
Krupa, Gene 63
Kuhn, Irene 187

Lady Be Good (1941) 95
The Lady Lies (1929) 19
"Lady Luck" 127
Lady of Burlesque (1944) 114
Laemmle, Carl 140, 156
Lahr, Bert 41, 156
Lake, Alice 93
Lake, Arthur 55, 93, 178
Lally, Kevin 70
Lamour, Dorothy 61, 95
Lane, Richard 165
Lanfield, Sidney 97
Lang, June 104, 106, 109
Lang, Walter 156
Langford, Frances 194
Lanza, Joseph 46
La Plante, Laura 10
Lasky, Jesse L. 117, 118, 143, 145
The Last Frontier (1932) 178
The Last Laugh (1924) 140
The Last Mile (play) 187
"The Last Round-Up" 65, 66, 68
"Laugh You Son of a Gun" 62
Laughing Irish Eyes (1936) 192
"The Laughing Song" 29
Laurel and Hardy 29, 33, 150, 173, 194
Lawrence, Fred 80, 81, **81**
Lawrence, Gertrude 17–20
Lax, Eric 120
"Lazy Breezes" 32
"Leave a Little Smile" 29
Lee, Dixie 65, 66, **67**, 67
Lee, Dorothy 185
Lee, Gwen 16
Lee, Rowland V. 143
Lee, Sammy 24
Leeds, Thelma 162, 165
Lees, Gene 85
Lehrman, Henry 96
Lemaire, Charles 72
LeRoy, Hal 55–58
"Let Me Sing You to Sleep with a Love Song" 66
"Let's Do It" 19
Let's Fall in Love (1933) 92–95, **94**
"Let's Fall in Love" 95
Let's Go Native (1930) 147

"Let's Go Places and Do Things" 176
Let's Love Tonight (1935) 146
Levine, Nat 167, 193
Lewis, Ted, and His Orchestra 194
Liberty (magazine) 90
Liberty Pictures Corporation 151, 166, 167, 183, 184
The Life and Death of 9413, a Hollywood Extra (1928) 17
Lightner, Winnie 29
Liliom (1934) 104
Lindsay, Margaret 101
"A Little Angel Told Me So" 66
Little Man, What Now? (1934) 104
*Little Miss Marker (1934) 58–59, 62–63
Little Miss Marker (1980) 63
Littlefield, Emma 153
Lloyd, Frank 8
Lloyd, Harold 34
Loder, Lotti 28, **28**, 29
Logan, Ella 156, 157, 158
Lombard, Carole 23, 46, 49, 94
Lombardo, Guy 65
"(Lookie, Lookie, Lookie) Here Comes Cookie" 66
Loos, Anita 129
*Lord Byron of Broadway (1930) 3, 20–25, **22**, 183
Lord Byron of Broadway (novel) 21
The Loria Brothers 164
Los Angeles Times (newspaper) 22, 27, 145, 151
*Lottery Lover (1935) 68–73, **71**, 99, 145, 146
Louis Prima and His Orchestra 194
Love, Bessie 21, 27
Love Among the Millionaires (1930) 34
Love and Hisses (1937) 61
The Love Boat (TV series) 118
*Love in Bloom (1935) 63–68, **67**
"Love in Bloom" 66
"Love Is Good for Anything That Ails You" 194
"Love Is Love Anywhere" 95
"Love Is Never Out of Season" 164
"Love Is the Thing" 184
The Love Life of a Crooner see *Wake Up and Dream*
Love Me Tonight (1932) 134
The Love of Sunya (1927) 104
"Low Down Lullaby" 62, 63
Lowe, Edmund 93, 95, 152, 153, 187
Lowe, Hite & Stanley 164
Luciano, Lucky 74
*Lucky Boy (1929) 10, 11–16, **14**, 116
Lucky in Love (1929) 17
Lucky Strike Hour (radio show) 15
Lugosi, Bela 131, 153, 154, **154**
Lukas, Paul 49, **154**, 155
Lunt, Alfred 96
Lupino, Ida 62, 117
Lyman, Abe 23
Lyon, Ben 134

MacDonald, J. Farrell 53
MacDonald, Jeanette 1
Mack, Helen **135**, 135–136
Mack, Tommy 162
Mack, Willard 52
Mack Sennett Studios 171, 175
Madden, Jeanne 1, 79–82, **81**
Madonna 129
Majestic Pictures Corporation 167, 172
"Mama, I Wanna Make Rhythm" 195
Mamba (1930) 31
Mamoulian, Rouben 117
Man Made Monster (1941) 178
The Man Who Found Himself (1937) 118
Mandel, Frank 34
Manhattan Love Song (1934) 67
Manhattan Merry-Go-Round (1937) 167, 190–196, **193**
Manhattan Tower (1932) 172
Mank, Gregory William 153
Manners, David 90, 91
Man's Castle (1933) 102
Mantell, Robert 15
Marafioti, P. Mario 105
The March of Time (1930) 127
Marianne (1929) 182
Mario, Queena 79
Maritza, Sari 131
Markey, Gene 17
Marquis, Rosalind 80, **81**
Marsh, Joan 174, 175
Marshall, Everett 117
Marshall, George 134
Marston, Christine 184
Martin, Francis 132
Martin, Keith 82
Martin, Nell 21
Martin, Paul 145
Martin, Tony 113
Martini, Nino 88, 116, **116**, 117, 118
"The Martinique" 184
The Marx Brothers 18, 136, 145
Mascot Pictures Corporation 167
Masuraca, Nicholas 134
Matthau, Walter 63
Maugham, Somerset 112
Mauvaise Graine (1934) 70
May, Joe 104
Mayer, Arthur 42
Mayfair, Mitzi 55
Maynard, Ken 172
Mayo, Archie 27
The Mayor of 44th Street (1942) 11
McCord, Ted 134
McCoy, Tim 172
McCrea, Joel 112, 113, **114**, 115, 170
McHugh, Jimmy 113, 156, 158
McKinney, Florine 183, **183**
McNally, Terrence 190
Medved, Harry 42, 119, 122

Medved, Michael 42, 119, 122
"Meet My Sister" 11
Meins, Gus 194
Melody Cruise (1933) 128, 133–137, **135**, 156
Melton, James 117
Men of the Sky (1931) 29
Menjou, Adolphe 62
Mercer, Johnny 84, 85
Merman, Ethel 62
Merrill, Dick 77
Merry-Go-Round (play) 19
Merry Mirthquakes (1953) 160
Metro-Goldwyn-Mayer (MGM) 2, 21, 22, 23, 24, 27, 29, 34, 37, 45, 52, 53, 68, 93, 95, 97, 99, 102, 104, 107, 118, 121, 123, 125, 127, 156, 196
Metropolis (1927) 140
Metropolitan (1935) 117
Meyer, Abe 14
MGM *see* Metro-Goldwyn-Mayer
Midnight (1934) 187
Midstream (1929) 15
Mike (magazine story) 90
Miles, Lillian 139, 140, 141, 183, 184, 185
Milland, Ray 65, 66
Miller, Ann 164, 165
Miller, Marilyn 5, 93, 132
Le Million (1931) 134
A Million to One (1937) 118
Mr. Smith Goes to Washington (1939) 126
Mitchell, Sidney 150
"Moanin' Low" 90
Modern Screen (magazine) 72, 104, 150
Molly and Me (1929) 15
Monogram Pictures Corporation 160, 166, 167, 168, 170
Montgomery, Douglass 104, 106, **154**
Montgomery, Robert 97
"Moon Song (That Wasn't Meant for Me)" 42
Moonlight and Pretzels (1933) 128, 137–141, **139**, 153, 184
Moonlight and Romance (1930) 117
"Moonlight in Heaven" 185
Moore, Colleen 104
Moore, Grace 74, 117
Moore, Victor 153
Moran, Polly **6**, 148, 150
Moreno, Antonio 98
Morgan, Frank 34, 36
Morgan, Helen 178, 184, 187, 188, **189**
Morning Matinee (radio show) 185
Morris, Chester **154**, 155, 187, 188, **189**
Morrison, Joe 1, 65–68, **67**
Mother Carey's Chickens (1938) 84
Mother Knows Best (1928) 10
Mother's Boy (1929) 17
Motion Picture (magazine) 70
Motion Picture Daily (periodical) 54, 80, 110, 189, 196
Motion Picture Herald (periodical) 170
Motion Picture News (periodical) 32

Moulin Rouge (1934) 45, 49, 95–98
Mountain Music (1937) 119
Movie Classic (magazine) 96
Mowbray, Alan 117
Mulhall, Jack 98, 180
The Mummy (1932) 140
Mundin, Herbert 102
Murphy, George 156, 157, **159**
Murphy, Ralph 156
Murray, Johnny 10
Music Box Revue (play) 22
Music for Madame (1937) 88, 115–118, **116**
The Music Goes 'Round (1936) 73–77, **75**
"The Music Goes 'Round and Around" 76, 77
Music in the Air (1934) 69, 70, 102–107, **105**
Music in the Air (play) 69
"My Blackbirds Are Bluebirds Now" 15
"My Green Fedora" 170
"My Heart Is an Open Book" 66
My Lady's Past (1929) 15
My Lips Betray (1933) 143
"My Love" 45
My Man Godfrey (1936) 156
"My Mother's Eyes" 14, 15, 16
My Weakness (1933) 99, 143
Myrt and Marge (Myrtle Vail and Donna Damerel) 1, 51–54
Myrt and Marge (1933) 50–54, 154, 175

Nagel, Anne 84
Nagel, Conrad 65
Nancy from Naples see *Oh, Sailor, Behave!*
NBC 45, 50, 79, 134, 175, 193, 194
Nelson, Harriet see Hilliard, Harriet
Nelson, Ozzie 162, 165
Neumann, Kurt 49
"New Faces" 164
New Faces of 1934 (play) 161
New Faces of 1936 (play) 162
New Faces of 1937 (1937) 160–165, **163**
New Moon (play) 34
New York Daily News (newspaper) 54
New York Sun (newspaper) 54
The New York Times (newspaper) 2, 10, 18, 24, 34, 36, 50, 54, 56, 60, 67, 76, 80, 102, 105, 122, 136, 138, 145, 147, 153, 157, 189, 194
The New Yorkers (play) 29
Newill, James 85
Newmeyer, Fred 34
Nichols, Nellie V. 195
Niesen, Gertrude 156
Nigh, William 21, 23, 183
"Night Flies By" 106
Night Must Fall (1937) 175
Night Owls (1930) 33
Nilsson, Anna Q. 98
Nina Rosa (play) 25
Nissen, Greta 136, 137
No More Ladies (1935) 118
No Red of Roses (book) 116

Nolan, Bob 185
Nolan, Doris 156, 157, 158, **159**
"None But the Weary Heart" 66
A Nous la Liberté (1931) 134
Novarro, Ramon 127, 192
Now and Forever (1934) 62
Nugent, Edward 69, 172, 173, 178, 185
Nugent, Frank S. 50, 76, 80, 157, 189

Oakie, Jack 59, 60, **60**, 61, 131
Oakland, Vivien 28, 29
"The Object of My Affection" 110
O'Brien, Pat 80
The O.C. (TV series) 81
O'Connell, Hugh 85, 153
O'Connor, Robert Emmett 101
O'Day, Dawn 55
O'Day, Molly 149
The Odd Couple (TV series) 81
Of Human Bondage (1934) 112
Of Mice and Men (1939) 180
Of Thee I Sing (play) 93
Oh, Sailor, Behave! (1930) 25–29, **28**
O'Hara, Maureen 77, 159
Oklahoma! (play) 36, 86
The Old Fashioned Way (1934) 65
The Old Homestead (1935) 180–182, 184–185
Olivette, Nina 36
Olsen, George 7, 65
Olsen, Ole 26–29, **28**
On Your Toes (1939) 86
Once in a Lifetime (play) 187
One Hour Late (1934) 63–66
"One More Dance" 105–106
One Night of Love (1934) 74, 117
One Night with You (1948) 118
Osborne, Vivienne 168
Oscar and Elmer 194

Pacino, Al 189
Paddy O'Day (1935) 107–108, 110–111
Page, Bradley 66
Paint Your Wagon (1969) 89
"Painting the Clouds With Sunshine" 27
Pal Joey (play) 24
Panama Hattie (1942) 95
Panama Hattie (play) 29
Pangborn, Franklin 132
Paradise Island (1930) 30–33, **32**
Paramount on Parade (1930) 34, 117, 127
Paramount Pictures/Paramount Publix Corporation 2, 17, 18, 19, 20, 34, 35, 37, 38, 40, 41, 42, 45, 46, 49, 59, 61, 62, 63, 65, 66, 67, 86, 90, 92, 101, 104, 117, 119, 127, 129, 130, 131, 132, 133, 134, 135, 138, 139, 141, 143, 147, 156, 162, 192, 194, 196
Parker, Frank 141
Parker, Max 145
Parkyakarkus (Harry Einstein) 162, 163, 165
Parsons, Loretta 99, 133, 183

Index

Passing the Buck (1932) 61
Paterson, Pat 69, 70, 73, 99, 100, 101, 146
Pathé Exchange 17, 25, 34, 186
Patrick, Gail 66, 168, 169
Patty and Fields 14
Pearce, Al 194
"Peckin'" 164
"Peg o' My Heart" 68
Pendleton, Nat 119, 120, **120**, 121
Penna, Dennis 46
Penner, Joe 162, 163, 164, 165
The Perils of Pauline (1933) 172
Perkins, Grace 90
Perrin, Jack 179
Petkere, Bernice 124
Petrie, Walter 19
Pfeiffer, Michelle 190
*The Phantom Broadcast (1933) 167–170, **169**
The Phantom of the Opera (novel and 1925 film) 168
Photoplay (publication) 10, 29, 62, 72, 97, 141, 150
Pick and Pat 194
"Pickaninnies' Heaven" 42
Pickford, Mary 117, 187
Pickin' a Winner (1932) 25
Picture Play (magazine) 61, 145
The Playboy see *Kicking the Moon Around*
"Plow Boy" 185
Podrecca's Piccoli Marionettes 144, 145
Pollack, Ben 164
Pommer, Erich 104, 105
Pons, Lily 117, 118
Porter, Cole 17, 20, 29, 156
Powell, Dick 1, 36, 79, 80, 85
Powell, Eleanor 37, 158
Preisser, June 55
Present Arms (play) 27
Presley, Elvis 189
Prevost, Marie 32
Prima, Louis, and His Orchestra 194
Prince, Frank see Lawrence, Fred
"Prisoner of Love" 45
The Prisoner of Zenda (1952) 175
Prisoners in Petticoats (1950) 160
Private Izzy Murphy (1926) 13
The Private Lives of Elizabeth and Essex (1939) 170
The Producers (1968) 161, 165
Producers Releasing Corporation (PRC) 160
Pryor, Arthur 138
Pryor, Roger 49, 138, 139, 140, **154**, 155
Purcell, Dick 25
Puttin' on the Ritz (1930) 74
Pygmalion (play) 143

Quality Street (1937) 118
*Queen High (1930) 7, 19, 33–37, **35**
Queen Kelly (1929) 103–104
Queen of the Night Clubs (1929) 48

Quigley, Eileen 86
Quimby, Margaret 14, 15, 16

Radio City Revels (1938) 165
Radio Guide (magazine) 52
Radio Mirror (magazine) 41
Radio Pictures see RKO
Raft, George 11
*Rainbow Over Broadway (1933) 171, 173–176
Rainger, Ralph 61, 62, 66, 90, 92
Rambeau, Marjorie 183
Rambling 'Round Radio Row (1932) 41
Ramona (1936) 110
Ramos, Josephine 170
Rapf, Harry 23, 123
Rasch, Albertina 24
Ratoff, Gregory 93, 156
Rawlinson, Herbert 139, 140
Rayart Pictures 168
Raymond, Gene 143, 144, **144**, 147
*Ready, Willing and Able (1937) 82–87, **83**
Reagan, Ronald 119, 121
Red Heads (1930) 25
Redheads on Parade (1935) 67
Reducing (1931) 52
Reed, Florence 187, 188–189
Reefer Madness (1936) 140, 184
"Reefer Man" 131
Regan, Phil 192, 193, **193**, 194, 196
Reisner, Charles F. 195
"Remember My Forgotten Man" 141
Remington Pictures 172
Remote Control (1930) 29
Republic Pictures 29, 82, 122, 160, 166, 167, 184, 186, 188, 190–196
The Return of Chandu (1934) 180
The Return of Dr. X (1939) 119
Revel, Harry 46, 66
"Rhapsody in Blue" 127
Rhodes, Erik 70, 117
Rice, Elmer 26
Richman, Harry 74–77, **75**
Riley, Michael 75, 76
Rio, Eddie 164
Rio Rita (1929) 28
Rio Rita (play) 22
Ritter, Tex 25
The River (1928) 169
RKO (Radio Pictures) 11, 17, 34, 45, 55, 58, 70, 84, 87, 96, 107, 112, 116, 117, 118, 133, 134, 135, 136, 137, 147, 148, 149, 151, 156, 159, 160, 161, 162, 163, 164, 165
Roberti, Lyda 91
Robertson, Willard 185
Robin, Leo 61, 62, 66, 90, 92
Robinson, Edward G. 11
Robson, E.W. 114
Rockabye (1932) 96
Rockett, Al 72
Rodgers, Richard 86, 159–160

Rogers, Buddy 17, 141
Rogers, Charles 156
Rogers, Ginger 1, 34, 36–37, 70, 86, 137, 140, 147, 156
Rogers, Roy 185
Rogers, Will 113, 145
Rolling Along see *The Music Goes 'Round*
"Rolling in Love" 65
Romance and Rhythm see *Hit Parade of 1941*
Romanoff, Michael 101
Romberg, Sigmund 25
Ronell, Ann 150
Rooney, Mickey 1
Roosevelt, Eleanor 121
Rose Marie see Baby Rose Marie
Rosen, Phil 168
Rosenblatt, Josef 10
Rosher, Charles 175
Ross, Lanny 62
Ross, Shirley 63
Roth, Lillian 141
Roth, Murray 55
Rowland, William 138, 141
Rubin, Benny 23, 164
Ruggles, Charles 19, 33–34, **35**, 36, 135, 136
Ruggles, Wesley 61
Rumann, Sig 14, 16
Runyon, Damon 62
Ruttenberg, Joseph 188
Ryan, Peggy 156, 157, 158

Saal, William 188
"St. Louis Blues" 113
Sally, Irene and Mary (1926) 96
Sandefur, W.A. 121
Sandrich, Mark 134, 136, 137
Santschi, Tom 31
The Sap from Syracuse (1930) 37
Sauber, Harry 195
Sawley, George 31
Say When (play) 74
Scarface (1932) 194
Scarlet Seas (1928) 10
Schallert, Edwin 145
Schenck, Joseph M. 74
Schertzinger, Victor 74
Scholl, Jack 80
School for Girls (1935) 151
Schotte, George 56
Schulz, Franz 70
Schünzel, Reinhold 123
Schwab, Laurence 34
Schwartz, Hanna 69
Scott, Fred 25
Scott, Randolph 42
A Scream in the Night (1936) 179, 180
Sea Racketeers (1938) 82
See Naples and Die see *Oh, Sailor, Behave!*
Seeley, Blossom 47, 48
Select Productions 188

Sennwald, Andre 60, 105
Sevely, Joe 14
Seymour, James 55
*The Shadow of Silk Lennox (1935) 176–177, 179–180
The Shadow Returns (1945) 160
"Shadows in the Night" (album) 158
The Shanghai Gesture (play) 189
Shaw, Wini **50,** 84
Shaw and Lee 85
She Done Him Wrong (1933) 186
She Loves Me Not (1934) 66
"She Was a China Tea-cup and He Was Just a Mug" 132
Shean, Al 104
Sheehan, Winifred 99, 109
The Sheik (1921) 178
Sherman, Lowell 28, 49
"She's Not the Type" 95
Shilling, Marion 3, **22**, 23
Shipstad, Eddie 124
Shipstad, Roy 124
Shirley, Eileen 86
*Shoot the Works (1934) 58–63, **60**, 66, 81
"Should I?" 24
Show Boat (1929) 10
Show Boat (1936) 50, 156, 188
Show Boat (play) 74
Show Girl (play) 19
The Show of Shows (1929) 11, 93, 127
The Show Off (1934) 102
Shutta, Ethel 65
Siegel, Al 139
Sillman, Leonard 161–162
Silver Screen (magazine) 92
Silvers, Louis 9
Silvers, Sid 99, 102
"Simple and Sweet" 57
Sinatra, Frank 158
"Singin' in the Rain" 127
Singin' in the Rain (1952) 5, 25
The Singing Buckaroo (1937) 25
The Singing Fool (1928) 13, 15
The Singing Marine (1937) 85
Singleton, Penny 121
Sinners' Holiday (1930) 172
Skipworth, Alison **60**
Skyscraper Symphony (1929) 17
Slide, Anthony 74, 158
Slightly French (1949) 95
Sloane, Paul 149
"The Slumber Boat" 90
Slye, Leonard see Rogers, Roy
Small, Edward 161, 165
Smart, Jack 156
Smeck, Roy 194
Smiles (play) 93
The Smiling Lieutenant (1931) 90
Smith, Kate 38, 39, 40–43, **40**
Smith, Paul Gerard 56

Smith, Stanley 7, 34, 36
Snyder, Gene 156
So This Is Harris! (1933) 134, 147
Some Like It Hot (1939) 63
"Something's Gotta Happen Soon" 124
Somnes, George 90
The Son of Kong (1933) 136
"The Song Is You" 104
"Sonny Boy" 15
Sons o' Guns (play) 25
The Sons of the Pioneers 185
The Sophomore (1929) 34
Sorrowful Jones (1949) 63
Sothern, Ann 74, 93–95, **94**
Sothern, E.H. 93
Sound Waves (magazine) 9
Soup to Nuts (1930) 34
"South Sea Bolero" 149, 150
Spaeth, Sigmund 187
Sparks, Ned 70, 148
Spectrum Pictures 25
Spencer, Norman 169
Sperber, A.M. 120
The Spoilers (1914) 31
Spring Is Here (1930) 182, 183
*Stage Struck (1936) 77, 79–80, 82
Stagecoach (1939) 30
Stahl, John M. 90
Stand Up and Cheer! (1934) 62
Stanwyck, Barbara 56, 112–115, **114**
Starling, Lynn 90
Start Cheering (1938) 55
Steamboat 'Round the Bend (1935) 113
Steele, Bob 179
Steinbeck, Elaine 86
Stella Dallas (1937) 115
Stevens, George 134
Stewart, James 123, 124, **125**, 126
Stockwell, Dean 36
Stockwell, Guy 36
Stokowski, Leopold 117
Stoopnagle and Budd *see* Colonel Stoopnagle and Budd
"Stormy Weather" 94
Strayer, Frank R. 171, 172
Street Girl (1929) 45
Street Scene (play) 27
Strike Me Pink (play) 56, 140
Strike Me Pink (1936) 162
Stroheim, Erich von 173
Stuart, Gloria 147, 153
Sunny (1930) 182
Sunnyside Up (1929) 99, 143
Sunset Blvd. (1950) 107
Sutherland, Edward 132
Svengali (1931) 168
Swanson, Gloria 88, 103–107, **105**
Swarthout, Gladys 117
"The Swede Is Not a Swede" 95
Sweepings (1933) 136
"Sweet and Lovely" 45
"Sweet Heartache" 194
Sweet Surrender (1935) 141
The Sweetheart of Sigma Chi (1933) 178–179
Sweetheart of the Campus (1941) 84
Sweetie (1929) 34, 58
Swerling, Jo 74
Swinburne, A.G. 9
*Swing Your Lady (1938) 88, 118–122, **120**
Symes, Marty 124
Syncopation (1929) 30

Take a Chance (1933) 141
Take a Chance (play) 140
"Take Me Out to the Ball Game" 176
Talbot, Lyle 98, 192
*Talent Scout (1937) 77–82, **81**
Talley, Marion 117, 167
Tamara 141
Tashman, Lilyan 47, 48, 131, 153, 187, 188
Taurog, Norman 13, 14
Tchaikovsky, Pyotr Ilyich 66
Ted Lewis and His Orchestra 194
Tell Your Children see Reefer Madness
Temple, Shirley 1, 62–63, 70, 91, 110–111, 164
Terhune, Max 194, 195
Terry, Ethelind 22–25, **22**
"Thank Heaven for You" 132
That Goes Double (1933) 45
"There Are No Two Ways About It" 158
"There'll Be No South" 76
"There's a Bit of Paree in You" 69, 72
"There's Nothing Else to Do in Malakamokalu But Love" 150
"They All Fall in Love" 19
They Met in Argentina (1941) 159
Thiele, Wilhelm 69, 70
This Is the Army (1943) 43
Thomas, Dan 72
Thompson, Kay 194
Thorpe, Richard 175
"Thou Art My Baby" 178
The Three Chocolateers 164–165
Three Little Pigs (1933) 150
Three on a Match (1932) 194
The Three Sailors 156
Three Smart Girls (1936) 156
The Three Stooges (act billed as such in *Gift of Gab*) 153, 154
The Three Stooges (Moe Howard, Larry Fine, Curly Howard) 51–54, 154
Thurman, Tedi 73
Tibbett, Lawrence 117
Tiffany-Stahl/Tiffany Pictures 13, 14, 15, 16, 30, 31, 166
"Tiger Rag" 185
Tilzer, Albert von 176
Tiomkin, Dimitri 24
"Tiptoe Through the Tulips" 27
Tobacco Road (1941) 113

Tobacco Road (play) 113, 186
Todd, Thelma 102
Tomlin, Pinky 110, 111
Tone, Franchot 97
Tonight or Never (1931) 103
"Too Beautiful for Words" 49
Too Many Girls (1940) 55
"Too Marvelous for Words" 84, 85
"Too Wonderful for Words" 85
*Top of the Town (1937) 128, 151, 155–160, **159**
Top Speed (1930) 27
Top Speed (play) 34
*Torch Singer (1933) 89–92, **91**
Tower of London (1939) 170
Tracy, Arthur 138
Tracy, Lee 139
Tracy, Spencer 88, 99–102
Transatlantic Wives (novel) 129
Treacher, Arthur 19
Treasure Girl (play) 17
The Trespasser (1929) 103, 104, 105
Tucker, Sophie 97, 173
"Tumbling Tumbleweeds" 185
Tupper, Tristram 169
Turner Classic Movies 2, 5, 25, 58, 151
Turner Network Television 5, 6, 25
Turpin, Ben 98
Twelvetrees, Helen 65, 66
20th Century–Fox *see* Fox Film Corporation
20th Century Pictures 46, 47, 48, 49, 96, 97, 98
20,000 Years in Sing Sing (1932) 102
Two Against the World (1932) 96
Tyler, Tom 179

UFA 104, 142, 146
*Under the Pampas Moon (1935) 107–110, **109**
Under Your Spell (1936) 117
United Artists 72, 74, 117, 134, 188
Universal Pictures 2, 10, 29, 34, 49, 50, 52, 53, 54, 63, 90, 92, 127, 138, 139, 140, 141, 148, 152, 153, 154, 156, 157, 158, 159, 170, 192
USA Network 158

Vail, Myrtle *see* Myrt and Marge
Valentino, Rudolph 49, 178
Vallee, Rudy 10, 45, 85, 132
The Vampire Bat (1933) 172
Variety (publication) 2, 10, 17, 21, 24, 25, 27, 32, 34, 48, 54, 68, 81, 84, 102, 114, 118, 119, 122, 151, 153, 157, 160, 162, 165, 175, 183, 189
Varsity Show (1937) 85
Veloz and Yolanda 110, 151
"Vesti la giubba" 117
Victor/Victoria (1982) 123
Viktor and Victoria (1933) 123
Vincent, Romo 118
Vine, Eddie 65
The Voice of Experience 194
The Voice of the City (1929) 52

Waggner, George 169, 178, 184
Wagner, Carl 62
"Waitin' at the Gate for Katy" 101
*Wake Up and Dream (1934) 43–45, 49–50, **50**
Wake Up and Live (1937) 61
Wald, Jerry 41, 153
Walker, Ray 66
Wallis, Hal 120
The War Song (play) 14
Ward, Edward 178
Warner, Harry 13
Warner, Jack L. 79, 101, 120
Warner Bros. Pictures 2, 9, 10, 11, 12, 13, 25, 26, 27, 28, 29, 36, 41, 48, 52, 55, 56, 58, 70, 79, 80, 81, 82, 84, 85, 86, 88, 93, 96, 97, 101, 102, 118, 120, 121, 122, 127, 138, 141, 147, 172, 192, 194, 196
Warren, Harry 97, 141
"Was I Drunk, and Was He Handsome?" 61
"Was It Rain?" 194
The Washington Post (publication) 162
Waters, Ethel 153
"Way Out There" 185
Wayne, John 86, 167, 192
"We Belong Together" 104
*Weary River (1929) 8–11, **8**
"Weary River" (song) 9–10
The Weaver Brothers, and Elviry 122
"The Wedding of the Painted Doll" 24
Weems, Ted 97
Welford, Nancy 98
We're Not Dressing (1934) 147
West, Mae 1, 61, 90, 175, 186
Wharf Angel (1934) 61
What a Widow! (1930) 103
"What Is Sweeter Than the Sweetness of I Love You?" 53
"What Makes My Baby Blue?" 19
What Price Hollywood? (1932) 96
Wheeler, Bert 28, 147, 149
"When I Am Housekeeping for You" 19
"When Love Comes in the Moonlight" 29
"When the Moon Comes Over the Mountain" 41
When Tomorrow Comes (1939) 170
"When You're in Love" 49
"Where Are You?" 158
"Where the Lazy River Goes By" 113
"Which One Do You Love?" 29
"Whistle and Blow Your Blues Away" 41
White, Alice 153
White, Sam 149
Whiteman, Paul, (and His Orchestra) 127, 140, 150
Whiting, Margaret 85
Whiting, Richard 84, 85
Whitley, Ray 159
"Who's Afraid of the Big Bad Wolf?" 150
"Why Can't I Remember Your Name?" 80
"The Widow in Lace" 164
Wilder, Billy 69, 70, 73, 104, 107

Wiley, Jan 164
Wilk, Max 86
Wilkerson, W.R. 38, 102
William, Warren 80
Williams, Frances 21
Williams, Guinn "Big Boy" 168
Williams, Hannah 23
Wilson, Charles C. 14
Winchell, Walter 46, 47, 48, 61
Wing, Toby 55, 66
"With My Eyes Wide Open I'm Dreaming" 61, 63, 66
Withers, Grant 172, 192
Withers, Jane 108, 110–111
"Without You" 20
Wodehouse, P.G. 184
The Wolf Man (1941) 178
Wolf Song (1929) 45
"The Woman in the Shoe" 24
The Women (1939) 126
Wonder Bar (1934) 55, 56
Wood, Helen 109
Woods, Donald 80, 81
Woollcott, Alexander 153

Woolsey, Robert 28, 147, 149
Words and Music (1948) 95
Wrigley, Philip K. 51
Wyman, Jane 85

The Yacht Club Boys 80
Yates, Herbert J. 166, 167, 188, 193
"You Call It Madness, But I Call It Love" 19, 45
You Can't Beat Love (1937) 118
"You'd Be Kinda Grandish" 80
Young, Loretta 42, 99, 110
Young, Victor 188
Young Man of Manhattan (1930) 34
Young Mr. Lincoln (1939) 30
Your Hit Parade (radio show) 193
"You're My Past, Present, and Future" 46
You're Telling Me! (1935) 175

Zanuck, Darryl F. 46, 47, 48, 96, 112
Ziegfeld, Florenz 22, 93, 94, 97
Ziegfeld Follies of 1917 (play) 129
Ziegfeld Follies of 1927 (play) 26
Ziegfeld Follies of 1931 (play) 55, 61
Zoo in Budapest (1933) 143

www.ingramcontent.com/pod-product-compliance
Lightning Source LLC
Chambersburg PA
CBHW032051300426
44116CB00007B/695